Travel Disco

This coupon entitles you to special discounts
when you book your trip through the

TRAVEL NETWORK®
RESERVATION SERVICE

Hotels ♦ Airlines ♦ Car Rentals ♦ Cruises
All Your Travel Needs

Here's what you get:*

♦ A discount of $50 USD on a booking of $1,000** or
more for two or more people!

♦ A discount of $25 USD on a booking of $500** or more
for one person!

♦ Free membership for three years, and 1,000 free miles
on enrollment in the unique Travel Network Miles-to-
Go® frequent-traveler program. Earn one mile for
every dollar spent through the program. Redeem
miles for free hotel stays starting at 5,000 miles. Earn
free roundtrip airline tickets starting at 25,000 miles.

♦ Personal help in planning your own, customized trip.

♦ Fast, confirmed reservations at any property
recommended in this guide, subject to availability.***

♦ Special discounts on bookings in the U.S. and around
the world.

♦ Low-cost visa and passport service.

♦ Reduced-rate cruise packages and special car rental
programs worldwide.

Visit our website at http://www.travelnetwork.com/Frommer
or call us globally at 201-567-8500, ext. 55. In the U.S., call
toll-free at 1-888-940-5000, or fax 201-567-1838. In Canada,
call at 1-905-707-7222, or fax 905-707-8108. In Asia, call
60-3-7191044, or fax 60-3-7185415.

* To qualify for these travel discounts, at least a portion of your trip must
include destinations covered in this guide. No more than one coupon discount
may be used in any 12-month period, for destinations covered in this guide.
Cannot be combined with any other discount or promotion.
**These are U.S. dollars spent on commissionable bookings.
*** A $10 USD fee, plus fax and/or phone charges, will be added to the cost of
bookings at each hotel not linked to the reservation service. Customers must
approve these fees in advance. If only hotels of this kind are booked, the traveler(s)
must also purchase roundtrip air tickets from Travel Network for the trip.

Valid until December 31, 1999. Terms and conditions of the Miles-to-
Go® program are available on request by calling 201-567-8500, ext 55.

HON234

Frommer's® 5th Edition

Honolulu, Waikiki & Oahu

by Jeanette Foster & Jocelyn Fujii

Macmillan • USA

ABOUT THE AUTHORS

A resident of the Big Island, **Jeanette Foster** has skied the slopes of Mauna Kea—during a Fourth of July ski meet, no less—and scuba dived with manta rays off the Kona Coast. A prolific writer widely published in travel, sports, and adventure magazines, she also co-authored *Frommer's Hawaii from $60 a Day* with Jocelyn Fujii.

Kauai-born **Jocelyn Fujii,** a resident of Honolulu, is one of Hawaii's leading journalists. She has authored *Under the Hula Moon: Living in Hawaii* and *The Best of Hawaii* as well as articles for *The New York Times, National Geographic Traveler, Islands, Condé Nast Traveler, Travel Holiday,* and other national and international publications.

MACMILLAN TRAVEL

A Simon & Schuster Macmillan Company
1633 Broadway
New York, NY 10019

Find us online at **www.frommers.com**

ISBN 0-02-861643-X
ISSN 1064-1238

Editors: Cheryl Farr and Kathy Iwasaki
Production Editor: Lori Cates
Design by Michele Laseau
Digital Cartography by Raffaele Degennaro & Ortelius Design

SPECIAL SALES

Bulk purchases (10+ copies) of Frommer's and selected Macmillan travel guides are available to corporations, organizations, mail-order catalogs, institutions, and charities at special discounts and can be customized to suit individual needs. For more information write to: Special Sales, Macmillan General Reference, 1633 Broadway, New York, NY 10019.

Manufactured in the United States of America

Contents

7   Dining   134

by Jocelyn Fujii

8   Fun in the Surf & Sun   165

by Jeanette Foster

9   Seeing the Sights   199

by Jeanette Foster

List of Maps

AN INVITATION TO THE READER

In researching this book, we discovered many wonderful places—hotels, restaurants, shops, and more. We're sure you'll find others. Please tell us about them, so we can share the information with your fellow travelers in upcoming editions. If you were disappointed with a recommendation, we'd love to know that, too. Please write to:

Jeanette Foster & Jocelyn Fujii
Frommer's Honolulu, Waikiki & Oahu, 5th Edition
Macmillan Travel
1633 Broadway
New York, NY 10019

AN ADDITIONAL NOTE

Please be advised that travel information is subject to change at any time—and this is especially true of prices. We therefore suggest that you write or call ahead for confirmation when making your travel plans. The authors, editors, and publisher cannot be held responsible for the experiences of readers while traveling. Your safety is important to us, however, so we encourage you to stay alert and be aware of your surroundings. Keep a close eye on cameras, purses, and wallets, all favorite targets of thieves and pickpockets.

WHAT THE SYMBOL MEANS

✪ Frommer's Favorites

Our favorite places and experiences—outstanding for quality, value, or both.

The following abbreviations are used for credit cards:

AE	American Express	ER	enRoute
CB	Carte Blanche	JCB	Japan Credit Bank
DC	Diners Club	MC	MasterCard
DISC	Discover	V	Visa
EC	Eurocard		

FIND FROMMER'S ONLINE

Arthur Frommer's Outspoken Encyclopedia of Travel (www.frommers.com) offers more than 6,000 pages of up-to-the-minute travel information—including the latest bargains and candid, personal articles updated daily by Arthur Frommer himself. No other Web site offers such comprehensive and timely coverage of the world of travel.

The Hawaiian Islands

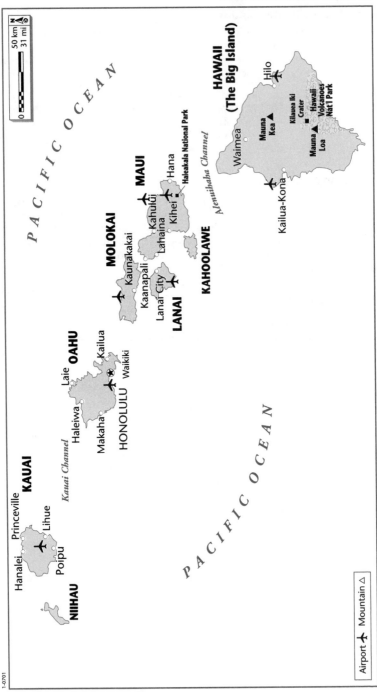

The Best of Oahu

by Jeanette Foster and Jocelyn Fujii

The island of Oahu, located literally in the middle of the most remote chain of islands on the planet, offers not just a vacation, a respite from work, a travel adventure, but also a sojourn into a dreamlike paradise. Imagine yourself hovering weightless over a rainbowed sea of tropical fish, sitting in a kayak watching the brilliant colors of dawn etch themselves across the sky, standing on the memorial where thousands of lives were lost and the course of history was changed, battling a magnificent game fish on a high-tech sportfishing boat, or listening to melodic voices chant the stories of a proud people and a proud culture that was overthrown little more than a century ago.

Everyone ventures to Honolulu, Waikiki, and Oahu looking for a different experience. Some talk about wanting to witness the "real" Hawaii, some are looking for heart-pounding adventure, some seek the relaxing and healing powers of this sacred place, and some are drawn by the indescribable, unexplainable concept of the aloha spirit, where harmony and love prevail.

This book is designed to help you find the paradise of your dreams. We have compiled everything for you to enjoy the island of Oahu. For those too excited to page through all the way, this chapter highlights what we think are the very best and the very finest of what this paradise has to offer.

1 The Best Beaches

To anyone unlucky enough to be landlocked, a beach is just a beach. But to Oahu residents there are beaches of all sizes, shapes, and colors, each one offering something different. Here's a list of our favorite beaches.

- **Lanikai Beach:** Hidden, off the beaten tourist path, this beach on the windward side is a mile of powder-soft sand that's safe for swimming and—with the prevailing trade winds—excellent for sailing and windsurfing. It's the perfect place to claim a quiet, isolated spot for a morning of swimming and relaxation. Sun-worshipers should arrive in the morning, as the Koolaus' shadow will block your rays in the afternoon. See chapter 8.

- **Kailua Beach:** Imagine a 30-acre public park with a broad, grassy area with picnic tables, a public boat ramp, rest rooms, a pavilion, a volleyball court, and food stands. Add a wide, sandy beach area, great for diving, swimming, sailing, snorkeling, and board and windsurfing, and presto!—you have Kailua Beach. On weekends, local families consider it *the* place to go. Great on weekdays, when you practically have the entire place to yourself. See chapter 8.

- **Kahana Beach:** If you didn't know you were in Hawaii, you would swear this beach was in Tahiti or Bora Bora. Picture salt-and-pepper sand, a crescent-shaped beach protected by ironwoods and *kamani* trees, and as a backdrop, a lush junglelike valley disturbed only by jagged cliffs. Kahana offers great swimming (even safe for children), good fishing, and perfect conditions for kayaking. Combine that with picnic areas, camping, and hiking trails, and you have one of the most attractive beaches on the island.

- **Malaekahana Beach:** If you would like to venture back to the Hawaii before jet planes brought millions of people to Oahu, back to the days when there were few footprints on the sand, then go north to the romantic wooded beach park at Malaekahana. This is a place to sit in quiet solitude or to beachcomb along the shore. Good swimming most of the time, good snorkeling when it is calm, but no lifeguard here. Surprisingly, very few visitors come to Malaekahana Beach, one of the best on Oahu—it's a true find. See chapter 8.

- **Waimea Bay:** Here is one of Oahu's most dramatic beaches. During much of the winter—October to April—huge waves come pounding in, creating strong rip currents. Even expert surfers think twice when confronted with 30-foot waves that crash on the shore with the force of a runaway locomotive. It's hard to believe that during the summer this same bay is glassy and calm, a great place for swimming, snorkeling, and diving. Oh, and by the way, despite what the Beach Boys croon in their hit song "Surfin USA" (why-a-MEE-ah), the name of this famous surfing beach is pronounced why-MAY-ah. See chapter 8.

- **Pokai Bay:** If your dream is of a powdered-sugar sand beach, a place you can swim, snorkel, and probably be the only visitor on the beach (on weekdays), try this off-the-beaten-path shoreline. Surrounded by a reef, the waters inside are calm enough for children and offer excellent snorkeling. Come with the aloha spirit and a respect for local customs—the local residents don't see too many visitors. See chapter 8.

- **Sunset Beach:** Surfers around the world know this famous site for the spectacular winter surf—the waves can be huge, thundering peaks reaching up to 15 to 20 feet. During the winter surf season, the best activity here is watching the professional surfers attack the giant waves. In the summer months, Sunset lies down and becomes a safe swimming beach. Great place to people watch year-round, everything from wanna-be *Baywatch* babes to King Kong–surfers. See chapter 8.

2 The Best Oahu Experiences

To have the absolute best travel experience on Oahu, imagine yourself in another country: Expect a different culture, language, cuisine, and way of doing things. Slow way, way down. You're now on an island that operates with its own rhythm—don't fight it, flow with the slower pace of life. To really experience the islands, we recommend the following:

- **Get Out on the Water:** View the islands the way Mother Nature does—from the sea. There are many different boats to choose from, ranging from tiny kayaks to 100-foot sightseeing vessels. Even state-of-the-art boats guaranteed to prevent seasickness are available. You'll take home memories of an emerald island rising out of the cobalt sea with white wispy clouds set against an azure sky or the Waikiki shoreline colored by the setting sun. See chapter 8.

- **Plunge Under the Water:** Don mask, fins, and snorkel and dive into the magical world beneath the surface, where clouds of colorful tropical fish flutter by, craggy old turtles lumber along, and tiny marine creatures hover over exotic corals. Can't swim?—no excuse, take one of the numerous submarines or semi-submersibles, but don't miss this opportunity. If you come to Hawaii and don't see the underwater world, you are missing half of the elixir that makes up this paradise. See chapter 8.
- **Meet Local Folks:** If you go to Hawaii and only see people like the ones back home, you might as well stay home. Extend yourself, leave the resorts and tourist quarters, go out and learn about Hawaii and its people. Just smile and say "howzit?"—which means "how is it?" "It's good," is the usual response—and you'll usually make a new friend. Hawaii is remarkably cosmopolitan; every ethnic group in the world seems to be here. It's delightful to discover the varieties of food, culture, language, and customs. The best place to start is Oahu's Polynesian Cultural Center. See chapter 9.
- **Drive to the North Shore:** Just an hour's drive from Honolulu, the North Shore is another world: a pastoral, rural setting with magnificent beaches and a slower way of life. During the winter months, stop and watch the professionals surf the ferocious monster waves. See chapter 9.
- **Watch the Hula Being Performed:** This is Hawaii, so you have to experience the hula. There's no excuse—many performances are free. For just about as long as we can remember, the Eastman Kodak Company has been hosting the **Kodak Hula Show** at Kapiolani Park. The show is really more '50s nostalgia than ancient culture, but it's a good bit of fun any way you slice it. Some 1,500 people flock to the shows at 10am every Tuesday, Wednesday, and Thursday; they last until 11:15am. See chapter 9.
- **Experience a Turning Point in America's History—the Bombing of Pearl Harbor:** The United States could no longer turn its back on World War II after December 7, 1941, the day that Japanese warplanes bombed Pearl Harbor. Standing on the deck of the USS *Arizona* Memorial, which straddles the eternal tomb for the 1,177 sailors and Marines trapped below deck when the battleship sank in 9 minutes, is a moving experience you'll never forget. Admission is absolutely free. See chapter 9.

3 The Best of Natural Oahu

This is Oahu as it was created by Mother Nature: the remains of once-steaming volcanoes, thundering waterfalls carved over a millennium, the dazzling array of tropical flora in full bloom, and the unexplainable pockets of beauty that continue to astound and amaze us all.

- **Volcanoes:** Oahu was born of volcanic eruptions—don't miss the opportunity to see the remains of a volcano up-close-and-personal. You can actually walk into the crater of Diamond Head. See chapter 8.
- **Waterfalls:** The thunder of millions of gallons of water dropping through space into freshwater pools is one of Oahu's most beautiful natural wonders. Hike to the awe-inspiring Sacred Falls where clear, cold water, originating from the top of the Koolau Mountains, descends down the Kaluanui Stream and cascades over Sacred Falls into a deep, boulder-strewn pool. See chapter 8.
- **Gardens:** Flowers are what Hawaii is about and there is no shortage of gardens on Oahu to show off this natural beauty. Foster Gardens is a 14-acre, leafy botanical oasis amid the high-rises of downtown Honolulu, showcasing 24 native

Hawaiian trees and the last stand of several rare trees, including an East African species whose white flowers bloom only at night. See chapter 9.

- **Marine Life Conservation Areas:** Oahu's underwater parks have such a unique marine environment that state law protects them. Submerged in a Neptunian underworld, these parks possess a sensual serenity unmatched in life above the waves. There are three underwater parks along Oahu's shorelines: Waikiki, Hanauma Bay, and Pupukea. See "Beaches" in chapter 8.
- **Natural Wonders:** Forget Old Faithful; the Halona Blowhole on the southeast side of Oahu features a geyser shooting into the air through a vent in the lava cliffs. (See chapter 9.) Other not-to-be-missed phenomena are the waterfalls that seem to flow uphill along the Nuuanu Pali highway. Gale-force winds sometimes howl through the mountain pass at this 1,186-foot-high perch guarded by 3,000-foot peaks; the result is waterfalls that are blown back up the mountain. See chapter 9.

4 The Best Snorkeling & Diving Sites

A different Hawaii greets anyone with a face mask, snorkel, and fins. Under the sea, you'll find schools of brilliant tropical fish, lumbering green sea turtles, quick-moving game fish, slack-jawed moray eels, and prehistoric-looking coral. It's a kaleidoscope of color and wonder.

- **Hanauma Bay:** It can get crowded, but for clear, warm, calm waters, an abundance of fish that are so friendly they'll swim right up to your face mask, a beautiful setting, and easy access, there's no place like Hanauma Bay. Just wade in waist-deep and look down to see more than 50 species of reef and inshore fish common to Hawaiian waters. Snorkelers hug the safe, shallow inner bay—it's really like swimming in an outdoor aquarium. Serious divers shoot "the slot," a passage through the reef, to gain access to Witch's Brew, a turbulent cove, and other outer reef experiences. See chapter 8.
- **Wreck of the Mahi:** Oahu is a wonderful place to scuba dive, especially for those interested in wreck diving. One of the more famous wrecks in Hawaii is the *Mahi,* a 185-foot former minesweeper, which is easily accessible just south of Waianae. Abundant marine life makes this a great place to shoot photos—schools of lemon butterfly fish and taape are so comfortable with divers and photographers that they practically pose. Eagle rays, green sea turtles, manta rays, and white-tipped sharks occasionally cruise by, and eels peer from the wreck. See chapter 8.
- **Kahuna Caynon:** For non-wreck diving, one of the best dive spots in the summer is Kahuna Canyon. In Hawaiian, Kahuna translates as priest, wise man, or sorcerer. This massive amphitheater, located near Mokuleia, is a perfect example of something a sorcerer might conjure up: Walls rising from the ocean floor create the illusion of an underwater Grand Canyon. Inside the amphitheater, crab, octopi, slipper and spiny lobsters abound (be aware that taking them in the summer is illegal), and giant trevally, parrot fish, and unicorn tangs congregate. Outside the amphitheater, you're likely to see the occasional shark in the distance. See chapter 8.
- **Shark's Cove:** The braver snorkelers among us may want to head to Shark's Cove, on the North Shore just off Kamehameha Highway, between Haleiwa and Pupukea. Sounds risky, we know, but we've never seen or heard of any sharks in this cove, and in summer this big, lava-edged pool is one of Oahu's best snorkel spots. Waves splash over the natural lava grotto and cascade like waterfalls into the pool full of tropical fish. There are deep-sea caves to explore to the right of the cove. See chapter 8.

- **Kapiolani Park Beach:** In the center of this beach park, a section known as Queen's Beach or Queen's Surf Beach, between the Natatorium and the Waikiki Aquarium, is great for snorkeling. We prefer the reef in front of the Aquarium because it has easy access to the sandy shoreline and the waters usually are calm. It also has the added advantage of being right next door to the Aquarium in case you see any flora or fauna that you would like more information about. See "Walking Tour: Kapiolani Park" in chapter 9.

5 The Best Golf Courses

Oahu is golf country with 5 municipal, 9 military, and 20 private courses to choose from. The courses range from 9-hole municipals, perfect for beginners, to championship courses that stump even the pros. Below is a range of selections; one will be just right for your game.

- **Ko Olina Golf Club** (☎ 808/676-5300): Here's a course that not only is in a beautiful setting, but it's downright challenging. In fact, *Golf Digest* named this 6,867-yard, par-72 course one of "America's Top 75 Resort Courses" when it opened in 1992. The rolling fairways and elevated tees and a few too many water features (always where you don't want them) will definitely improve your game or humble your attitude. See chapter 8.
- **Turtle Bay Hilton Golf & Tennis Resort** (☎ 808/293-8574): Of the two courses to choose from here, we recommend the 18-hole **Links at Kuilima,** designed by Arnold Palmer and Ed Seay—*Golf Digest* rated it the fourth best new resort course in 1994. Palmer and Seay never meant for golfers to get off too easy; this is a challenging course. The front 9 holes, with rolling terrain, only a few trees, and lots of wind, play like a British Isles course. The back 9 holes have narrower, tree-lined fairways and water. In addition to ocean views along the course, it also circles Punahoolapa Marsh, a protected wetland for endangered Hawaiian waterfowl. See chapter 8.
- **Sheraton Makaha Golf Club** (☎ 800/757-8060 or 808/695-9544): The readers of a local city magazine recently named this challenging course as "The Best Golf Course on Oahu" and the readers of *Golfweek* rated it as one of Hawaii's top 10. Away from the crowds of Honolulu, about an hour's drive, this William Bell–designed course is in Makaha Valley on the leeward side of the island. Incredibly beautiful, sheer, 1,500-foot, volcanic walls tower over the course and swaying palm trees and neon-bright bougainvillea surround it; an occasional peacock will even strut across the fairways. "I was distracted by the beauty" is a great excuse for your score at the end of the day. See chapter 8.
- **Olomana Golf Links** (☎ 808/259-7926): This is a gorgeous course located in Waimanalo, on the other side of the island from Waikiki. The low-handicap golfer may not find this course difficult, but the striking views of the craggy Koolau mountain ridges are worth the greens fees alone. The par-72, 6,326-yard course is very popular with local residents and visitors. The course starts off a bit hilly on the front 9, but flattens out by the back 9. The back 9 have their own special surprises, including tricky water hazards. See chapter 8.

6 The Best Walks

The weather on Oahu usually is sunny with trade winds providing cooling breezes, perfect conditions to take a walk and enjoy the island's beauty. Below are some of our favorite walks, from city strolls to trails through rain forests.

- **Diamond Head Crater:** Everyone can make this easy walk to the summit of Hawaii's most famous landmark. Kids love the top of the 760-foot volcanic cone, where they have 360° views of Oahu up the leeward coast from Waikiki. The 1.4-mile round-trip will take about an hour. See chapter 8.
- **Makiki-Manoa Cliff Trails:** Just a 15-minute drive from downtown Honolulu is an incredible walk through a rain forest and along a ridgetop with nonstop views. This somewhat strenuous loop trail is one you'll never forget; however it is more than 6 miles, gains 1,260 feet in elevation, and takes about 3 hours to complete. This trail is part of the labyrinth of trails found in this area. The views of the city and the shoreline are spectacular. See chapter 8.
- **Chinatown:** Honolulu's Chinatown appeals to the senses, with the pungent aroma of Vietnamese *pho* mingling with the ever-present sweet scent of burning incense; a jumble of streets that come alive every day with bustling residents and visitors from all over the world; a cacophony of sounds in the air, from the high-pitched bleating of vendors in the open market to the lyrical dialects of the retired men talking story over a game of mah-jongg; and brilliant reds, blues, and greens trimming buildings and goods everywhere you look. No trip to Honolulu is complete without a visit to this exotic, historic district. See chapter 9.
- **Manoa Falls Trail:** This easy, eight-tenths of a mile (one-way) hike is terrific for families; it takes less than an hour to reach idyllic Manoa Falls. The often-muddy trail follows Waihi Stream and meanders through the forest reserve past guava and mountain apple trees and wild ginger. The forest is moist and humid and inhabited by nothing more dangerous than giant bloodthirsty mosquitoes, so bring repellent. See chapter 8.

7 The Best Views

Oahu has many extraordinary lookouts. How can you have a bad view in paradise? Here are just a few of our favorites.

- **Puu Ualakaa State Park:** Watching the sun set into the Pacific from a 1,048-foot hill named after a sweet potato is actually much more romantic that it sounds. Puu Ualakaa State Park translates into "rolling sweet potato hill," which was how the early Hawaiians harvested the crop. Don't miss the sweeping panoramic views from this hill, which extend from Diamond Head across Waikiki and downtown Honolulu, over the airport and Pearl City, all the way to the Waianae range. Great photo opportunities during the day, romantic sunset views in the evening, and starry skies at night. See chapter 9.
- **Nuuanu Pali Lookout:** Oahu's best-looking side, the Windward Coast, can be seen in its full natural glory from the Nuuanu Pali Lookout, a gusty perch set amid jagged jade cliffs that pierce the puffy white clouds that go scudding by. A thousand sheer feet below, the island is a carpet of green that runs to an azure Pacific dotted by tiny offshore islets. You'll feel like you're standing on the edge of the world. See chapter 9.
- **Diamond Head Crater:** The view from atop this world-famous 720-foot-tall sleeping volcano is not to be missed. The 360-degree view from the top is worth the 560-foot hike. You can see all the way from the Koko Crater to Barbers Point and the Waianae mountains. See chapter 9.
- **Lanikai Beach:** This is one of the best places on Oahu to greet the sunrise. Watch the sky slowly move from pitch black to wisps of gray to burnt orange as the sun begins to rise over the two tiny offshore islands of Mokulua. This is a five-senses experience: birds singing the sun up; a gentle breeze on your face; the taste of salt

in the air; the smell of the ocean, the sand, and the fragrant flowers near by; and the kaleidoscope of colors as another day dawns. See chapter 8.

- **Puu O Mahuka Heiau:** Once the largest sacrificial temple on Oahu, today Puu O Mahuka Heiau is a state historical site. Located on a 300-foot bluff, the Heiau encompasses some 5 acres. People still come here to pray—you may see offerings such as ti-leaves, flowers, and fruit left at the Heiau. Don't disturb the offerings or walk on the stones (it's very disrespectful). The view from this bluff is awe-inspiring: from Waimea Bay all the way to Kaena Point. See chapter 9.

8 The Best Adventures for Thrill Seekers

- **Soar in Silence in a Glider:** Imagine soaring through silence on gossamerlike wings, with a panoramic view of Oahu. A ride on a glider is an unforgettable experience. Glider rides are available at Dillingham Air Field, in Mokuleia, on Oahu's North Shore. The glider is towed behind a plane; at the right altitude, the tow is dropped, and you (and the glider pilot) are left to soar in the thermals. See chapter 8.
- **Surf Waikiki in a Hawaiian Outrigger Canoe:** It's summertime and there's a South Pacific swell rolling into Waikiki from Tahiti; here's your chance to try surfing—in a Hawaiian outrigger canoe. Numerous beach concessions on Waikiki Beach offer the chance to paddle an outrigger canoe and surf back into Waikiki. Not only do you get a great view of Waikiki Beach from offshore, but also the thrill of actually catching a wave and gliding back into shore. See chapter 8.
- **Float on the Thermals on a Tandem Hang Glider:** See things from a bird's-eye view (literally) as you and your instructor float high above Oahu on a tandem hang glider. See chapter 8.
- **Leap into the Ocean:** Even though all the signs say "Dangerous, stay off the rocks," a favorite pastime on Oahu is climbing the stone precipice next to Waimea Bay and leaping into the ocean. This is a summer-only experience, as the thundering winter waves drive everyone from the sea, except the professional surfers and the very, very stupid. See chapter 8.
- **Venture into the Neptunian Underworld:** It's Hawaii—you have to see what it is like under the waves. Try scuba diving; you can enjoy a "scuba experience" with absolutely no previous diving experience. Here's your opportunity to glide weightlessly through the azure sea stopping to admire the multicolored marine creatures. See chapter 8.

9 The Best Places to Discover the Real Oahu

Oahu isn't just any other beach destination. It has a wonderfully rich, ancient history and culture, and people who are worth getting to know while you're visiting in the islands. If you want to meet the "local" folks who live on Oahu, check out the following:

- **Watch the Ancient Hawaiian Sport of Canoe Paddling:** From February to September, on weekday evenings and weekend days, hundreds of canoe paddlers gather at Ala Wai Canal and practice the Hawaiian sport of canoe paddling. Find a comfortable spot at Ala Wai Park, next to the canal, and watch this ancient sport come to life. See chapter 8.
- **Attend a Hawaiian-Language Church Service: Kawaiahao Church** (☎ 808/ 522-1333) is the Westminster Abbey of Hawaii; the vestibule is lined with portraits of the Hawaiian monarchy, many of whom were coronated in this very

building. The coral church is a perfect setting to experience an all-Hawaiian service, held every Sunday at 10:30am, complete with Hawaiian song. Admission is free; let your conscience be your guide as to a donation. See chapter 9.

- **Buy a Lei from Vendors in Chinatown:** There's actually a host of cultural sights and experiences to be had in Honolulu's Chinatown. Wander through this several-square-block area with its jumble of exotic shops offering herbs, Chinese groceries, and acupuncture services. Before you leave, be sure to check out the lei sellers on Maunakea Street (near N. Hotel Street), where Hawaii's finest leis go for as little as $2.50. See chapter 9.

- **Observe the Fish Auction:** There is nothing else quite like the Honolulu Fish Auction at the United Fishing Agency, 117 Ahui St. (below John Dominis Restaurant), Honolulu, HI 96814 (☎ **808/536-2148**). The fishermen bring their fresh catch in at 5:30am (sharp), Monday to Saturday, and the small group of buyers wanders from big fat tunas to weird looking hapupu, bidding on the price of each fish. Don't be surprised if you don't recognize much of the language the bidders are using; it is an internal dialect developed over decades, which only the buyers and the auctioneer understand. The auction lasts until all the fish are sold. It is well worth getting up early to enjoy this unique cultural experience.

- **Get a Bargain at the Swap Meet:** For 50 cents admission, it's an all-day show at the Aloha Stadium parking lot, where more than 1,000 vendors are selling everything from junk to jewels. Go early for the best deals. Open Wednesday, Saturday, and Sunday from 6am to 3pm.

10 The Best Luxury Hotels & Resorts

No Hawaiian king or queen ever had it this good. Great luxury resort hotels stand like temples of hedonism on the waterfront. Here are our favorites:

- **Halekulani** (☎ **808/923-2311**): For the ultimate in a "heavenly" Hawaii vacation, this is the place. In fact, Halekulani translates into "House Befitting Heaven," an apt description. When money is no object, Oahu's only five-diamond resort is the place to stay. This luxury 456-room resort is spread over 5 acres of Waikiki beachfront property. The atmosphere of elegance envelops you as soon as you step into the lobby. Even if you don't stay here, drop by at sunset to sip on a Mai Tai and listen to Sonny Kamehele sing Hawaiian songs as a graceful hula dancer sways to the music. See chapter 6.

- **Kahala Mandarin Oriental Hawaii** (☎ **800/367-2525** or 808/739-8888): Formerly the Kahala Hilton, this luxury property reopened in March 1996, after $75 million in renovations. Since 1964, when Conrad Hilton first opened the hotel as a place for rest and relaxation, far from the crowds of Waikiki, the Kahala has always been rated as one of Hawaii's premier hotels. A venerable who's who of celebrities have stayed at the hotel, including every president since Richard Nixon, a host of rock stars from the Rolling Stones to the Beach Boys, and a range of actors from John Wayne to Bette Midler. The Mandarin has retained the traditional feeling of an earlier time in Hawaii, which defined the Kahala for a generation, and has combined it with exotic Asian touches, creating a resort hotel for the 21st century, but with the grace and elegance of a softer, gentler time in the islands. See chapter 6.

- **Royal Hawaiian** (☎ **800/325-3535** or 808/923-7311): Hidden in the jungle of concrete buildings that make up Waikiki is an oasis of verdant gardens and a shockingly pink building. The Royal Hawaiian Hotel, affectionately called the pink palace, is known around the world as a symbol of luxury. Since the first day it opened in 1927, the Royal has been the place to stay for celebrities, including Clark

Gable, Shirley Temple, President Franklin Roosevelt, the Beatles, Kevin Costner, and others. The location is one of the best spots on Waikiki Beach. There's no place else like it. See chapter 6.

- **Sheraton Moana Surfrider Hotel** (☎ 800/325-3535 or 808/922-3111): Step back in time to old Hawaii at the Sheraton Moana Surfrider Hotel. Built in 1901, this was Waikiki's first hotel. Those days of yesteryear live on today at this grand hotel. Entry is through the original colonial porte-cochere, past the highly polished wooden front porch, with white wood rocking chairs, and into the perfectly restored lobby with its detailed millwork and intricate plaster detailing on the ceiling. Time seems to slow down here, tropical flowers arranged in huge sprays are everywhere, and people in the lobby all seem to be smiling. At check-in guests are greeted with a lei and a glass of fruit juice. This is a hotel not only with class, but with historical charm. See chapter 6.

- **Hilton Hawaiian Village** (☎ 800-HILTONS or 808/949-4321): This is Waikiki's biggest resort—so big it even has its own post office. Some 2,545 rooms, spread over 20 acres with tropical gardens, thundering waterfalls, exotic wildlife, award-winning restaurants, nightly entertainment, 100 different shops, children's programs, fabulous ocean activities, a secluded lagoon, three swimming pools, Hawaiian cultural activities, two mini-golf courses, and Waikiki Beach. This place is so big and so complete, you could spend your entire vacation here and never leave the property. See chapter 6.

- **Ihilani Resort & Spa** (☎ 800/626-4446 or 808/679-0070): Located in the quiet of Oahu's west coast, some 17 miles and 25 minutes west of Honolulu International Airport—and worlds away from the tourist scene of Waikiki—the Ihilani (which means "heavenly splendor") is the first hotel in the 640-acre Ko Olina Resort and features a luxury spa and fitness center, and championship tennis and golf. It's hard to get a bad room here; some 85% of guest rooms enjoy lagoon or ocean views. The luxuriously appointed rooms are larger than most (680 square feet), with huge lanais complete with extremely comfortable cushioned teak furniture (chaise lounge, chairs, and table). Luxurious marble bathrooms have deep soaking tubs, separate glass-enclosed showers, hair dryers, and Yukata robes. Who misses Waikiki with luxury like this? See chapter 6.

11 The Best Moderately Priced Hotels & Resorts

It is possible to stay in paradise without having to take out a second mortgage. You can choose from an elegant boutique hotel in Waikiki, a historical bed-and-breakfast in Manoa, or a tropical accommodation reminiscent of the Hawaii of yesteryear, all at affordable prices.

- **The Royal Garden at Waikiki** (☎ 800/367-5666 or 808/943-0202): Deals, deals, deals—that's what you'll find at this elegant boutique hotel, tucked away on a quiet, tree-lined side street in Waikiki. There's a deal for everyone: room/car packages start at $135 (that's a $130 standard room, plus a car for only $5 extra); a family plan, which gives you a second room at 50% off the rack rate; and the Young-at-Heart Package, which allows seniors to book rooms starting at $91 (they also get a 10% discount at Royal Garden restaurants). See chapter 6.

- **The New Otani Kaimana Beach Hotel** (☎ 800/35-OTANI or 808/923-1555): This is one of Waikiki's best-kept secrets: a boutique hotel just outside of Waikiki nestled right on the beach at the foot of Diamond Head. The airy lobby opens to the open-air Hau Tree Lanai restaurant, under the same tree that sheltered Robert Louis Stevenson a century ago. Double rooms in this quiet section of Waikiki start at $110. Since the hotel overlooks Kapiolani Park, guests have easy access to such activities as golf, tennis, kite flying, jogging, and bicycling. See chapter 6.

- **Hawaiiana Hotel** (☎ 800/535-0085 or 808/923-3811): The lush tropical flowers and carved tiki at the entrance on tiny Beach Walk set the tone for this intimate low-rise hotel. The hotel's slogan says it all: "The spirit of old Hawaii." From the moment you arrive, you'll experience the aloha spirit here: At check-in, guests are given a pineapple; every morning, complimentary Kona coffee and tropical juice are served poolside; at check-out, flower leis are presented to the women as a fragrant reminder of their vacation at the Hawaiiana. The concrete hollow-tile rooms, which start at $109 double, feature a kitchenette and a view of the gardens and swimming pool. See chapter 6.

- **Prince Kuhio, A Royal Outrigger Hotel** (☎ **800/OUTRIGGER** or 808/922-0811): The Prince Kuhio is one of the best hotels in the Outrigger chain, which is famous for comfortable accommodations at reasonable prices. Up the escalator to the second-floor lobby, the marble floors, chandelier, handwoven rugs, and artful decor offer a hint of your accommodations. Completely renovated in 1997, the 37-story Prince Kuhio is located just blocks from Waikiki Beach, the Honolulu Zoo, and the heart of Waikiki shopping. A room for two starts at $125. See chapter 6.

- **Manoa Valley Inn** (☎ 800/535-0085 or 808/947-6019): It's completely off the tourist trail and far from the beach, but that doesn't stop travelers from heading to this historic 1915 Carpenter Gothic home on a quiet residential street near the University of Hawaii. This eight-room Manoa landmark—it's on the National Register of Historic Places—offers a glimpse into the lifestyles of the rich and famous in early Honolulu. Each room has its own unique decor and has been named for a prominent figure in Hawaii's history: The John Guild suite, for instance, has a turn-of-the-century parlor with antiques and old-fashioned rose wallpaper; the adjoining bedroom has a king-size koa bed, and the bath features an old-style tub as well as a separate modern shower. As the sun sets, complimentary wine and cheese are served on the quiet veranda. Rates are $99 to $120 double with shared bath; $140 to $190 double with private bath. See chapter 6.

12 The Best Places to Stay Beyond Waikiki

Waikiki is the draw, but there are other parts of Oahu that are worth equal consideration. There are adorable B&Bs on the North Shore, practical two-bedroom apartments in Honolulu, a studio with a swimming pool overlooking Pearl Harbor, and a luxury resort on the north end of the island.

- **Santa's By the Sea** (☎ 800/262-9912 or 808/885-4550): This certainly must be where Santa Claus comes to vacation, and for good reason—St. Nick knows a bargain when he sees it: $99 for two for this apartment right on the ocean on the North Shore. The location, price, and style make this place a must-stay if you plan to see the North. Santa's is located on not just any beach, but the famous Banzai Pipeline. You can go from your bed to the sand in less than 30 seconds to watch the sun rise over the Pacific. See chapter 6.

- **Prospect House** (☎ 800/262-9912 or 808/885-4550): On a quiet residential street near Punchbowl, the Prospect House has a two-bedroom apartment with a spectacular view of Honolulu and the Pacific for just $85 for two. The apartment has its own private entrance, outside deck, and hot tub with city view. There's even a small breakfast nook outside where you can sit and watch the city wake up as you sip your morning coffee. To top it all off, the location is great: 15 minutes from the airport and Waikiki, and just minutes from Honolulu's attractions. See chapter 6.

- **Rainbow Inn** (☎ 808/488-7525): This private tropical garden studio, downstairs from the home of retired military officer Gene Smith and his wife Betty, has panoramic views of Pearl Harbor, the entire south coast of Oahu, and the Waianae and Koolau mountains. A large deck and full-sized pool are just outside the apartment's door. Located close to Pearl Ridge Shopping Center, Rainbow Inn is freeway-close to all of Oahu's attractions, yet far enough away to provide you with lots of peace and quiet. And at $65 a night, this is one of Oahu's best bed-and-breakfast deals. See chapter 6.

- **Lanikai Bed & Breakfast:** (☎ 800/258-7895 or 808/261-1059): This old-time bed-and-breakfast, a *kamaaina* (native-born) home that reflects the Hawaii of yesteryear, is now into its second generation. The recently renovated 1,000-square-foot upstairs apartment is decorated in old Hawaii bungalow style and rents for $85 for two. Or, you can follow the ginger- and ti-lined path to a 540-square-foot honeymooner's delight, at $65 for two. Access to picture-perfect white-sand Lanikai Beach is right across the street, bus routes are close by, and a 2¹/₂-mile biking-walking loop is immediately accessible. See chapter 6.

- **Hulakai Hale** (☎ 808/235-6754): Hulakai Hale ("house of the dancing waters") sits right on Kaneohe Bay, with picture-postcard views in every direction. The view from the swimming pool deck of the bay and the yacht club next door is worth the incredible price of $55 to $65 for two. Located at the end of a private road, Hulakai Hale is well away from traffic, but just minutes from the restaurants and shops of Kaneohe. Each of the two well-furnished units has a small fridge, microwave, coffeemaker, full bath, and a private outdoor entrance, plus breakfast (tropical juice, fresh fruit, a variety of breads, cereal, coffee, and tea) is served every morning on the pool deck or in the formal dining area. See chapter 6.

- **Turtle Bay Hilton Golf and Tennis Resort** (☎ 800/HILTONS or 808/293-8811): An hour's drive from Waikiki and eons away is this luxurious oceanfront resort out in the country. Sitting on 808 acres, this is a resort filled with activities: 27 holes of golf, 10 tennis courts, and 5 miles of shoreline with secluded white-sand coves. Choose from the spacious guest rooms, suites, or oceanside cabanas—all have oceanfront views starting at $155 for two. See chapter 6.

13 The Best Culinary Experiences

Oahu's dining scene falls into several categories: Waikiki restaurants, chef-owned glamour restaurants, neighborhood eateries, fast-food joints, and ethnic restaurants. One of Honolulu's greatest assets is the range of restaurants in all of these categories. Here's a sampling of Oahu's finest.

- **Akasaka** (1646B Kona St.; ☎ 808/942-4466): The spicy tuna hand roll, hamachi sushi, clam miso soup, and sizzling tofu and scallops are among life's greatest pleasures. The tiny sushi bar is hidden among the shadowy nightclubs of Kona Street—off the beaten track, yet always jumping with regulars. See chapter 7.

- **Alan Wong's Restaurant** (1857 S. King St., 5th Floor; ☎ 808/949-2526): Master strokes at this shrine of Hawaii Regional Cuisine: crispy ahi lumpia; warm California roll made with salmon roe, wasabi, and Kona lobster instead of rice; and ginger-crusted fresh onaga. Fresh "day boat" scallops in season are a must, grilled lamb chops a perennial. The menu changes daily, but the flavors never lose their sizzle. See chapter 7.

- **Hawaii Seafood Paradise** (1830 Ala Moana Blvd.; ☎ **808/946-4514**): Nine kinds of roast duck, including a peerless Peking, are reason enough to go there. But the sizzling platters, seafood fried rice, spicy prawn soup, and kung pao scallops take Cantonese/Szechuan to new heights. A few Thai dishes spice up the menu. See chapter 7.
- **Jimbo's Restaurant** (1936 S. King St.; ☎ **808/947-2211**): Life's simple pleasures: homemade broth, homemade noodles, light-as-air tempura, nabeyaki of the gods. All in a cozy room accented with bamboo, calligraphy, and folk art. See chapter 7.
- **Kahala Moon Café** (4614 Kilauea Ave.; ☎ **808/732-7777**): The grilled lamb chops are the way to go, and the lemongrass crème brûlée and mango bread pudding are the guiltless finale. In between, feast on whole-leaf Caesar salad, sautéed salmon with wild mushroom stuffing, pasta, and crab cakes in a windowless but pleasing room. See chapter 7.
- **Roy's Restaurant** (6600 Kalanianaole Hi.; ☎ **808/396-7697**): The pioneer of Hawaii Regional Cuisine still reigns at his busy, noisy flagship Hawaii Kai dining room with the trademark open kitchen. Roy's deft way with local ingredients, ethnic preparations, and fresh fish make his menu, which changes daily, a novel experience every time.
- **Singha Thai Cuisine** (Canterbury Place, 1910 Ala Moana Blvd.; ☎ **808/ 941-2898**): Thai chili fresh fish and blackened ahi summer rolls are among Singha's big hits—and there are many. The Thai fusion menu uses local organic ingredients and many varieties of fresh Island fish, as well as the bold spices and flavorings of Thai cuisine. The Royal Thai Dancers are a feast for the eyes. See chapter 7.

14 The Best of Oahu for Kids

Oahu isn't for adults only—there are plenty of activities to keep the keikis (kids) as well as the kids-at-heart busy.

- **Swim at Waikiki Beach:** Waikiki Beach offers a lot more than just swimming for the kids, they can boogie board, learn to surf, take a ride on an outrigger canoe or sailing catamaran, snorkel, or build sand castles. See chapter 8.
- **Explore the Bishop Museum:** There are some 1,180,000 Polynesian artifacts, 13,500,000 different insect specimens, 6,000,000 marine and land shells, 490,000 plant specimens, 130,000 fish specimens, and 85,000 birds and mammals all in the Bishop Museum. Kids can explore interactive exhibits, see a 50-foot sperm whale skeleton, and check out a Hawaiian grass hut. There's something for everyone here. See chapter 9.
- **Walking Through a Submarine:** The USS *Bowfin* Submarine Museum Park offers kids an interactive museum and a real submarine that served in some of the fiercest naval battles in World War II. Kids can explore the interior of the tightly packed submarine that housed some 90 to 100 men, seeing the stacked bunks where the men slept, the radar and electronics in the command center, and where the torpedoes were stored and launched. See chapter 9.
- **Dream at the Hawaii Maritime Center:** Kids will love the Kalakaua Boathouse, the two-story museum of the Maritime Center with exhibits that include the development of surfing, the art of tattooing, and artifacts from the whaling industry. Next door is the fully rigged, four-masted *Falls of Clyde*. Built in 1878, it served as a cargo-and-passenger liner and a sailing tanker before being declared a National Historic Landmark. If it's not out sailing, moored next to the *Falls* is the *Hokule'a*, the re-creation of a traditional double-hulled sailing canoe, which in 1976 made

the 6,000-mile round-trip voyage to Tahiti, following only ancient navigational techniques—the stars, the wind, and the sea. See chapter 9.

- **Watch the Fish and Sharks at the Waikiki Aquarium:** Much more than just a big fish tank, the Waikiki Aquarium will astound, and at the same time educate, your youngsters. They can probably sit for hours staring at the sharks, turtles, eels, rays, and fish swimming in the main tank. For a few laughs, wander out to the monk seal area and watch the antics of these endangered seagoing clowns. See chapter 9.

- **Snorkel at Hanauma Bay:** Kids will be enthralled at the underwater world that can be accessed in this marine park teeming with tropical fish. The shallow waters near the beach are perfect for neophyte snorkelers to learn in. The long (2,000-foot) beach has plenty of room for kids to take off and run. Get there early; it can get crowded. See chapter 8.

- **Explore the Depths in a Submarine Dive:** Better than a movie, more exciting than a video game, both the Atlantis and Voyager submarines journey down to 100 feet below the waves and explore the Neptunian world of tropical reef fish, turtles, huge manta rays, and even an occasional shark or two. See chapter 8.

- **See Sea Creatures at Sea Life Park:** Kids will love this 62-acre ocean theme park that features orca whales, dolphins, seals, and penguins going through their hoops to the delight of kids of all ages. There's a Hawaiian Reef Tank full of native tropical fish, a "touch" pool where you can grab a real sea cucumber (commonly found in tide pools), and a Bird Sanctuary where you can see birds like the red-footed booby and the Frigate bird that usually are seen overhead. The chief curiosity, though, is the world's only "wolphin"—a cross between a false killer whale and an Atlantic bottle-nosed dolphin. See chapter 9.

15 The Best Shopping

In this land of the alluring outdoors, few people like to admit that shopping is a major activity—or, some would say, distraction. Truth be known, the proliferation of top-notch made-in-Hawaii products, the vitality of the local crafts scene, and the search for mementos of the islands lend a new respectability to shopping here.

- **Academy Shop** (900 S. Beretania St., Honolulu Academy of Arts; ☎ **808/ 523-8703**): What's here: ethnic and contemporary gift items representing the art and craft traditions of the world, from books and jewelry to basketry, beadwork, ikats, saris, ethnic fabrics, and fiber vessels and accessories. What you'll want: everything. See chapter 10.

- **Avanti Fashion** (2229 Kuhio Ave., ☎ **808/924-1688;** 2270 Kalakaua Ave., Waikiki Shopping Plaza, ☎ 808/922-2828): In authentic prints from the 1930s and 1940s reproduced on silk, Avanti aloha shirts and sportswear elevate tropical garb from high kitsch to high chic. Casual, comfortable, easy care, and light as a cloud, the silks look vintage but cost a fraction of collectibles prices. The nostalgic treasures are available in retail stores statewide, but the best selection is at the two Avanti retail stores in Waikiki. See chapter 10.

- **Contemporary Museum Gift Shop** (2411 Makiki Heights Rd., Contemporary Museum; ☎ **808/523-3447**): It gets our vote as the most beautiful setting for a gift shop, and its contents are a bonus: extraordinary art-related books, avant-garde jewelry, cards and stationery, home accessories, and gift items made by artists from Hawaii and across the country. Only the best here. See chapter 10.

- **Island Provision Co. at Vagabond House** (1200 Ala Moana Center, Ward Centre; ☎ **808/593-0288**): The theme of gracious island living means home accessories, one-of-a-kind island crafts, fine porcelain and pottery, children's books, luxury soaps, hand-screened table linens, china, furniture, and everything from toys to teapots. A browser's (and shopper's!) paradise. See chapter 10.

- **Native Books & Beautiful Things** (222 Merchant St., Downtown; ☎ **808/ 599-5511;** 1525 Bernice St., Kalihi, at Bishop Museum, ☎ 808/845-8949): Hawaii is the content and the context in this shop of books, crafts, and gift items made by Island artists and crafters. Musical instruments, calabashes, jewelry, leis, books, fabrics, clothing, home accessories, jams and jellies—they're all high quality and made in Hawaii—a celebration of Hawaiiana. See chapter 10.
- **Silk Winds** (1016 Kapahulu Ave., Kilohana Square; ☎ **808/735-6599**): Cricket cages, mah-jongg tiles, jade, porcelain, Buddhas, and beads await the fortunate shopper who stumbles upon this treasure trove of new and old collectibles. See chapter 10.
- **Strawberry Connection of Hawaii** (1931 Kahai St., Kalihi; ☎ **808/842-0278**): This is paradise for foodies, chefs, aspiring chefs, and those on the hunt for the best in Hawaii food products. This warehouse in industrial Honolulu rewards your search with thousands of the best gifts to go, from tropical fruit vinegars and preserves to gourmet honeys, chocolates, and made-in-Hawaii sauces and marinades. See chapter 10.

16 The Best Spots for Sunset Cocktails

Need we say more?

- **House Without a Key** (2199 Kalia Rd., Halekulani; ☎ **808/923-2311**): Oahu's quintessential sunset oasis claims several unbeatable elements: It's outdoors on the ocean, with a view of Diamond Head, and it offers great hula and steel guitar music—and the best Mai Tais on the island. You know it's special when even jaded Honoluluans declare this their favorite spot for send-offs, reunions, and an everyday gorgeous sunset. See chapter 11.
- **Mai Tai Bar** (2259 Kalakaua Ave., Royal Hawaiian Hotel; ☎ **808/923-7311**): This bar without walls is perched a few feet from the sand, with sweeping views of the south shore and the Waianae Mountains. Surfers and paddlers ride the waves while the light turns golden and Diamond Head acquires a halo. This is one of the most pleasing views of Waikiki Beach; sip a mighty Mai Tai while Carmen and Keith Haugen serenade you. See chapter 11.
- **Duke's Canoe Club** (2335 Kalakaua Ave., Outrigger Waikiki Hotel; ☎ **808/ 923-0711**): It's crowded at sunset, but who can resist Moe Keale or Brother Noland's music in this upbeat atmosphere a few feet from the sands of Waikiki? Come in from the beach or from the street—it's always a party at Duke's. Entertainment here is tops, and it reaches a crescendo at sunset. See chapter 11.
- **Sunset Lanai** (2863 Kalakaua Ave., New Otani Kaimana Beach Hotel; ☎ **808/ 923-1555**): The hau tree shaded Robert Louis Stevenson as he wrote poems to Princess Kaiulani. Today it frames the ocean view from the Sunset Lanai, next to the Hau Tree Lanai restaurant. Sunset Lanai is the favorite watering hole of Diamond Head–area beachgoers who love Sans Souci Beach, the ocean view, the consummate Mai Tais, and the live music during weekend sunset hours. See chapter 6.
- **Jameson's by the Sea** (62–540 Kamehameha Hi., Haleiwa; ☎ **808/637-6272**): The Mai Tais here are dubbed the best in surf city, and the view, though not perfect, isn't hurting either. Across the street from the harbor, this open-air roadside oasis is a happy stop for North Shore wave watchers and sunset-savvy sightseers. See chapter 7.

Oahu, the Gathering Place

2

by Jeanette Foster

A wise Hawaiian *kupuna* once told me that the islands are like children—that each is special yet different, that each is to be loved for its individual qualities. One thing's for sure: You will never find another island like Oahu, the commercial and population center of Hawaii.

It's astounding to spend hours flying across the barren blue of the Pacific and then to see suddenly below you the whites and pastels of Honolulu, the most remote big city on earth, a 26-mile-long metropolis of some 875,000 souls living in the middle of nowhere. Once on its streets, you'll find bright city lights, five-star restaurants, nearly all-night nightclubs, world-class shopping, great art and architecture, and grand old hotels.

Nine out of ten visitors to Hawaii—some 5 million a year—stop on Oahu, and most of them end up along the busy streets of Waikiki, Honolulu's famous hotel district and its most densely populated neighborhood. Some days it seems like the entire world is sunning itself on Waikiki's famous beach.

Beyond Waikiki, Honolulu is clean and easy to enjoy. Founded by King Kamehameha, "reformed" by Boston missionaries, and once dominated by the "Big Five" cartels, Honolulu has come of age just in time for the 21st century. The old port town has reshaped its waterfront, altered its skyline, and is building a convention center and opening new world-class hotels—all the while trying to preserve its historic roots and revive its Polynesian heritage.

Out in the country, Oahu can be as down-home as the music of a slack-key guitarist. That's where you'll find a big blue sky, perfect waves, empty beaches, rainbows and waterfalls, sweet tropical flowers, and fiery Pacific sunsets. In fact, nowhere else within 60 minutes of a major American city can you snorkel in a crystal-clear lagoon, climb an old volcano, surf monster waves, fish for record-sized marlin, kayak to a desert isle, picnic on a sandbar, soar in a glider over tide pools, skin dive over a sunken airplane, bicycle through a rain forest, golf a championship course, or sail into the setting sun.

And weatherwise, no other Hawaiian island has it as nice as Oahu: The Big Island is hotter, Kauai is wetter, Maui has more wind, and Molokai and Lanai are drier. But Oahu enjoys a kind of perpetual late spring, with light trade winds and 82°F days almost year-round. In fact, the climate is supposed to be the best on the planet. Once you have that, the rest is easy.

1 Honolulu & Oahu Today

Not just another pretty place in the sun, America's only island state is emerging as the cultural center and meeting place of the Pacific Rim, with an international cast of characters playing key roles.

Even busy Waikiki is cleaning up its act, replacing time-share vendors with flower lei stands, and offering authentic chant and hula in traditional costumes nightly at sunset. It is no longer a place of tacky T-shirts and souvenir stands, evolving into the shopping capital of the Pacific, where people fly in to browse European designer boutiques like Cartier, Dunhill, Ferragamo, and Ettore Bugatti. A new $214 million Hawaii Convention Center rising at the gateway to Waikiki will enhance the state's position as a crossroad between East and West. Completion of the four-story, 1.1-million-square-foot center is scheduled for July 1998.

Hawaii now has some of the world's newest and finest world-class beach resorts, contemporary palaces that would astound even the islands' hedonistic kings. Here you can dine on the freshest seafood and island-grown fruits and vegetables, receive the attention of your own butler, and while away lazy days in secret gardens and private pools.

And the old and new are combining to create a level of style and service that only enhances Oahu's own aloha spirit. Oahu is not just a place where East meets West but where the tropical past is carried forward into the future.

"Our goal is to teach and share our culture," says Gloriann Akau, who is an island manager for the Aloha Festivals. "In 1946, after the war, Hawaiians needed an identity. We were lost and needed to regroup. When we started to celebrate our culture, we began to feel proud. We have a wonderful culture that had been buried for a number of years. This brought it out again. Self-esteem is more important than making a lot of money."

In 1985, as glitzy megaresorts with borrowed cultures began to appear in the islands, native Hawaiian educator, author, and *kupuna* George Kanahele started infusing Hawaiian values into hotels. (A *kupuna* is an elder with leadership qualities who commands great respect; Kanahele is a *kupuna* with a Ph.D. from Cornell University.)

"You have the responsibility to preserve and enhance the Hawaiian culture, not because it's going to make money for you but because it's the right thing to do," Kanahele told the Hawaii Hotel Association. "Ultimately, the only thing unique about Hawaii is its Hawaiianess. Hawaiianess is our competitive edge."

From general managers to maids, employees at two major resorts took 16 hours of Hawaiian cultural training. They held focus groups to discuss the meaning of aloha—the Hawaiian concept of unremitting love. They applied aloha to their work and their lives. Kaanapali Beach Hotel on Maui was the first to instill Hawaiian ways in their hotel staff, followed by the Outrigger Hotel chain, one of the biggest in Hawaii. Many others have joined the movement.

Impressions

If paradise consists solely of beauty, then these islands were the fairest that man ever invaded, for the land and sea were beautiful and the climate was congenial.

—James A. Michener, *Hawaii*

No longer content with trying hula as a joke, visitors can now learn from real *kumu hula* (hula teachers), or visit a *heiau* (Hawaiian temple) with a kupuna, and try native Hawaiian medicine from the rain forest.

THE QUESTION OF SOVEREIGNTY

The cultural renaissance has made its way into politics, so don't be surprised if you see clenched-fisted native Hawaiians taking to the streets and beaches to call for independence for their homeland. Under the banner of sovereignty, many *kanaka maoli*—or native people, as they call themselves—are demanding the restoration of rights taken away more than a century ago when the United States overthrew the Hawaiian monarchy and claimed the islands. In the past few years, members of about 30 activist groups have invaded Waikiki Beach to hand out sovereignty leaflets and tell sun-worshipping tourists to "Go Home Now." Thousands recently blocked Kalakaua Avenue, Waikiki's main drag, for 2 hours on a protest march. They demonstrated before 400 delegates at a state-sponsored congress intended to promote tourism. Then-governor John Waihee, the first person with Hawaiian blood ever elected to the office, raised the Hawaiian flag instead of the Stars and Stripes over the statehouse at the 100-year observance of the U.S. overthrow of the Hawaiian monarchy. In a 1994 rally on Iolani Palace grounds, where the monarchy was toppled, some 500 Hawaiians known as the Ohana Council declared independence from the United States and claimed the land as their own.

Their demands for sovereignty were not lost on President Bill Clinton, who was picketed at a Democratic political fund-raiser at Waikiki Beach in July 1993. Four months later, Clinton signed a law that stated the U.S. Congress "apologizes to Native Hawaiians on behalf of the people of the United States for the overthrow of the Kingdom of Hawaii on January 17, 1893, with the participation of agents and citizens of the United States, and deprivation of the rights of Native Hawaiians to self-determination."

While that could be construed to mean a return to the way things were in Hawaii a century ago with kings and queens and a royal court, not even neonationalists are convinced that's possible. First, the Hawaiians themselves must decide if they want sovereignty, since each of the 30 identifiable sovereignty organizations, and more than 100 splinter groups, has a different view of self-determination. They range from total independence from the United States to a nation-within-a-nation similar to the status of American Indians.

2 History 101

by Rick Carroll

Paddling outrigger canoes, the first ancestors of today's Hawaiians followed the stars and birds across a trackless sea to Hawaii, which they called "the land of raging fire." Those first settlers were part of the great Polynesian migration that settled the vast triangle of islands stretching from New Zealand in the southwest to Easter Island in the east to Hawaii in the north. No one is sure when they arrived in Hawaii from Tahiti and the Marquesas Islands, some 2,500 miles to the south, but a dog-bone fish hook found at the southernmost tip of the Big Island has been carbon-dated to A.D. 700.

An entire Hawaiian culture arose over the next 1,500 years. The settlers built temples, fishponds, and aqueducts to irrigate taro plantations. Sailors became farmers and fishermen. Each island was a separate kingdom. The *alii* (high ranking chiefs) created a caste system and established taboos. Violators were strangled. High priests asked the gods Lono and Ku for divine guidance. Ritual human sacrifices were common.

THE "FATAL CATASTROPHE"

No ancient Hawaiian ever imagined a *haole* (a person with "no breath") would ever appear on "a floating island." But then one day in 1779 just such a white-skinned person sailed into Waimea Bay on Kauai, where he was welcomed as the god, Lono.

The man was 50-year-old Capt. James Cook, already famous in Britain for "discovering" much of the southern Pacific. Now on his third great voyage of exploration, Cook had set sail from Tahiti northward across uncharted waters to find the mythical Northwest Passage linking the Pacific and Atlantic oceans. On his way, Cook stumbled upon the Hawaiian Islands quite by chance. He named them the Sandwich Islands, for the Earl of Sandwich, First Lord of the Admiralty, who had bankrolled his expedition.

Overnight, Stone Age Hawaii entered the age of iron. Gifts were presented and trade established: nails for fresh water, pigs, and the affections of Hawaiian women. The sailors brought syphilis, measles, and other diseases to which the Hawaiians had no natural immunity, thereby unwittingly wreaking havoc on the native population. (While on a trip to Europe in 1825, King Kamehameha II and his queen Kamamalu died of measles in London.)

After an unsuccessful attempt to find the Northwest Passage, Cook returned to Kealakekua on the Big Island, where a fight broke out. The great navigator was killed by a blow to the head. After this "fatal catastrophe," the British survivors sailed home.

Hawaii was now on the sea charts. French, Russian, and American traders on the fur route between Canada's Hudson's Bay Company and China anchored in Hawaii to get fresh water. More trade and more disastrous liaisons ensued.

Two more sea captains left indelible marks on the islands: The first was American John Kendrick, who in 1791 filled his ship with sandalwood and sailed to China. By 1825, Hawaii's sandalwood forests were gone, enabling invasive plants to run amok on the islands. The second was Englishman George Vancouver, who in 1793 left cows and sheep, which nibbled the islands to the high-tide line. The king sent to Mexico and Spain for cowboys to round up the wild cattle, thus beginning the islands' *paniolo* (cowboy) tradition.

The tightly woven Hawaiian society, enforced by royalty and religious edicts, began to unravel after the death in 1819 of King Kamehameha I, who had used guns seized from a British ship to unite the islands under his rule. His successor, Queen Kaahumanu, abolished the old taboos, thus opening the door for a religion of another form.

STAYING TO DO WELL

In April of 1820, god-fearing missionaries arrived from New England bent on converting the pagans. "Can these be human beings?" exclaimed their leader, the Rev. Hiram Bingham, upon first glance of "the almost naked savages" whose "appearance of destitution, degradation, and barbarism" he found "appalling."

Intent on instilling their brand of rock-ribbed Christianity in the islands, the missionaries clothed the natives, banned them from dancing the hula, and nearly dismantled their ancient culture. They tried to keep the whalers and sailors out of the bawdy houses, where a flood of whiskey quenched fleet-size thirsts and where the virtue of native women was never safe.

The missionaries taught reading and writing, created the 12-letter Hawaiian alphabet, started a letter press, and began writing the islands' history, which was until then only an oral account in half-remembered chants.

Children of the missionaries became the islands' business leaders and politicians. They married Hawaiians and stayed on in the islands, causing one wag to remark that the missionaries "came to do good and stayed to do well."

In 1848 King Kamehameha III proclaimed the Great Mahele (division) that enabled commoners and eventually foreigners to own crown land. In two generations more than 80% of all private land was in haole hands. Sugar planters imported waves of immigrants to work the fields as contract laborers. The first Chinese came in 1852, followed by 7,000 Japanese in 1885 and the Portuguese in 1878.

King David Kalakaua was elected to the throne in 1874. This popular "Merrie Monarch" built Iolani Place in 1882, threw extravagant parties, and restored the hula and other native arts to grace. For this he was much loved. He also gave Pearl Harbor to the United States; it became the westernmost bastion of the U.S. Navy—and the bull's-eye of the infamous Japanese air raid on the sleepy Sunday of December 7, 1941. In 1891, King Kalakaua visited chilly San Francisco, caught a cold, and died in the royal suite of the Sheraton Palace. His sister, Queen Liliuokalani, assumed the throne.

A SAD FAREWELL

On January 17, 1893, a group of American sugar planters and missionary descendants, with the support of gun-toting marines, imprisoned Queen Liliuokalani in her own palace. The monarchy was dead.

A new republic was established, controlled by Sanford Dole, a powerful sugarcane planter. In 1898 Hawaii became an American territory ruled by Dole and his fellow sugarcane planters and the Big Five, a cartel that controlled banking, shipping, hardware, and every other facet of economic life in the islands.

Oahu's central Ewa Plain soon filled with row crops. The Dole family planted pineapple on their vast acreage. Planters imported more contract laborers from Puerto Rico (1900), Korea (1903), and the Philippines (1907–1931). Most of the new immigrants stayed on to establish families and become a part of the islands. Meanwhile, the native Hawaiians became a landless minority in their own homeland.

For a half century sugar was king, generously subsidized by the U.S. federal government. The sugar planters dominated the territory's economy, shaped its social fabric, and kept the islands in a colonial plantation era with bosses and field hands. But the workers eventually struck for higher wages and improved working conditions; the planters were unable to compete with cheap third-world labor costs, and their market share was shrinking. Hawaii's lush fields of sugar and pineapple gradually went to seed, and the plantation era ended.

THE TOURISTS ARRIVE

Tourism proper began in the 1860s. Kilauea became the world's prime attraction for adventure travelers who rode on horseback 29 miles from Hilo to peer into the boiling hell fire of Halemaumau. The journal of missionary William Ellis, the first American to see the Kilauea volcano in 1823, inspired many to visit it. "Astonishment and awe for some moments rendered us mute and like statues we stood," he wrote. "Our eyes riveted on the abyss below . . . one vast flood of burning matter . . . rolling to and fro its fiery surge and flaming billows." In 1865, a grass version of Volcano House was built on the Halemaumau Crater rim to shelter them. It was Hawaii's first tourist hotel.

But Hawaii's tourism really got off the ground with the demise of the plantation era, and it has shaped the islands' history in ways that sugarcane and pineapples never did.

In 1901, W. C. Peacock built the elegant beaux arts Moana Hotel on Waikiki Beach, and W. C. Weedon convinced Honolulu businessmen to bankroll his plan to advertise Hawaii in San Francisco. Travelers were going to California, and Weedon meant to persuade them to see Hawaii, too. Armed with a stereopticon and tinted photos of Waikiki, Weedon sailed off in 1902 for 6 months of lecture tours to introduce "those remarkable people and the beautiful lands of Hawaii." He drew packed houses. A tourism promotion bureau was formed in 1903, financed by the port's rat-control plague tax. About 2,000 visitors came to Hawaii that year.

Steamships were Hawaii's tourism lifeline. It took $4^{1/2}$ days to sail from San Francisco to Honolulu. Streamers, leis, pomp, and a warm "Boat Day" welcomed each Matson Liner at downtown's Aloha Tower. Well-heeled visitors brought trunks, servants, even their Rolls, and stayed for months. Hawaii amused the idly rich with personal tours, floral parades, and shows spotlighting that naughty dance, the hula.

Beginning in 1935 and running for the next 40 years, Webley Edwards's weekly live radio show, "Hawaii Calls," planted the sounds of Waikiki—surf, sliding steel guitar, sweet Hawaiian harmonies, drumbeats—in the hearts of millions of listeners in America, Australia, and Canada.

In 1936, visitors could fly to Honolulu on the *Hawaii Clipper*, a seven-passenger Pan American Martin M-130 flying boat, for $360 one way. The flight took 21 hours, 33 minutes. Modern tourism was born, with five flying boats providing daily service between San Francisco and Honolulu. The 1941 visitor count was a brisk 31,846 through December 6.

REMEMBER PEARL HARBOR!

On December 7, 1941, Japanese Zeros came out of the rising sun to bomb American warships based at Pearl Harbor. It was the "day of infamy" that plunged the United States into World War II and gave the nation its revenge-laced battle cry, "Remember Pearl Harbor!"

The aftermath of the attack brought immediate changes to the islands. Martial law was declared, thus stripping the Big Five cartels of their absolute power in a single day. Feared to be spies, Japanese-Americans from Hawaii and California were sent to internment camps. Hawaii was "blacked out" at night, Waikiki Beach was strung with barbed wire, and Aloha Tower was painted in camouflage. Only young men bound for the Pacific came to Hawaii during the war years. Tens of thousands returned to graves in a Honolulu cemetery called The Punchbowl.

The postwar years saw the beginnings of Hawaii's faux culture. Harry Yee invented the Blue Hawaii cocktail and dropped in a tiny Japanese parasol. Vic Bergeron created the Mai Tai, a rum-and-fresh-lime-juice drink, and opened Trader Vic's, America's first theme restaurant that featured the art, decor, and food of Polynesia. Arthur Godfrey picked up a ukulele and began singing hapa-haole tunes on early television shows. Burt Lancaster and Deborah Kerr made love in the surf at Hanauma Bay in the 1954 movie *From Here to Eternity.* In 1955, Henry J. Kaiser built the Hilton Hawaiian Village, and the 11-story high-rise Princess Kaiulani Hotel opened on a site where the real princess once played. Hawaii greeted 109,000 visitors that year.

STATEHOOD!

In 1959 Hawaii became the last star on the Stars and Stripes, the 50th state of the union. But that year also saw the arrival of the first jet airliners, which brought

250,000 tourists to the fledgling state. The personal touch that had defined aloha gave way to the sheer force of numbers. Waikiki's room count virtually doubled in 2 years, from 16,000 in 1969 to 31,000 units in 1971, and more followed before city fathers finally clamped a growth lid on the world's most famous resort. By 1980, the number of annual arrivals reached 4 million.

In the early 1980s, the Japanese government decided its citizens should travel overseas, and out they went. Waikiki was one of their favorite destinations, and they brought lots of spending money. The effect on sales in Hawaii was phenomenal: European boutiques opened stores in Honolulu, and duty-free shoppers became the main supporter of Honolulu International Airport. Japanese investors competed for the chance to own or build part of Hawaii. Hotels sold so quickly and at such unbelievable prices that heads began to spin with dollar signs.

In 1986, Hawaii's visitor count surpassed 5 million. Two years later, it went over 6 million. Expensive fantasy megaresorts bloomed on the neighbor islands like giant artificial flowers, swelling the luxury market with ever swankier accommodations.

The highest visitor count ever recorded hit 6.9 million in 1990, but the bubble burst in early 1991 with the Gulf War and worldwide recessions. In 1992, Hurricane Iniki devastated Kauai, and airfare wars sent Americans to Mexico. Overbuilt with luxury hotels, Hawaii slashed its room rates, enabling visitors to reside in luxury digs at affordable prices—a trend that continues.

3 Life & Language

by Rick Carroll

Plantations brought so many different people to Hawaii that the state is now a rainbow of ethnic groups. No one group is a majority; everyone's a minority. Living here are Hawaiians, Caucasians, African-Americans, American Indians, Eskimos, Aleuts, Japanese, Chinese, Filipinos, Koreans, Tahitians, Asian Indians, Vietnamese, Guamanians, Samoans, Tongans, and other Asian and Pacific islanders. Add a few Canadians, Dutch, English, French, German, Irish, Italians, Portuguese, Scottish, Puerto Ricans, and Spanish.

More than a century ago, W. Somerset Maugham noted that "All these strange people live close to each other, with different languages and different thoughts; they believe in different gods and they have different values; two passions alone they share: love and hunger." More recently, noted travel journalist Jan Morris said of Hawaii's population: "Half the world's races seem to be represented and interbred here, and between them they have created an improbable microcosm of human society as a whole."

In combination, it's a remarkable potpourri. Most retain an element of the traditions of their homeland. Some Japanese-Americans of Hawaii, even after three and four generations removed from the homeland, are more traditional than the Japanese of Tokyo. And the same is true of many Chinese, Korean, Filipinos, and the rest of the 25 or so ethnic groups that make Hawaii a kind of living museum of various Asian and Pacific cultures.

WHAT *Haole* MEANS

When Hawaiians first saw Western visitors, they called the pale-skinned, frail men *haole* because they looked so out of breath. In Hawaiian, *ha* means breath, *ole* means an absence of what precedes it. In other words, a lifeless-looking person.

Today, the term haole is generally a synonym for Caucasian or foreigner and is used casually without intending to cause any disrespect. However, if uttered by an

Real Hawaiian Style

With 25 different ethnic groups, including the largest Asian mix in the United States, Hawaii has a real diffusion of styles and cultures. Yet out of this rich melange there emerges a distinct Hawaiian style. Sooner or later everyone, even the visitor, picks up on it and puts it into practice. It's speech, body language, local habits, and a way of life that distinguishes those who live in the islands from those who visit.

It's a mix of surfer, Hawaii hang-loose, traditional Chinese, and coastal haole. There's Aloha Friday (every Friday), pidgin ('Eh fo'real, brah), and the shaka greeting (stick out your pinky and thumb, pull in your three middle fingers, and shake—hang loose, brah).

People stand in line at noon to order plate lunches, ask for "two scoops rice," like to eat Spam, and drink Budweiser beer. They seldom honk their car horns (it's considered rude). They're at home with chopsticks. They barbecue in public beach parks, and hold baby luaus for kids when they turn 1 year old.

They vote Democratic, check the surf report on "Good Morning Hawaii," listen to Hawaiian music on KCCN, and register their opinion on The Hawaii Poll. They worry about the high cost of housing and the loss of jobs.

They wear shower sandals known as *zoris* outdoors but never indoors, and they often go barefoot. They specify "aloha attire" at the funeral when their *tutu* (grandmother) dies, but only businessmen, lawyers, and other professionals tuck their aloha shirts into their pants. Everyone else leaves them out.

Some young men wear queues—the long plait of hair hanging down their backs that their Asian grandfathers gladly shed—as a sign of ethnic pride. Some now affect the traditional Polynesian zigzag tattoos that English sailors first saw in Tahiti in 1767.

Although women in old Hawaii went topless, young women today wear the long muumuu dresses introduced by the missionaries. The only bare breasts you'll see today are on nude beaches, which technically are illegal, but never mind that.

Everyone wears flowers, in their hair or around their neck. Men and women often tuck a single blossom over their ear. It's very Polynesian, and a clue to your current status with the opposite sex: Over the right ear means available, over the left means spoken for.

Make eye contact and say hello by raising your eyebrows with a smile. That's Hawaiian-style. Try it—it works.

---

angry stranger who adds certain adjectives like stupid or dumb, the term haole can be construed as a mild racial slur.

THE HAWAIIAN LANGUAGE

Almost everyone here speaks English, so except for pronouncing place names, you should have no trouble communicating in Hawaii. Many folks in Hawaii now speak Hawaiian, for the ancient language is making a comeback. Everybody who visits Hawaii, in fact, will soon hear the words *aloha, mahalo, wahine,* and *kane.* If you just arrived, you're a *malihini.* Someone who's been here a long time is a *kamaaina.*

When you finish a job or your meal, you are *pau* (over). On Friday it's *pau hana,* work over. You put *pupus* (that's Hawaii's version of hors d'oeuvres) in your mouth when you go *pau hana.* Pupus are easier to spell—and eat.

The Hawaiian alphabet, created by the New England missionaries, has only 12 letters—the 5 regular vowels (a, e, i, o, and u) and 7 consonants (h, k, l, m, n, p, and w). The vowels are pronounced in the Roman fashion, that is, *ah, ay, ee, oh,* and *oo* (as in "too")—not *ay, ee, eye, oh,* and *you,* as in English. For example, *huhu* is pronounced "who-who." Almost all vowels are sounded separately, although some are pronounced together, as in Kalakaua: *Kah lah cow ah.*

SOME HAWAIIAN WORDS

Here are basic Hawaiian words, with their English meanings, that you will often hear in Hawaii and see throughout this book:

ali'i   Hawaiian royalty

aloha   greeting or farewell

ewa   in the direction of Ewa, an Oahu town; generally meaning west ("Drive ewa 5 miles.")

hala   the pandanus tree, the leaves of which are used for weaving

halau   school

hale   house or building

haole   foreigner, Caucasian

heiau   Hawaiian temple or place of worship

holoholo   to have fun, relax

hoolaulea   celebration

hui   a club, assembly

hula   native dance

imu   underground oven lined with hot rocks, used for cooking the luau pig

kahili   royal standard of red and yellow feathers

kahuna   priest or expert

kalua   to bake underground in the imu (as in kalua pig)

kamaaina   old-timer

kanaka maoli   native Hawaiians

kane   man

kapa   tapa, bark cloth

kapu   taboo, forbidden

keiki   child

kokua   help, cooperate

kumu hula   teacher of Hawaiian dance

kupuna   an elder with leadership qualities who commands great respect; grandparent

lanai   porch or veranda

lei   garland

lomilomi   massage

luau   feast

mahalo   thank you

makai   a direction, toward the sea

malihini   stranger, newcomer

malo   loin cloth

mana   spirit power

mauka   direction, toward the mountains

mele   song or chant

muumuu   loose fitting gown or dress

nene   official state bird, a goose

ohana   family

ono   delicious

pahu   drum

pau   finished, done

pali   cliff

poi   crushed taro root, made into a starchy paste

pupu   hors d'oeuvre

wahine   woman

PIDGIN: 'EH FO'REAL, BRAH

As you get to know Hawaii, you'll reach beyond "aloha" and "mahalo" and discover words like *da kine,* an ubiquitous multipurpose term that can mean "that thing over there," or the "whatchamacallit," or "the very best," as in "when you care enough to send da kine card." Da kine is from Hawaii's other native tongue: pidgin English.

Pidgin developed as a means for sugar planters to communicate with their Chinese laborers in the 1800s. Today pidgin is spoken by people who grew up in Hawaii to talk with their peers. It's a manner of speaking that seems to endure despite efforts to suppress it. At a local ball game, fans may shout **"Geevum!"** (Give 'em what-for). A ruffled clerk may tell her friend someone gave her **"stink eye"** (a dirty look). **"No huhu"**(don't get mad), soothes the friend. You could be invited to hear an elder **"talk story"** (relating memories) or to enjoy local treats like **"shave ice"** (tropical snow cone) and **"crack seed"** (highly seasoned preserved fruit). Local residents also punctuate their speech by inserting a word like "yeah" into sentences for emphasis, or as a segue meaning "do you know what I mean?" For example: "Got to be there 6am, you know. Junk, yeah? Maybe humbug, but, boss's speech, 'ats why."

Action words undergo a kind of poetic squeeze, so that each has a lot of meanings. Take the word **"broke."** It's immortalized in the most famous pidgin phrase of all— the motto of the 442nd Infantry Battalion, World War II's fearless band of Japanese-American heroes from Hawaii and California who risked their lives to prove their loyalty: "Go For Broke." Then there's **"wen' go broke"** (something got busted or torn, or simply stopped).

"Broke da mouth" (tastes really good) is the favorite pidgin phrase of Dr. Derek Bickerton, professor of linguistics at University of Hawaii, who teaches a course on Creole languages. He says Hawaiian pidgin is more than a makeshift list of sing-song terms used to bridge a language gap. Over decades, a real Creole language developed with its own order and syntax, relying not only on English and Hawaiian but borrowing words and some grammar from several languages—Japanese, Chinese, Filipino, Portuguese, and the tongues of all the other ethnic groups who came to work the sugarcane fields a century ago.

Today, although the plantations are almost gone, the next generations and the new immigrants continue the pidgin tradition in their own way. However, modern pressures may be driving pidgin underground. Pure pidgin speakers these days tend to be older people in remote areas. Visitors to Waikiki will be lucky to hear the real thing at all.

A FEW MORE PIDGIN WORDS & PHRASES

> *'owzit!*   How's it?
> **laters**   See you later.
> **chance em**   Go for it.
> **moah bettah**   the best
> **cheeken skeen**   goose bumps
> **Eh, fo' real, brah**   It's true, brother.

4 A Taste of Hawaii

by Jocelyn Fujii

THE NEW GUARD: HAWAII REGIONAL CUISINE

A decade ago, visitors could expect to find frozen mahimahi beurre blanc with frozen or canned vegetables as the premium dish on a fine-dining menu in Hawaii. But not anymore. It's a whole new world in Hawaii's restaurant kitchens.

Today, you can expect to encounter Indonesian sates, Chinese stir-frys, Polynesian imu-baked foods, and guava-smoked meats in sophisticated presentations in the state's finest dining rooms. If there's pasta or risotto or rack of lamb on the menu, it could be nori (seaweed) linguine with opihi (limpet sauce), or risotto with local seafood served in taro cups, or a rack of lamb in Cabernet and Hoisin sauce (fermented soybean, garlic, and spices), or with macadamia nuts and coconut.

It has been called many things: Euro-Asian, Pacific Rim, Pacific Edge, Euro-Pacific, Fusion cuisine, Hapa cuisine. By whatever name, Hawaii regional cuisine has evolved as Hawaii's singular cooking style, what some say is the last American regional cuisine, this country's final gastronomic, as well as geographic, frontier. This cuisine highlights the fresh seafood and produce of Hawaii's rich waters and volcanic soil, the cultural traditions of Hawaii's ethnic groups, and the skills of well-trained chefs—such as Roy Yamaguchi (Roy's on Oahu, Big Island, Maui, and Kauai), Peter Merriman (Merriman's on the Big Island), and Jean-Marie Josselin (A Pacific Cafe on Kauai, Maui, and Oahu)—who broke ranks with their European predecessors to forge new ground in the 50th state.

Fresh ingredients are foremost, and farmers and fishermen work together to provide steady supplies of just-harvested seafood, seaweed, fern shoots, vine-ripened tomatoes, goat cheese, lamb, herbs, taro, gourmet lettuces, and countless harvests from land and sea that wind up in myriad forms on ever-changing menus, prepared in Asian and Western culinary styles.

Fresh fruit salsas and sauces (mango, lychee, papaya, pineapple, guava), ginger-sesame-wasabi flavorings, corn cakes with sake sauces, tamarind and fish sauces, coconut-chili accents, tropical-fruit vinaigrettes, and other local and newly arrived seasonings from Southeast Asia and the Pacific impart unique qualities to the preparations.

Here's a sampling of what you can expect to find on a Hawaii Regional menu: Seared Hawaiian fish with lilikoi shrimp butter; tiger shrimp in sake-uni (sea urchin) beurre blanc; taro cakes and Pahoa corn cakes; Molokai sweet-potato vichychoisse; Ka'u orange sauce and Kahua Ranch lamb; pot stickers with ginger sauce; fern shoots from Waipio Valley; Maui onion soup and Hawaiian bouillabaisse, with fresh snapper, Kona crab, and fresh aquacultured shrimp; gourmet Waimanalo greens, picked that day. With menus that often change daily, and the unquenchable appetites that the leading chefs have for cooking on the edge, the possibilities for once-in-a-lifetime dining adventures are more available than ever in Hawaii.

PLATE LUNCHES & MORE: LOCAL FOOD

Although Hawaii regional cuisine has put Hawaii on the epicurean map, at the other end of the spectrum is the cuisine of the hoi polloi, the vast and endearing world of "local food." By that we mean plate lunches and poke, shave ice and saimin, bento lunches and manapua, cultural hybrids all.

Reflecting a polyglot population of many styles and ethnicities, Hawaii's idiosyncratic dining scene is eminently inclusive. Consider Surfer Chic: barefoot in the sand, in swimsuit, chowing down on a plate lunch ordered from a lunch wagon, consisting of fried mahimahi, "two scoops rice," macaroni salad, and a few leaves of green, typically julienned cabbage. (Generally, teriyaki beef or shoyu chicken are options.) Greasy gravy is often the condiment of choice, accompanied by a soft drink in a paper cup. Like saimin—the local version of noodles in broth topped with scrambled egg, green onions, and sometimes pork—the plate lunch is Hawaii's version of high camp.

Because this is Hawaii, at least a few licks of *poi*, the Hawaiian staple of cooked, pounded taro, and the other examples of indigenous cuisine are de rigeuer, if not at a corny luau, then at least in a Hawaiian plate lunch. The native samplers include foods from before and after Western contact, such as *lau lau* (pork, chicken, or fish steamed in ti leaves), *kalua* pork (pork cooked in a Polynesian underground oven known here as an *imu), lomi* salmon (salted salmon with onions, tomatoes, and green onions), chicken long rice, squid *luau* (octopus cooked in coconut milk and taro tops), *poke* (cubed raw fish seasoned with onions and seaweed and the occasional sprinkling of roasted *kukui* nuts), *haupia* (creamy coconut pudding), and *kulolo* (steamed pudding of coconut, brown sugar, and taro).

Bento, another popular choice for the dine-and-dash set, is also available throughout Hawaii. The compact, boxed assortment of picnic fare usually consists of neatly arranged sections of rice, pickled vegetables, and fried chicken, beef, or pork. The

Ahi, Ono & Opakapaka: A Hawaiian Seafood Primer

The fresh seafood in Hawaii has been described as the best in the world. In the pivotal book, *The New Cuisine of Hawaii* by Janice Wald Henderson, acclaimed chef Nobuyuki Matsuhisa (chef-owner of Matsuhisa in Beverly Hills and Nobu in Manhattan) wrote, "As a chef who specializes in fresh seafood, I am in awe of the quality of Hawaii's fish; it is unparalleled anywhere else in the world." Without doubt, the surrounding waters, the waters of the Northwestern Hawaiian Islands, and a growing aquaculture industry are fertile grounds for this most important of Hawaii's food resources.

The reputable restaurants in Hawaii buy fresh fish daily at predawn auctions or from local fishermen. Some chefs even spearfish their ingredients themselves. "Still wiggling" is the ultimate term for freshness in Hawaii. The fish can then be grilled over *kiawe* (mesquite) or prepared in innumerable ways.

Although most menus include the western description for the fresh fish used, most often the local nomenclature is listed, turning dinner for the uninitiated into a confusing, quasi-foreign experience. To help familiarize you with the menu language of Hawaii, here's a basic glossary of island fish:

Ahi: yellowfin or bigeye tuna, important for its use in sashimi and poke, at sushi bars, and in Hawaii Regional Cuisine.

Aku: skipjack tuna, frequently utilized by local families in home cooking and poke.

Ehu: red snapper, delicate and sumptuous, yet lesser known than opakapaka (see below).

Hapuupuu: grouper, a sea bass whose use is expanding from ethnic to nonethnic restaurants.

Hebi: spearfish, mildly flavored and frequently featured as the "catch of the day" in upscale restaurants.

---

bento is a derivative of the "kau kau tin" that served as the modest lunch box for Japanese immigrants who labored in the sugar and pineapple fields. Today you'll find bentos dispensed ubiquitously throughout Hawaii, from department stores like Daiei and Shirokiya (bento bonanzas) to corner delis and supermarkets.

Also from the plantations come *manapua*, a bready, doughy round with tasty fillings of sweetened pork or sweet beans. In the old days, the Chinese "manapua man" would make his rounds in the camps and villages with bamboo containers balanced on a rod over his shoulders. Today you'll find white or whole-wheat manapua containing chicken, vegetables, curry, and other savory fillings.

The daintier Chinese delicacy, dim sum, is made of translucent wrappers filled with fresh seafood, pork hash, and vegetables, served for breakfast and lunch in Chinatown restaurants. The Hong Kong–style dumplings are ordered fresh and hot from bamboo steamers from invariably brusque servers who move their carts from table to table. Much like hailing a taxi in Manhattan, you have to be quick and loud for dim sum.

TASTY TREATS: SHAVE ICE & MALASSADAS

For dessert or a snack, particularly in Haleiwa, the prevailing choice is shave ice, the Island version of a snow cone. At places like Matsumoto Store in Haleiwa and Waiola Store in McCully, particularly on hot, humid days, long lines of shave ice lovers

Kajiki: Pacific blue marlin, also called au, with firm flesh and high fat content that make it a plausible substitute for tuna in some raw fish dishes and as a grilled item on menus.

Kumu: goatfish, a luxury item on Chinese and upscale menus, served en papillote or steamed whole, Oriental-style, with sesame oil, scallions, ginger, and garlic.

Mahimahi: dolphinfish (the gamefish, not the mammal) or dorado, a classic sweet, white-fleshed fish requiring vigilance among purists because it is often disguised as fresh when it's actually "fresh-frozen"—a big difference.

Monchong: bigscale or sickle pomfret, an exotic, tasty fish, scarce but gaining a higher profile on island menus.

Nairagi: striped marlin, also called au; good as sashimi and in poke, and often substituted for ahi in raw fish products.

Onaga: ruby snapper, a luxury fish, versatile, moist, and flaky; top-of-the-line.

Ono: wahoo, firmer and drier than the snappers, often served grilled and in sandwiches.

Opah: moonfish, rich and fatty, versatile; cooked, raw, smoked, and broiled.

Opakapaka: pink snapper, light, flaky, and luxurious, suited for sashimi, poaching, sautéing, and baking; the best-known upscale fish.

Papio: jack trevally, light, firm, and flavorful, and favored in island cookery.

Shutome: broadbill swordfish, of beeflike texture and rich flavor.

Tombo: albacore tuna, with a high fat content, suitable for grilling and sautéing.

Uhu: parrot fish, most often encountered steamed, Chinese style.

Uku: gray snapper of clear, pale-pink flesh, delicately flavored and moist.

Ulua: large jack trevally, firm-fleshed and versatile.

gather for their cones of rainbow-colored, finely shaved ice topped with sweet tropical syrups. The fast-melting mounds require prompt, efficient consumption and are quite the local summer ritual for sweet tooths. Aficionados order shave ice with ice cream and sweetened azuki beans plopped in the middle.

You may also encounter malassadas, the Portuguese version of a doughnut, and if you do, it's best to eat them immediately. A left-over malassada has all the appeal of a heavy, lumpy cold doughnut. When fresh and hot, however, as at school carnivals (where they attract the longest lines), or at bakeries and roadside stands (such as Agnes Portuguese Bake Shop in Kailua), the sugary, yeasty doughnut-without-a-hole is enjoyed by many as one of the enduring legacies of the Portuguese in Hawaii.

PINEAPPLES, PAPAYAS & OTHER FRESH ISLAND FRUITS

Lanai isn't growing pineapples commercially anymore, but low-acid, white-fleshed, wondrously sweet Hawaiian Sugarloaf pineapples are being commercially grown, on a small scale, on Kauai as well as the Big Island.

That is just one of the developments in a rapidly changing agricultural scene in Hawaii, where the lycheelike Southeast Asian rambutan; longan (Chinese dragon's eye lychees); 80-pound Indian jackfruits; starfruit; luscious, custardy mangosteen; and the usual mangoes, papayas, guava, and *lilikoi* (passion fruit) make up the dazzling array of fresh Island fruit that come and go with the seasons.

Papayas, bananas, and pineapples grow year-round, but pineapples are always sweetest, juiciest, and yellowest in the summer. While new papaya hybrids are making their way into the marketplace, the classic bests include the fleshy, firm-textured Kahuku papayas, the queen of them all; the Big Island's sweet Kapoho and Puna papayas; and the fragile, juicy, and red Sunrise papayas from Kauai. Apple bananas are smaller, firmer, and tarter than the standard and are a local specialty among the dozens of varieties (20 types grow wild) that flourish throughout the Islands.

Lychees and mangoes are long-awaited summer fruit. Mangoes begin appearing in late spring or early summer and can be found at roadside fruit stands in windward Oahu, at Chinatown markets, and at health food stores, where the high prices may shock you. My favorite is the white pirie, rare and resiny, fiberless, and so sweet and juicy it makes the high-profile Hayden seem prosaic. White piries are difficult to find but occasionally appear, along with lychees and other coveted seasonal fruit, at the Maunakea Marketplace in Chinatown or at Paradise Produce Company nearby.

Molokai watermelons are a summer hit and the best watermelons in the state. But Kahuku watermelons, available from stands along Oahu's north shore roadside in the summer months, give them a run for their money; they're juicy and sweet, and the season is woefully short-lived.

In the competitive world of oranges, the Kau Gold navel oranges from southern Big island put Sunkist to shame. Grown in the volcanic soil and sunny conditions of the South Point region (the southernmost point in the United States), the oranges, a winter crop, are brown, rough, and anything but pretty. But the browner and uglier they are, the sweeter and juicier. Because the thin-skinned oranges are tree-ripened, they're fleshy and heavy with liquid, and will spoil you for life.

If you're eager to sample the newly developed crops of South American and Southeast Asian fruit with unpronounceable names that are appearing in Island cuisine, check out Frankie's Nursery in Waimanalo. It's the hot spot of exotic fruit, *the* place to sate your curiosity and your palate.

5 The Natural World: An Environmental Guide to the Islands

The Oahu of today—with its crescent-shaped coves gently encircling azure water, thundering waterfalls exploding into cavernous pools, whispering palms bordering moonlit beaches, and vibrant rainbows arching through the early morning mist— differs dramatically from the island that came into being at the dawn of time.

Born of violent volcanic eruptions from deep beneath the ocean's surface, the first Hawaiian islands emerged about 70 million years ago—more than 200 million years after the major continental land masses had been formed. Two thousand miles from the nearest continent, Mother Nature's fury began to carve beauty from barren rock. Untiring volcanoes spewed forth curtains of fire that cooled into stone. Severe tropical storms, some with hurricane-force winds, battered and blasted the cooling lava rock into a series of shapes. Ferocious earthquakes flattened, shattered, and reshaped the islands into precipitous valleys, jagged cliffs, and recumbent flatlands. Monstrous surf and gigantic tidal waves rearranged and polished the lands above and below the reaches of the tide.

A geological youngster, Oahu itself was born only 3 to 5 million years ago, when the Waianae volcano spewed lava above the ocean's surface. It continued to erupt until 2$^{1}/_{2}$ million years ago; after the volcano was done, erosion and the whims of Mother Nature worked at it until only a crescent-shaped piece on its eastern rim, now known as the Waianae Range, remained. Nearby, between 1 and 3 million years later, the Koolau volcano erupted. The new series of eruptions created the plateau between the two volcanoes, joining them together and forming the flat central part of the island of Oahu. Finally, about 1.1 million years ago, several cone-building eruptions began on the southeast end of the young island. The cones remaining after the eruptions (which ended around 31,000 years ago) can be seen today: Diamond Head, Koko Head, Koko Crater, and Hanauma Bay.

It took many more years to chisel the dramatic cliffs of the west and east ends of the island, to form the majestic peak of Mt. Kaala, to create the deeply cut waterfalls of the north side of the island, to form the reefs of Hanauma Bay, and to shape the coral-sand beaches that ring Oahu. The result is an island like no other on the planet—a tropical dream rich in unique flora and fauna, surrounded by a vibrant underwater world, and covered with a landscape that will haunt your memory forever.

THE LANDSCAPE

Oahu, the island where the major metropolis of Honolulu is located, is the third largest island in the Hawaiian archipelago (after the Big Island and Maui). It's also the most urban, with a resident population of nearly 850,000; in fact, nearly half of the population of the entire state of Hawaii resides in just one quarter of Oahu, in Honolulu and Waikiki. Pearl Harbor, with its naturally deep waters, is the key to Oahu's dominant position in the state. Ancient Hawaiians using outrigger canoes could maneuver easily in fairly shallow waters, but European ships, with deep keels, needed a deep-draft harbor. Pearl Harbor was perfect: It has three deep lochs, which are actually river valleys gouged out during the ice age when the sea level was lower.

The island, which is 40 miles long by 26 miles wide, is ringed by more than 130 sandy beaches and defined by two mountain ranges: the Waianae Ridge (Mt. Kaala, at 4,050 feet, is the highest point on the island) in the west and the jagged Koolaus in the east, which form a backdrop for the city of Honolulu. These two ranges divide the island into three different environments. The Koolaus, with their spectacular peaks, fluted columns, lone spires, and steep verdant valleys, keep the naturally rainy windward side of the island lush and beautiful with tropical vegetation and flowing waterfalls. Mist frequently forms around the peaks like an ethereal lei, rainbows pour from the sky, and continuous but gentle rain blesses the land. On the other side of the island, the area between the Waianae Range and the ocean (known as the leeward side) is drier; it's an arid landscape with little rainfall and sparse vegetation. Powdery sand beaches, one after another, line the shoreline. Perpetually sunny days and big, thundering surf mark the Waianae coastline.

In between the two mountain ranges lies the central valley, moderate in temperature and vibrant with tropical plants and verdant agricultural fields. As farming centers and military bases (which occupied this area for decades) begin to diminish, housing tracts are slowly moving in. Red dirt and dust have previously kept this area from becoming highly populated, but as the amount of available land on Oahu shrinks and real estate prices continue their astronomic climb, Oahu's central plain is becoming an increasingly attractive suburban alternative.

Oahu is not only surrounded by water; it permeates the landscape. Natural lakes and human-made reservoirs supply water not just for living purposes but also recreational opportunities, especially for fishing enthusiasts. Streams abound on the island, and many have waterfalls, from Sacred Falls' spectacular cascades to the gentle, meandering Nuuanu Stream, which feeds into the "Jackass Ginger" swimming hole.

Hawaii's most well-known area, Waikiki, which lies along the western end of the island's southern coast, hasn't always been home to the soft sand and swaying palms that are its trademark. In fact, its name, meaning "spouting water," came from the gushing springwaters that kept the area a perpetual swamp. Until the 1920s, Waikiki was populated by noisy ducks, enormous toads, and other water creatures that inhabited the area's fishponds, damp taro patches, and waterlogged rice paddies. But in 1922, the swamps were drained to make way for the Waikiki reclamation project. Sand was imported to create the "Waikiki Beach" we see today. Anchoring one end of Waikiki Beach is Oahu's world-famous symbol, Diamond Head. The Hawaiians called this crater *lae'ahi*, which means brow (*lea*) of the *ahi* fish. Some years later, map makers shortened this name to *Leahi*. Today, we know the crater as Diamond Head because some British sailors in 1825, who had perhaps overindulged in liquid libations during shore leave, mistakenly thought that the glittering—but worthless—calcite crystals they found in the crater were diamonds. Despite their error, the name stuck.

THE FLORA OF OAHU

The Oahu of today radiates with sweet-smelling flowers, lush vegetation, and exotic plant life. Some of the more memorable trees, plants, and flowers on the islands include:

African Tulip Trees   Even at a long distance, you can see the flaming red flowers on these large trees, which can grow over 50 feet tall. Children love the trees because the buds hold water—they use them as water pistols.

Angel's Trumpet   This is a small tree that can grow up to 20 feet tall, with an abundance of large pendants (up to 10 inches in diameter)—white or pink flowers that resemble, well, trumpets. The Hawaiians call this *nana-honua,* which means "earth gazing." The flowers, which bloom continually from early spring to late fall, have a musky scent. However, beware: All parts of the plant are poisonous, and all parts contain a strong narcotic.

Anthuriums   One of Hawaii's most popular cut flowers, anthuriums originally came from the tropical Americas and the Caribbean islands. There are more than 550 species, but the most popular are the heart-shaped flowers (red, orange, pink, white, even purple) with a tail-like spath (green, orange, pink, red, white, purple, and in combinations thereof). Look for the heart-shaped green leaves in shaded areas. These exotic plants have no scent, but will last several weeks as cut flowers.

Banyans   Among the world's largest trees, Banyans have branches that grow out and away from the main trunk. These branches form descending roots that grow down to the ground to form and feed additional trunks, making the tree very stable during tropical storms.

Bird of Paradise   This native of Africa has become something of a trademark of Hawaii. They're easily recognizable by the orange and blue flowers nestled in gray-green bracts, looking somewhat like birds in flight.

Bougainvillea   Originally from Brazil and named for the French navigator Louis A. de Bougainville, these colorful, tissue-thin bracts (ranging in color from majestic purple to fiery orange) hide tiny white flowers.

Bromeliads   The pineapple plant is the best known bromeliad—native to tropical South America and the Caribbean islands, there are more than 1,400 species. "Bromes," as they are affectionately called, are generally spiky plants ranging in size from a few inches to several feet in diameter. They're popular not only for their unusual foliage but also for their strange and wonderful flowers. The flowers range from colorful spikes to delicate blossoms resembling orchids. Bromeliads are widely used in landscaping and as interior decoration, particularly in resort areas like Waikiki.

Gingers   Some of Hawaii's most fragrant flowers are white and yellow gingers (which the Hawaiians call *'awapuhi-ke'oke'o* and *'awapuhi-melemele*). Usually found in clumps, growing 4- to 7-feet tall, in the areas blessed by rain, these sweet-smelling, 3-inch wide flowers are composed of three dainty petal-like stamen and three long, thin petals. White and yellow gingers are so prolific that many people assume they are native to Hawaii; actually, they were introduced in the 19th century from the Indo-Malaysia area. Look for yellow and white ginger from late spring to fall. If you see them on the side of the road, stop and pick a few blossoms—your car will be filled with a divine fragrance for the rest of the day. The only downside of white and yellow ginger is that, once picked, they'll live only briefly.

Other members of the ginger family frequently seen on Oahu (there are some 700 species) include red ginger, shell ginger, and torch ginger. Red ginger consists of tall, green stalks with foot-long red "flower heads." The red "petals" are actually bracts; inch-long white flowers are protected by the bracts and can be seen if you look down into the red head. Red ginger (*'awapuhi-'ula'ula* in Hawaiian), which unfortunately does not share the heavenly smell of white ginger, will last a week or longer when cut. Look for red ginger from spring through late fall. Cool, wet mountain forests are the ideal condition for shell ginger; Hawaiians called it *'awapuhi-luheluhe,* which means "drooping" ginger. Natives of India and Burma, these plants, with their pearly white, clam shell–like blossoms, bloom from spring to fall.

Perhaps the most exotic gingers are the red or pink torch gingers. Cultivated in Malaysia as seasoning (the young flower shoots are used in curries), torch ginger rises directly out of the ground; the flower stalks (which are about 5 to 8 inches in length) resemble the fire of a lighted torch. One of the few gingers that can bloom year-round, the Hawaiians call this plant *'awapuhi-ko'oko'o,* or "walking-stick" ginger.

Heliconias   Some 80 species of the colorful heliconia family came to Hawaii from the Caribbean and Central and South America. The brightly colored bract (yellow, red, green, orange, etc.) overlap and appear to unfold like origami birds as they climb up (or down, as heliconias have both erect and pendant bracts). The most obvious heliconia to spot is the lobster claw, which resembles a string of boiled crustacean pincers—the brilliant crimson bracts alternate on the stem. Another prolific heliconia is the parrot's beak. Growing to about hip height, the parrot's beak is composed of bright-orange flower bracts with black tips, not unlike the beak of a parrot. Look for parrot's beak in the spring and summer, when it blooms in profusion.

Hibiscus   One variety of this year-round blossom is the official state flower: the yellow hibiscus. The 4- to 6-inch hibiscus flowers come in a range of colors, from lily-white to lipstick-red. The flowers resemble crepe paper, with stamens and pistils protruding spirelike from the center. Hibiscus hedges can grow up to 15 feet tall. Once plucked, the flowers wither quickly.

Jacaranda   Beginning about March and sometimes lasting until early May, these huge, lacy-leaved trees metamorphose into large clusters of spectacular lavender-blue sprays. The bell-shaped flowers drop quickly, leaving a majestic purple carpet beneath the tree.

Marijuana   Also known as *pakalolo* ("crazy weed" in Hawaiian), this plant is illegally cultivated throughout the islands. You probably won't see it as you drive along the roads, but if you go hiking, you may glimpse the feathery green leaves with tight clusters of buds. Despite years of police effort to eradicate the plant, the illegal industry continues. Don't be tempted to pick a few buds, as the purveyors of this nefarious industry don't take kindly to poaching.

Monkey-pod trees   One of Hawaii's most majestic trees, they grow more than 80 feet tall and 100 feet across and are often seen near older homes and in parks. The leaves of the monkey pod drop in February and March. The wood from the tree is a favorite of woodworking artisans.

Night-Blooming Cereus   Look along rock walls for this spectacular night-blooming cactus flower. Originally from Central America, this vinelike member of the cactus family has green scalloped edges and produces foot-long white flowers that open as darkness falls and wither as the sun rises. The plant also bears a red fruit that is edible.

Orchids   In many minds, nothing says Hawaii more than orchids. Yet the orchid family is the largest in the entire plant kingdom; orchids are found in most parts of the world. There are some species that are native to Hawaii, but they're inconspicuous in most places, so people may overlook them. The most widely grown orchid—and the major source of flowers for leis and garnish for tropical libations—are the vanda orchids. The vandas used in Hawaii's commercial flower industry are generally lavender or white, but they grow in a rainbow of colors, shapes, and sizes. The orchids used for corsages are the large, delicate cattleya; the ones used in floral arrangements—you'll probably see them in your hotel lobby—are usually dendrobiums.

Plumeria   Also known as frangipani, this sweet-smelling, five-petal flower, found in clusters on trees, is the most popular choice of lei makers. The Singapore plumeria has five creamy-white petals, with a touch of yellow in the center. Another popular variety, ruba—with flowers from soft pink to flaming red—is also used in making leis. When picking plumeria, be careful of the sap from the flower, as it is poisonous and can stain clothes.

Proteas   Originally from South Africa, this unusual plant comes in more than 40 different varieties. Proteas are shrubs that bloom into a range of flower types. Different species of proteas range from those resembling pincushions to a species that looks just like a bouquet of feathers. Proteas are long-lasting cut flowers; once dried, they will last for years.

Taro   Around pools, streams, and in neatly planted fields, you'll see the green heart-shaped leaves of taro. Taro was a staple to ancient Hawaiians, who pounded the root into poi. Originally from Sri Lanka, taro is not only a food crop, but also grown as an ornamental.

FRUIT TREES

Banana   Edible bananas are among the oldest of the world's food crops. By the time Europeans arrived in the islands, the Hawaiians had more than 40 different types of bananas planted. Most banana plants have long green leaves hanging from the tree, with the flower giving way to fruit in clusters.

Breadfruit   A large tree—over 60-feet tall—with broad, sculpted, dark-green leaves. The fruit is round and about 6 inches or more in diameter. The ripe fruit, a staple in the Hawaiian diet, is whitish-yellow.

Lychee   This evergreen tree, which can grow to well over 30 feet across, originated in China. Small flowers grow into panicles about a foot long in June and July. The round, red-skinned fruit appears shortly afterward.

Mango   From the Indo-Malaysian area comes the delicious mango, a fruit with peachlike flesh. Mango season usually begins in the spring and lasts through the summer, depending on the variety. The trees can grow to more than 100 feet tall. The tiny reddish-flowers give way to a green fruit that turns red-yellow when ripe. Some people enjoy unripe mangoes, sliced thin or in chutney as a traditional Indian preparation. The mango sap can cause a skin rash on some.

Papaya   Yellow pear-shaped fruit (when ripe) found at the base of the large, scalloped-shaped leaves on a pedestal-like, nonbranched tree. Papayas ripen year-round.

THE FAUNA OF OAHU

When the Polynesians from the Society Islands arrived in Hawaii, around A.D. 1000, they found only two endemic mammals: the **hoary bat** and the **monk seal.** The Hawaiian monk seal, a relative of warm-water seals previously found in the Caribbean and Mediterranean, was nearly slaughtered into extinction for its skin and oil during the 19th century. Recently these seals have experienced a minor population explosion in a few of their haunts, forcing relocation of some males from their protected homes in the inlets north of the main Hawaiian Islands. Periodically, these endangered marine mammals turn up at various beaches throughout the state. They are protected under federal law by the Marine Mammals Protection Act. If you're fortunate enough to see a monk seal, just look; don't disturb one of Hawaii's living treasures.

What's perhaps even more astonishing is what the first Polynesians didn't find—there were no reptiles, amphibians, mosquitoes, lice, no fleas, not even a cockroach. They did bring a few creatures from home: dogs, pigs, and chickens (all were for eating). A stowaway on board the Polynesian sailing canoes was the rat. Oahu still has feral goats and wild pigs, which generally make a nuisance of themselves by destroying the rain forest and eating native plants. Non-native game birds (ring-neck pheasants, green pheasants, Erkel's francolins, Japanese quail, spotted doves, and zebra doves) are also found on Oahu.

The Hawaiian islands have only one tiny earthwormlike snake. Strict measures are taken to keep other snakes out of Hawaii. On the island of Guam, the brown tree snake has obliterated most of the bird population. Officials in Hawaii are well aware of this danger to Hawaii and are vigilant to prevent snakes from entering the state.

Two non-native creatures that visitors to Oahu are likely to see are:

Geckos   These harmless, soft-skinned, insect-eating lizards come equipped with suction pads on their feet, enabling them to climb walls and windows so they can reach tasty insects like mosquitoes and cockroaches. You'll see them on windows outside a lighted room at night, or hear their cheerful chirp.

Mongooses   The mongoose is a mistake. It was brought here in the 19th century to counteract the ever-growing rat problem. But rats are nocturnal creatures, sleeping during the day and wandering at night. Mongooses are day creatures. Instead of getting rid of the rat problem, the mongooses eat bird eggs, contributing to the deterioration of the native bird population in Hawaii.

BIRDS

The inspiration for the first Polynesian voyages to Hawaii may have come from the **Kolea,** or Pacific golden plover—a homely speckled bird that migrates from Siberia and Alaska every year, traveling through Hawaii and down to the Marquesas, Tahiti, and New Zealand. Historians wonder if the Marquesans, watching the birds arrive and depart, speculated where they came from and what that place was like. When the first Marquesans arrived in Hawaii between A.D. 500 and 800, scientists say they found 67 varieties of endemic Hawaiian birds, a third of which are now believed to be extinct, including the **koloa** (the Hawaiian duck).

In the last 200 years, more native species of birds have become extinct in the Hawaiian Islands than anywhere else on the planet. Of the 67 native Hawaiian species, 23 are extinct, 29 are endangered, and one is threatened (*'alala,* the Hawaiian crow). Two native birds that have managed to survive are the:

Nene   Endemic to Hawaii, the nene is Hawaii's state bird. It is being brought back from the brink of extinction through captive breeding and the implementation of strenuous protection laws. A relative of the Canada goose, the nene stands about two feet high and has a black head and yellow cheeks, a buff neck with deep furrows, a grayish-brown body, and clawed feet. It gets its name from its two syllable, high nasal call "nay-nay." Although they're not found on Oahu, the approximately 500 nenes alive today can be seen at Haleakala National Park on Maui, at Mauna Kea State Park bird sanctuary, and on the slopes of Mauna Kea on the Big Island.

Pueo   The Hawaiian short-eared owl, which grows to about 12 to 17 inches in size, can be seen at dawn and dusk on Kauai, Maui, and the Big Island. The brown-and-white bird with a black bill goes hunting for rodents at night. Pueos were highly regarded by Hawaiians: According to legend, spotting a Pueo is a good omen.

SEABIRDS   On the east coast of Oahu, from Kahuku to Makapuu Point, are numerous small islands, islets, and rocks that are nesting areas for seabirds native to the region. Once part of the island of Oahu, these small land masses, some just a few hundred yards offshore, are environmentally necessary for the survival of these birds. The seabird population has suffered since the arrival of people to the Hawaiian Islands, as coastal areas have been altered for human use. Many seabirds are ground nesters, making them easy prey for nonindigenous animals like dogs, cats, rats, and mongooses. Nonindigenous plants, such as sea grape and lantana, have encroached upon the nesting grounds as well.

Because of their ecological importance, the offshore islands dotting Oahu's windward coast have been made part of the Hawaii State Seabird Sanctuary. Shearwaters, noddies, and petrels are among the birds that use the protected islands for roosting and nesting, and migratory birds like ruddy turnstones, wandering tattlers, and golden plovers forage along the shore. The islands also provide protected environments for native coastal vegetation. Because the nesting grounds are fragile environments, access to the offshore islands is limited; visitors should observe all posted signs. Many seabirds build their nests under dense vegetation or in shallow, sandy burrows that cannot be seen by unwary hikers and sightseers. Human disturbance can cause birds to abandon their nests, leaving eggs and chicks exposed.

The seabirds found on these offshore islands include the:

Great Frigatebird ('Iwa)   The Hawaiian name, *iwa,* meaning thief, refers to the frigatebirds' habit of snatching food from other birds in midair. Frigatebirds are superb flyers and so well adapted to life in the air that they can barely walk on land. They are often seen soaring above Waimanalo Bay on the island's windward side.

Wandering Tattler ('Ulili)   Wandering tattlers are migrants who travel annually over 2,000 miles from Alaska to Canada to Hawaii, where they spend their winters foraging for insects and fish. They're usually solitary and can be seen hunting for food along rocky shorelines and tidal flats. Their Hawaiian name, *'ulili,* mimics their unique call.

Sooty Tern *('Ewa'ewa)* These seabirds nest in large numbers on the offshore islands of Manana and Moku Manu. They lay single, camouflaged eggs directly on the ground, and are easily disturbed by curious humans.

Ruddy Turnstones *('Akekeke)* These winter visitors, who fly from their Arctic nesting grounds to Hawaii in August and September, can be seen probing with their bills in search of insects and tiny crustaceans along Oahu's shorelines.

Bristle-thighed Curlew *(Kioea)* In early August, the *kioea* leave their nesting grounds in the Alaskan tundra and fly to Hawaii (as well as to other islands in the Pacific). They prefer undisturbed sandy shorelines and secluded grassy meadows.

Wedge-tailed Shearwater *('Ua'u kani)* The most common birds found on the offshore islands, these birds get their Hawaiian name from their eerie, drawn-out call.

Red-footed Booby *('A)* These large white birds are often seen flying low over the water, far out to sea, in search of fish and squid. Fishermen love to spot these birds because *'a* often circle and feed directly over schools of tuna or mahimahi.

Red-tailed Tropicbird *(Koa'e'ula)* Distinguished by their white plumage and long red-tail feathers, these birds nest not only on the offshore islands but also on Oahu's cliffs.

Brown Noddy *(Nolo koha)* These common birds nest in small colonies on the open ground and raise their single offspring on a diet of small fish and crustaceans.

Bulwer's Petrel *('Ou)* These birds spend most of their life at sea, returning to land—usually back to the island where they were born—only to mate. They're nocturnal feeders, spending nights hunting for small surface-water fish.

SEALIFE

Oahu has an extraordinarily unique world to explore offshore, beneath the sea. Approximately 680 species of fish are known to inhabit the underwater world around the Hawaiian islands. Of those, approximately 450 species stay close to the reef and inshore areas.

Coral The reefs surrounding Hawaii are made up of various coral and algae. The living coral grow through sunlight that feeds a specialized algae, called zooxanthellae, which in turn allows the development of the coral's calcareous skeleton. It takes thousands of years for reefs to develop. The reef attracts and supports fish and crustaceans, which use the reef for food, habitat, mating, and raising their young. Mother Nature can cause the destruction of the reef with a strong storm or large waves, but humans—through a seemingly unimportant act such as touching the coral, or allowing surface runoff of dirt, silt, or chemicals to blanket the reef and cut off the life-giving light—have proven even more destructive to the fragile reefs.

The coral most frequently seen in Hawaii are hard, rocklike formations named for their familiar shapes: antler, cauliflower, finger, plate, and razor coral. Wire coral, looks just like its name—a randomly bent wire growing straight out of the reef. Some coral appear soft, such as tube coral; it can be found in the ceilings of caves. Black coral, which resemble winter-bare trees or shrubs, are found at depths of over 100 feet.

Reef Fish Of the approximately 450 reef fish, about 27% are native to Hawaii and found nowhere else on the planet. This may seem surprising for a string of isolated islands, 2,000 miles from the nearest land mass. But over the millions of years of gestation of the Hawaiian islands, as they were born from the erupting volcanoes, ocean currents—mainly from the Indo-Malay Pacific region—carried the larvae of thousands of marine animals and plants to Hawaii's reef. Of those, approximately 100 species not only adapted, but thrived. Some species are much bigger and more plentiful than their Pacific cousins; many developed unique characteristics. Some, like the lemon or milletseed butterfly fish, are not only particular to Hawaii but also unique within their larger, worldwide family in their specialized schooling and feeding behaviors.

Another surprising thing about Hawaii endemics is how common some of the native fish are. You can see the saddleback wrasse on virtually any snorkeling excursion or dive in Hawaiian waters. Some of the reef fish you might encounter in the waters off Oahu are:

Angel Fish   Often mistaken for butterfly fish, angel fish can be distinguished by looking for the spine, located low on the gill plate. Angel fish are very shy; several species live in colonies close to coral for protection.

Blennys   Small, elongated fish, blennys range from 2 to 10 inches long, with the majority in the 3-to-4-inch range. Blennys are so small that they can live in tide pools. Because of their size, you might have a hard time spotting one.

Butterfly Fish   Some of the most colorful of the reef fish, butterfly fish are usually seen in pairs (scientists believe they mate for life) and appear to spend most of their day feeding. There are 22 species of butterfly fish, of which three (bluestripe, lemon or milletseed, and multiband or pebbled butterfly fish) are endemic. Most butterfly fish have a dark band through the eye and a spot near the tail resembling an eye in order to confuse their predators (the moray eel loves to lunch on butterfly fish).

Eels   Moray and conger eels are the common eels seen in Hawaii. Morays are usually docile unless provoked or if there is food or an injured fish around. Unfortunately, some morays have been fed by divers and—being intelligent creatures—associate divers with food; thus, they can become aggressive. But most morays like to keep to themselves, hidden in a hole or crevice. While morays may look menacing, conger eels look downright happy, with big lips and pectoral fins (situated so that they look like big ears) that give them a perpetually smiling face. Conger eels have crushing teeth so they can feed on crustaceans; in fact, since they're sloppy eaters, they usually live with shrimp and crabs, who feed off the crumbs they leave.

Parrot Fish   One of the largest and most colorful of the reef fish, parrot fish can grow as large as 40 inches long. Parrot fish are easy to spot—their front teeth are fused together, protruding like buck teeth and resembling a parrot's beak. These unique teeth allow the parrot fish to feed by scraping algae from rocks and coral. The rocks and coral pass through the parrot fish's system, resulting in fine sand. In fact, most of the sand found in Hawaii is parrot fish waste; one large parrot fish can produce a ton of sand a year. Hawaiian native parrot fish species include yellowbar, regal, and spectacled.

Scorpion Fish   This is a family of what scientists call "ambush predators." These fish hide under camouflaged exteriors and ambush their prey when they come along. Several sport a venomous dorsal spine. These fish don't have a gas bladder, so when they stop swimming, they sink—that's why you usually find them "resting" on ledges and on the ocean's bottom. Although they are not aggressive, an inattentive snorkeler or diver could inadvertently touch one and feel the effects of those venomous spines—so be very careful where you put your hands and feet while you're in the water.

Surgeon Fish   Sometimes called tang, the surgeon fish get their name from the scalpel-like spines located on each side of their bodies near the base of their tails. Some surgeon fish have a rigid spine; others have the ability to fold their spine against their body until it's needed for defense purposes. Some surgeon fish, like the brightly colored yellow tang, are boldly colored. Others are adorned in more conservative shades of gray, brown, or black. The only endemic surgeon fish—and the most abundant in Hawaiian waters—is the convict tang (*manini* in Hawaiian), a pale white fish with vertical black stripes (like a convict's uniform).

Wrasses   This is a very diverse family of fish, ranging in size from 2 to 15 inches. Several wrasses are brilliantly colored and change their colors through aging and sexual dimorphism (sex changing). Wrasses have the unique ability to change gender from female (when young) to male with maturation. There are several wrasses that are endemic to Hawaii: the Hawaiian cleaner, shortnose, belted, gray (or old woman), psychedelic, pearl, flame, and the most common Hawaiian reef fish, the saddleback.

GAME FISH   Fishers have a huge variety to choose from in the waters off Oahu, from pan-sized snapper to nearly one-ton marlin. Hawaii is known around the globe as *the* place for big game fish—marlin, swordfish, and tuna—but its waters are also great for catching other offshore fish (like mahimahi, rainbow runner, and wahoo), coastal fish (barracuda, scad), bottom fish (snappers, sea bass, and amberjack), and inshore fish (trevally, bonefish, and others), as well as freshwater fish (bass, catfish, trout, bluegill, and oscar).

Billfish are caught year-round. There are six different kinds of billfish found in the offshore waters around the islands: Pacific blue marlin, black marlin, sailfish, broadbill swordfish, striped marlin, and shortbill spearfish. Hawaii billfish range in size from the 20-pound shortbill spearfish and striped marlin to an 1,805-pound Pacific blue marlin, the largest marlin ever caught on rod and reel anywhere in the world. **Tuna** ranges in size from small (a pound or less) mackerel tuna used as bait (Hawaiians call them *oioi*), to 250-pound yellowfin ahi tuna. Other species of tuna found in Hawaii are bigeye, albacore, kawakawa, and skipjack.

Some of the best eating fish are also found in offshore waters: **mahimahi** (also known as dolphin fish or dorado) in the 20- to 70-pound range, **rainbow runner** (*kamanu*) from 15 to 30 pounds, and **wahoo** (*ono*) from 15 to 80 pounds. Shoreline fishers are always on the lookout for **trevally** (the state record for giant trevally is 191 pounds), **bonefish, ladyfish, threadfin, leatherfish,** and **goatfish.** Bottom fishermen pursue a range of **snappers**—red, pink, gray, and others—as well as **sea bass** (the state record is a whopping 563 pounds) and **amberjack,** which weigh up to 100 pounds.

Reservoirs on Oahu are home to Hawaii's many freshwater fish: **bass** (large, smallmouth, and peacock), **catfish** (channel and Chinese), **rainbow trout, bluegill sunfish, pungee,** and **oscar.** The state record for freshwater fish is the 43-pound, 13-ounce channel catfish caught in Oahu's Lake Wilson.

WHALES   Humpbacks   The most popular visitors to Hawaii come every year in the winter, around November, and stay until the springtime (April or so) when they return to their summer home in Alaska. Humpback whales—some as big as a city bus and weighing many tons—migrate to the warm, protected Hawaiian waters in the winter to mate and calve. You can take whale-watching cruises that will let you observe these magnificent leviathans close up on every island, or you can spot their signature spouts of water from shore as they expel water in the distance. Humpbacks grow to up to 45 feet long, so when they breach (propel their entire body out of the water) or even wave a fluke, you can see it for miles.

Other whales   Humpbacks are among the biggest whales found in Hawaiian waters, but other whales—like pilot, sperm, false killer, melon-headed, pygmy killer, and beaked whales—can be seen year-round. These whales usually travel in pods of 20 to 40 animals and are very social, interacting with each other on the surface.

SHARKS   Yes, Virginia there are sharks in Hawaii. But chances are you won't see a shark unless you specifically go looking for one. The ancient Hawaiians had great respect for sharks and believed that some sharks were reincarnated relatives who had returned to assist them.

About 40 different species of shark inhabit the waters surrounding Hawaii; they range from the totally harmless whale shark—at 60 feet, the world's largest fish—which has no teeth and is so docile that it frequently lets divers ride on its back, to the not-so-docile, infamous—and extremely uncommon—great white shark. The most common sharks seen in Hawaii are white-tip reef sharks, gray reef sharks (about 5 feet long), and blacktip reef sharks (about 6 feet long). Since records have been kept, starting in 1779, there have been only about 100 shark attacks in Hawaii, of which 40% have been fatal. The biggest number of attacks occurred after someone fell into the ocean from the shore or from a boat. In these cases, the sharks probably attacked after the person was dead.

General rules for avoiding sharks are: Don't swim at sunrise, sunset, or where the water is murky due to stream runoff—sharks may mistake you for one of their usual meals. And don't swim where there are bloody fish in the water (sharks become aggressive around blood).

OAHU'S ECOSYSTEM PROBLEMS

Oahu may be paradise, but even paradise has its problems. The biggest threat Oahu's natural environment faces is human intrusion—simply put, too many people want to experience paradise firsthand. From the magnificent underwater world to the breathtaking rain forest, the presence of people isn't always benign, no matter how cautious or environmentally aware they might be.

Marine Life   Hawaii's beautiful and abundant marine life has attracted so many visitors that they threaten to overwhelm it. A great example of this over enthusiasm is Oahu's Hanauma Bay, a marine preserve. Thousands of people flock to this beautiful bay, which features calm, protected swimming and snorkeling areas loaded with tropical reef fish. An overabundance of visitors forced government officials to limit the number of people entering the bay at any one time. Commercial tour operators have been restricted entirely in an effort to balance the people-to-fish ratio.

People who fall in love with the colorful tropical fish and want to see them all the time back home are also thought to be impacting the health of Hawaii's reefs. The growth in home, office, and decor aquariums has risen dramatically in the last 20 years. As a result, more and more reef fish collectors are taking a growing number of reef fish from Hawaiian waters.

The reefs surrounding the islands have faced increasing ecological problems over the years. Runoff of soil and chemicals from construction, agriculture, erosion, and even heavy storms can blanket and choke a reef, which needs sunlight to survive. In addition, the intrusion of foreign elements—like breaks in sewage lines—can cause problems for Hawaii's reef. Human contact with the reef can also upset the ecosystem. Coral, the basis of the reef system, is very fragile; snorkelers and divers grabbing on to coral can break off pieces that took decades to form. Feeding fish can also upset the balance of the ecosystem (not to mention upsetting the digestive system of the fish). One glass-bottom boat operator on the Big Island reported that they fed an eel for years, considering it their "pet" eel. One day the eel decided that he wanted more than just the food being offered and bit the diver's fingers. Divers and snorkelers report that in areas where the fish are routinely fed the fish have become more aggressive; schools of certain reef fish—normally shy—surround divers, demanding to be fed.

Flora   One of Hawaii's most fragile environments is the rain forest. Any intrusion—from hikers carrying seeds on their shoes to the rooting of wild boars—can upset the delicate balance in these complete ecosystems. In recent years, development has moved closer and closer to the rain forest.

Fauna   The biggest impact on the fauna in Hawaii is the decimation of native birds by feral animals, which have destroyed the birds' habitats, and by mongooses that have eaten the birds' eggs and young. Government officials are vigilant about snakes because of the potential damage tree snakes can do to the remaining birdlife.

Vog   When the trade winds stop blowing for a few days, Oahu begins to feel the effects of the volcanic haze—caused by gases released by the continuous eruption of the volcano on the flank of Kilauea, on the Big Island, and the smoke from the fires set by the lava—that has been dubbed "vog." The hazy air, which looks like smog from urban pollution, limits viewing from scenic vistas and plays havoc with photographers trying to get clear panoramic photographs. Some people claim that the vog has even caused bronchial ailments.

Culture   Virtually since the arrival of the first Europeans, there has been a controversy over balancing the preservation of history and indigenous cultures and lifestyles with economic development. The question of what should be preserved—and in what fashion—is continually debated in Hawaii's rapidly growing economy. Some factions argue that the continuously developing tourism economy will one day destroy the very thing that visitors come to Hawaii to see; another sector argues that Hawaii's cost of living is so high that new development and industries are needed so residents can earn a living.

3

Planning a Trip to Oahu

by Jeanette Foster

Oahu has so many places to explore, things to do, sights to see—planning your trip can be bewildering with so much vying for your attention. Where to start? That's where we come in. In the pages that follow, we've compiled everything you need to know to plan your ideal trip to Hawaii: airlines, seasons, a calendar of events, and much more (even how to get married in the islands). We'll show you how to do it without going broke: You'll find lots of great money-saving tips and insider advice on how to get the most out of your vacation time and money.

Remember that the planning process can be part of the excitement of your trip. So, in addition to reading this guide, we suggest that you spend some time either on the Internet looking at sites (we've included Web site addresses throughout this book) or calling and writing for brochures. We fully believe that searching for the best bargains and planning your dream vacation to Hawaii should be half the fun.

1 Visitor Information & Money

SOURCES OF INFORMATION

For information about traveling in Hawaii, contact the **Hawaii Visitors and Convention Bureau (HVCB),** Suite 801, Waikiki Business Plaza, 2270 Kalakaua Ave., Honolulu, HI 96815 (☎ **800/GO-HAWAII** or 808/923-1811; Web site: http://www.visit.hawaii.org). Among other things, the bureau publishes the helpful *Accommodations and Car Rental Guide* and supplies free brochures, maps, and *Islands of Aloha* magazine, the official HVCB magazine.

The HVCB also has a U.S. mainland office at 180 Montgomery St., Suite 2360, San Francisco CA 94104 (☎ **800/353-5846**). All other HVCB offices on the mainland have been closed due to budget constraints.

If you want information about working and living in Hawaii, contact **The Chamber of Commerce of Hawaii,** 1132 Bishop St., Suite 200, Honolulu, HI 96815 (☎ **808/545-4300**).

You can also surf the web for information on Hawaii:

- **Hawaii State Vacation Planner:** http://www.hshawaii.com
- **Travel and Visitor Information:** http://www.planet-hawaii.com
- **Outrigger Hotels:** http://www.outrigger.com/infoweb

- **Hawaii Yellow Pages:** http://www.surfhi.com
- **Holo Hawaii/Marine and Ocean Sports News and Weather:** http://www.holo.org
- **NASA's Virtually Hawaii:** http://www.satlab.hawaii.edu/space/hawaii
- **Great Outdoor Adventures of Hawaii:** http://www.cyber-hawaii.com/travel
- **Backpacking information:** http://www.backpackers-hawaii.com

MONEY

Hawaii pioneered the use of automatic teller machines (ATMs) nearly two decades ago, and now they're everywhere on Oahu. You'll find them at most banks, in supermarkets, at Long's Drug stores, at Honolulu International Airport, and in some resorts and shopping centers like Ala Moana Center and Aloha Tower Market Place. It's actually cheaper and faster to get cash from an ATM than to fuss with traveler's checks; and credit cards are accepted just about everywhere. To find the location of the ATM nearest you, call ☎ 800/424-7787 for the **Cirrus** network, or ☎ 800/843-7587 for the **Plus** system.

The United States dollar is the accepted currency in Hawaii, but you can easily exchange most major foreign currencies (see "Money" and "Fast Facts" in chapter 4).

2 When to Go

The majority of visitors don't come to Hawaii when the weather's best in the islands; rather, they come when it's at its worst everywhere else. Thus, the "high" season—when prices are up and resorts are booked to capacity—is generally from mid-December through March or mid-April. The last two weeks of December, in particular, are prime time for travel to Hawaii. If you're planning a holiday trip, make your reservations as early as possible, expect to travel with holiday crowds, and expect to pay top dollar for accommodations and airfare.

The best bargains are available in the spring (from mid-April to mid-June) and fall (from September to mid-December)—a paradox, since these are the best seasons in Hawaii, in terms of reliably great weather. If you're looking to save money, or if you just want to avoid the crowds, this is the time to visit. Hotel rates tend to be significantly lower during this "off" season. Airfares also tend to be lower—sometimes substantially—and good packages and special deals are often available. (*Note*: If you plan to come to Hawaii between the last week in April and mid-May, be sure to book in advance your accommodations, interisland air reservations, and car rental. Waikiki is especially busy during this time because the Japanese, who are on holiday for "Golden Week", are also booking reservations.)

Due to the large number of families traveling in summer (June through August), you won't get the fantastic bargains of spring and fall. However, you'll still do much better on accommodations and airfare than you will in the winter months.

CLIMATE

Since Hawaii lies at the edge of the tropical zone, it technically has only two seasons, both of them warm. There's a dry season that corresponds to summer, while the rainy season generally runs during the winter from November to March. It rains every day somewhere in the islands anytime of the year, but the rainy season can cause "gray" weather and spoil your tanning opportunities. Fortunately, it seldom rains for more than three days straight.

The year-round temperature usually varies no more than 10°F, but it depends on where you are. Oahu is like a ship in that it has a leeward and a windward side.

What Things Cost in Waikiki	U.S. $
Taxi from Honolulu International Airport to Waikiki	$23.00
Shuttle Van from Honolulu International Airport to Waikiki	$8.00
Local telephone call (on same island)	.25
Double at Aloha Punawai (budget)	$ 60.00
Double at The Breakers (inexpensive)	$91.00
Double at Double Tree Alana Waikiki (moderate)	$135.00
Double at Hilton Hawaiian Village (expensive)	$189.00
Double at Halekulani (very expensive)	$295.00
Lunch for one (ramen special) at Ezogiku (cheap)	$7.00
Lunch for one (salad and seafood spaghetti) at Arancino (affordable)	$12.50
Lunch for one (salad or soup; a hoagie, fresh fish, or fettuccine entree; and dessert) at Orchids (pricey)	$27.00
Dinner for one (deluxe cheeseburger) at Planet Hollywood (cheap)	$8.95
Dinner for one (filet mignon) at Hy's Steak House (pricey)	$32.50
Coca-Cola	$1.50
Draft beer	$2.50
Cup of coffee	$1.25
Admission to Bishop Museum, Honolulu	$8.00
Movie Ticket	$7.00

The leeward side (the west and south, from Waianae to Honolulu and Waikiki) is usually hot and dry, while the windward side (east and north, from Haleiwa to Waimanalo) is generally cooler and moist. When you want arid, sun-baked, desertlike weather, go leeward. When you want lush, often wet, junglelike weather, go windward.

Hawaii is also full of microclimates thanks to its interior valleys, coastal plains, and mountain peaks. It can be pouring rain at the University of Hawaii in Manoa and sunny and dry in Waikiki, a 15-minute drive away.

The best months to be in Hawaii are April, May, September, and October, when the nearly perfect weather is even better—not so windy, not so humid, but just right. It's off-season, kids are in school, and the tourists have thinned out. The state's "carrying capacity," as they say here, isn't maxed out. Hotels, restaurants, and attractions aren't as crowded, and everyone is more relaxed.

On rare occasions the weather can be disastrous, like when Hurricane Iniki, the most powerful Pacific storm in history, crushed Kauai in September 1992 with 225-mile-an-hour winds. The official hurricane season is June to November. Tsunamis, huge tidal waves caused by far-off earthquakes, have swept the shores of the islands. But those are extreme exceptions. Mostly, one day follows another here in glorious sunny procession, each quite like the other. You have only to decide where and how to spend them.

HOLIDAYS

When Hawaii observes holidays, especially those over a long weekend, travel between the islands increases, interisland airline seats are fully booked, rental cars are at a premium, and hotels and restaurants will be busier than at other times.

Federal, state, and county government offices are closed on all federal holidays: January 1 (New Year's Day); third Monday in January (Martin Luther King, Jr. Day); third Monday in February (Presidents' Day, Washington's Birthday); last Monday in May (Memorial Day); July 4 (Independence Day); first Monday in September (Labor Day); second Monday in October (Columbus Day); November 11 (Veteran's Day); fourth Thursday in November (Thanksgiving Day); and December 25 (Christmas).

State and county offices are also closed on local holidays. These include: Prince Kuhio Day (March 26), honoring the birthday of Hawaii's first delegate to the U.S. Congress; King Kamehameha Day (June 11), a statewide holiday commemorating Kamehameha the Great, who united the islands and ruled from 1795 to 1819; and Admission Day (third Friday in August), which honors Hawaii's admission as the 50th state in the U.S. on August 21, 1959.

Other special days celebrated by many people in Hawaii that don't involve the closing of federal, state, and county offices are: Chinese New Year (in January or February), Girl's Day (March 3), Buddha's Birthday (April 8), Father Damien's Day (April 15), Boy's Day (May 5), Samoan Flag Day (in August), Aloha Festivals (September to October), and Pearl Harbor Day (December 7).

OAHU CALENDAR OF EVENTS

For information on sporting events see "Sports Calendar of Events" in chapter 8.

January

- **Annual Cherry Blossom Festival,** Bishop Museum, Honolulu. A culture and craft fair celebrating aspects of Japanese culture. Entertainment, games, and demonstrations. January through March. Call ☎ **808/949-2255.**
- **Narcissus Festival,** Honolulu. Around Chinese New Year, this cultural festival includes a queen pageant, cooking demonstrations, and cultural fair. January or February depending on Chinese New Year. Call ☎ **808/9533-3181.**
- ✪ **Ala Wai Challenge,** Ala Wai Park, Waikiki. This all-day event features ancient Hawaiian games like *ulu maika* (bowling a round stone through pegs), *oo ihe* (spear throwing at an upright target), *huki kaula* (tug of war), and a quarter-mile outrigger canoe race. This is a great place to hear Hawaiian music. Call ☎ **808/923-1802.**

February

- ✪ **Punahou School Carnival,** Punahou School, Honolulu. Everything you can imagine in a school carnival, from high-speed rides to homemade jellies, all benefiting scholarship funds for Hawaii's most prestigious school. Call ☎ **808/944-5753.**

March

- **Annual Merchant Street St. Patrick's Day Block Party,** Merchant St., between Nuuanu Ave and Bethel St., Honolulu. In the evening, the downtown streets of Honolulu become Irish for one evening in celebration of St. Patty's day. There's live entertainment, food, and drinks. Call ☎ **808/734-6900.**
- **Prince Kuhio Celebration,** commemorates the birth of Jonah Kuhio Kalanianaole, born March 26, 1871. He might have been one of Hawaii's kings if the Hawaiian monarchy had not been overthrown. After Hawaii's annexation to the United States, Prince Kuhio was elected to Congress (1902). Ceremonies are held at the Prince Kuhio Federal Building, at Kuhio Beach in Waikiki, and other locations throughout Oahu. Check the local newspapers for details.
- **Sand Castle Building Contest,** Kailua Beach Park. Students from the University of Hawaii School of Architecture compete against professional architects to see who

Cyber Deals for Net Surfers

It's possible to get some great deals on airfare, hotels, and car rentals via the Internet. So grab your mouse and start surfing before you hit the real waves in Hawaii—you could save a bundle on your trip. The Web sites we've highlighted below are worth checking out, especially since all services are free (but don't forget that time is money when you're on-line).

Microsoft Expedia (http://www.expedia.com)   The best part of this multipurpose travel site is the "Fare Tracker": You fill out a form on the screen indicating that you're interested in cheap flights to Hawaii from your hometown, and, once a week, they'll e-mail you the best airfare deals. The site's "Travel Agent" will steer you to bargains on hotels and car rentals, and you can book everything, including flights, right on-line. This site is even useful once you're booked: Before you go, log on to Expedia for oodles of up-to-date travel information, including weather reports and foreign exchange rates.

Preview Travel (http://www.reservations.com and http://www.vacations.com) Another useful travel site, "Reservations.com" has a "Best Fare Finder," which will search the Apollo computer reservations system for the three lowest fares for any route on any days of the year. Say you want to go from Chicago to Honolulu and back between December 6 and 13: Just fill out the form on the screen with times, dates, and destinations, and within minutes, Preview will show you the best deals. If you find an airfare you like, you can book your ticket right on-line—you can even reserve hotels and car rentals on this site. If you're in the preplanning stage, head to Preview's "Vacations.com" site, where you can check out the latest package deals for Hawaii and other destinations around the world by clicking on "Hot Deals."

Travelocity (http://www.travelocity.com)   This is one of the best travel sites out there. In addition to its "Personal Fare Watcher," which notifies you via e-mail of the lowest airfares for up to five different destinations, Travelocity will track the three lowest fares for any routes on any dates in minutes. You can book a flight right then and there, and if you need a rental car or hotel, Travelocity will find you the best deal via the SABRE computer reservations system (a huge database used by travel agents worldwide). Click on "Last Minute Deals" for the latest travel bargains, including a link to "H.O.T. Coupons" (**http://www.hotcoupons.com**), where you can print out electronic coupons for travel in the U.S. and Canada, including Hawaii.

can build the best, most unusual, and most outrageous sand sculpture. Call ☎ **808/956-7225.**

✪ **Kamehameha Schools Song Contest,** Neal Blaisdell Center, Honolulu. For more than three-quarters of a century, Hawaii's top Hawaiian school has conducted this traditional Hawaiian chorale contest. Call ☎ **808/842-8338.**

April

- **Easter Sunday,** National Cemetery of the Pacific, Punchbowl, Honolulu. For a century, people have gathered at this famous cemetery for Easter sunrise services. Call ☎ **808/293-9788.**
- **Buddha Day,** at various Hongwanji missions throughout the island. Some Buddhist missions have a flower pageant honoring the birth of Buddha. April 6. Call ☎ **808/595-2144.**

Trip.Com (http://www.thetrip.com)   This site is really geared toward the business traveler, but vacationers-to-be can also use Trip.Com's valuable fare-finding engine, which will e-mail you every week with the best city-to-city airfare deals on your selected route or routes.

Discount Tickets (http://www.discount-tickets.com)   Operated by the ETN (European Travel Network), this site offers discounts on airfares, accommodations, car rentals, and tours. It deals in flights between the U.S. and other countries, not domestic U.S. flights, so it's most useful for travelers coming to Hawaii from abroad.

E-SAVERS PROGRAMS   Several major airlines, most of which service the Hawaiian islands, offer a free e-mail service known as **E-Savers,** on which they'll send you their best bargain airfares on a weekly basis. Here's how it works: Once a week (usually Wednesday), subscribers receive a list of discounted flights to and from various destinations, both international and domestic. But there's a catch: These fares are only available if you leave the very next Saturday (or sometimes Friday night) and return on the following Monday or Tuesday. It's really a service for the spontaneously inclined and travelers looking for a quick getaway (for Hawaii, that usually means travelers from the West Coast). But the fares are cheap, so it's worth taking a look. If you have a preference for certain airlines (in other words, the ones you fly most frequently), sign up with them first. Another caveat: You'll get frequent-flier miles if you purchase one of these fares, but you can't use miles to buy the ticket.

Here's a list of airlines and their Web sites, where you can not only get on the e-mailing lists, but also book flights directly:

- **American Airlines:** http://www.americanair.com
- **Continental Airlines:** http://www.flycontiental.com
- **TWA:** http://www.twa.com
- **Northwest Airlines:** http://www.nwa.com
- **US Airways:** http://www.usairways.com

Epicurious Travel (http://travel.epicurious.com), another good travel site, allows you to sign up for all of these airline e-mail lists at once.

—Jeanette Foster

- **Hawaiian Slack Key Concert,** Honolulu Academy of Arts, Honolulu. A great opportunity to listen to this traditional form of music. The date of the concert varies from year to year; call ☎ **808/532-8701** for details.

May

○ **Annual Lei Day Celebration.** May Day is Lei Day in Hawaii, celebrated with lei making contests, pageantry, arts and crafts, and a concert at the Waikiki Shell. May 1. Call ☎ **808/924-8934.**

○ **World Fire-Knife Dance Championships & Samoan Festival,** Polynesian Cultural Center, Laie. Junior and adult fire-knife dancers from around the world converge on the Center in the most amazing performance you'll ever see. Authentic Samoan food and cultural festivities. Mid-May. Call ☎ **808/293-3333.**

- **State Fair,** Aloha Stadium, Honolulu. The annual state fair is a great one, with the biggest rides and shows. Check out the livestock contests, orchid displays, food booths, and local music and hula performances. Last Saturday in May through mid-June. Call ☎ **808/488-3389.**
- **Memorial Day,** National Memorial Cemetery of the Pacific, Punchbowl, Honolulu. The Armed Forces have a ceremony recognizing those who have died for their country. Call ☎ **808/566-1430.**

June

❂ **King Kamehameha Celebration,** a state holiday with a massive floral parade, *hoolaulea* (party), and much more. First weekend in June. On Oahu call ☎ **808/586-0333.**

- **King Kamehameha Hula Competition,** Neal Blaisdell Center, Honolulu. One of the top hula competitions with dancers from as far away as Japan. Third weekend in June. Call ☎ **808/586-0333.**

❂ **Taste of Honolulu,** Civic Center Grounds, Honolulu. Benefiting the Easter Seals campaign, Hawaii's premier outdoor food festival features tastings from 30 restaurants. Entertainment, beer and wine tasting, cooking demos, gourmet marketplace, and children's activities. End of June. Call ☎ **808/536-1015.**

July

- **Pacific Island Taro Festival,** Windward Community College, Kaneohe. Music, storytelling, dance, an arts-and-crafts fair, and a farmers market help to explain and celebrate the cultures and traditions of the Pacific Islands. Usually first Saturday in July. Call ☎ **808/235-7433.**
- **Fourth of July Fireworks,** Desiderio and Sills Field, Schofield Barracks, Wahiawa. A day-long celebration with entertainment, food, and games that ends with spectacular fireworks. Free and open to the public. Call ☎ **808/665-0143.**
- **Na Wahine O' Hawaii,** McCoy Pavilion, Ala Moana Park, Honolulu, Oahu. This all-female competition focuses on all aspects of the performing arts. Early July. Call ☎ **808/239-4336.**
- **Hawaii Seafood Festival.** Celebrations, cooking contests, demonstrations, theme restaurant meals, and more throughout the island. First or second weekend in July. Call ☎ **808/587-2683.**
- **Hawaii International Jazz Festival,** Sheraton Waikiki, Waikiki. Evening concerts and daily jam sessions, scholarship giveaways, the USC jazz band, along with many popular jazz and blues artists. Mid-July. Call ☎ **808/941-9974.**
- **Ukulele Festival,** Kapiolani Bandstand, Waikiki. This annual event features 400 children and special guest stars. Presented by Sheraton Hotels in Waikiki. End of July. Call ☎ **808/732-3739.**

August

- **Admissions Day,** Hawaii became the 50th state on August 21, 1959, so the state takes a holiday (all state-related facilities and the local banks are closed) on the third Friday in August.

❂ **Hawaiian Slack-Key Guitar Festival.** Five-hour festival held annually at a different location on Oahu, presenting the best of Hawaii's slack-key guitar players. Call ☎ **808/239-4336.**

September

❂ **Aloha Festivals,** various sites across Oahu. Parades and other events celebrate Hawaiian culture. Call ☎ **800/852-7690** or **808/545-1771** for a schedule of events.

October
- **Makahiki Festival,** Waimea Valley. Hawaiian games, crafts, music, and food, all in a tremendous natural setting. The Hula Kahiko Competition is a major highlight. First weekend in October. Call ☎ **808/638-8511.**

November
- **Hawaii International Film Festival,** various locations in Honolulu. A cinema festival with a cross-cultural spin featuring filmmakers from Asia, the Pacific Islands, and the U.S. First two weeks in November. Call ☎ **808/528-FILM.**
- **World Invitational Hula Festival,** Waikiki Shell. Competitors from all over the world dance for the prizes. Early to mid-November. Call ☎ **808/486-3185.**

December
- **Festival of Trees,** Honolulu. Downtown display of one-of-a-kind decorated trees, wreaths, and decorations to benefit Queen's Medical Center. First or second week of the month. Call ☎ **808/547-4780.**
- ✪ **First Night,** downtown Honolulu. A festival of arts and entertainment. For 12 hours, musicians, dancers, actors, jugglers, magicians, and mimes perform, food is available, and fireworks bring in the New Year. Alcohol-free. December 31. Call ☎ **808/532-3131.**

3 Health & Insurance

STAYING SAFE & HEALTHY

While some Hawaii-bound adventurers may worry about shark bites, the most common cause of injury in the islands is sunburn. Hawaii lies south of the Tropic of Cancer, only about 1,400 miles north of the equator at the edge of the tropical zone. So the sun is extremely harsh, and only intermittent clouds and trade winds keep the islands from having stifling temperatures. Apply plenty of sunscreen with a high SPF, and wear a hat and sunglasses. The worst time to be in the sun in Hawaii is between 10am and 3pm (some dermatologists now suggest staying out of the sun until after 4pm). If you're outside during these hours, put on sunscreen and cover up. Experts say that most of us do not use enough sunscreen—they recommend one tablespoon of sunscreen per limb; reapply it every two hours, even if it is waterproof. If you do get a burn, apply liberal amounts of aloe vera—Hawaii's favorite local remedy to ease the pain.

DRINKING WATER   You can drink the water. Oahu's water, naturally purified by 30 years of filtering through the volcanic rock of the Koolau Mountains before it comes out of the tap, is regularly judged America's best-tasting water in blind tastings. However, if you go camping, you must treat all water from waterfalls and streams; it can be contaminated by wild pigs, goats, and cattle.

HIKING SAFETY   Hikers should let someone know when they're going, where they're heading, and when they plan to return. Too many hikers are lost on Oahu because they don't let others know their basic plans. Check weather conditions with the **National Weather Service** (☎ **808/973-4381**) before you go. Hike with a pal, never alone. Wear hiking boots, a sun hat, and clothes to protect you from the sun and from scratches. Take water. Stay on the trail. Watch your step. It's easy to slip off precipitous trails and into steep canyons, with often disastrous, and even fatal results. Incapacitated hikers are often plucked to safety by Fire and Rescue squads, who must use helicopters to gain access to remote sites. Today, many experienced hikers and boaters pack a cellular phone in case of emergency. Just call ☎ 911.

OCEAN SAFETY   Don't worry about sharks. Unless you specifically go looking for sharks, you're unlikely to even see one during your trip. People have lived in Hawaii their entire lives and spent every weekend in the water without seeing a shark. However, always keep these other considerations in mind when you're at the beach:

Never, ever, turn your back on the ocean—big waves can come seemingly out of nowhere and travel far up the shore in a matter of minutes. Always keep an eye on the ocean, even if you are taking a casual stroll along the water's edge; monitor the waves constantly. Also, remember that ocean conditions can change in a few hours. Surf that was placid and safe for swimming one day can become dangerous the next. If you don't have any experience with waves, get out of the water when the swells start coming in.

The best places to swim are at beaches with lifeguards. Always swim with a partner. When swimming at an unfamiliar beach, ask the lifeguard about the ocean conditions and where the safest place to swim is. If the beach doesn't have a lifeguard, ask the local beachgoers. If there's no one around to ask, stay out of the water: Hidden rip currents, undertows, and submerged rocks may turn a pleasant dip into a disaster.

Be aware of the potential dangers in the water. During the winter months, storms and winds bring Portuguese Man-of-War and other stinging jellyfish close to shore. (The lifeguards will often close down a beach when these stinging critters move in.) While they are floating in the water, it's difficult to see the 1- to 4-inch-long, violet-blue floating jellyfish, with their several-foot-long tentacles. The stings are quite painful and can produce red welts on the skin. The best treatment is to sprinkle the affected area with unseasoned meat tenderizer, which helps to neutralize the poison.

Coral cuts are a common problem for active oceangoers. A good way to prevent cuts is to wear protective shoes in the water. Try to avoid touching coral altogether, since it's a living (and growing) organism—it's very easy for you to damage coral and vice versa. Any ocean-related cut is susceptible to infection and is usually slow to heal. Any wound you receive near the ocean should be scrubbed immediately with soap and water and hydrogen peroxide to remove the foreign material. Apply an antiseptic ointment as soon as possible.

Another common danger is sea urchin spines. If you even brush against these sharp, needlelike spines, they can break off into your skin. They're not easy to remove. Believe it or not, one of the best remedies is to urinate on the affected part, which seems to aid the dissolution of the spines; an alternative is to pour vinegar on the spot.

OUTDOOR ETIQUETTE

Act locally, think globally, and carry out what you carry in. Find a rubbish container for all your litter (including cigarette butts—it's very bad form to throw them out of your car window). Observe *kapu* and no trespassing signs. Don't climb on ancient Hawaiian heiau walls and temples, or carry home rocks, all of which belong to the Hawaiian Volcano Goddess Pele. Some say it's just a silly superstition or coincidence, but each year the U.S. Park Service gets boxes of lava rocks sent back to Hawaii by visitors who've experienced unusually bad luck.

INSURANCE

Your current policies may be adequate, but before you leave home, ask your insurance company if it will cover you while driving a rental car in Hawaii (where car insurance is mandated by law); review your homeowners' policy to make sure that any theft or loss (luggage, cameras, etc.) is covered; and finally, check your health insurance to ensure that medical problems will be covered. Hawaii law mandates that all employers provide health insurance coverage for employees, so most health care providers insist on health insurance. Without health insurance, you may have a problem finding a medical provider.

If you need additional coverage, you can contact the following (*warning:* always read the small print to make sure that you are getting the kind of insurance you want):

Access America, 6600 W. Broad St., P.O. Box 11188, Richmond, VA 23230 (☎ **800/284-8300** or 804/285-3300), not only offers travel insurance and 24-hour emergency travel, medical, and legal assistance, but also has a hotline center, which will refer you to the nearest physician, hospital, or legal advisor. They will also assist in obtaining emergency cash or in the replacement of lost travel documents.

Carefree Travel Insurance, P.O. Box 9366, Garden City, NY 11530 (☎ **800/323-3149**), offers policies on baggage loss or delays, trip cancellation, medical insurance, and accidental death and dismemberment. They also have a telephone hotline for help with any medical, travel, and legal problems before and during your trip.

Travel Guard International, 1145 Clark St., Stevens Point, WI 54481 (☎ **800/826-1300**), features comprehensive insurance programs on basically everything: trip cancellation, lost luggage, medical coverage, and accidental death. They also have a 24-hour emergency hotline.

4 Tips for Travelers with Special Needs

FOR TRAVELERS WITH DISABILITIES

Travelers with disabilities are made to feel very welcome in Hawaii. There are more than 2,000 ramped curbs on Oahu alone, hotels are usually equipped with wheelchair-accessible rooms, and tour companies provide many special services. **The Commission on Persons with Disabilities,** 919 Ala Moana Blvd., Honolulu, HI 96814 (☎ **808/586-8121**), and the **Hawaii Center for Independent Living,** 677 Ala Moana Blvd., Suite 118, Honolulu, HI 96813 (☎ **808/537-1941**) can provide information and send you a copy of the *Aloha Guide to Accessibility* ($3).

HandiCabs of the Pacific (☎ **808/524-3866**) provides wheelchair taxi service and a variety of wheelchair-accommodated activities on Oahu, including sightseeing tours, luaus, and cruises. Airport pickup to a Waikiki hotel costs $35 one-way. On Oahu, you can also book transportation to a specific destination (not for sightseeing purposes) in vans complete with lifts and lock-downs with **HandiVans** (☎ **808/832-0777**)

For disabled travelers who wish to do their own driving, hand-controlled cars can be rented from **Avis** (☎ **800/331-1212**) and **Hertz** (☎ **800/654-3131**). The number of hand-controlled cars in Hawaii is limited, so they should be booked well in advance. Hawaii recognizes other states' windshield placards indicating that the car's driver is disabled. Use them to park in specially marked handicapped stalls.

FOR SENIORS

Discounts for seniors are available at almost all of Hawaii's major attractions, and occasionally at hotels and restaurants. Always ask when making hotel reservations.

Members of the **American Association of Retired Persons (AARP),** 601 E St. NW, Washington, D.C. 20049 (☎ 800/424-3410 or 202/434-2277) are usually eligible for such discounts. Organized tour packages at moderate rates are also available through the AARP Travel Service. The **National Council of Senior Citizens,** 1331 F St. NW, Washington, D.C. 20004 (☎ 202/347-8800) also offers travel discounts to seniors.

There are some great, low-cost trips to Hawaii available for people 60 and older through **Elderhostel,** 75 Federal St., Boston, MA 02110 (☎ 617/426-7788), a nonprofit group that offers travel and study programs around the world. Trips are usually unbelievably cheap and include moderate accommodations and meals in one low package price.

If you're planning to visit Hawaii's national parks, you can save sightseeing dollars if you're 62 or older by picking up a **Golden Age Passport** from any national park, recreation area, or monument. This lifetime pass has a one-time fee of $10 and provides free admission to the parks, plus 50% savings on camping and recreation fees. You can pick one up at the park entrances.

5　Planning an Island Wedding

Fragrant blossoms, lush vegetation, perfect sun-kissed days, whatever your dreams, Hawaii is a great place for a wedding. Not only do the islands exude romance and beauty, but after the ceremony, you're only a few steps from the perfect honeymoon. And your family, friends, and members of your wedding party will probably be delighted—you've given all of them the perfect excuse for their own island vacations.

Couples can get married, or remarried, in historic Hawaiian churches; on the beach; under a waterfall in a rain forest; on horseback in a pasture with an ocean view; in a lush tropical garden; on a sailboat, with Diamond Head as a backdrop; on a deserted islet; underwater with a school of brilliant-colored fish for witnesses; barefoot on the beach at sunset and draped in fragrant leis; or in full regalia on formal parade from chapel to luxury hotel.

It happens every day of the year in Hawaii, where more than 20,000 marriages are performed each year, most of them on the island of Oahu. Nearly half (44.6%) of the couples married here are from somewhere else. This booming business has spawned more than 70 companies that can help you organize a long-distance event and stage an unforgettable wedding, Hawaiian-style or your style (see "Wedding Planners," below). However, you can also plan your own island wedding, even from afar, and not spend a fortune doing it.

THE PAPERWORK

The state of Hawaii has minimal procedures for obtaining a marriage license. The first thing you should do is contact the **Honolulu Marriage License Office,** State Department of Health Building, 1250 Punchbowl St., Honolulu, HI 96813 (☎ 808/586-4545; open Monday through Friday from 8am to 4pm, except holidays). They'll mail you their brochure, *Getting Married,* and direct you to the marriage licensing agent closest to where you'll be staying in Hawaii.

Upon arrival in Hawaii, the prospective bride and groom must go together to the marriage licensing agent to get a license. A license costs $25 and is good for 30 days; if you don't have the ceremony within the time allotted, you'll have to pay another $25 for another license. The only requirements are that both parties must be 18 years of age or older, and not more closely related than first cousins. That's it.

And Fragrant Flowers Fill the Airport: The Welcoming Lei

When you arrive in Hawaii, the air is fragrant with flowers. Sweet scents are everywhere, in a profusion of perfumes from gardens, street trees, and fields—and around your neck in a welcoming flower lei.

A tradition born in the Pacific and cherished by all who love Hawaii, the lei is a garland of fresh, fragrant flowers. It's given to honor guests and to celebrate birthdays, weddings, graduations, triumphs, and farewells. Bus drivers tuck fragrant blossoms behind their ears or onto their dashboards. Musicians hang leis from their microphones. The dance isn't really hula without leis, and no woman is fully dressed for evening unless she's wearing flowers.

Lei making is a tropical art form. All are fashioned by hand in a variety of traditional patterns. Some leis are sewn of hundreds of tiny blooms or shells, or bits of ferns and leaves. Some last only a few hours. The memory lasts forever.

Every island has its own special flower lei. On Oahu, the choice is *ilima,* a small orange flower. On Kauai, it's the *mokihana,* a fragrant green vine and berry. Big Islanders prefer the *lehua,* a large delicate red puff. Maui likes the *lokelani,* a small rose. Molokai prefers the *kukui,* the white blossom of a candlenut tree. And Lanai's lei is made of *kaunaoa,* a bright yellow moss, while Niihau utilizes its abundant seashells to make leis once prized by royalty and now worth a small fortune.

Leis are available at the lei stands at the Honolulu International Airport. Other places to get creative, inexpensive leis are the half-dozen lei shops on Maunakea Street in Honolulu's Chinatown, and Flowers by Jou & T Jr., 2653 S. King St. (near University Ave.).

So pick up a lei and feel the spirit of Aloha. Welcome to Hawaii!

Contrary to some reports from the media, gay couples cannot marry in Hawaii. Although the state courts ruled a few years ago that the state of Hawaii had to show a compelling reason why the state wouldn't issue a marriage license to gay couples, the state legislature passed a law in 1997 specifying that a marriage license would only be issued to a man and a woman.

PLANNING THE WEDDING
DOING IT YOURSELF

The marriage licensing agents, which range from the Governor's satellite office in Kona to private individuals, are usually friendly, helpful people who can steer you to a nondenominational minister or marriage performer who's licensed by the state of Hawaii to perform the ceremony. These marriage performers are great sources of information for budget weddings. They usually know great places to have the ceremony for free or a nominal fee.

If you don't want to use a wedding planner (see below) but want to make arrangements before you arrive in Hawaii, our best advice is to get a copy of the daily newspapers on the island where you want to have the wedding. People willing and qualified to conduct weddings advertise in the classifieds. They're great sources of information, as they know the best places to have the ceremony and can recommend caterers, florists, and everything else you'll need. Check out the ***Honolulu Advertiser,*** P.O. Box 3110, Honolulu, HI 96802 (☎ **808/525-8000**), the ***Honolulu Star Bulletin,*** P.O. Box 3080, Honolulu, HI 96802 (☎ **808/525-8000**); and *MidWeek,* 45-525 Luluku Rd., Kaneohe, HI 96744 (☎ **808/235-5881**).

USING A WEDDING PLANNER

Wedding planners—many of whom are marriage licensing agents themselves—can arrange everything for you, from a small private outdoor affair to a full-blown formal ceremony in a tropical setting. They charge anywhere from $450 to a small fortune—it all depends on what you want. The Hawaii Visitors and Convention Bureau (see "Visitor Information & Money," above) can provide contact information on wedding coordinators.

If you want to get married at sea, call Capt. Ken Middleton, of **Tradewind Charters,** 1833 Kalakaua St., Suite 612, Honolulu, HI 96815 (☎ **800/829-4899** or 808/973-0311) for a private wedding and reception on the ocean waves.

Or for a wedding conducted entirely in Hawaiian, contact **Traditional Hawaiian Weddings,** 94-1054 Paha Pl., Waipahu, HI 96794 (☎ **808/671-8420**).

For a wedding and reception in Waimea Falls Park, contact the wedding coordinator, **Waimea Falls Park,** 59-88864 Kamehameha Hwy., Haleiwa, HI 96712, at ☎ **808/638-8511.**

If you want a romantic wedding in an exotic setting like near a waterfall, on the beach, or in a garden chapel, **AAA Above Heaven's Gate,** ☎ **800/800-2WED** or 808/259-5429, can arrange it

Other wedding planners include: **Affordable Weddings of Hawaii,** P.O. Box 26475, Honolulu, HI 96825, (☎ **800/942-4554** or 808/923-4876); **Aloha Wedding Planners,** 1860 Ala Moana Blvd., Suite 115, Honolulu, HI 96815 (☎ **800/288-8309** or 808/943-2711); and **Wedding Planning Made Easy,** 258 Moomuku Pl., Honolulu, HI (☎ **808/395-0536**).

6 Getting There & Getting Around

ARRIVING IN THE ISLANDS

All major American and many international carriers fly to Honolulu International Airport.

United Airlines (☎ 800/225-5825) offers the most frequent service from the U.S. mainland, but **American Airlines** (☎ 800/433-7300), **America West** (☎ 800/235-9292), **Continental Airlines** (☎ 800/231-0856), **Delta Air Lines** (☎ 800/221-1212), **Northwest Airlines** (☎ 800/225-2525), and **Trans World Airlines** (☎ 800/221-2000) all have regular flights.

Based in Honolulu, **Hawaiian Airlines** (☎ 800/367-5320 or 808/537-5100) offers nonstop service on wide-body DC-10s from San Francisco, Seattle, Los Angeles, Portland, and Las Vegas. Hawaiian works with Fly AAway Vacations, the tour unit of American Airlines. For information about its package tours, phone **Hawaiian Airlines Vacations** at ☎ 800/353-5393, or ask your travel agent.

Airlines serving Hawaii from other than the U.S. mainland include **Air Canada** (☎ 800/776-3000), **Canadian Airlines International** (☎ 800/426-7000), **Air New Zealand** (☎ 800/262-1234), **Qantas** (☎ 800/227-4500), **Japan Airlines** (☎ 800/525-3663), **All Nippon Airways** (☎ 808/695-8008), **China Airlines** (☎ 800/227-5118), **Garuda Indonesian** (☎ 800/231-0856), **Korean Airlines** (☎ 800/223-1155 on the East Coast, 800/421-8200 on the West Coast), and **Philippine Airlines** (☎ 800/435-9725). *Note:* You can fly to Hawaii from the U.S. mainland on one of these foreign carriers only if you're continuing on with them to—or returning with them from—an overseas destination.

AIRFARE DEALS

To save money on tickets, check out the prices from a consolidator, which are wholesalers who buy tickets directly from the airlines in bulk at heavy discounts, and then resell them. The tickets are usually heavily restricted (ask about all the details), but you may save a bundle—usually 20% to 35%. Reliable consolidators include **Cheap Tickets** (☎ **800/377-1000** or 212/570-1179); **TFI Tours International** (☎ **800/745-8000** or 212-736-1140); **1-800-FLY-CHEAP** (Web site: http://www.websrus.com/flycheap); and **1-800-FLY-4-LESS** (e-mail: fly4less@juno.com).

AGRICULTURAL SCREENING AT THE AIRPORTS   At Honolulu International and the neighbor-island airports, baggage and passengers bound for the mainland and other countries must be screened by agricultural officials before boarding. This takes a little time, but isn't a problem unless you happen to be carrying a football-sized local avocado home to Aunt Emma. Officials will confiscate fresh avocados, bananas, mangoes, and many other kinds of local produce in the name of fruit-fly control. Pineapples, coconuts, and papayas inspected and certified for export; boxed flowers; leis; and processed foods (macadamia nuts, coffee, jams, dried fruit, and the like) will pass. Call federal or state agricultural officials before leaving for the airport if you're not sure about your trophy.

INTERISLAND FLIGHTS

If you want to see another island while you are in Hawaii, access is via airlines. Don't expect to jump a ferry between any of the Hawaiian islands. Today, everyone island-hops by plane. In fact, almost every 20 minutes of every day from just before sunrise to well after sunset (usually around 8pm), a plane takes off or lands at Honolulu International Airport on the interisland shuttle service. If you miss a flight, don't worry; they're like buses—another one will be along real soon.

Aloha Airlines (☎ **800/367-5250** or 808/484-1111; http://www.alohaair.com) is the state's largest provider of interisland air transport service. It offers 275 regularly scheduled daily jet flights throughout Hawaii and enjoys one of the lowest complaint records in the airline industry. Aloha's sister company, **Island Air** (☎ **800/323-3345** or 808/484-2222), operates eight deHavilland Twin Otter turboprop aircraft and serves Hawaii's small interisland airports in West Maui, Hana (Maui), Lanai, and Molokai.

Hawaiian Airlines (☎ **800/367-5320** or 808/835-3700; http://www.hawaiianair.com; e-mail: webmaster@hawaiianair.com), Hawaii's oldest interisland airline, has carried more than 100 million passengers around the state on its jets and prop planes. It's one of the world's safest airlines, never having had a fatal incident since it started flying in 1929.

Mahalo Air (☎ **800/277-8333** or 808/833-5555), Hawaii's youngest interisland carrier, usually charges the lowest fares for round trips to all islands except Lanai in its 50-seat turboprop Fokker aircraft. If you're in no hurry and can travel midweek, Mahalo is the thrifty alternative. Exteriors of their eye-catching planes feature renditions of Hawaii's endangered species like the nene goose, Hawaiian owl, green sea turtle, and humpback whale.

CAR RENTALS

All major rental car agencies are represented at Honolulu International Airport and most neighbor-island airports, including **Alamo** (☎ 800/327-9633), **Avis** (☎ 800/321-3712), **Budget** (☎ 800/935-6878), **Dollar** (☎ 800/800-4000), **Enterprise**

(☎ 800/325-8007), **Hertz** (☎ 800/654-3011), **National** (☎ 800/227-7368), **Payless** (☎ 800/729-5377), **Sears** (☎ 800/527-0770), and **Thrifty** (☎ 800/367-2277). It's almost always cheaper to rent a car at the airport than in Waikiki or through your hotel.

To rent a car in Hawaii, you must be at least 25 years of age and have a valid driver's license and a credit card. Your valid home-state license will be recognized here.

INSURANCE   Hawaii is a no-fault state, which means that if you don't have collision damage insurance, you are required to pay for all damages before you leave the state, whether the accident was your fault or not. Your personal car insurance may provide rental-car coverage—read your policy or call your insurer before you leave home. Bring your identification card if you decline the optional insurance, which usually costs from $12 to $20 a day. Obtain the name of your company's local claim representative before you go. Some credit-card companies also provide collision damage insurance for their customers; check with yours before you rent.

DRIVING RULES   Hawaii has a mandatory seat belt law; if you're caught not buckled up, you'll get a $50 ticket. Infants must be strapped in car seats. Pedestrians always have the right of way, even if they're not in the crosswalk. You can turn right on red from the right lane after a full and complete stop, unless there is a sign forbidding you to do so.

ROAD MAPS   The best and most detailed island maps are by Honolulu-based cartographer James A. Bier and are published by University of Hawaii Press. Updated periodically, they include a detailed network of island roads, large-scale insets of towns, historical and contemporary points of interest, parks, beaches, and hiking trails. They cost about $3 each, or about $15 for a complete set. If you can't find them in a bookstore near you, write to **University of Hawaii Press,** 2840 Kolowalu St., Honolulu, HI 96822.

If you seek topographical maps of the Hawaiian Islands, go to the **Hawaii Geographic Society,** 49 S. Hotel St., Honolulu, HI 95813, or write to them at P.O. Box 1698 Honolulu, HI, 96806 (☎ **808/546-3952;** fax 808/536-5999). Old road maps and sea charts are available at **Tusitala Bookshop,** 116 Hekili St., Kailua, HI 96734 (☎ **808/262-6343**).

For Foreign Visitors 4

by Jeanette Foster

Although American fads and fashions have spread across Europe and other parts of the world so that the United States may seem like familiar territory before your arrival, there are still many peculiarities and uniquely American situations that any foreign visitor will encounter, especially in this island state.

1 Preparing for Your Trip

ENTRY REQUIREMENTS

Immigration laws are a hot political issue in the United States these days, and the following requirements may have changed somewhat by the time you plan your trip. Check at any U.S. embassy or consulate for current information and requirements.

DOCUMENT REGULATIONS Citizens of Canada and Bermuda may enter the United States without visas, but they will need to show proof of nationality, of which the most common and hassle-free form is a passport. The U.S. State Department has a **Visa Waiver Pilot Program** allowing citizens of certain countries to enter the United States without a visa for stays of fewer than 90 days of holiday travel. At press time these included Andorra, Argentina, Australia, Austria, Belgium, Brunei, Denmark, Finland, France, Germany, Iceland, Ireland, Italy, Japan, Liechtenstein, Luxembourg, Monaco, the Netherlands, New Zealand, Norway, San Marino, Spain, Sweden, Switzerland, and the United Kingdom. (The program as applied to the United Kingdom refers to British citizens who have the "unrestricted right of permanent abode in the United Kingdom," that is, citizens from England, Scotland, Wales, Northern Ireland, the Channel Islands, and the Isle of Man; and not, for example, citizens of the British Commonwealth of Pakistan.) Citizens from these countries need only a valid passport and a round-trip air or cruise ticket in their possession upon arrival. If they first enter the United States, they may then visit Mexico, Canada, Bermuda, and/or the Caribbean islands and return to the United States without needing a visa. Further information is available from any U.S. embassy or consulate. Citizens of countries other than those specified above, or those traveling to the U.S. for reasons or length of time outside the restrictions of the Visa Waiver program, or those who require waivers of inadmissibility must have two documents:

- a valid passport, with an expiration date at least 6 months later than the scheduled end of the visit to the United States (some countries are exceptions to the 6-month validity rule. Contact any U.S. embassy or consulate for complete information.); and
- a tourist visa, available from the nearest U.S. consulate. To obtain a visa, the traveler must submit a completed application form (either in person or by mail) with a 1½-inch square photo and the required application fee. There may also be an issuance fee, depending on the type of visa and other factors. Usually you can obtain a visa right away or within 24 hours, but it may take longer during the summer rush period (June to August). If you cannot go in person, contact the nearest U.S. embassy or consulate for directions on applying by mail. Your travel agent or airline office may also be able to provide you with visa applications and instructions. The U.S. consulate or embassy that issues your visa will determine whether you will be issued a multiple- or single-entry visa. The Immigration and Naturalization Service officers at the port-of-entry in the U.S. will make an admission decision and determine your length of stay.

Foreign driver's licenses are recognized in Hawaii, although you may want to get an international driver's license if your home license is not written in English.

Medical Requirements   Inoculations are not needed to enter the United States unless you are coming from, or have stopped over in, areas known to be suffering from epidemics, particularly cholera or yellow fever.

If you have a disease requiring treatment with medications containing narcotics or drugs requiring a syringe, carry a valid signed prescription from your physician to allay suspicions that you are smuggling drugs.

Customs Requirements   Every adult visitor may bring in free of duty: 1 liter of wine or hard liquor; 200 cigarettes or 100 cigars (but no cigars from Cuba) or 3 pounds of smoking tobacco; $100 worth of gifts. These exemptions are offered to travelers who spend at least 72 hours in the United States and who have not claimed them within the preceding 6 months. It is altogether forbidden to bring into the country foodstuffs (particularly cheese, fruit, cooked meats, and canned goods) and plants (vegetables, seeds, tropical plants, and so on). Foreign tourists may bring in or take out up to $10,000 in U.S. or foreign currency with no formalities; larger sums must be declared to customs on entering or leaving.

In addition, you cannot bring fresh fruits and vegetables into Hawaii, even if you're coming from the U.S. mainland and have no need to clear customs. Every passenger is asked shortly before landing to sign a certificate declaring that he or she does not have fresh fruits and vegetables in their possession. The form also asks questions for the Hawaii Visitors Bureau about your visit, such as how long you plan to stay, which island or islands you will visit, and how many times you have been to Hawaii.

Insurance   There is no nationwide health system in the United States, and the cost of medical care in Hawaii is extremely high. Accordingly, we strongly advise every traveler to secure health insurance coverage before setting out.

You may want to take out a comprehensive travel policy that covers (for a relatively low premium) sickness or injury costs (medical, surgical, and hospital); loss or theft of your baggage; trip-cancellation costs; guarantee of bail in case you are arrested; costs of accident, repatriation, or death. Such packages (for example, "Europe Assistance" in Europe) are sold by automobile clubs at attractive rates, as well as by insurance companies and travel agencies.

MONEY

CURRENCY The American monetary system has a decimal base: one U.S. **dollar** ($1) = 100 **cents** (100¢). Dollar bills commonly come in $1 ("a buck"), $5, $10, $20, $50, and $100 denominations (the last two are not welcome when paying for small purchases and are not accepted in taxis or movie theaters).

There are six denominations of coins: 1¢ (one cent or a "penny"), 5¢ (five cents or a "nickel"), 10¢ (ten cents or a "dime"), 25¢ (twenty-five cents or a "quarter"), 50¢ (fifty cents or a "half-dollar"), and the rare $1 piece.

Exchanging Currency Unlike most other states, in which exchanging foreign currency for U.S. dollars can be a pain, you can easily change most currencies in Hawaii. Most major banks provide this service. In downtown Honolulu, you also can get reliable currency service at **Thomas Cook Currency,** 1000 Bishop St., Bishop Trust Building, Ground Level, facing King Street (☎ **808/523-1321**). In Waikiki, go to **A1 Foreign Exchange,** which has offices in the Royal Hawaiian Shopping Center, 2259 Kalakaua Ave., and in the Hyatt Regency Waikiki Tower, 2424 Kalakaua Ave. (☎ **808/922-3327**); or to **Monyx International,** 307 Royal Hawaiian Ave. (☎ **808/923-6626**).

Traveler's Checks It's actually cheaper and faster to get cash at an automatic teller machine (ATM) than to fuss with traveler's checks, as noted in "Visitor Information & Money" in chapter 3.

Hawaii has ATMs almost everywhere except on Lanai. If you do bring them, traveler's checks denominated in U.S. dollars are readily accepted at most hotels, restaurants, and large stores. Do not bring traveler's checks denominated in currencies other than U.S. dollars.

Credit Cards The method of payment most widely used is the credit card: Visa (BarclayCard in Britain), MasterCard (EuroCard in Europe, Access in Britain, Chargex in Canada), American Express, Diners Club, Discover, and Carte Blanche. You can save yourself trouble by using "plastic money" rather than cash or traveler's checks in most hotels, restaurants, and retail stores (a growing number of food and liquor stores now accept credit cards). Also, you must have a credit card to rent a car in Hawaii.

SAFETY

GENERAL While tourist areas are generally safe, crimes occur everywhere, and Hawaii is no exception. Visitors should always stay alert. It's wise to ask the island tourist office if you're in doubt about which neighborhoods are safe. Avoid deserted areas, especially at night. Don't go into any city park at night unless there's an event that attracts crowds—for example, the Waikiki Shell concerts in Kapiolani Park. Generally speaking, you can feel safe in areas where there are many people and open establishments.

Avoid carrying valuables with you on the street, and don't display expensive cameras or electronic equipment. Hold onto your pocketbook, and place your billfold in an inside pocket. In theaters, restaurants, and other public places, keep your possessions in sight.

Recently there have been a series of purse-snatching incidents on Oahu. Thieves, in slow-moving cars or on foot, have snatched handbags from female pedestrians (in some instances dragging women, who refuse to let go of their pocketbooks, down the street). The Honolulu police department advises women to carry their purses on the shoulder away from the street, or better yet to wear the strap across your chest instead of on one shoulder. Women with clutch bags should hold their bags close to their chest.

Remember that hotels are open to the public, and in a large establishment, security may not be able to screen everyone entering. Always lock your room door—don't assume that once inside your hotel you are automatically safe and no longer need to be aware of your surroundings.

DRIVING　Safety while driving is particularly important. Question your rental agency about personal safety, or ask for a brochure of traveler safety tips when you pick up your car. Obtain written directions or a map with the route marked in red from the agency showing how to get to your destination.

Recently more crime has involved burglary of tourist rental cars in hotel parking structures and at beach parking lots. Park in well-lighted and well-traveled areas if possible. If you leave your rental car unlocked and empty of your valuables, you are probably safer than locking your car with valuables in plain view. Never leave packages or valuables in sight. If someone attempts to rob you or steal your car, do not try to resist the thief/carjacker—report the incident to the police department immediately.

2　Getting To & Around the United States

Travelers from overseas can take advantage of the **APEX (Advance Purchase Excursion)** fares offered by all major U.S. and European carriers. Aside from these, attractive values are offered by **Icelandair** on flights from Luxembourg to New York and by **Virgin Atlantic Airways** from London to New York/Newark. You can then catch a connecting domestic flight to Honolulu. Advance purchase fares are available to travelers from Australia via **Qantas Airways,** which runs daily flights from Sydney to Honolulu (plus additional flights 4 days a week); they are also available for travelers from New Zealand via **Air New Zealand,** which runs 40 flights per week from Auckland.

Some large American airlines (for example, TWA, American Airlines, Northwest, United, and Delta) offer travelers on transatlantic or transpacific flights special discount tickets under the name **Visit USA,** allowing travel between any U.S. destinations at reduced rates. They're not on sale in the United States and must, therefore, be purchased before you leave your foreign point of departure. This system is the best, easiest, and fastest way to see the United States at low cost. You should obtain information well in advance from your travel agent or the office of the airline concerned, since the conditions attached to these discount tickets can be changed without advance notice.

The ETN (European Travel Network), operates a Web site called **Discount Tickets (http://www.discount-tickets.com)**, which offers discounts on international airfares to the United States, accommodations, car rentals, and tours.

The visitor arriving by air should cultivate patience and resignation before setting foot on U.S. soil. Getting through immigration control may take as long as 2 hours on some days, especially summer weekends. Add the time it takes to clear customs and you'll see that you should make very generous allowances for delay in planning connections between international and domestic flights—an average of 2 to 3 hours at least.

For further information about travel to Hawaii, see "Getting There & Getting Around" in chapter 3.

FAST FACTS: For the Foreign Traveler

Automobile Organizations　Auto clubs will supply maps, suggested routes, guidebooks, accident and bail-bond insurance, and emergency road service. The major auto club in the United States, with 955 offices nationwide, is the **American Automobile Association** (AAA; often called "triple A"). Members of some foreign auto clubs have reciprocal arrangements with the AAA and enjoy its services at no charge. If you belong to an auto club, inquire about AAA reciprocity before you leave. The AAA can provide you with an **International Driving Permit** validating your foreign license. You may be able to join the AAA even if you are not a member of a reciprocal club. To inquire, call ☎ **800/336-4357.** In Hawaii, the local office of the AAA is at 590 Queen St., Honolulu (☎ **808/528-2600**). In addition, some automobile rental agencies now provide these services, so you should inquire about their availability when you rent your car.

Automobile Rentals   See "Getting There & Getting Around" in chapter 3.

Business Hours   See "Fast Facts: Oahu" in chapter 5.

Climate   See "When to Go" in chapter 3.

Currency & Currency Exchange   See "Preparing for Your Trip," above.

Electricity   Hawaii, like the U.S. mainland and Canada, uses 110–120 volts, 60 cycles, compared to 220–240 volts, 50 cycles, as in most of Europe and in other areas of the world including Australia and New Zealand. In addition to a 100-volt transformer, small appliances of non-American manufacture, such as hair dryers or shavers, will require a plug adapter, with two flat, parallel pins.

Embassies & Consulates   All embassies are located in the national capital, Washington, D.C. Some consulates are located in major cities, and most nations have a mission to the United Nations in New York City. Listed here are the embassies and some consulates of the major English-speaking countries. Travelers from other countries can obtain telephone numbers for their embassies and consulates by calling directory information for Washington, D.C. (☎ **202/555-1212**).

The embassy of **Australia** is at 1601 Massachusetts Ave. NW, Washington, D.C. 20036 (☎ **202/797-3000**). There is also an Australian consulate in Hawaii at 1000 Bishop St., Penthouse Suite, Honolulu, HI 96813 (☎ **808/524-5050**).

The embassy of **Canada** is at 501 Pennsylvania Ave. NW, Washington, D.C. 20001 (☎ **202/682-1740**). Canadian consulates are also at 1251 Avenue of the Americas, New York, NY 10020 (☎ **212/768-2400**), and at 550 South Hope St., 9th floor, Los Angeles, CA 90071 (☎ **213/346-2700**).

The embassy of the **Republic of Ireland** is at 2234 Massachusetts Ave. NW, Washington, D.C. 20008 (☎ **202/462-3939**). There's a consulate office in San Francisco at 44 Montgomery St., Suite 3830, San Francisco, CA 94104 (☎ **415/392-4214**).

The embassy of **New Zealand** is at 37 Observatory Circle NW, Washington, D.C. 20008 (☎ **202/328-4800**). The only New Zealand consulate in the United States is at 12400 Wilshire Blvd., Los Angeles, CA 90025 (☎ **310/207-1605**).

The embassy of the **United Kingdom** is at 3100 Massachusetts Ave. NW, Washington, D.C. 20008 (☎ **202/462-1340**). British consulates are at 845 Third Ave., New York, NY 10022 (☎ **212/745-0200**), and 11766 Wilshire Blvd., Suite 400, Los Angeles, CA 90025 (☎ **310/477-3322**).

The embassy of **Japan** is at 2520 Massachusetts Ave. NW, Washington, D.C. 20008 (☎ **202/939-6700**). The consulate general of Japan is located at 1742 Nuuanu Ave., Honolulu, HI 96817 (☎ **808/536-2226**). There are several other consulates, including one in New York at 299 Park Ave., New York, NY 10171 (☎ **212/371-8222**).

Emergencies   Call ☎ **911** to report a fire, call the police, or get an ambulance. If you encounter problems while traveling, check the local directory to find an office of the **Traveler's Aid Society,** a nationwide, nonprofit, social-service organization geared to helping travelers in difficult straits. Their services might include reuniting families separated while traveling, providing food and/or shelter to people stranded without cash, or even emotional counseling. If you're in trouble, seek them out.

Gasoline (Petrol)   One U.S. gallon equals 3.8 liters, while 1.2 U.S. gallons equals one Imperial gallon. You'll notice there are several grades (and price levels) of gasoline available at most gas stations. And you'll also notice that their names change from company to company. The ones with the highest octane are the most expensive, but most rental cars take the least expensive "regular" gas with an octane rating of 87.

Holidays   See "When to Go" in chapter 3.

Languages   English is the official language. Major Hawaii hotels may have multilingual employees, and most Honolulu and Waikiki shops have multilingual staff who speak English, Japanese, Korean, and several dialects of the Philippines. Unless your language is very obscure, they can usually supply a translator on request. See "Life & Language" in chapter 2 for information about the Hawaiian language and the local version of pidgin.

Legal Aid   The ordinary tourist will probably never become involved with the American legal system. If you are pulled over for a minor infraction (for example, driving faster than the speed limit), never attempt to pay the fine directly to a police officer; you may wind up arrested on the much more serious charge of attempted bribery. Pay fines by mail or directly into the hands of the clerk of the court. If accused of a more serious offense, it's wise to say and do nothing before consulting a lawyer (you have a right to both remain silent and to consult an attorney under the U.S. Constitution). Under U.S. law, an arrested person is allowed one telephone call to a party of his or her choice. Call your embassy or consulate.

Mail   If you want your mail to follow you on your vacation and you aren't sure of your address, your mail can be sent to you, in your name, c/o **General Delivery** at the main post office of the city or region where you expect to be. The addressee must pick it up in person and produce proof of identity (driver's license, passport, etc.).

Mailboxes are generally found at intersections, are blue with a blue-and-white eagle logo, and carry the inscription "U.S. Postal Service." If your mail is addressed to a U.S. destination, don't forget to add the five-figure postal code, or **zip code,** after the two-letter abbreviation of the state to which the mail is addressed. The abbreviation for Hawaii is **HI.**

International air mail rates are 60¢ for half-ounce letters (40¢ for letters going to Mexico and 46¢ for letters to Canada) and 50¢ for postcards (35¢ to Mexico and 40¢ to Canada). All domestic first-class mail goes from Hawaii to the U.S. mainland by air, so don't bother paying the extra amount to send a letter back to a friend in Michigan.

Newspapers/Magazines   National newspapers include the *New York Times,* (often available at hotels in a condensed fax edition), *USA Today,* and the *Wall Street Journal.* These are available in major hotels, as are the larger West Coast newspapers like the *San Francisco Chronicle* and the *Los Angeles Times.* National news weeklies include *Newsweek, Time,* and *U.S. News and World Report. The Honolulu Advertiser* and the *Honolulu Star-Bulletin* are the major local newspapers on Oahu.

Radio & Television   The United States has numerous coast-to-coast television networks—ABC, CBS, NBC, Fox, the Public Broadcasting System (PBS), CNN, ESPN, MSNBC, MTV, and other cable networks play a major part in American life. In Honolulu, televiewers have a choice of about two dozen TV channels, most of them transmitting all day long, not counting the pay-TV channels showing recent movies or sports events. All options are usually indicated on your hotel TV set. You'll also find a wide choice of local radio stations, each broadcasting particular kinds of talk shows and/or music—classical, country, jazz, pop, gospel—punctuated by news broadcasts and frequent commercials. For more information, see "Fast Facts: Oahu" in Chapter 5.

Safety   See "Safety" under "Preparing for Your Trip," above.

Taxes   The United States has no VAT (Value-Added Tax) or other indirect taxes at a national level. Every state, and each city in it, has the right to levy its own local tax on all purchases, including hotel and restaurant checks, airline tickets, and so on. In Hawaii, sales tax is 4%; there's also a 6% hotel room tax, so the total tax on your hotel bill will be 10%.

Telephone & Fax   The telephone system in the United States is run by private corporations, so rates, particularly for long-distance service and operator-assisted calls, can vary widely—especially on calls made from public telephones. Local calls made from public phones in Hawaii cost 25¢.

Generally, hotel surcharges on long-distance and local calls are astronomical. You are usually better off using a **public pay telephone,** which you will find clearly marked in most public buildings and private establishments as well as on the street.

Most **long-distance and international calls** can be dialed directly from any phone. For calls to Canada and to other parts of the United States, dial 1 followed by the area code and the seven-digit number. For international calls, dial 011 followed by the country code, city code, and the telephone number of the person you wish to call.

In Hawaii, interisland phone calls are considered long-distance and often are as costly as calling the U.S. mainland.

For **reversed-charge** or **collect calls** and for **person-to-person calls,** dial 0 (zero, not the letter "O") followed by the area code and number you want; an operator will then come on the line, and you should specify that you are calling collect, or person-to-person, or both. If your operator-assisted call is international, ask for the overseas operator.

Note that all phone numbers with the area code 800 or 888 are toll-free.

For **local directory assistance** ("information"), dial 411; for **long-distance information,** dial 1, then the appropriate area code and 555-1212.

Fax facilities are widely available and can be found in most hotels and many other establishments. Try **Mailboxes Etc.** or any photocopying shop.

Telephone Directory   There are two kinds of telephone directories in the United States. The general directory is the so-called *White Pages,* in which private and business subscribers are listed in alphabetical order. The inside front cover lists the emergency number for police, fire, and ambulance, and other vital numbers (like the Coast Guard, poison-control center, crime-victims hotline, and so on). The first few pages are devoted to community-service numbers, including a guide to long-distance and international calling, complete with country codes and area codes.

The second directory, printed on yellow paper (hence its name, *Yellow Pages*), lists all local services, businesses, and industries by type of activity, with an index at the back. The listings cover not only such obvious items as automobile repairs by make of car, or drugstores (pharmacies), often by geographical location, but also restaurants by type of cuisine and geographical location, bookstores by special subject and/or language, places of worship by religious denomination, and other information that a visitor might otherwise not readily find. The *Yellow Pages* also includes city plans or detailed maps, often showing postal zip codes and public transportation routes.

Time   See "Fast Facts: Oahu" in chapter 5.

Tipping   It's part of the American way of life to tip, on the principle that you must expect to pay for any service you get. Many personnel receive little direct salary and must depend on tips for their income. In fact, the U.S. federal government imposes income taxes on service personnel based on an estimate of how much they should have earned in tips relative to their employer's total receipts. In other words, they may have to pay taxes on a tip you didn't give them!

Here are some rules of thumb:

In **hotels,** tip bellhops at least $1 per piece of luggage ($2 to $3 if you have a lot of luggage) and tip the chamber staff $1 per day. Tip the doorman or concierge only if he or she has provided you with some specific service (for example, calling a cab for you or obtaining difficult-to-get theater tickets). Tip the valet parking attendant $1 every time you get your car.

In **restaurants, bars,** and **nightclubs,** tip service staff 15% to 20% of the check, tip bartenders 10% to 15%, and tip valet-parking attendants $1 per vehicle. Tip the doorman only if he has provided you with some specific service (such as calling a cab for you). Tipping is not expected in cafeterias and fast-food restaurants.

Tip **cab drivers** 15% of the fare.

As for **other service personnel,** tip skycaps at airports at least $1 per piece ($2 to $3 if you have a lot of luggage), and tip hairdressers and barbers 15% to 20%.

Tipping ushers at movies and theaters and gas-station attendants is not expected.

Toilets   Foreign visitors often complain that public toilets are hard to find in most U.S. cities. True, there are none on the streets, but the visitor can usually find one in a bar, restaurant, hotel, museum, department store, or service station—and it will probably be clean (although the last-mentioned sometimes leaves much to be desired). Note, however, a growing practice in some restaurants and bars of displaying a notice that "toilets are for the use of patrons only." You can ignore this sign, or better yet, avoid arguments by paying for a cup of coffee or soft drink, which will qualify you as a patron. The cleanliness of toilets at parks and beaches is more open to question. Some public places are equipped with pay toilets, which require you to insert one or more coins into a slot on the door before it will open.

Getting to Know Oahu 5

by Jeanette Foster

Oahu—just letting the name roll off your tongue is a bit like blowing smoke rings as the round vowels line up one after another. Oahu is not the biggest island in the Hawaiian chain (the Big Island of Hawaii holds that distinction) or the oldest (Kauai wins by a few million years), but it certainly is the best known. The business and financial center of the state, Oahu is also the population center with nearly 875,000 residents, 75% of the total state population.

Actually it is a relatively small island, measuring some 44 miles across at its widest to 26 miles long, totaling 608 square miles of land, with 112 miles of coastline. From outer space, Oahu looks somewhat like a frayed Indian arrowhead with two mountain ridges shoring up each side: the 4,000-foot Waianae Mountains on the leeward (western) coast and the 3,000-foot Koolau Mountains on the windward (eastern) side. At night you can see the lights of the encroaching urban areas pouring down and out of the mountain valleys and blanketing the shoreline.

In most people's minds it's hard to separate Oahu's most famous city, Honolulu, from the island. In fact, some people think the name of the island is Honolulu, a misnomer further compounded by the islandwide county calling itself the "City and County of Honolulu." The population of Honolulu is 377,059, the largest urban area not only on Oahu but in the entire state. Honolulu's equally well-known neighbor, Waikiki, a mere 500 acres of land (and 133 acres of that is Kapiolani Park), has a resident population of some 19,768 with an additional 83,400 tourists visiting on an average day.

To help you navigate around the nearly one million people on this 608-square-mile island we have provided information in this chapter to help you make your way from the airport and give you a feel for the lay of the land. We've also made some recommendations regarding what to see if your time is limited, and offered logistical advice for getting around the island. Finally, we've provided some handy facts and phone numbers to make your trip as hassle free as possible.

1 Arriving

Honolulu International Airport sits on the south shore of Oahu, west of downtown Honolulu and Waikiki, near Pearl Harbor. All major American and many international carriers fly to Honolulu from the mainland: **United Airlines** (☎ 800/225-5825) offers the most frequent service from the U.S. mainland, but **American Airlines** (☎ 800/433-7300), **America West** (☎ 800/235-9292), **Continental Airlines** (☎ 800/231-0856), **Delta Air Lines** (☎ 800/221-1212), **Northwest Airlines** (☎ 800/225-2525), and **Trans World Airlines** (☎ 800/221-2000) all have regular flights.

Based in Honolulu, **Hawaiian Airlines** (☎ 800/367-5320 or 808/537-5100) offers nonstop service on wide-body DC-10s from San Francisco, Seattle, Los Angeles, Portland, and Las Vegas. Hawaiian works with Fly AAway Vacations, the tour unit of American Airlines. For information about its package tours, phone **Hawaiian Airlines Vacations** at ☎ 800/353-5393, or ask your travel agent.

Airlines serving Hawaii from other than the U.S. mainland include **Air Canada** (☎ 800/776-3000), **Canadian Airlines International** (☎ 800/426-7000), **Air New Zealand** (☎ 800/262-1234), **Qantas** (☎ 800/227-4500), **Japan Airlines** (☎ 800/525-3663), **All Nippon Airways** (☎ 808/695-8008), **China Airlines** (☎ 800/227-5118), **Garuda Indonesian** (☎ 800/231-0856), **Korean Airlines** (☎ 800/223-1155 on the East Coast, 800/421-8200 on the West Coast), and **Philippine Airlines** (☎ 800/435-9725). *Note:* You can fly to Hawaii from the U.S. mainland on one of these foreign carriers only if you're continuing on with them to—or returning with them from—an overseas destination.

LANDING AT HONOLULU INTERNATIONAL AIRPORT

Landing in Honolulu is like arriving in a foreign country—the airport is full of exciting strangers from every corner of the world. On any given day, it's probably the most cosmopolitan spot in the Pacific.

While the airport is large and constantly expanding, the layout is quite simple and easy to navigate. You can walk or take the **Wiki-Wiki Bus,** a free airport shuttle, from your arrival gate to the main terminal and baggage claim, which is on the ground level. After collecting your bags, exit to the palm-lined street, where uniformed attendants flag down taxis, Waikiki shuttles, and rental car vans; they can also direct you to TheBUS (for transportation information, see "Getting to & from the Airport," below).

GETTING TO & FROM THE AIRPORT

BY RENTAL CAR All major rental companies have cars available at Honolulu International Airport (see "Getting Around," below). Rental agency vans will pick you up at the middle curbside outside baggage claim and take you to their off-site lot.

BY TAXI Taxis are abundant at the airport; an attendant will be happy to flag one down for you. Taxi fare from Honolulu International to downtown Honolulu is about $16, to Waikiki about $23. If you need to call a taxi, see "Getting Around," below, for a list of cab companies.

BY AIRPORT SHUTTLE Shuttle vans operate 24 hours a day every day of the year between the airport and all 350 hotels and condos in Waikiki. At a rate of $8 one-way to Waikiki and $13 round-trip, it's a much better bargain than taking a taxi—if there's only one or two of you. If you're in a group of three or more, it's probably more cost-efficient to grab a cab. **Trans-Hawaiian Services** (☎ 808/566-7000) serves the airport with passenger vans every 20 to 30 minutes, depending on traffic. Children small enough to sit on your lap ride for free. No reservation is necessary, but do book ahead for hotel pickup for a departing flight. Look for attendants in red shirts that say "shuttle vehicle"; pickup is at the middle curb outside baggage claim. You can board with two pieces of luggage and a carry-on at no extra charge; surfboards and bicycles are prohibited for safety reasons. Backpacks are okay. Tips are welcome.

BY TheBUS TheBUS is by far the cheapest way to get to Waikiki—but you've got to be traveling light to use it. Bus nos. 19 and 20 (Waikiki Beach and Hotels) run from the airport to downtown Honolulu and Waikiki. The first bus from Waikiki to the airport is at 4:50am on weekdays and 5:25am on weekends; the last bus departs the airport for Waikiki at 11:45pm on weekdays, 11:15pm on weekends. There are two bus stops on the main terminal's upper level; a third is on the second level of the Inter-Island terminal.

You can board TheBUS with a carry-on or small suitcase as long as it fits under the seat and doesn't disrupt other passengers; otherwise, you'll have to take a shuttle or taxi. The approximate travel time to Waikiki is an hour. The one-way fare is $1, 50¢ for students (exact change only). For information on routes and schedules, call **TheBUS** at ☎ **808/848-5555.**

2 Orienting Yourself: The Lay of the Land

VISITOR INFORMATION

The **Hawaii Visitors and Convention Bureau (HVCB)** is at 2270 Kalakaua Ave., 7th floor, Suite 801, Honolulu, HI 96815 (☎ **800/GO-HAWAII** or 808/923-1811), and on the net at http://www.visit.hawaii.org. The bureau supplies free brochures, maps, accommodation guides, and *Islands of Aloha,* the official HVCB magazine. **Waikiki Oahu Visitors Association,** 1001 Bishop St., Pauahi Tower, Suite 47, Honolulu, HI 96813 (☎ **800/OAHU-678** or 808/524-0722) distributes a free 64-page visitors booklet.

A number of free publications, including *This Week* and *Guide to Oahu,* are packed with money-saving coupons offering discounts on dining, shops, and activities around the island; look for them on the visitors' publication racks at the airport and around town.

THE ISLAND IN BRIEF

HONOLULU

America's 11th largest city looks like any other big metropolitan center with tall buildings. In fact, some cynics refer to it as "Los Angeles West." But within Honolulu's metes and bounds you'll find rain forests, deep canyons, valleys and waterfalls, a nearly mile-high mountain range, coral reefs, and gold-sand beaches. The city proper—where most of Honolulu's 850,000 residents live—is approximately 12 miles wide and 26 miles long, running east–west roughly between Diamond Head and Pearl Harbor (you'll see Pearl Harbor from the left side of your airplane on your final approach into Honolulu International). It folds over seven hills laced by seven streams that run to Mamala Bay.

Up close, Honolulu becomes exceedingly complex: Downtown, street vendors sell papayas from a truck on skyscraper-lined concrete canyons, where professional women wear muumuus and carry briefcases. Joggers and BMWs rush by a lacy palace where champions of liberty stole the kingdom. Burly bus drivers sport fragrant white ginger flowers on their dashboards, Methodist churches look like Asian temples, businessmen wear aloha shirts to billion-dollar meetings. Doctors and dope dealers share surfing spots, and the entire social spectrum spreads mats edge to edge on a lawn to hear folksy Hawaiian music and watch hula under the stars. Tokyo teenagers sun on the beach in bikinis while their older Hawaiian cousins carry parasols for shade, and waiters, if asked, will stand and recite their 14 cultural antecedents in a tradition as old as Polynesia. What under the tropical sun is this place? The third world's American capital, mankind's hope for the future, or just the stuff between the

Oahu

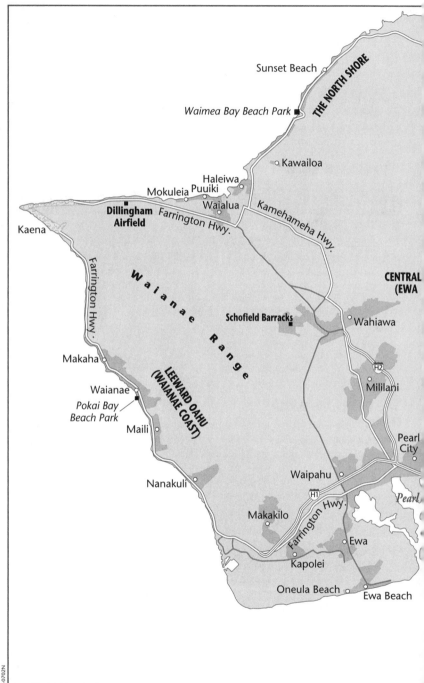

Sunset Beach

THE NORTH SHORE

Waimea Bay Beach Park ■

Kawailoa

Haleiwa
Mokuleia Puuiki
Dillingham Waialua
Airfield Farrington Hwy.

Kaena

Kamehameha Hwy.

CENTRAL
(EWA

Farrington Hwy.

W a i a n a e

R a n g e

Schofield Barracks ■

Wahiawa

Makaha

LEEWARD OAHU
(WAIANAE COAST)

H2

Mililani

Waianae

*Pokai Bay
Beach Park* ■

Maili

Pearl
City

Waipahu

Nanakuli

H1

Farrington Hwy.

Pearl

Makakilo

Ewa

Kapolei

Oneula Beach

Ewa Beach

1-0702N

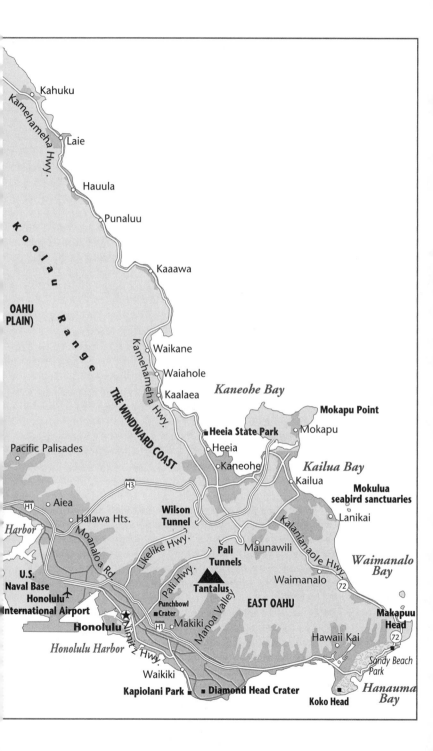

airport and the beach at Waikiki? Watch out while you find out; some cities tug at your heart, but Honolulu is a whole love affair.

WAIKIKI

When King Kalakaua played in Waikiki, it was "a hamlet of plain cottages . . . its excitements caused by the activity of insect tribes and the occasional fall of a coconut." The Merrie Monarch, who gave his name to Waikiki's main street, would love the scene today. It's where all the action is. Waikiki is an urban beach backed by 175 high-rise hotels with more than 33,000 guest rooms, all in a 1 1/2-square-mile beach zone. The beach district boasts 279 drinking establishments, 240 restaurants, 90 hotels, and four churches. Waikiki is honeymooners and sun seekers, bikinis and bare buns, a round-the-clock beach party every day of the year. And it's all because of a thin crescent of imported sand.

Some say Waikiki is past its prime and that everybody goes to Maui now. But Waikiki is the very incarnation of Yogi Berra's comment about Toots Shor's famous New York restaurant: "Nobody goes there anymore. It's too crowded."

HONOLULU BEYOND WAIKIKI

DOWNTOWN   Now a tiny cluster of high-rise offices west of Waikiki, downtown Honolulu is the financial, business, and government center of Hawaii. Fort Street runs inland from the iconic 1926-vintage Aloha Tower, once the tallest building on Oahu.

The history of Hawaii can be read architecturally downtown, where Italianate Monarchy style buildings stand next to New England Mission Houses and the 1920s buildings of the "Big Five" cartel. There's a Carnegie-built Mediterranean library, a Spanish-style City Hall, a Julia Morgan YWCA, and a State Capitol designed by John Carl Warnecke that looks like a volcano. And there's the gingerbread palace that became a prison for Hawaii's last queen.

CHINATOWN HISTORIC DISTRICT   In Chinatown, on the edge of downtown, you can buy thousand-year-old duck eggs or fresh flower leis, find an ancient potion, get a $3 haircut, play pool in a 1930s bar, get treated by an acupuncturist, buy fresh Chinese *manapua,* eat Vietnamese *pho,* or browse Oahu Market, where 17 vendors sell fish, ducks, spices, fresh fruits, and vegetables under a tin roof. Founded in 1860 by Chinese immigrants, it's the oldest Chinatown in America and still one of Honolulu's liveliest neighborhoods. A quaint village of tin-roofed sheds, brightly painted shops, and often crowded streets, this historic 15-block district is a nonstop pageant of people, sights, sounds, smells, and tastes—not all Chinese, now that Southeast Asians, including many Vietnamese, share the old storefronts. Go on Saturday morning when everyone shops in Chinatown for fresh goods like ginger root, fern fronds, and hogsheads.

ALA MOANA   A great beach as well as a famous shopping center, Ala Moana is the retail and transportation heart of Honolulu, a place where you can both shop and suntan in one afternoon. All bus routes lead to the open-air Ala Moana Shopping Center, a modern mall across the street from Ala Moana Beach, a wonderful family playground. This 50-acre, 200-shop emporium attracts 56 million customers a year; people fly up here from Tahiti just to buy their Christmas gifts. Every European designer from Armani to Vuitton has a shop here, and Neiman-Marcus will open in 1998. It's Honolulu's answer to Beverly Hills' Rodeo Drive.

MANOA VALLEY   First inhabited by white settlers, the Moana Valley above Waikiki still has vintage *kamaaina* (native-born) homes, one of Hawaii's premier botanical gardens in the Lyon Arboretum, ever-gushing Manoa Falls, and the 320-acre campus of the University of Hawaii, where 50,000 students hit the books when they're not on the beach and where scholars develop solutions to third-world problems at the East-West Center, a major Pacific Rim education and research center.

TO THE EAST: KAHALA Just beyond Diamond Head you'll find one of Oahu's top-drawer neighborhoods, where the grandiose estates of world-class millionaires line the beach. In between the gated mansions are narrow sand alleys that lead to the thin, gnarly beach that fronts the mansions. The only hotel here is the newly opened—and very pricey—Mandarin Oriental.

EAST OAHU

Beyond Kahala lie East Honolulu and the suburban bedroom communities of Aina Haina, Niu Valley, Kuliouou, Hawaii Kai, Portlock, and Kalama Valley, all linked by Kalanianaole Highway and each chockablock with homes, condos, fast-food joints, and shopping malls. It looks like southern California on a good day. The only reasons you're likely to find yourself out here are to splurge on lunch or dinner at Roy's, the original and still-outstanding Hawaii Regional restaurant, in Hawaii Kai; if you're bound for Hanauma Bay for some great snorkeling or heading to Sandy Beach to watch daredevil surfers risk their necks; or if you're just looking to enjoy the natural splendor of the lovely coastline, which might include a hike to Makapuu Lighthouse.

THE WINDWARD COAST

For years, travel writers—hoping, no doubt, to keep a great secret—portrayed Oahu's northeastern side as wet, windy, and unappealing to visitors. Well, the secret's out. The Windward Coast looks like the South Pacific of the travel posters: green and lush, backed by the awesome cliffs of the Koolau Range, with plenty of sun, cool trade winds, and miles of empty coral-sand beaches fronted by bays and reefs. This is Oahu's natural state, a place of beauty not yet violated by high-rise hotels—but you will find plenty of beach cottages (some for rent) and B&Bs in little villages on big beaches.

KAILUA The biggest little beach town in Hawaii, Kailua sits at the foot of the sheer green Koolau Mountains, on a great bay with two of Hawaii's best beaches. The town itself is a low-rise cluster of time-worn shops and homes. Kailua has become the bed-and-breakfast capital of Hawaii; it's an affordable alternative to Waikiki, with rooms and vacation rentals from $50 a day and up. It's a funky little town full of fun restaurants like Buzz's (where President Clinton ate when he came to town), the publike Kailua Beach Grill, and Brent's, an authentic New York style deli. With the prevailing trade winds whipping up a cooling breeze, Kailua attracts windsurfers from around the world.

KANEOHE Helter-skelter suburbia sprawls around the edges of Kaneohe, one of the most scenic bays in all the Pacific. After you clear the trafficky maze of Kaneohe, you return to Oahu's more natural state. This great bay beckons you to get out on it, and you can depart from Heeia Boat Harbor on snorkeling or fishing charters and visit Ahu o Laka ("the altar of Laka," a canoe-sailing god), the sandbar that appears and disappears in the middle of the bay. From out there, you'll get a panoramic view of the Koolau Range.

KUALOA/LAIE The upper northeast shore is one of the most sacred places on Oahu. It's an early Hawaiian landing spot where even kings dipped their sails, the cliffs hold ancient burial sites, and ghosts still march in the night.

Honolulu's Neighborhoods in Brief

Legend
Airport ✈
Church ✝
Information ⓘ

Neighborhoods:
Ala Moana ⓫
Chinatown
  Historic District ❸
Downtown ❺
Kahala ㉒

Kaimuki–Kapahulu ⓴
Makiki Valley ⓭
Manoa Valley ⓮
Moiliili–Makiki ⓯
Waikiki ⓰

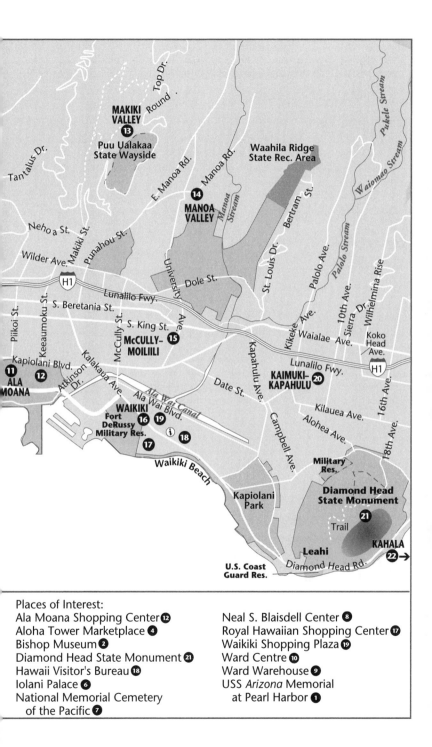

Places of Interest:
Ala Moana Shopping Center **12**
Aloha Tower Marketplace **4**
Bishop Museum **2**
Diamond Head State Monument **21**
Hawaii Visitor's Bureau **18**
Iolani Palace **6**
National Memorial Cemetery
 of the Pacific **7**

Neal S. Blaisdell Center **8**
Royal Hawaiian Shopping Center **17**
Waikiki Shopping Plaza **19**
Ward Centre **10**
Ward Warehouse **9**
USS *Arizona* Memorial
 at Pearl Harbor **1**

Sheer cliffs stab this sea coast fringed by coral reef. Old fishponds are tucked along the two-lane coast road that weaves around beautiful Kahana Bay and by empty gold-sand beaches in towns with too many vowels, like Kaaawa. Thousands "explore" the South Pacific at the Polynesian Cultural Center, in Laie, a Mormon settlement with its own Tabernacle Choir of sweet Samoan harmony.

THE NORTH SHORE

Only 28 miles from downtown Honolulu, the little beach town of Haleiwa and the surrounding shoreline seems like a separate paradise; once some people get the roar of the surf in their head, they never leave. They come to see the big waves roll up on world-famous beaches like Sunset Beach and Banzai Pipeline, go deep-sea fishing, visit the island's biggest *heiau*, explore Oahu's Waimea Falls, shop and eat shave ice in artsy Haleiwa town, and stay in affordable beachfront cottages on the edge of the roaring surf.

CENTRAL OAHU: THE EWA PLAIN

Flanked by the Koolau and Waianae mountain ranges, the hot, sun-baked Ewa Plain runs up and down the center of Oahu. Once covered with the sandalwood forests hacked down for the China trade, and later the sugarcane and pineapple backbone of Hawaii, Ewa today sports a new crop: suburban houses stretching to the sea. But let your eye wander west to the Waianae Range and Mount Kaala, the highest summit on Oahu at 4,020 feet. Up there in the misty rain forest, native birds thrive in the hummocky bog.

Hawaiian chiefs once fought on the Ewa Plain for supremacy of Oahu. In 1928 the U.S. Army pitched a tent camp on the plain. It became Schofield Barracks, which author James Jones called "the most beautiful army post in the world." Hollywood filmed Jones's *From Here to Eternity* here, thus launching crooner Frank Sinatra on his comeback.

LEEWARD OAHU: THE WAIANAE COAST

The west coast of Oahu is a hot and dry place of naturally spectacular beauty: big beaches, steep cliffs, and wildness. The rustic villages of Nanakuli, Waianae, and Makaha are the last stands of native Hawaiians. This side of Oahu is seldom visited, except by surfers bound for Yokohama Bay and anyone else who wants to see needle-nose Kaena Point (the island's westernmost outpost) and a coastal wilderness park under a 768-foot peak named for the endangered Hawaiian owl.

3 Oahu in a Nutshell: Suggested Itineraries for 1 to 5 Days

If You Have 1 Day

No question—drive around the island of Oahu. If you don't have a car, take TheBus 52 or 55 (see the "By Bus" section below). If you do have a car, take off across the middle of Oahu and go to Haleiwa for breakfast. Spend the morning stopping at as many beaches as you have time for. Wander into the Polynesian Cultural Center in the early afternoon. Drive along the windward side for a late afternoon dip at Lanikai Beach. Head back to Honolulu and Waikiki as the sun is setting, and plan on dinner at Roy's in Hawaii Kai to finish your perfect day.

If You Have 2 Days

Spend the first day driving around the island (see above). On the second day, get up early and go to the USS *Arizona* Memorial at Pearl Harbor (get there early as the lines

⭐ Frommer's Favorite Honolulu & Oahu Experiences

Snorkeling Hanauma Bay. It has a reputation of being too crowded—but for clear, warm water and an abundance of fish that are so friendly they'll eat out of your hand, there's no place like Hanauma Bay. The best thing about this underwater park is that anyone can join the fun: Just wade in and look down to see the kaleidoscope of fish that call Hawaii's waters home. Go early to avoid the crush.

Climbing Diamond Head. The hike to the summit of this 760-foot-high volcanic crater takes about 45 minutes, but the reward is a breathtaking 360° view—with Waikiki, Honolulu, and the Pacific Ocean at your feet. This one's for everyone, especially kids.

Watching the North Shore Waves. Humongous. Totally awesome. No other words describe the monster winter waves of Oahu's north shore. You've seen it on TV, in the opening shot of *Hawaii Five-0:* blue-green water in a perfect tube. But see it in person for the full effect: It snarls out of the Pacific like a tsunami and roars like a 50-foot-high freight train before smashing almost at your feet in foam. The surfers who take them on will keep you spellbound for hours.

Exploring Oahu's Rain Forests. In the misty sunbeams, colorful birds flit among giant ferns and hanging vines, and towering tropical trees form a thick canopy that shelters all below in cool shadows. This emerald world is a true Eden. For the full experience, try Manoa Falls Trail, a walk of about a mile that ends at a freshwater pool and waterfall.

Wearing an Aloha Shirt. Aloha shirts are one of the best things about tropical Honolulu. They're light, colorful, and fun. You don't have to button them or tuck them in. Some think only tourists wear them; it's not true. In Honolulu, the aloha-shirt capital of the world, men wear bright floral-print shirts to work every day. Invitations to many of Honolulu's exclusive social engagements specify "aloha attire." Funeral notices in Honolulu even suggest aloha attire for those who attend, as well as the recently departed.

get longer as the day goes on); be sure to check out the USS *Bowfin* submarine next door. In the afternoon hit either Waikiki Beach or Hanauma Bay for snorkeling and swimming. Head for Waikiki at sunset for sweet Hawaiian music and a night on the town.

If You Have 3 Days

See above for the first two days. On day three, put on your walking shoes and explore Honolulu: downtown (take in the cultural sites from the Iolani Palace to the Mission Museum House), Chinatown (where the smells will compel you to stop for lunch), and the Waterfront area. In the afternoon check out the Waikiki Aquarium. Take in a luau in the evening.

If You Have 5 Days or More

See above for the first three days. On day four, you might want to consider driving to Southeast Oahu and going to Sea Life Park in the morning, with a quick swim at one of the many beaches lining the coast. In the afternoon explore Kailua and Kaneohe: Wander through Heeia State Park, check out the replica of the 900-year-old Byodo-In in the Valley of the Temples, bike or horseback ride in Senator Fong's Plantation and Gardens, or take windsurfing lessons at Kailua Beach.

The next day return to the North Shore, spending time at all the activities at Waimea Valley, stopping to watch the surfers during the winter, or snorkeling the incredible reefs in the summer.

4 Getting Around

BY CAR

Oahu residents own 600,000 registered vehicles, but they have only 1,500 miles of mostly two-lane roads. That's 400 cars for every mile, a fact that becomes abundantly clear during morning and evening rush hours. You can avoid the gridlock by driving between 9am and 3pm or after 6pm.

State law mandates that all passengers in a car must wear a seat belt. The law is enforced with vigilance and the fine is quite stiff—so buckle up.

CAR RENTALS All of the major car-rental firms have agencies on Oahu, at the airport and in Waikiki, including **Alamo** (☎ 800/327-9633); **Avis** (☎ 800/321-3712), **Budget** (☎ 800/935-6878); **Enterprise** (☎ 800/325-8007); **Hertz** (☎ 800/654-3011); **National** (☎ 800/227-7368); **Payless** (☎ 800/729-5377); **Sears** (☎ 800/527-0770); and **Thrifty** (☎ 800/367-2277). For tips on saving money on car rentals in the islands, see "Car Rentals" under "Getting There & Getting Around" in chapter 3.

Most of the local, "Rent-A-Wreck" type car rental companies have gone by the wayside on Oahu (even Tropical Rent-a-Car has closed); however, one reliable, affordable, and accessible company remains: **Tradewinds,** 2875-A Koapaka St., Honolulu, HI 96819 (☎ **888/388-7368** or 808/834-1465; e-mail: Rent-a-Car@gte.net), a small, family-run company with a fleet of some 300 cars. Depending on the time of year, daily rentals will be at least $5 less than what the national chains charge; weekly and monthly rentals at Tradewinds offer super savings; and collision coverage is also cheaper—$9 per day vs. $14 to $20. It's best to book in advance. When you arrive at Honolulu airport, get your luggage, go to the courtesy phones for car rentals, and push the button for Tradewinds—they'll send a van to pick you up.

MOTORCYCLE RENTALS If your dream is to go screaming down the highway on the back of a big Harley Hog, here's your chance; rent a motorcycle. **Island Motorcycle**, 512-B Atkinson Dr. (at Kapiolani Blvd.), Honolulu, HI 96814 (☎ **808/957-0517**) has Harley Heritage, Heritage Classic, Fat Boy and Bad Boy cycles starting at $98 for 4 hours, $138 for 8 hours, and $188 for 24 hours (insurance is included in the price). In Waikiki try **Thrifty's,** 1778 Ala Moana Blvd. (Discovery Bay Plaza), Honolulu, HI 96815 (☎ **808/971-2660**), which has brand-new Harley Fat Boys, Wide Glides, and Heritages starting at $149 a day (includes helmet) or **Coconut Cruisers,** 2301 Kalakaua Ave. (across the street from the International Market Place), Honolulu, HI 96815 (☎ **808/924-1644**), which has a range of bikes from $135 to $220 a day. You must have a valid motorcycle license to rent a bike.

MAIN STREETS & HIGHWAYS

Navigating around Oahu is actually easy, there are only a few roads that circle the perimeter of the island and a handful that cut across the island.

TO AND FROM THE AIRPORT The main thoroughfare that runs from the airport to Honolulu and Waikiki is the H-1 Freeway. The H-1 also runs in the opposite direction to Pearl Harbor and Ewa. The artery that runs from the airport to Honolulu and Waikiki is Nimitz Highway (which has stoplights). In downtown Honolulu, Nimitz Highway becomes Ala Moana Boulevard.

Finding Your Way Around, Oahu Style

Local residents give directions a bit differently than what mainlanders are used to. Seldom will you hear east, west, north, and south; instead, islanders refer to directions as either *makai* (MA-kae), meaning toward the sea, or *mauka* (MOW-kah), toward the mountains. In Honolulu, people use "Diamond Head" as a direction referring to the east (in the direction of the world-famous crater called Diamond Head), and "Ewa" as a direction referring to the west (in the direction of the town called Ewa, on the other side of Pearl Harbor).

So if you ask a local for directions, this is what you're likely to hear: "Drive 2 blocks makai (toward the sea), then turn Diamond Head (east) at the stoplight. Go 1 block, and turn mauka (toward the mountains). It's on the Ewa (western) side of the street."

HONOLULU The myriad of one-way streets in Honolulu can be confusing and frustrating. If you wish to travel in the Diamond Head direction, King Street is one-way going toward Diamond Head. Beretania Street is one-way in the opposite or Ewa direction. In the mauka and makai direction: Punchbowl and Bishop streets run toward the ocean (makai), and Alakea and Bethel streets run toward the mountains (mauka).

WAIKIKI There are three parallel main streets in Waikiki: Kalakaua Avenue (which is one-way going toward Diamond Head and eventually fronts Waikiki Beach), Kuhio Avenue (1 block mauka of Kalakaua Avenue, which has two-way traffic), and Ala Wai Boulevard (which fronts the Ala Wai Canal and runs one-way in the Ewa direction).

AROUND OAHU From Waikiki, Hi. 72 (Kalanianaole Hwy.) takes you around Makapuu Point into Kailua and Kaneohe. From Kailua and Kaneohe, Hi. 83 (Kamehameha Hwy.) takes you around the north shore to Haleiwa, where it is still called the Kamehameha Hwy., but the number of the highway changes to 99, and then cuts through mid-Oahu past Schofield Barracks, Wahiawa, and swings out to Pearl City. On the leeward coast, H-1 Freeway becomes two-lane Hi. 93 (Farrington Hwy.); after Makaha the number changes to Hi. 930, but it is still called Farrington Hwy. all the way out to Kaena Point. Although you cannot drive around Kaena Point, Farrington Hwy. (still called Hi. 930) picks up on the north side of the point and goes through Mokuleia and Waialua.

ACROSS OAHU Highways that cut across the island are Hi. 99 (see above), the Likelike Hwy. (also called Hi. 63, which goes from Honolulu to Kaneohe), and the Pali Hwy. (also called Hi. 61, which goes from Honolulu to Kailua). At the end of 1997 the H-3 Freeway will open; it will start at Pearl Harbor and travel to Kaneohe and Kailua.

STREET MAPS

One of the best general maps of the island is the *Map of Oahu,* cartography by James A. Bier, published by the University of Hawaii Press, available at bookstores or by writing the Marketing Department, University of Hawaii Press, 2840 Kolowalu St., Honolulu, HI 96822 (☎ **808/956-8255**). For a more specific street map, the best one we have found is *TMK Maps: Oahu Streets and Condos,* published by Hawaii TMK Service, Inc., 222 S. Vineyard St., Suite 401, Honolulu, HI 96813 (☎ **808/533-4601**).

TheBUS

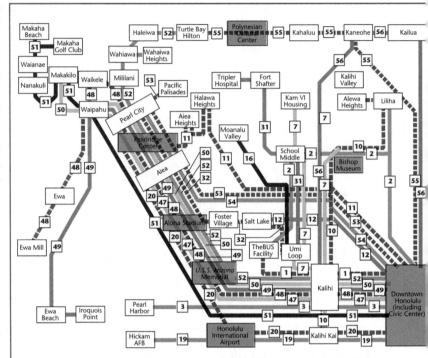

Common Bus Routes (all routes originate from Kuhio Avenue in Waikiki):

Ala Moana Shopping Center: Take bus #8 & #58 ALA MOANA CENTER, #19 & #20 AIRPORT or #47 WAIPAHU. Return #8 WAIKIKI or #19 WAIKIKI, or across Ala Moana Blvd. #20 & #47.

Bishop Museum: Take #2 SCHOOL STREET get off at Kapalama St., cross School St., walk down Bernice St. Return to School St. and take #2 WAIKIKI.

Byodo-In Temple: Take bus #2 to Hotel-Alakea St. (TRF) to #55 KANEOHE-KAHALUU. Get off at Valley of the Temple cemetery. Also #19 & #20 AIRPORT to King-Alakea St., (TRF) on Alakea St. to #55 KANEOHE-KAHALUU.

Circle Island: Take a Bus to ALA MOANA CENTER (TRF) to #52 WAHIAWA CIRCLE ISLAND or #55 KENEOHE CIRCLE ISLAND. This is a four-hour bus ride.

Chinatown or Downtown: Take any #2 bus going out of Waikiki, to Hotel St. Return take #2 WAIKIKI on Hotel St., or #19, #20, #47 WAIKIKI on King St.

Contemporary Museum & Punchbowl (National Cemetery of the Pacific): Take #2 bus (TRF) at Alapai St. to #15 MAKIKI-PACIFIC HGTS. Return, take #15 and get off at King St., area (TRF) #2 WAIKIKI.

Diamond Head Crater: #22 or #58 HAWAII KAI-SEA LIFE PARK to the crater. Take a flashlight. Return to the same area and take #22 WAIKIKI or #58 ALA MOANA.

Dole Plantation: Take bus to ALA MOANA CENTER (TRF) to #52 WAHIAWA CIRCLE ISLAND.

Foster Botanic Gardens: Take #2 bus to Hotel-Riviera St. Walk to Vineyard Blvd. Return to Hotel St. Take #2 WAIKIKI, or take #4 NUUANU and get off at Nuuanu-Vineyard. Cross Nuuanu Ave. and walk one block to the gardens.

Hawaii Maritime Center: Take #19-#20 AIRPORT, #47 WAIPAHU and get off at Alakea–Ala Moana. Cross the Street to the Aloha Tower.

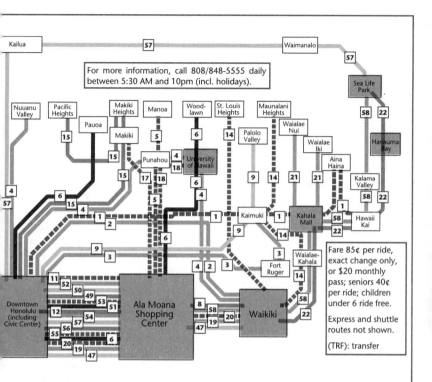

Honolulu Zoo: Take any bus on Kuhio Ave. going DIAMOND HEAD direction to Kapahulu Ave.

Iolani Palace, also **State Capitol, Kawaihao Church, Mission Houses, King Kamehameha Statue, State Judiciary Bldg:** take any #2 bus and get off at Punchbowl and Beretania St. Walk to King St. Return #2 WAIKIKI on King St.

Kodak Hula Show: (Tues-Thurs 10AM.) Free. Take #8, #19, #20, #47 WAIKIKI or #2 KAPIOLANI PARK to Kapiolani Park. Walk to the Waikiki Shell.

Pearl Harbor (USS *Arizona* Memorial): Open Daily 8AM to 3PM. Free. Take #20 AIRPORT or #47 WAIPAHU. Get off across from Memorial, or take a bus to Ala Moana Center (TRF) to #49, #50 or #52.

Polynesian Cultural Center: Take a bus to ALA MOANA CENTER (TRF) to #55 KANEOHE CIRCLE ISLAND. Bus ride takes two hours one way. PCC opens at 12:30PM. Closed on Sundays.

Queen Emma's Summer Palace: Take #4 NUUANU and it will take you there, or board a bus to ALA MOANA CENTER (TRF) to #55 KANEOHE, #56-#57 KAILUA.

Sea Life Park: #22-#58 HAWAII KAI-SEA LIFE PARK. #22 will stop at Hanauma Bay enroute to the park.

University of Hawaii: Take #4 NUUANU. The bus will go to the University enroute to Nuuanu.

Waimea Falls Park: Take a bus to ALA MOANA CENTER (TRF) to #52 WAHIAWA CIRCLE ISLAND or #55 KANEOHE CIRCLE ISLAND.

BY BUS

One of the best deals anywhere, **TheBUS** (☎ **808/848-5555,** or 808/296-1818 for recorded information) will take you around the whole island for $1. In fact, on a daily basis, more than 260,000 people use the system's 68 lines and 4,000 bus stops. TheBUS goes almost everywhere almost all the time. The most popular route is no. 8 (Waikiki/Ala Moana), which shuttles people between Waikiki and Ala Moana Center every 10 minutes or so (the ride is 15 to 20 minutes). The no. 19 (Airport/Hickam), no. 20 (Airport/Halawa Gate), no. 47 (Waipahu), and no. 58 (Waikiki/Ala Moana) also cover the same stretch. Waikiki service begins daily at 5am and runs until midnight; buses run about every 15 minutes during the day and every 30 minutes in the evening.

The Circle Island–North Shore route is no. 52 (Wahaiwa/Circle Island); it leaves from Ala Moana Shopping Center every 30 minutes and takes about $4^1/_2$ hours to circle the island. The Circle Island–South Shore route is no. 55 (Kaneohe/Circle Island) and also leaves Ala Moana every half-hour and takes about 3 to $4^1/_2$ hours to circle the island. *Warning:* Some visitors waiting for a bus along the North Shore have been attacked and robbed in broad daylight recently. You might want to consider splurging on a rental car to visit the North Shore.

You can buy a **Visitors Pass** for $10 at any ABC store in Waikiki (ABC stores are literally everywhere in Waikiki). It's good for unlimited rides anywhere on Oahu for 4 days.

BY TROLLEY

It's fun to ride the 34-seat, open-air, motorized **Waikiki Trolley** (☎ **800/824-8804** or 808/596-2199), which looks like a San Francisco cable car. It loops around Waikiki and downtown Honolulu, stopping every 40 minutes at 12 key places: Hilton Hawaiian Village, Iolani Palace, Wo Fat's in Chinatown, the State Capitol, King Kamehameha's Statue, the Mission House Museum, Aloha Tower, Honolulu Academy of Arts, Hawaii Maritime Museum, Ward Centre, Fisherman's Wharf, and Restaurant Row. A 1-day pass at $17 for adults, $5 for children under 12, allows you to jump on and off all day long. Five-day passes cost $30 for adults, $10 for children under 12.

BY TAXI

Oahu's major cab companies offer islandwide, 24-hour radio-dispatched service, with multilingual drivers, air-conditioned cars, limos, vans, and vehicles equipped with wheelchair lifts. Fares are standard for all taxi firms; from the airport, expect to pay about $23 (plus tip) to Waikiki, about $16.50 to downtown, about $35 to Kailua, about $35 to Hawaii Kai, and about $75 to the North Shore. Try **Aloha State Cab** (☎ 808/847-3566), **Charley's Taxi & Tours** (☎ 808/531-1333), **City Taxi** (☎ 808/524-2121), **Royal Taxi & Tour** (☎ 808/944-5513), **Sida Taxi & Tours** (☎ 808/836-0011), **Star Taxi** (☎ 808/942-7827), or **TheCab** (☎ 808/422-2222). **Coast Taxi** (☎ 808/261-3755) serves Windward Oahu; **Hawaii Kai Hui/Koko Head Taxi** (☎ 808/396-6633) serves East Honolulu/Southeast Oahu.

FAST FACTS: Oahu

American Express The Honolulu office is at 1440 Kapiolani Blvd., Suite 104 (☎ **808/946-7741**).

Area Code All of the Hawaiian Islands, including Oahu, are in the **808** area code.

Business Hours Most offices open at 8am and close by 5pm. The morning commute usually runs from 6am to 8am, while the evening rush is from 4pm to 6pm. Many people work at two or three jobs and drive their children to and from private schools, which creates extra traffic. Bank hours are Monday to Thursday from 8:30am to 3pm, Fridays from 8:30am to 6pm. Some banks open on Saturdays. Shopping centers open Monday to Friday from 10am to 9pm, Saturdays from 10am to 5:30pm, and Sundays from noon to 5pm or 6pm.

Dentists If you need dental attention while you're on Oahu, contact the **Hawaii Dental Association** (☎ **808/536-2135**).

Doctors Doctors on Call has offices at the Hyatt Regency Waikiki, Diamond Head Tower, 4th floor (☎ **808/971-8001**); Hawaiian Regent Hotel, 2nd floor (☎ **808/923-3666**); Hilton Hawaiian Village, Rainbow Bazaar (☎ **808/923-5252**); Outrigger Waikiki (☎ **808/971-6000**); and the Royal Hawaiian Medical Center, Royal Hawaiian Hotel (☎ **808/923-4499**).

Emergencies Call ☎ **911** for police, fire, and ambulance.

Hospitals Hospitals offering 24-hour emergency care include **Queens Medical Center**, 1301 Punchbowl St. (☎ 808/538-9011); **Kaiser Permanente Medical Center,** Honolulu Clinic, 1010 Pensacola St. (☎ 808/593-2950); **Kuakini Medical Center,** 347 Kuakini St. (☎ 808/536-2236); **Straub Clinic and Hospital,** 888 S. King St. (☎ 808/522-4000); **Moanalua Medical Center,** 3288 Moanalua Rd. (☎ 808/834-5333); **Kapiolani Medical Center for Women and Children,** 1319 Punahou St. (☎ 808/973-8511); and **Kapiolani Medical Center** at Pali Momi, 98-1079 Moanalua Rd. (☎ 808/486-6000). In Central Oahu go to **Wahiawa Gen-eral Hospital,** 128 Lehua St. (☎ 808/621-8411). On the windward side go to **Castle Medical Center,** 640 Ulukahiki St., Kailua (☎ 808/263-5500).

Electricity Like the rest of the United States, Hawaii's electric power is 110 volts, 60 cycles.

Legal Aid Call the Legal Aid Society of Hawaii, 1108 Nuuanu Ave., Honolulu HI 96817 (☎ **808/536-4302**).

Liquor Laws The legal drinking age in Hawaii is 21.

Newspapers The *Honolulu Advertiser* and *Honolulu Star-Bulletin* are Oahu's daily papers. *Midweek, Pacific Business News,* and *Honolulu Weekly* are weekly papers. *Honolulu Weekly,* available free at restaurants, clubs, shops, bookstores, and newspaper racks around Oahu, is the best source for what's going on around town. It features discriminating restaurant reviews and an informed critique of the nightclub scene, plus a weekly Calendar of Events that lists concerts, theater and dance performances, gallery and museum shows, workshops, children's events, hikes and walks, and often neighbor island events, too.

Poison Control Center At 1319 Punahou St. (☎ 808/941-4411).

Post Office To find the location nearest you, call ☎**808/423-3990** (the phone number for all Honolulu Post Office branches). The downtown location is in the old U.S. Post Office, Customs, and Court House Building at 335 Merchant St. (across from the Iolani Palace and next to the Kamehameha Statue; TheBUS: 2). Referred to as the "old Federal Building," this building was designated as a Historic Customs House in 1977. Other convenient locations include the Waikiki Post Office, 330 Saratoga Ave. (Diamond Head side of Fort DeRussy; TheBUS: 19 or 20); and the Ala Moana Shopping Center branch (TheBUS: 8, 19, or 20).

Radio & TV Honolulu has a score of radio stations that broadcast in English, Hawaiian, Japanese, and Filipino throughout the islands. The most popular are KCCN (1420 AM), which features Hawaiian music; KHPR (88.1 or 90.7 FM), the National Public Radio station; KGU (760 AM), for news and talk radio; KUMU (94.7 FM), for easy listening; and KSSK (590 AM), the pop-music station and the top morning drive disc-jockeys.

All major Hawaiian islands are equipped with cable TV and receive major mainland network broadcast programs, which local stations delay by several hours so they will appear as "prime time" in Hawaii's time zone. This includes sports events, so fans who wish to follow their teams "live" should seek out establishments with satellite dishes. CNN is the prime source of 24-hour news.

Safety Although Hawaii is generally a safe tourist destination, visitors have been crime victims, so stay alert. The most common crime against tourists is rental car break-ins. Never leave any valuables in your car, not even in your trunk. Thieves can be in and out of your trunk faster than you can open it with your own keys. Be leery of high risk areas, such as beaches and resort areas. Also, never carry large amounts of cash in Waikiki and other tourist zones. Stay in well-lighted areas after dark. Don't hike on deserted trails alone.

Smoking It's against the law to smoke in public buildings, including the airports, grocery stores, retail shops, movie theaters, banks, and all government buildings and facilities. Hotels have nonsmoking rooms available, restaurants have nonsmoking sections, and car rental agencies have nonsmoking cars. Most bed-and-breakfasts prohibit smoking inside their buildings.

Taxes Hawaii's sales tax is 4%. Hotel occupancy tax is 6%, and hoteliers are allowed by the state to tack on an additional .001666% excise tax. Thus, expect taxes of about 10.17% to be added to every hotel bill.

Telephone Hawaii's telephone system operates like any other state's. Long distance calls may be directly dialed to the islands from the U.S. mainland and from most foreign countries. The international country code is 1, the same as for the rest of the United States and for Canada. Local calls costs 25¢ at a pay phone (if you can find one). Interisland calls are billed at the same rate as long distance. Hotels add a surcharge on local, interisland, mainland, and international calls.

Time For the time, call ☎ **808/983-3211.**

Hawaii standard time is in effect year-round. Hawaii is 2 hours behind Pacific standard time and 5 hours behind Eastern standard time. In other words, when it's noon in Hawaii, it's 2pm in California and 5pm in New York during standard time on the mainland. There's no daylight saving time here, so when daylight saving time is in effect on the mainland, Hawaii is 3 hours behind the West Coast and 6 hours behind the East Coast—so in summer, when it's noon in Hawaii, it's 3pm in California and 6pm in New York.

Hawaii is east of the international dateline, putting it in the same day as the U.S. mainland and Canada, and a day behind Australia, New Zealand, and Asia.

Transit Info For information on TheBUS, call ☎ **808/848-5555.**

Weather Reports For National Weather Service recorded forecasts for Honolulu, call ☎ **808/973-4380;** for marine reports, call ☎ **808/973-4382;** for surf reports, call ☎ **808/973-4383;** for coastal wind reports, call ☎ **808/973-6114.**

Accommodations 6

by Jeanette Foster

The island of Oahu, while not the biggest in the Hawaiian chain, offers the widest choices in accommodations. You can stay in near-palatial royal surroundings where kings, heads of state, billionaires, and rock stars have spent the night, or in a quaint bed-and-breakfast on the North Shore where the rolling surf lulls you to sleep at night. You can opt for the bright lights and action of Waikiki, the quiet comforts of Kahala, the rural calm of the windward side, or the breathtaking beauty of the North Shore. Oahu has the perfect place for everyone.

Waikiki Some 5 million tourists visit Oahu every year, and nine out of ten of them choose accommodations in Waikiki. This is where the action is: restaurants from fast food to fine dining, nightlife including everything from the sweet sounds of Hawaiian melodies to spicy dancing music, shopping from bargains to brand names, and every ocean activity you can imagine from sunning to surfing. Staying in Waikiki puts you in the heart of it all, but also be aware that Waikiki is an on-the-go city with traffic noise 24 hours a day, has its share of crime, and is almost always crowded.

Honolulu & Neighborhoods The city of Honolulu occupies a good portion of Oahu and houses the majority of its population. Downtown Honolulu is a relatively small area occupying a handful of blocks, which houses the financial, government, and corporate headquarters of businesses in the islands. A plethora of neighborhoods surround the downtown area ranging from the quiet suburbs of Hawaii Kai to the old kamaaina neighborhoods like Manoa. With the exception of staying right downtown, these neighborhoods are generally quieter than Waikiki, more residential, yet within minutes of beaches, shopping, and all the activities Oahu has to offer.

Windward On the opposite side of the island from Waikiki, the windward side is where the trade winds blow, rain squalls bring lush, tropical vegetation, and miles of subdivisions dot the landscape. The communities of Kailua and Kaneohe dominate here. This is the place for "island" experiences. Numerous bed-and-breakfasts (ranging from oceanfront estates to tiny cottages on quiet residential streets) abound. Vacations here are filled with ocean activities, exploring the surrounding areas, and quick, 15-minute drives into Waikiki and Honolulu.

North Shore Here's the Hawaii of Hollywood—giant waves, surfers galore, tropical jungles, waterfalls, and mysterious Hawaiian temples. If you are looking for a quieter vacation, closer to nature, filled with swimming, snorkeling, diving, surfing, or just plain hanging out on some of the world's most beautiful beaches, the North Shore is your place. Many of the advantages of the city (restaurants, shopping, and cultural activities), but with the quiet of country living, the North Shore offers an alternative place to spend your vacation. Bed-and-breakfasts are the most common accommodations, but there is one first-class hotel, some vacation rentals, and even a budget place to consider. Be forewarned that it is a long trip, nearly an hour's drive, from the North Shore to Honolulu and Waikiki.

Leeward A new frontier for Oahu visitors. Currently only one exquisite resort offers accommodations in this beach-lined rural section of Oahu, but more are planned. Here's a chance to truly escape to a quiet resort area, far, far from the hustle and bustle of Waikiki. This is the sunny side of the island, with little rain and lots of sandy beaches. People who love to play golf, enjoy the ocean, and explore cultural activities will have plenty to do. However, outside of the Ko Olina Resort area, there is little in the way of fine dining or interesting shopping.

To help you find your dream accommodations, we have divided this section not only by geographic area, but also by the dent it will make in your pocketbook. For those dream vacations where money is no object, look in the **Very Expensive** category, where rooms begin at more than $200 a night. For those wanting a dream vacation, but having some spending limits, the **Expensive** category lists accommodations where rates start at $150 to $200 a night. For a vacation that won't mean taking out a second mortgage, look at the **Moderate** category where rates start at $100 to $150 a night. For those on a frugal budget, check out the good buys in the **Inexpensive** (rates starting from $75 to $100 a night) and the **Budget** (rates starting at under $75 a night) categories.

Combined within these categories are a variety of accommodations: hotels, vacation rentals, bed-and-breakfast units, apartments, condominium units, and—in the budget divisions—hostels and the "Y."

Before you reach for the phone to book a place, consider when you will be traveling to Hawaii. Hawaii has two seasons—high and low. The highest season, where rooms are always booked and rates are at the top end, is mid-December to March. The second "high" season, when rates are high, but bookings are somewhat easier is summer, June to September. The low season, with fewer tourists, cheaper rates—and sometimes, even "deals" on rooms—is April to June and September to mid-December.

The last word on rates is Hawaii's hotel and room tax: Be sure to add 10.17% to all the listed rates to get a true picture of your bill. Don't forget to include parking, which, at Waikiki hotels, can quickly add up.

1 Waikiki

WAIKIKI: EWA END

All of the hotels listed below are located between Ala Wai Boulevard and the Ala Wai Yacht Harbor, and between Ala Wai Terrace in the Ewa direction (or western side of Waikiki) and Olohana Street and Fort DeRussy Park in the Diamond Head direction (or western side of Waikiki).

VERY EXPENSIVE

Hawaii Prince Hotel. 100 Holomoana St. (just across the Ala Wai Canal bridge, ocean side of Ala Moana Blvd., turn right on Holomoana St.), Honolulu, HI 96815. ☎ **800/321-OAHU** or 808/965-1111. Fax 808/946-0811. 464 rms, 57 suites. A/C TV TEL. $240–$390 double; $500–$2,500 suite. Extra person $40. Children 17 or younger free in parents' room with existing bedding. AE, DISC, MC, V. Valet parking $12; self-parking $8. TheBUS: 19 or 20.

The first hotel at the entrance to Waikiki, just across the Ala Wai Canal, is the $150 million, twin–33-story Hawaii Prince Hotel. A strikingly stunning modern structure, the Prince opened in April 1990. The high-ceilinged lobby is a mass of pink Italian marble with English slate accents. A grand piano sits in the midst of the raised seating area, where high tea is served every afternoon.

A glass-encased elevator outside the building takes guests up to their rooms. All of the rooms face the yachts in the Ala Wai Yacht Harbor, with floor-to-ceiling sliding glass windows to enjoy the view. The rooms are all basically the same, and in 1997 they underwent renovations. The price difference is based on where the room is located—the higher the floor, the higher the price of the room. The comfortably appointed rooms have nightly turndown service (where they not only leave a bedtime sweet, but also a small booklet of short stories), in-room safes, hair dryers, and the bathrooms have both showers and tubs. On the "hokulea" floors, guests are given additional amenities such as a welcome basket filled with snacks, a coffeemaker, tea service, a toothbrush and razor, logo bathrobes, and a CD player for an additional $40 a night.

The level of service at the hotel is set by Japanese standards: no detail is ignored, no request too small. A business floor can handle any business request from use of a computer to secretarial services. The location is perfect for shopping—Ala Moana shopping center is just a 10-minute walk (or via the hotel's shuttle bus service). Waikiki's beaches are just a 5-minute walk (or via the hotel's shuttle bus service). In addition, the Prince has its own 27-hole Hawaii Prince Golf Club in Ewa Beach, with shuttle service from the hotel to the golf course.

Dining/Entertainment: The Prince Court, located on the third floor with floor-to-ceiling windows looking out on the Ala Wai Yacht Harbor, offers casual bistrolike fare. The Hakone Japanese Restaurant serves traditional cuisine prepared by master chefs. Casual Japanese dining is available at the Takanawa Sushi Bar and Restaurant. The outdoor Promenade Deck is the place for cafe-style dining and tropical drinks.

Services: Concierge desk, room service, complimentary newspaper, amenity basket, baby-sitting services, and hot towels (oshibori) upon arrival.

Facilities: Business center, fitness room, full-service beauty shop.

EXPENSIVE

Ilikai. 1777 Ala Moana Blvd. (ocean side of Ala Moana Blvd., at Hobron Lane), Honolulu, HI 96815. ☎ **800/367-8434** or 808/949-3811. Fax 808/947-0892. 800 rms, 52 suites. A/C TV TEL. $198–$295 double; $485–$855 suite. Rates include continental breakfast. Extra person $25. AE, CB, DC, DISC, JCB, MC, V. Parking $7. TheBUS: 19 or 20.

This hotel could be fabulous. It has almost everything: excellent location, ocean views, huge rooms with spacious lanais, and all the activities, restaurants, and shops you can imagine. There is only one thing stopping this from being one of the best hotels in all of Waikiki, and that is the attitude of the staff. We have not found the aloha spirit here, instead, on several occasions, the staff appears distracted, uninterested in guests' problems and in some cases, just too busy to bother.

We hope that management can correct this lapse in service because the property really is beautiful and the rooms are extraordinarily spacious, with wall-mounted hair dryers, in-room safes, and large lanais overlooking the ocean and the mountains. Some of the top rooms have whirlpool spas in the bathroom, desktop fax machines, and a minilibrary of best-sellers for purchase.

Complimentary continental breakfast is included in the room price. The daily newspaper is delivered to your room and telephone access fees are waived. There are great deals for seniors, with rooms starting at $148.50 and good family packages starting at $639 for 4 days/3 nights that include rooms with a full kitchen, a midsized car, free parking, and $100 credit for dinner at Canoes restaurant.

Dining/Entertainment: Much of the Ilikai's excitement is in its restaurants and nightclubs. Its casual restaurant, Canoes, looks out over the Ala Wai Yacht Harbor, and is perfect for moderately priced, open-air family-style dining; it also offers a fabulous Sunday brunch. Serento's Top of the I is an Italian restaurant accessible by an outside glass elevator that takes you up 30 stories with a view of all of Waikiki. Tanaka of Tokyo West specializes in Japanese seafood and steaks. Nightfall signifies the start of the hotel's traditional torch-lighting ceremony. For drinks and dancing, the Ilikai has Coconut's Night Club.

Services: Next Club for business travelers, business class floors with in-room fax, modem capability and office supplies, express checkouts, 24-hour medical services, voice mail, shopping arcade.

Facilities: Waikiki's most complete tennis resort with six newly resurfaced Plexipave courts overlooking Waikiki and the yacht marina, full-time tennis staff, pro services, tennis clinics, a sports and fitness center, swimming in two pools and a nearby blue lagoon, plus sailing, surfing, and scuba diving.

MODERATE

✪ **Doubletree Alana Waikiki.** 1956 Ala Moana Blvd. (on the Ewa side of Ala Moana Blvd., between Ena Rd. and Kalakaua Ave.), Honolulu, HI 96815. ☎ **800/367-6070** or 808/ 941-7275. Fax 808/949-0996. 268 rms, 45 suites. TV TEL. $135–$215 double; $250–$550 suite. Children 18 or younger free in parents' room. Extra person $25. AE, CB, DC, DISC, JCB, MC, V. Parking $7. TheBUS: 19 or 20.

In 1997, the Doubletree chain (known for giving guests a freshly baked chocolate-chip cookie every night), took over this boutique hotel. Located within walking distance of the beach, the Alana Waikiki is a welcome oasis of beauty, comfortable accommodations, and prompt service. The elegant lobby is located up the escalators on the second floor where original Picasso ceramics and other works of art are spread throughout the public areas. The interior decorator decided to give the rooms a more homey feel than is usually found in hotel rooms. Soft pastel colors dominate the co-ordinated wall coverings, drapes, and bedding. The result is a comfortable room that feels so inviting, you may want to curl up with a good book. Room amenities include two queen-size beds, two-line telephones, voice mail, computer-fax outlets, flashlights, and coffee/tea makers. The bathrooms are compact, yet outfitted with everything you need, including a phone.

The staff is attentive to details and willing to go to any length to make guests happy. Want The *New York Times* delivered to your room? No problem. Need secretarial help? Within minutes it's available. A good percentage of the guests are business travelers who expect top drawer service and the Alana Waikiki delivers.

Dining/Entertainment: Harlequin, the restaurant on the street level, and Café Picasso, located off the lobby, both offer superb Pacific Rim cuisine.

Services: Concierge, room service.

Facilities: Business center, with secretarial and translation services, computers, fax, and more; fitness center with Universal equipment, cedar sauna, and massage rooms (massage service in guest rooms is also available); Art Gallery, 24-hour reading room with major international newspapers and magazines; and heated swimming pool.

Holiday Inn—Waikiki. 1830 Ala Moana Blvd. (between Hobron Lane and Kalia Rd.), Honolulu, HI 96815. ☎ **888/9WAIKIKI** or 808/955-1111. Fax 808/947-1799. Web page: http:// www.holiday-inn.com. 199 rms. A/C TV TEL. $110 standard double; $120 deluxe double; $130 superior deluxe double. Extra person $15. AE, CB, DC, DISC, JCB, MC, V. Parking $5. TheBUS: 19 or 20.

Holiday Inn—with its dependable quality, amenities, and service—is now in charge of the former Hawaii Dynasty Hotel. In 1994, the chain spent some $6 million to totally renovate the aging hotel. Just 2 blocks from the beach, 2 blocks from Ala Moana Shopping Center, and a 7-minute walk from the Convention Center, it's well-placed for anyone's vacation. All the rooms, which have a modern Japanese look, come with either a king or two double beds plus TV, voice mail, computer jacks, coffeemaker with complimentary coffee, safe, and refrigerator. The property sits back from the street, so noise is at a minimum. The staff is unbelievably friendly (much, much more so than at the Airport Holiday Inn). Children 19 and under stay for free, as long as they share a room with their parents and use the existing bedding.

✪ **The Royal Garden at Waikiki.** 440 Olohana St. (between Kuhio Ave. and Ala Wai Blvd.), Honolulu, HI 96815. ☎ **800/367-5666** or 808/943-0202. Fax 808/946-8777. 220 rms. A/C TV TEL. $130–$180 double; $295 one-bedroom suite for 2; $500 two-bedroom suite (sleeps up to 4). Room/car package $135; Family Plan 50% off second room; Young-at-Heart package (for seniors 55 and over) $91 double. Rates include continental breakfast. Extra person $20. AE, DC, DISC, JCB, MC, V. Parking $7. TheBUS: 19 or 20.

Deals, deals, deals—that's what you'll find at this elegant boutique hotel, tucked away on a quiet, tree-lined side street in Waikiki. There's a deal for everyone: room/car packages start at $135 (that's a $130 standard room, plus a car for only $5 extra); a family plan, which gives you a second room at 50% off the rack rate; and the Young-at-Heart Package, which allows seniors to book rooms starting at $91 (they also get a 10% discount at Royal Garden restaurants).

You won't believe what you get for your money: The 25-story hotel has a lobby filled with European marble and chandeliers, and plush rooms featuring a pantry kitchenette (refrigerator, wet bar, coffeemaker), sitting area, marble bath, lots of closet space, and a lanai; voice mail and computer/fax hookups are welcomed amenities. Facilities include two restaurants (Cascada, serving country-French cuisine, and Shizu, serving Japanese specialties); two freshwater swimming pools (one with cascading waterfall); two Jacuzzis; two saunas; and a fitness center. Complimentary shuttle service to Kapiolani Park, Ala Moana Shopping Center, Royal Hawaiian Shopping Center, and Duty Free Shoppers is included.

INEXPENSIVE

Inn on the Park. 1920 Ala Moana Blvd. (at Kalia Rd.), Honolulu, HI 96815. ☎ **800/367-5004** or 808/946-8355. Fax 800/477-2329 or 808/946-4839. 238 rms. A/C TV TEL. Low season $85 standard double; $100 ocean-view double; $110 deluxe double studio with kitchenette. High season $95 standard double; $110 ocean-view double; $120 deluxe double studio with kitchenette. Extra person $17. AE, CB, DC, JCB, MC, V. Parking $8. TheBUS: 19 or 20.

This hotel, built in 1979, is well-located, just across the street from Fort DeRussy and a couple of blocks from the beach. The rooms are minuscule, so don't expect to squeeze more than two in; families might want to look elsewhere, or rent two rooms. Even the lanais are small—there's barely room for a chair. Most rooms have refrigerators; the studios have kitchenettes with cook top, toaster, and coffeemaker. The 5th-floor swimming pool has a grand view of Fort DeRussy and the Waikiki skyline. Among the shops in the lobby is a moped rental shop, for those wanting to explore Oahu on a motorized two-wheeler; there's also an Italian restaurant. If you don't mind small rooms—you're in Hawaii, so how much time are you going to spend in your room anyway?—the price here can't be beat.

✪ **Outrigger Ala Wai Tower.** 1700 Ala Moana Blvd. (between Hobron Lane and Ala Wai Canal), Honolulu, HI 96815. ☎ **800/OUTRIGGER** or 808/942-7722. Fax 800/622-4852 or 808/943-7272. E-mail: reservations@outrigger.com. Web page: http://www.outrigger.com. 167 rms. A/C TV TEL. $85–$95 standard double with kitchenette; $90–$100 ocean-view double with kitchenette; $160 one-bedroom suite for 2. Rates include continental breakfast buffet. Extra person $15. AE, CB, DC, DISC, JCB, MC, V. Parking $8. TheBUS: 19 or 20.

🅜 Family-Friendly Hotels

If you're traveling with the kids, you'll be welcomed with open arms by many of Oahu's resorts, condos, and B&Bs. Our favorite family-friendly accommodations on the island are listed below. If you're looking for a hotel that has supervised activities for your youngster, you might want to consider the **Sheraton Moana Surfrider,** which has a great children's program. We've listed other options below. If you're looking for a more moderately priced option, look at the **Aston Pacific Monarch** in Waikiki, **Backpacker Vacation Inn** on the North Shore, and **J&B's Place** vacation rental in Kailua, all of which love to accommodate kids and their well-behaved parents.

Waikiki Hotels

Halekulani *(see p. 90)* Halekulani has a complimentary program for children ages 6 to 11 during the summer from early June to mid-August and at Christmas from December 18 to December 30. Daily programs include crafts, games, sightseeing, and excursions. This is a complimentary service for hotel guests; the only charges are for lunch and admission to excursions. Parents will like the "Heavenly Summer Program," which allows them to pay $295 for a second room, no matter what the cost of the first room (available to U.S. and Canadian residents only).

Hilton Hawaiian Village *(see p. 93)* The Rainbow Express is the Hilton's year-round, 7 days a week program of activities for children ages 5 to 12. The program has a wide range of educational and fun activities, such as Hawaiiana arts and crafts, environmental nature walks, wildlife feeding, shell hunting, fishing, peeking at sea creatures at the Waikiki Aquarium, roaming through the Honolulu Zoo, and exploring the world with a computer. Costs start at $17 for a half day including lunch, and go up to $32 for a full day with lunch.

Ilima Hotel *(see p. 104)* When the Teruya brothers, who own a local supermarket chain, built this high-rise condo-hotel, they designed it with families in mind. The units are large, and all have full-sized kitchens. Although there are no formal supervised children's program, there is free HBO, Disney Channel, and Super Nintendo video games in each room. The coin-operated laundry is a big help. The beach and International Market Place are both just a short walk away, and TheBUS stop is just outside. Very popular with neighbor-island families.

Outrigger Reef Tower *(see p. 99)* This hotel offers something for everyone, including nightlife for mom and dad and baby-sitting for the kids. Just 1 1/2 blocks from the beach, the Outrigger Reef Towers also has a good-sized swimming pool on-site. The larger rooms come with kitchenettes, which let you save on food by preparing some meals for yourself.

Royal Kuhio *(see p. 103)* If you have active kids, this is the place for you. The seventh-floor recreation area has volleyball courts, billiards, basketball courts, shuffle-board, an exercise room, even a putting green. Located just across the street from the International Market Place and 2 blocks from the beach, the Royal Kuhio features one-bedroom apartments (with sofa sleeper in the living room) with full kitchens. Rates allow up to four people in a unit, and will sleep five for an extra charge of $15 for the rollaway or crib.

Sheraton Waikiki Hotel *(see p. 95)* During the summer (from mid-June to mid-August), the Keiki Aloha Sunshine Club offers activities for children ages 5 to 12 consisting of boogie boarding, kite-flying, catamaran sailing, a photo contest, and nightly movies. Also, on arrival, the kids are greeted with a complimentary candy lei.

Outside of Waikiki

Kahala Mandarin Oriental Hawaii *(see p. 119)* The Keiki Club is the year-round activity program for children ages 5 to 12 years. Children dance the hula, make leis, design sand sculptures, construct origami figures, participate in making puppets and putting on puppet shows, strum ukuleles, produce shell art, make fish prints, listen to Hawaiian folk tales and legends, play Hawaiian games, participate in the beach Olympics, and a host of other activities. Rates are $30 for the first child, $20 for each additional child for the half-day program; $50 for the first child, $35 for each additional child for the full-day program that includes lunch.

North Shore

Rodeway Inn Hukilau Resort *(see p. 127)* Children are not only welcome here, there's no charge for kids under 18 at this two-story, plantation-style hotel. Within walking distance of the Polynesian Cultural Center, the Rodeway is set up for families, with features like free continental breakfast, pool, and laundry. To top it all off, a terrific white-sand beach is just across the street.

Turtle Bay Hilton Golf and Tennis Resort *(see p. 125)* The Turtle Bay offers a year-round program for children ages 5 to 12 years called the Turtle Keiki Program. Their activities include Hawaiian-style arts and crafts, coconut painting, sand sculpturing, swimming, various games, sports, movies, and storytelling. The daylong activities, including lunch, cost $30.

Leeward

Ihilani Resort & Spa *(see p. 128)* The Keiki Beachcomber Club, available every day of the year, has its own facility for children from 4 to 12 years. Outdoor activities include kite-flying, tide pool exploration, snorkeling, golf, tennis, swimming, aerobics, and international games like les boules (similar to bocce ball), Indian kick ball, and tinikling (a bamboo dance from the Philippines). Hawaiian cultural activities feature lei making and hula dancing. There's a state-of-the-art Computer Learning Center (complete with Sega Genesis, CD-ROM, and Super Nintendo) and a host of other activities. Cost start at $30 for a half day and go up to $55 for a full day including lunch.

Windward

Sheffield House *(see p. 123)* Paul and Rachel Sheffield, who have three children of their own, welcome families with children to their bed-and-breakfast. Their one-bedroom unit is equipped to sleep four. The large yard is filled with children's toys, and the three younger Sheffields are usually available to play with visiting kids.

Waikiki Accommodations

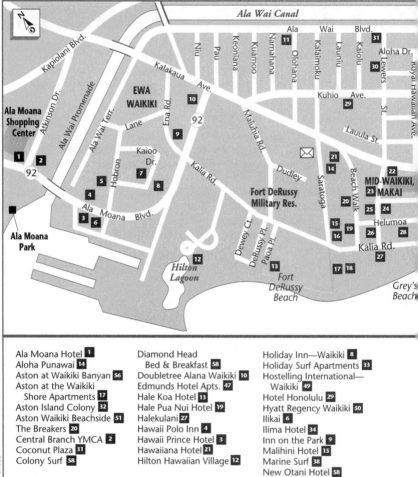

Ala Moana Hotel **1**
Aloha Punawai **14**
Aston at Waikiki Banyan **56**
Aston at the Waikiki
  Shore Apartments **17**
Aston Island Colony **32**
Aston Waikiki Beachside **51**
The Breakers **20**
Central Branch YMCA **2**
Coconut Plaza **31**
Colony Surf **58**

Diamond Head
  Bed & Breakfast **58**
Doubletree Alana Waikiki **10**
Edmunds Hotel Apts. **47**
Hale Koa Hotel **13**
Hale Pua Nui Hotel **19**
Halekulani **27**
Hawaii Polo Inn **4**
Hawaii Prince Hotel **3**
Hawaiiana Hotel **21**
Hilton Hawaiian Village **12**

Holiday Inn—Waikiki **8**
Holiday Surf Apartments **33**
Hostelling International—
  Waikiki **49**
Hotel Honolulu **29**
Hyatt Regency Waikiki **50**
Ilikai **6**
Ilima Hotel **34**
Inn on the Park **9**
Malihini Hotel **15**
Marine Surf **38**
New Otani Hotel **58**

This skyscraper complex, which sits back from busy Ala Moana Boulevard, is just 4 blocks from the beach and close to Ala Moana Shopping Center and the highlights of Waikiki. The rooms were renovated in 1995; views are stunning from the upper floors. The studio-type doubles with kitchenettes are in the 40-story Tower, whose glass elevators offer breathtaking views every time you ride up and down (but with 40 floors and only two elevators, the wait for an elevator can challenge your patience); each has a dishwasher, disposal, refrigerator, stove, coffeemaker, microwave, and cooking utensils. The one-bedroom condo-style units are in the 16-story Annex; these have a separate bedroom, living room, lanai, and kitchen with a four-burner stove, oven, refrigerator, and cooking utensils. (Mobility-impaired travelers should book in the Tower, as you have to climb a flight of stairs to reach the elevator in the Annex.)

The property boasts a pool, spa, sauna, tennis courts, and laundry facilities. There are no restaurants, but the management offers a complimentary continental buffet every morning, which makes this budget hotel an even better deal. *Hot tip for views:*

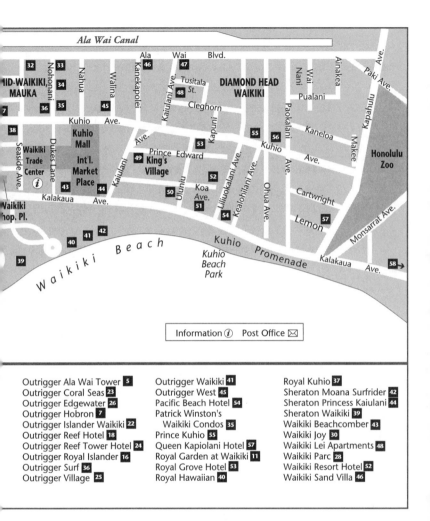

Information (i)   Post Office ⊠

Outrigger Ala Wai Tower **5**
Outrigger Coral Seas **23**
Outrigger Edgewater **26**
Outrigger Hobron **7**
Outrigger Islander Waikiki **22**
Outrigger Reef Hotel **18**
Outrigger Reef Tower Hotel **24**
Outrigger Royal Islander **16**
Outrigger Surf **36**
Outrigger Village **25**

Outrigger Waikiki **41**
Outrigger West **45**
Pacific Beach Hotel **54**
Patrick Winston's
   Waikiki Condos **35**
Prince Kuhio **55**
Queen Kapiolani Hotel **57**
Royal Garden at Waikiki **11**
Royal Grove Hotel **53**
Royal Hawaiian **40**

Royal Kuhio **37**
Sheraton Moana Surfrider **42**
Sheraton Princess Kaiulani **44**
Sheraton Waikiki **39**
Waikiki Beachcomber **43**
Waikiki Joy **30**
Waikiki Lei Apartments **48**
Waikiki Parc **28**
Waikiki Resort Hotel **52**
Waikiki Sand Villa **46**

In the Tower, the best views are from floors 21 and above; ask for a room facing Ewa (west) for spectacular sunset views. In the Annex, the best views are from floors five and above, which overlook the Ala Wai Yacht Harbor and Ala Moana Beach Park.

BUDGET

Hawaii Polo Inn. 1696 Ala Moana Blvd. (between Hobron Lane and Ala Wai Canal), Honolulu, HI 96815. ☎ **800/669-7719** or 808/949-0061. Fax 808/949-4906. E-mail: hipolo@lava.net. 68 rms (with shower only). TV TEL. $49–$59 superior double; $59–$69 deluxe double; $69–$79 studio double; $95–$135 one-bedroom suite for 2. AE, DC, DISC, JCB, MC, V. Parking $7. TheBUS: 19 or 20.

Until recently, the Hawaii Polo Inn was just another aging hotel going to seed. Then along came the brand-new Hawaii Convention Center—opening in mid-1998 just a few blocks away—and the management saw new potential in their property. It still isn't the Ritz, but this boutique hotel, located within walking distance of Ala Moana Shopping Center, offers nicely decorated rooms with modern conveniences at budget prices. The rooms have been redone with new tile, new furniture, all-new amenities, and a fresh tropical motif. Walls were removed from the suites, making them bigger and airier. All rooms come with TVs, coffeemakers, and refrigerators; the suites have microwaves and hot plates. Ala Moana Boulevard is still noisy, but the minute you step inside the rattan-furnished lobby, you'll feel like you're in another world. Staff members are fluent in Spanish, German, and Japanese, and all seem knowledgeable about local adventures and activities. There's a small swimming pool, a travel desk, and a self-serve Laundromat.

Outrigger Hobron. 343 Hobron Lane (just off Ala Moana Blvd.), Honolulu, HI 96815. ☎ **800/OUTRIGGER** or 808/942-7777. Fax 808/943-7373 or 800/622-4852. E-mail: reservations@outrigger.com. Web page: http://www.outrigger.com. 612 rms. A/C TV TEL. $65–$85 double; $75–$100 double with kitchenette; $140 ocean-view studio with kitchenette (sleeps up to 4); $180 two-bedroom suite with kitchenette (sleeps up to 4); $210 three-bedroom suite with kitchenette (sleeps up to 6). Extra person $15. AE, CB, DC, DISC, JCB, MC, V. Parking $8. TheBUS: 19 or 20.

This 44-story outpost of the reliable Outrigger chain is located on a quiet side street, just a 10-minute walk from Waikiki Beach or the Ala Moana Shopping Center. There are 16 rooms on each floor: Four rooms have ocean views, four look toward the mountains, four face Diamond Head, and the last four show you Honolulu's city lights. The top five floors were renovated in 1991, and the 5th to the 38th floors were renovated in 1993. The rooms are small, with not a lot of dancing room between the bed and the walls; the studios are a bit larger, and have kitchenettes equipped with a two-burner hot plate, refrigerator, sink, coffeepot, cooking utensils, and toasters. You might want to invest in ear plugs—the walls seem paper-thin. But at $65 a day for a couple or $180 to $210 for a family of four to six, you're really getting a lot of bang for your buck at this budget hotel. There's a restaurant, a swimming pool, a sauna, and laundry facilities on the premises.

MID-WAIKIKI, MAKAI

All of the hotels listed below are between Kalakaua Avenue and the ocean, and between Fort DeRussy in the Ewa direction and Kaiulani Street in the Diamond Head direction.

VERY EXPENSIVE

✪ **Halekulani.** 2199 Kalia Rd. (Diamond Head end of road, ocean side with entrance across from Lewers St.), Honolulu, HI 96815. ☎ **800/367-2343** or 808/923-2311. Fax 808/926-8004. Web page: http://www.halekulani.com/. 456 rms and suites. A/C MINIBAR TV TEL. $295–$520 double; $700–$4,500 suite. Extra person $125. One child under 17 free in parents' room with existing bedding. Maximum 3 persons per room. AE, CB, DC, JCB, MC, V. Parking $10. TheBUS: 19 or 20.

For the ultimate in a "heavenly" Hawaii vacation, this is the place. In fact, Halekulani translates as "House Befitting Heaven," an apt description. This luxury 456-room resort is spread over 5 acres of Waikiki beachfront property. The five buildings of the hotel are interconnected by open courtyards and lush tropical gardens. The elegant atmosphere envelopes you as soon as you step into the lobby, done in Italian terrazzo and wood. There are no long registration lines, because guests are immediately personally escorted to their rooms, where the details of registration are done in the comfort and privacy of your own room.

There are so many things that set this luxury hotel apart from the others, the most important being the rooms. First, most rooms (about 90%) face the ocean. Second, the rooms are big (519 to 720 square feet) with separate sitting areas with love seat, chairs, coffee table, and business desk. Every room has a large lanai with table and chairs. The bathrooms feature a deep-soaking tub, separate glassed-in shower, and marble basin. Other amenities include: refrigerator, three telephones, safe, luxurious bathrobes, twice-daily maid service, complimentary daily newspaper, and complimentary local phone calls.

The resort offers a package deal for lovers, called "Heaven on Waikiki," which consists of chilled French champagne on arrival, a bouquet of flowers in the room, and an intimate breakfast for two served on the room's lanai. The cost is $1,539 for 3 nights or $3,159 for 7 nights. During the summer months, they offer an excellent package called the "Heavenly Summer Program," where you pay $295 for a second room, no matter what the cost of your first room (available to U.S. and Canadian residents only).

Dining/Entertainment: Dining facilities are superb: there's Orchids, the oceanside main dining room, which serves all three meals and highlights locally grown produce in its Indo-Pacific cuisine; the award-winning neoclassic French restaurant, La Mer, which offers a superb ala carte menu and two prix fixe dinners, both three-hour haute-cuisine experiences at $85 and $105; and ✪ **House Without a Key,** an oceanside restaurant under a century-old kiawe tree, surely one of the world's most romantic spots for sunset cocktails, light meals, and Hawaiian entertainment.

Services: Concierge desk, business and secretarial services, free daily newspapers, twice-daily maid and turndown service, free local telephone calls.

Facilities: Fitness room, running sessions and aerobic workouts, in-room massage by professional therapists, magnificent oceanside swimming pool, easy access to superb stretch of Waikiki Beach.

✪ **Royal Hawaiian.** 2259 Kalakaua Ave. (makai end of Royal Hawaiian Ave., Diamond Head side of the Sheraton Waikiki, and ocean side of the Royal Hawaiian Shopping Center), Honolulu, HI 96815. ☎ **800/325-3535** or 808/923-7311. Fax 808/924-7098. 527 rms and suites. A/C MINIBAR TV TEL. $290 Historic Wing double; $365 Historic Garden Wing double; $490 Historic Ocean Wing double; $490 tower oceanfront double; $540 luxury ocean double; $475–$3,000 suites. Extra person $50. Inquire about Sheraton's "Sure Saver" rates, available at different times of the year, which could mean as much as 32% in savings. AE, MC, V. Valet parking $18; self-parking at Sheraton Waikiki $9. TheBUS: 19 or 20.

Hidden in the jungle of concrete buildings that make up Waikiki is an oasis of verdant gardens and a shockingly pink building. The Royal Hawaiian Hotel, affectionately called the "pink palace," is known around the world as a symbol of luxury. Built by the owners of the Matson steamship lines as a luxury hotel for their passengers, the Royal opened on February 1, 1927, on the same spot that Queen Kaahumanu had her summer palace. Influenced by the popular silent screen star Rudolph Valentino and his Arabic escapades, the Spanish-Moorish, six-story, 400-room hotel cost $4 million to build.

Entry into the hotel is past the lush gardens, with its spectacular banyan tree, into the black terrazzo-marble lobby, with handwoven pink carpets, and giant, 10-foot tall flower arrangements. Guests are given a traditional lei and escorted to the front desk for check-in. Every room in the Royal is enchanting, but our hearts were won over by the Historic wing: carved wooden doors, four-poster wooden canopy beds, flowered wall paper, and period furniture. The guest amenities list is lengthy: freshly baked banana bread (made from the hotel's original 1927 recipe) on arrival, daily newspaper, 24-hour room service, even preferential tee times at Makaha Resort and Golf Club.

The beach fronting the Royal is perfect for sunbathing, and the Royal provides all the necessary beach accessories from deck chairs to umbrellas. Every Monday, Wednesday, and Friday, the Royal invites local artists to display their Hawaiian crafts such as Hawaiian quilts, leis, weaving, and more.

If you are planning to stay 4 nights, the Royal offers a celebration package that includes a bottle of pink champagne, a romantic dinner for two (that can be served in the privacy of your room), a pass on the Waikiki Trolley, a commemorative farewell gift, and your fifth night free.

Dining/Entertainment: The Surf Room, on the ocean, offers all three meals and is known for its elaborate seafood buffets. The ✪ **Mai Tai Bar** is one of the most popular places in Waikiki for the namesake drink, which is reputed to have originated here. The Royal Hawaiian Luau, done in the grand style, is held on Monday nights.

Services: Multilingual concierge desk, 24-hour room service, 24-hour medical service, baby-sitting, preferential tee-off times at Makaha Resort and Golf Club.

Facilities: Freshwater swimming pool, business center, hospitality suite for early arrivals and late check-outs, shops, and one of the best stretches of Waikiki Beach.

✪ **Sheraton Moana Surfrider Hotel.** 2365 Kalakaua Ave. (ocean side of the street, across from Kaulani St.), Honolulu, HI 96815. ☎ **800/325-3535** or 808/922-3111. Fax 808/923-0308. 747 rms and 44 suites. A/C MINIBAR TV TEL. $250 city view; $290 large city view; $385 ocean view in Banyan Wing; $410 partial ocean view in Tower Wing; $485 deluxe ocean view in Tower and Diamond Wings. Extra person and rollaway bed $40. Children under 18 free in parents' room with existing bedding. Inquire about Sheraton's "Sure Saver" rates, available at different times of the year, which could mean as much as 32% in savings. AE, CB, DC, MC, V. Parking $10. TheBUS: 19 or 20.

Step back in time to old Hawaii at Waikiki's first hotel, originally built in 1901. Those days of yesteryear live on at this grand hotel. Entry is through the original colonial porte-cochere, past the highly polished wooden front porch, with white-wood rocking chairs, and into the perfectly restored lobby with its detailed millwork and intricate plaster detailing on the ceiling. Time seems to slow down here, tropical flowers arranged in huge sprays are everywhere, and the people in the lobby all seem to be smiling. At check-in, on the Ewa side of the lobby, guests are greeted with a lei and a glass of fruit juice. This is a hotel not only with class, but with historical charm.

Opened on March 11, 1901, the then-four story, 75-room hotel was Hawaii's largest and one of the more elaborate buildings at the time. Considered an innovative hotel in the travel industry back then, the Moana (as it was once known) featured a private bath and a telephone in each guest room (an unheard of luxury at the turn of the century). The first guests thought the rooms were a bit "pricey" ($1.50 a night), but worth it. Today the hotel is listed on the National Register of Historic Places, and consists of three wings: the original (and totally restored) Banyan Wing, the Diamond Wing, and the Tower Wing. The Banyan Wing gets its name from the tree in the courtyard, which was planted in 1885. When the hotel opened, the courtyard immediately became a favorite gathering place for visitors and Honolulu's hoi polloi. From 1935 to 1975, the Banyan Court became well known to millions of people across the country when a radio announcer proclaimed every week: "From the Banyan Court of the Moana Hotel, overlooking bee-you-tee-full Waikiki Beach, it's Hawaii Calls!"

It's hard to get a bad room here: The majority of the rooms have ocean views and they all come with such amenities as refrigerators, iron and ironing boards, hair dryers, plush robes, complimentary safes, and voice mail. But, we are especially taken with the rooms in the original Banyan Wing. The handcrafted colonial armoire hides the television, a small panel of controls next to the bed activates the lights, air-conditioning, and television. The fixtures in the smallish bathrooms are modern-day replicas of the 19th-century hardware.

Dining/Entertainment: The Beachside Café, overlooking the ocean, is great for a casual breakfast, lunch or dinner, as is W. C. Peacock and Co., Ltd., also at the ocean's edge in a tropical garden setting, featuring fresh fish and carefully cooked steaks. The Banyan Veranda is the setting for breakfast, Sunday brunch, high tea, and afternoon cocktails, located on the porch overlooking the Banyan Court. The Moana's fine dining restaurant, the Ship's Tavern, features contemporary cuisine. The Beach Bar and a poolside snack bar are outdoors.

Services: Free, year-round, supervised children's program offers not only on-site activities, but also excursions to the Zoo and the Waikiki Aquarium. Daily guest activities feature Hawaiian arts and crafts such as coconut-palm weaving and Hawaiian quilting.

Facilities: Beach, fitness center, and freshwater swimming pool.

EXPENSIVE

Aston at the Waikiki Shore Apartments. 2161 Kalia Rd. (Ewa side of the Outrigger Reef Hotel, on the ocean across the street from Saratoga Rd. and Fort DeRussy), Honolulu, HI 96815. ☎ **800/367-2353** or 808/926-4733. Fax 808/922-2902. 76 apts. A/C TV TEL. $160–$175 studio apt (sleeps 2); $220–$250 one-bedroom apt (sleeps 4); $305–$350 two-bedroom apt (sleeps 6); $350–$525 two-bedroom, two-bath, ocean-view apt (sleeps 6). Ask about the "Mix 7" rates, where you stay 7 or more consecutive nights with Aston and get 20–30% off rates. AE, CB, DC, DISC, JCB, MC, V. Limited parking $7. TheBUS: 19 or 20.

Entry to the rooms is through a locked gate and keyed elevators, security is tight. You'll see why everyone wants to stay here—a panoramic vista of the entire shoreline from Diamond Head to Honolulu. The apartments, which are privately owned and decorated and then rented out through Aston, range in size from studio to two-bedroom. Each has fully equipped tiled kitchens, big lanais, spacious sitting areas, and those fabulous views. Reservations are hard to get; book way in advance.

There are full-time residents who live in this complex, so the units tend to be quiet. The building sits on an excellent beach and the location is close to all of Waikiki's restaurants and shops. Daily maid services and plenty of assistance from the front desk gives this condominium stay all the benefits of hotel service.

✪ **Hilton Hawaiian Village.** 2005 Kalia Rd. (Ala Moana Blvd.), Honolulu, HI 96815. ☎ **800-HILTONS** or 808/949-4321. Fax 808/947-7898. Web page: http://www.hilton.com/. 2,545 rms, 365 suites. A/C MINIBAR TV TEL. $189–$335 double; $219–$365 Ali'i Tower; $415–$3,400 suite. Extra person $30. Children 18 and under free in parents' room. AE, CB, DISC, ER, JCB, MC, V. Valet parking $12; self-parking $9. TheBUS: 19 or 20.

This is Waikiki's biggest resort—so big it even has its own post office. It includes some 2,545 rooms spread over 20 acres with tropical gardens, thundering waterfalls, exotic wildlife, award-winning restaurants, nightly entertainment, 100 different shops, children's programs, fabulous ocean activities, a secluded lagoon, three swimming pools, Hawaiian cultural activities, two minigolf courses, and Waikiki beach.

The Hawaiian Village dates back to 1955 when Henry J. Kaiser planned a Hawaiian vacation village that would have everything a visitor could possibly want. The original "Village" consisted of thatched guest cottages, hand-built by Samoans from Windward Oahu. In 1961, hotelier Conrad Hilton bought the "Village" and made a few changes, added a few rooms, a few towers, until it became the complete Hawaiian vacation village that Kaiser envisioned in 1955.

Like everything else in the "Village," there is also a wide choice of accommodations, ranging from simply lovely to absolutely breathtaking. There are four towers to choose from: Rainbow Tower, Tapa Tower, Diamond Head Tower, and Alii Tower. All the rooms are large and beautifully furnished, and offer views that range from court and garden to yacht harbor and ocean. No smoking rooms and disabled-accessible rooms are available throughout the complex. Of all the rooms, we highly recommend the ones in the Alii Tower. Located right on the ocean, the

348 ultradeluxe guest rooms and suites offer the royal treatment that the name implies, including in-room registration, exclusive health club and swimming pool, and the attention of a multilingual concierge staff. Each room has a fully stocked refreshment center, in-room coffee services, no fewer than three phones (one of which is PC-compatible), and even a mini-TV on the bathroom vanity.

In addition to the luxurious rooms, the Hilton Hawaiian Village offers guests a range of on-property activities from Atlantis Submarine rides to a host of free activities (tai chi classes, lei making, and hula lessons to name a few). Their year-round children's program is one of Waikiki's best, featuring such activities as a wildlife and ecology tour, eating healthy and keiki cooking classes, a parade, and a Diamond Head hike.

Dining/Entertainment: Both the Golden Dragon (excellent Cantonese and Szechuan cuisine in exquisite oriental surroundings) and the romantic Bali-by-the-Sea, with ocean views and gourmet cuisine, are named among Honolulu's best restaurants year after year. Illusionist John Hirokawa and "The Magic of Polynesia" are featured at the Hilton Dome. The beachfront Hau Tree Bar, the Paradise Lounge, the Shell Bar, and the Tapa Bar are all favorite nightspots. Other restaurants include: Rainbow Lanai (casual cafe atmosphere), Tapa Café (featuring a "fitness-first" menu), and the Village Steak & Seafood Restaurant (steaks, seafood, and a California salad bar).

Services: Multilingual concierge staff; in-room fax and computer hookups in many rooms; daily bilingual activities for kids 4 to 12; walking tours for adults; free fitness classes in tai chi, stretching, aquacise, and yoga; classes in lei making, hula, and the ukulele; in-room massage; room service.

Facilities: Business center, fitness center, three swimming pools, scores of shops (including those in the Rainbow Bazaar), and easy access to a superb stretch of Waikiki Beach.

✪ **Outrigger Reef Hotel.** 2169 Kalia Rd. (ocean side of Kalia Rd., Ewa side of the Halekulani Hotel, and across the street from Beach Walk), Honolulu, HI 96815. ☎ **800/OUTRIGGER** or 808/923-3111. Fax 800/622-4852. E-mail: reservations@outrigger.com. Web page: http://www.outrigger.com/. 883 rms, 47 suites. A/C TV TEL. $145–$320 double; $190–$345 Voyagers Club; $260–$1,000 suite. Extra person $25. Children under 17 free in parents' room with existing bedding. Seniors 50 and older 20% off, AARP members 25% off. Ask about room-and-breakfast packages. Free rent-a-car when booking at rack rates. AE, CB, DC, DISC, JCB, MC, V. Parking $10. TheBUS: 19 or 20.

Location, location, location! This Outrigger is right on Waikiki Beach, across from Ft. DeRussy. Yet it remains a moderately priced hotel with beautifully appointed rooms, excellent service, and a myriad of activities, shops, and restaurants. This is a big hotel with three towers (5, 10, and 17 floors each) and a megalobby connecting them. Off the lobby is an enormous swimming pool, with some 300 chaise lounges surrounding it, three whirlpool spas, and food and cocktail service within hailing distance. Throughout the lobby are enough shops to qualify as a mini–shopping mall. And of course, beautiful Waikiki Beach is in the backyard.

The rooms have the usual well-designed, well-appointed Outrigger furnishings and decorations with great views and plenty of extra room to have a couple of kids bedding down. Room amenities include refrigerators, blackout drapes, coffeemakers, safes, irons and ironing boards. Coin-operated laundry facilities are available as is a hospitality room for early check-ins or late check-outs. No smoking and handicapped-accessible rooms are also available.

Dining/Entertainment: At poolside is the Chief's Hut for casual, family dining for breakfast, lunch, and dinner. At oceanside you'll find The Shorebird Beach

Broiler, an immensely popular spot offering buffet breakfasts and broil-your-own dinners. The Shorebird Prime Rib & Pasta Company is open for dinner only. The Aloha Lobby features Hawaiian entertainment, the Shorebird Beach Bar also has live entertainment, and the Pool Terrace is a poolside sports bar with big screen TV.

Services: Many beach services, including catamaran sailing, canoe rides, and surfboard lessons; room service; fitness center; and concierge desk.

Facilities: One of the largest freshwater swimming pools in Waikiki, and a business center with state-of-the-art equipment and the assistance of a full-time secretary.

✪ **Outrigger Waikiki.** 2335 Kalakaua Ave. (between Royal Hawaiian Shopping Center and the Sheraton Moana Surfrider Hotel, on the ocean side of the street), Honolulu, HI 96815. ☎ **800/OUTRIGGER** or 808/923-0711. Fax 800/622-4852. E-mail: reservations@ outrigger.com. Web page: http://www.outrigger.com/. 477 rms, 53 suites. A/C TV TEL. $160–$350 double; $215–$530 Voyager Club rooms and suites; $500–$530 suite. Seniors 50 and older get 20% off, AARP members get 25% off. Children 17 and under free when sharing rooms with parents with existing bedding. Free rent-a-car when booking at rack rates. Extra person $25. AE, CB, DC, DISC, JCB, MC, V. Parking $10. TheBUS: 19 or 20.

The same value and quality that we have come to expect in every Outrigger is definitely in evidence here, only multiplied by a factor of 10. The newly renovated rooms are big and comfortable with huge closets, roomy bathrooms, and plenty of amenities (refrigerator, iron, hair dryer, safe, and coffeemaker). All the rooms have spacious lanais and the price of your room will be dependent on the view. Rooms on the top four floors are considered part of the "Voyagers Club," and have the use of the private lounge that serves continental breakfast and complimentary pupus in the evening.

The beachfront location makes this one of the most attractive Outrigger properties. Additionally, there are plenty of shops, restaurants, and entertainment on the property. Other services include room service, fitness center, hospitality room, business center, and medical services.

Dining/Entertainment: Duke's Canoe Club serves island-style seafood and steaks at its beachfront location; Monterey Bay Canners and Chuck's Steakhouse are both popular places for seafood and steaks; Brass Rail is a "Cheers"-like pub and deli; Pai's Health Foods serves up healthy sandwiches and other healthy food; and the Outrigger Snack Shop features fast food served on the beach. Entertainment includes the talented Society of Seven performing in the Showroom.

Services: Room service, concierge desk, beauty salon, shopping galleria with many shops, Doctors on Call medical clinic, ATM machine, business center and hospitality room for early check-ins and late check-outs.

Facilities: An 800-square-foot fitness center, beautifully landscaped pool area with adjacent Jacuzzi, easy access to prime stretch of Waikiki Beach.

Sheraton Waikiki. 2255 Kalakaua Ave. (makai end of Royal Hawaiian Ave., Ewa side of the Sheraton Royal Hawaiian, and ocean side of the Royal Hawaiian Shopping Center), Honolulu, HI 96815. ☎ **800/325-3535** or 808/922-4422. Fax 808/923-8785. 1,852 rms, 130 suites. A/C MINIBAR TV TEL. $150 double Sheraton Manor; $195–$430 double, $600–up suite. Extra person $40. Inquire about Sheraton's "Sure Saver" rates, available at different times of the year, which could mean as much as 32% in savings. AE, CB, DC, DISC, JCB, MC, V. Valet parking $13; self-parking $9. TheBUS: 19 or 20.

The Sheraton chain owns a substantial portion of Waikiki with some 4,371 rooms in three hotels on the beach and one across the street. The Sheraton Waikiki is by far the biggest of the four—1,852 rooms spread over two 30-story towers. The bank of 11 elevators will give you a feel for the sheer size of the place. It is also host to numerous large conventions. If big crowds, especially conventioneers, is not your idea of a Hawaiian vacation, this may not be the place for you. However, size has its advantages and the Sheraton Waikiki has everything from free programs for the kids to historical walks for the grandparents.

The lobby is immense, filled with shopping arcades, people, groups, travel desks, and now a three-dimensional turtle sculpture at the entrance. It's hard to get a bad room here. Of the 1,852 guest rooms, 1,200 of them have some sort of ocean view and 650 rooms have a view of Diamond Head. There is a saying on the Waikiki strip that a lot of hotels have great views of the Sheraton, but the Sheraton guests have views of the beach and Diamond Head all to themselves.

The rooms are large with big lanais to take in those magnificent views. The room amenities include minibars/refrigerators (if you want the refrigerator to store your own food and drinks, call housekeeping to clear out the refrigerator), safes, and coffeemakers. The bathrooms have both showers and tubs for those wanting a long soak.

For the budget-conscious, the Sheraton Manor Hotel occupies a separate wing adjacent to the Sheraton Waikiki, and offers all the services and beachfront of the Sheraton Waikiki. The views aren't the best—overlooking the porte cochere—and the rooms are small (maximum of two people) with modest appointments, air-conditioning, and no lanai. At the other end of the spectrum, the Sheraton has the "Suite Impressions" program, a sort of a hotel-within-a-hotel, where 70 double-sized oceanfront rooms (going for $900 a night for two) include not only hotel room but also complimentary luxury limousine pick-up and return to the airport, champagne, snack basket and flowers on arrival, and complimentary parking.

The Sheraton's new slogan is the "heartbeat of excitement, the center of entertainment." They offer free programs for children ages 5 to 12 that include a candy lei on arrival, boogie boarding, kite flying, catamaran sailing, a photo contest, and a nightly movie. Other activities for those over 12 include: free cooking demonstrations, Hawaiian arts and crafts demonstrations, complimentary fun runs, aerobic exercise, and even a walking tour of the Waikiki of yesteryear.

Last but never least, a few words about the beach—it's just steps from the rooms. Here is the real reason that the Sheraton appears to be filled with guests—world-famous Waikiki Beach is at the doorstep.

Dining/Entertainment: There's the open-air Ocean Terrace for casual buffet meals, the glamorous Hanohano Room for gourmet dining in a spectacular setting 30 stories up (take the glass elevator just for the view), as well as Ciao! (Italian cuisine), and Esprit nightclub for dancing, drinks, and entertainment. Near the pool is Kau Kau Express for snacks and the Sand Bar for liquid libations.

Services: If you decide to leave "home," you can, of course, "play and charge" at the other Sheraton hotels in Waikiki as well as at the Makaha Golf Club's golf and tennis facilities. A multilingual staff and business center are also available.

Facilities: You'll probably spend a lot of time right at the hotel, what with all those great shops in the lobby, that vast expanse of beach at your doorstep, and one of the biggest and sunniest pools along the Waikiki beachfront. There is a fitness center on the property, too.

✪ Waikiki Parc. 2233 Helumoa Rd. (Lewers St.), Honolulu, HI 96815. **☎ 800/422-0450** or 808/921-7272. Fax 808/923-1336. 298 rms. A/C MINIBAR TV TEL. $170–$230 double; $195–$255 deluxe. Extra person $30. Children 14 and under free in parents' room. Inquire about room-and-car packages, bed-and-breakfast packages, and 50%-off second-room packages. AE, CB, DC, DISC, JCB, MC, V. Valet parking $9. TheBUS: 19 or 20.

This hotel, located just 100 yards from the beach, is for people who love the elegance, grace, and comfort of the Halekulani, but just can't quite afford their rates. Tucked just behind the Halekulani, and owned and operated by the same company, the Waikiki Parc offers luxury and beautifully appointed rooms at an affordable price. Opened in 1987, the 298-room hotel was a success from the first day.

The guest rooms all have lanais with either ocean, mountain, or city views. The compact rooms have ceramic tile floors with plush carpeting, a conversation area with writing desk, and a rattan couch and chair. Room amenities include refrigerator, minibars, two telephones, a safe, and adjustable floor-to-ceiling shutters for those who want to sleep in.

The Waikiki Parc has the same level of service that has made the Halekulani famous. On a recent visit, we asked room services for a few items that were not exactly on the menu. They not only happily complied, but the manager checked back later to make sure we got what we wanted. We requested an out-of-town newspaper one day; the next day the bellman said he would deliver it to our room everyday, no problem. We called the valet desk and asked directions to get to an out-of-the-way location on Oahu. When we picked up our car, the valet desk handed us a map with the route highlighted in yellow.

Dining/Entertainment: Waikiki Parc has two excellent restaurants. Parc Café, with its garden-terrace atmosphere, serves fabulous buffet-style meals, featuring island specialties. Don't miss the seafood buffet on Friday, Saturday, and Sunday and the Hawaiian luncheon buffet on Wednesday and Friday. Kacho, one of Hawaii's few Kyoto-style restaurants, is a charming oasis for true devotees of sushi and Japanese seafood dishes.

Services: Concierge desk, twice-daily maid service, secretarial and other business services, wheelchair accessibility to all public areas, room service.

Facilities: Freshwater pool on the eighth-floor recreation deck, a great stretch of Waikiki beach nearby.

MODERATE

✪ **Hawaiiana Hotel.** 260 Beach Walk (near Kalakaua Ave.), Honolulu, HI 96815. ☎ **800/535-0085** or 808/923-3811. Fax 808/926-5728. E-mail: marc@aloha.net. 95 rms (some with shower only). A/C TV TEL. Low season, $109–$219 double. High season, $119–$229 double. Extra person $15. AE, DC, DISC, JCB, MC, V. Parking $8. TheBUS: 19 or 20.

The lush tropical flowers and carved tiki at the entrance on tiny Beach Walk set the tone for this intimate low-rise hotel. The hotel's slogan says it all: "The spirit of old Hawaii." From the moment you arrive, you'll experience the aloha spirit here: At check-in, guests are given a pineapple; every morning, complimentary Kona coffee and tropical juice are served poolside; and at check-out, flower leis are presented to the women as a fragrant reminder of their vacation at the Hawaiiana. The concrete hollow-tiled rooms feature a kitchenette (small refrigerator, two-burner hot plate, toaster oven, and coffeemaker), two beds (a double and a single), TV, phone, and a view of the gardens and swimming pool. The staff provides complimentary use of the washer and dryers. Hawaiian entertainment is featured every week. The hotel is about a block from the beach and within walking distance of Waikiki shopping and nightlife.

Outrigger Islander Waikiki. 270 Lewers St. (entry on ocean, Ewa side of Lewers St. at Kalakaua Ave.), Honolulu, HI 96815. ☎ **800/OUTRIGGER** or 808/923-7621. Fax 800/622-4852. E-mail: reservations@outrigger.com. Web page: http://www.outrigger.com/. 287 rms. A/C TV TEL. $95–$135 double; $140–$150 studio. Extra person $15. Children 17 and under stay free when using existing bedding. Seniors 50 and older 20% discount, AARP members 25% discount. Ask about room-and-breakfast packages. Free rent-a-car when booking at rack rates. Parking $8. TheBUS: 19 or 20.

If you're looking for a moderately priced hotel in the midst of Waikiki, here's your place—Waikiki's newest hotel. In 1997, the Outrigger chain completely gutted the old Pleasant Holiday Isle Hotel, then dropped more than $7 million for renovations to bring the property up to Outrigger standards. The location on Lewers and Kalakaua is fabulous: just across the street from the Royal Hawaiian Shopping Center, and 1 block to the beach. An escalator takes you up to the glass-encased lobby, with the pool at one end and shops and a restaurant at the other. (As we went to press, the restaurant and lobby shops were not yet open.)

The rooms, which are all interconnected, range in size from 240 to 342 square feet, and have been refurbished in Berber carpets, with Italian tile entryways, blond island-style furniture, and matching wallpaper and artwork by Hawaii's artists. All rooms have small semicircle balconies, either king or two double beds, coffeemakers, safes, hair dryers, and irons and ironing boards. Also available: rooms with bath tubs, no-smoking rooms, and wheelchair-accessible rooms.

INEXPENSIVE

The Breakers. 250 Beach Walk (between Kalakaua Ave. and Kalia Rd.), Honolulu, HI 96815. ☎ **800/426-0494** or 808/923-3181. Fax 808/923-7174. Web page: http://www. travelweb.com/thisco/lri/64039/64039_b.html. 64 rms (with shower only). A/C TV TEL. $88–$95 single; $91–$97 double. Extra person $8. AE, DC, MC, V. Limited free parking; parking $6 across the street. TheBUS: 19 or 20.

A little gem in the midst of high-rise Waikiki, The Breakers is full of old-fashioned Hawaiian aloha—and it's only steps from the beach. This two-story hotel has a friendly staff and a loyal following, with more than 70% returning for another stay. Its six buildings are set around a pool and a tropical garden blooming with brilliant red and yellow hibiscus; wooden jalousies and shoji doors further the tropical ambiance. The tastefully decorated, slightly oversized rooms come with a lanai and a kitchenette with two-burner stove, toaster oven, and fridge. The poolside bar and grill serves cocktails and heavy pupus. Every Wednesday and Friday, you're invited to a formal Japanese tea ceremony from 10am to noon.

✪ **Outrigger Coral Seas.** 250 Lewers St. (between Kalakaua Ave. and Helumoa St.), Honolulu, HI 96815. ☎ **800/OUTRIGGER** or 808/923-3881. Fax 800/622-4852 or 808/922-2330. E-mail: reservations@outrigger.com. Web page: http://www.outrigger.com. 109 rms (with shower only). A/C TV TEL. $75–$85 double; $85–$95 double with kitchenette; $130 one-bedroom with kitchenette (sleeps up to 4). Extra person $15. AE, CB, DC, DISC, JCB, MC, V. Parking $8. TheBUS: 19 or 20.

In the heart of Waikiki, on a busy little street lined with a number of Outriggers, you'll find this small, clean hotel. It's one of the area's great bargains, especially in the spring and fall, when rooms go for $75 a night. Last renovated in 1993, the rooms are small but comfortable, with two double beds, a desk, TV, phone, and safe. Rooms with kitchenettes are equipped with refrigerator, microwave, sink, and cooking utensils. They don't have ocean views and aren't grand, but the hotel's location can't be beat. If you get a room overlooking Lewers Street, you can sit on your semiprivate lanai and watch the incredible parade of humanity go by—Lewers may be noisy, but it's the best free show in town. The hotel has several restaurants, including a moderately priced steak-and-seafood house, an all-you-can-eat buffet, and a Chinese place. There's no pool, but you're welcome to use the one at the Outrigger Village next door.

Outrigger Edgewater. 2168 Kalia Rd. (at Beach Walk), Honolulu, HI 96815. ☎ **800/ OUTRIGGER** or 808/922-6424. Fax 800/622-4852 or 808/924-6354. E-mail: reservations@outrigger.com. Web page: http://www.outrigger.com. 184 rms. A/C TV TEL. $78–$98 double; $88–$98 double with kitchenette; $145 one-bedroom with kitchenette (sleeps up to 4). Extra person $15. AE, CB, DC, DISC, JCB, MC, V. Parking $8. TheBUS: 19 or 20.

Although this one is closer to the beach, we don't think it's as nice as the numerous Outriggers on Lewers Street, nor does it have the amenities they offer (for one, no coffeemakers). The Edgewater is an older building with small rooms (renovated in 1993) and tiny lanais. Still, as in all Outrigger hotels, the rooms are tastefully decorated and come with TV, phone, and safe; those with kitchenettes have an oven, three-burner stove, sink, fridge, and cooking utensils.

The shortage of elevators—only two for seven floors and 184 rooms—can cause long, long waits. The hotel shares a swimming pool with the adjacent Outrigger Waikiki Tower. The location really can't be beat—just cross the street and walk behind the Outrigger Reef to get to the beach. It's also convenient to restaurants, nightlife, and shopping; but with four on-site restaurants, ranging from a deli to Italian seafood, you can even opt to stay in for dinner.

Outrigger Reef Tower Hotel. 227 Lewers St. (near Helumoa Rd.), Honolulu, HI 96815. ☎ **800/OUTRIGGER** or 808/924-8844. Fax 800/622-4852 or 808/924-6042. E-mail: reservations@outrigger.com. Web page: http://www.outrigger.com. 480 rms. A/C TV TEL. $85–$110 double; $95–$115 double with kitchenette; $130 studio with kitchenette (sleeps up to 4); $140 one-bedroom with kitchenette (sleeps up to 4). Seniors 50 and older get 20% off room rates, AARP members get 25% off. Ask about room-and-breakfast packages. Free rent-a-car when booking at rack rates. Children under 17 stay free with existing bedding. Extra person $15. AE, CB, DC, DISC, JCB, MC, V. Parking $8. TheBUS: 19 or 20.

This is a great deal for families: Four of you can easily stay here for $130 or $140, with the advantage of a kitchenette to help keep dining costs down. The Reef is one of Outrigger's larger hotels, consisting of two 13-story towers. The rooms—renovated in 1994 and '95—are larger than those at some nearby Outriggers, and come with a few more amenities than those in the chain's lower-priced hotels. The lanais, however, are very small. The kitchenettes come with microwave or stove/oven and fridge (toasters are available on request). The huge lobby is filled with shops, and four restaurants, ranging from Cajun to coffee shop, are on hand; you'll also find an activities desk and a cocktail lounge. The Polynesian Showroom features some of Hawaii's top entertainers. You can order room service from the Waikiki Broiler; baby-sitting is available if you want a night on the town. There's also an on-site pool.

✪ **Outrigger Royal Islander.** 2164 Kalia Rd. (at Saratoga Rd.), Honolulu, HI 96815. ☎ **800/OUTRIGGER** or 808/922-1961. Fax 800/622-4852 or 808/923-4632. Web page: http://www.outrigger.com. E-mail: reservations@outrigger.com. 101 rms (with showers only). A/C TV TEL. $75–$110 double; $155 ocean-view triple suite; $160 one-bedroom triple suite (3 people will feel cramped) with kitchenette. Extra person $15. AE, CB, DC, DISC, JCB, MC, V. Parking $8. TheBUS: 19 or 20.

This is about as close as you can get to the beach and still pay budget prices: The sand is just across the street and through the beach access walkway. The elegant lobby of this boutique hotel gives it the look of a luxury hotel. The rooms, renovated in 1992, are small—two people will be comfortable, a threesome will be really tight—but decorated in the same tasteful fashion that all Outriggers, from budget to expensive, are done in. You can request coffeemakers from housekeeping, or just bop down to the lobby in the morning, where coffee awaits. Since the Royal Islander is such a small hotel, it shares some services (such as a swimming pool and spill-over parking) with the beachfront Outrigger Reef across the street. Dozens of restaurants are within a 5-minute walk.

Outrigger Village. 240 Lewers St. (near Helumoa Rd.), Honolulu, HI 96815. ☎ **800/OUTRIGGER** or 808/923-3881. Fax 800/622-4852 or 808/922-2330. E-mail: reservations@outrigger.com. Web page: http://www.outrigger.com. 440 units (with showers only). A/C TV TEL. $85–$110 double; $95–$115 double with kitchenette; $130–$140 triple studio with kitchenette. Seniors 50 and older get 20% off room rates, AARP members get 25% off. Ask about room-and-breakfast packages. Free rent-a-car when booking at rack rates.

Children under 17 stay free with existing bedding. Extra person $15. AE, CB, DC, DISC, JCB, MC, V. Parking $8. TheBUS: 19 or 20.

Deep in the heart of Outrigger country, along a stretch of Lewers Street where Outrigger hotels dominate (the chain seems to own the street), one will find another recommendable one. The Outrigger Village is less than 2 blocks from the beach and in the midst of Waikiki's restaurant, shopping, and nightlife scene. All of the Outriggers are dependable, tastefully decorated, and offer good value. The Village is considered a moderate Outrigger hotel: the rooms are small but cozy. There are no in-room coffeemakers, but you can get your morning cup at the breakfast-only coffee shop. The pool sits in the middle of the open-air lobby, which makes for interesting people-watching as you work on your tan. Because the hotel rooms only sleep two, families of three might consider the studio kitchenettes, which come with a microwave and refrigerator. *Helpful hint:* If you prefer a king bed, request one when reserving your room, as the hotel has a limited number of them.

BUDGET

Aloha Punawai. 305 Saratoga Rd. (across from Ft. DeRussy and the Waikiki Post Office, between Kalia Rd. and Kalakaua Ave.), Honolulu, HI 96815. ☎/fax **808/923-5211.** 18 units (studios have showers only). TV. $52–$57 single studios without A/C; $60–$65 double without A/C; $57–$62 single studios with A/C; $65–$70 double with A/C; $62–$67 one-bedroom single, $70–$75 double (sleeps up to 4); $70–$75 large one-bedroom single, $78–$83 double (sleeps up to 5). Extra person $8. Children under 15 stay free. 3-night minimum; discounts for week-long (or longer) stays. No credit cards. Parking $5. TheBUS: 19 or 20.

Here's one of Waikiki's best-kept secrets: A low-profile, family-operated (since 1959) apartment hotel just 2 blocks from the beach and within walking distance of most Waikiki attractions. Aloha Punawai has the lowest prices in Waikiki, bar none (if you stay a week, prices drop even more). And the location is great, just across the street from Ft. DeRussy park and 2 blocks to Grey's Beach—the same great beach facing the luxury Halekulani and Sheraton Waikiki hotels. The apartments have a mishmash of furniture and come with complete kitchens, private bath, lanai, and TV. Towels and linen are provided, and a coin-operated washer and dryer are on the property. The phone wiring has been installed and is ready for service; you have to pay for hook-up.

Hale Pua Nui Hotel. 228 Beach Walk (across from Helumoa St.), Honolulu, HI 96815. ☎ **808/923-9693.** Fax 808/923-9678. E-mail: halepua@aloha.net. 22 units, with showers only. TV TEL. Low season $45 double; high season $57 double. 3-night minimum. MC, V. Parking $5. TheBUS: 19 or 20.

This four-story studio-apartment complex is a real find for budget travelers. Don't expect the luxury of the Halekulani—or even the modern look of a budget Outrigger. Built motel-style (with a series of doors down an outside hallway), Hale Pua Nui features clean, older units at 1970s prices. The large studios have seen better days—the furniture's worn and the carpet is showing its age—but the bargain prices make up for the lack of luxury. The one-room units have two single beds, a TV, a small table, a kitchenette (small refrigerator, oven, stove, and toaster), a phone, and a bath with shower only. The Beach Walk location puts you just 1 1/2 blocks from the beach, 1 1/2 blocks from a bus stop, and with walking distance of restaurants, nightclubs, and other Waikiki activities.

Malihini Hotel. 217 Saratoga Rd. (across from Ft. DeRussy, near Kalia Rd.), Honolulu, HI 96815. ☎ **808/923-9644.** 28 units (some with shower only). TV TEL. $45–$85 double. Extra person $2–$5. 3-night minimum Dec–Apr. No credit cards. Parking $7–$10. TheBUS: 19 or 20.

The promotional literature for this two-story hotel describes it as a "small, plain hotel with no extra frills, just a place to stay in an excellent location." That just about sums it up. The location is excellent: a half-block from the beach(!), with shopping and restaurants (including McDonald's) just around the corner. A solid lava wall blocks out the noise of busy Saratoga Road—as soon as you enter in the brick courtyard, with its red picnic tables and brick barbecue, the only sounds you'll hear are the chirps of the hotel's parakeets. Three types of units are available: compact studios, lanai studios, and one-bedroom apartments. The compact studios have either twin beds or a king, plus a shower and a kitchenette (small refrigerator, oven, four-burner stove, and toaster). The lanai studios are larger and have their own lanai or garden patio that allows cross-ventilation from the trade winds. The one-bedroom apartments, which can sleep up to five, have a separate bedroom, a full bath, additional twin beds in the living room, and a full kitchen. The decor isn't fancy—linoleum floors, well-used furniture, and just the basics. But hey, for $45 a night, you'll get more than get your money's worth here.

A HOTEL FOR THE MILITARY

Hale Koa Hotel. 2055 Kalia Rd. (across from Ft. DeRussy, between Dewey Way and Saratoga Rd.), Honolulu, HI 96815. ☎ **800/367-6027** or 808/955-0555. Fax 800/HALE-FAX. 814 rms. A/C TV TEL. $53–$78 standard double; $60–$87 moderate double; $66–$96 superior double; $70–$102 partial ocean-view double; $77–$112 ocean-view double; $83–$121 deluxe ocean-view double; $91–$132 oceanfront double; $97–$142 deluxe oceanfront double. Rates include continental breakfast and orientation the morning after check-in. Extra person $10; singles deduct $2 from double rate. AE, DC, DISC, MC, V. Parking $3. TheBUS: 19 or 20.

We wish we could stay here—but we're not allowed. This is a very exclusive hotel, for active-duty and retired military personnel and their families only. This is a first-class hotel, right on Waikiki Beach, with the grassy lawns of Fort DeRussy on the other side. The price structure, which depends on military rank (lower ranks get cheaper rates), is 50% to 75% less than what comparable Waikiki hotels charge. The facilities here include three swimming pools, 66 landscaped acres with picnic tables and barbecues, health club, Jacuzzi, sauna, jogging trails, four lighted tennis courts, racquetball courts, volleyball courts, four restaurants, and the lounges. The only drawback is that the hotel is always booked; some guests reserve up to a year in advance.

MID-WAIKIKI, MAUKA

These mid-Waikiki hotels, on the mountain side of Kalakaua Avenue, are a little farther away from the beach than those listed above. They're all between Kalakaua Avenue and Ala Wai Boulevard, and between Kalaimoku Street in the Ewa direction and Kaiulani Street in the Diamond Head direction.

EXPENSIVE

Sheraton Princess Kaiulani Hotel. 120 Kaiulani Ave. (at Kalakaua Ave., across the street from the Sheraton Moana Surfrider), Honolulu, HI 96815. ☎ **800/325-3535** or 808/922-5811. Fax 808/923-9912. 1,150 rms. A/C TV TEL. $180–$280 double; $485–up suites. Extra person $40. Children under 18 free in parents' room with existing bedding. Inquire about Sheraton's "Sure Saver" rates, available at different times of the year, which could mean as much as 32% in savings. AE, CB, DC, JCB, MC, V. Parking $8. TheBUS: 19 or 20.

Portraits of the hotel's namesake, Princess Kaiulani, heir to the throne who died in 1899 at the age of 24, fill the large open-air lobby. Her regal, youthful face looks out on the site that was once her royal estate. A huge swimming pool sits behind a row of restaurants and shops facing Kalakaua Avenue. The open-air lobby connects the three buildings of the Princess Kaiulani: the 11-story original hotel that opened in 1955, and the 11-story Kaiulani wing and the 29-story Ainahau Tower that both opened in 1960.

The rooms have been recently renovated and double insulated doors with sound-proofing has been added. We wish every hotel in noisy Waikiki had this feature—the rooms really are soundproof. You can't hear the constant noise on Kaulakaua Avenue, the blaring of sirens, or the sound of garbage cans being emptied at 3am. Other amenities include lanais, coffeemakers, safes, refrigerators, hair dryers, and irons and ironing boards.

Dining/Entertainment: Pikake Terrace offers casual dining in a poolside garden; Lotus Moon features Mandarin cuisine from Northern China; Momoyama specializes in Japanese dishes; and Minute Chef is an international food court with everything from burgers to stir-fry. The Polynesian Revue features nightly shows on the dances, songs, culture, and drama of Polynesia.

Services: Multilingual staff and Keiki Aloha Club, a free kids' program available daily.

Facilities: Pool, shops, and restaurants.

Waikiki Beachcomber. 2300 Kalakaua Ave. (at Duke's Lane), Honolulu, HI 96815. ☎ **800/ 622-4646** or 808/922-4646. Fax 808/923-4889. E-mail: beach@dps.net. 500 rms. A/C TV TEL. Low season $150–$195 double room; $285 double suite. High season $160–$205 double room; $295 double suite. Room/car packages from $119.95. Extra person $18. 2-night minimum for packages. AE, DC, JCB, MC, V. Parking $6. TheBUS: 19 or 20.

The room/car package makes this stylish Waikiki hotel a real deal. One of its main plusses is the great location: 1 block from Waikiki Beach, just across the street from the upscale Royal Hawaiian Shopping Center, and next door to bargain shopping at the International Market Place. All 500 rooms were upgraded in 1996 with Berber carpets, new beds, TV armoires, contemporary furniture, handheld showers, convenient hot pots for making coffee or tea, and a state-of-the-art voice messaging system.

The Beachcomber is Waikiki's only hotel with its own rooftop vegetable farm—yes, a farm in Waikiki. This urban hydroponic project has been so successful that it's now a two-level, 3,000-square-foot garden growing a variety of lettuces, gourmet cucumbers, cherry tomatoes, and a host of herbs. Want to sample the goods? The hotel's Hibiscus Cafe features the hydroponic produce.

Yet another reason to stay at this conveniently located hotel: It's the home of the legendary Don "Tiny Bubbles" Ho Show.

✪ Waikiki Joy. 320 Lewers St. (at Kuhio Ave.), Honolulu, HI 96815. ☎ **800/92-ASTON** or 808/923-2300. Fax 808/924-4010 or 808/922-8785. 242 rms. A/C TV TEL. $155–$190 double; $175–$190 club suite; $210–$220 junior suite with kitchen for up to 4 people; $240–$260 one-bedroom executive suite with kitchen for up to 3 people. Rates include continental breakfast. Extra person $18. Ask about the "Mix 7" rates, where you stay 7 or more consecutive nights with Aston and get 20%–30% off rates. AE, CB, DC, JCB, MC, V. Parking $10. TheBUS: 19 or 20.

This is one hotel that truly deserves its name. An oasis right in the heart of busy Waikiki, this hidden jewel offers not only outstanding personal service but also a Bose entertainment system and a Jacuzzi in every room! The Italian marble–accented open-air lobby and the tropical veranda, with swimming pool, sauna, and furnished deck, set the scene for the beautifully decorated guest rooms. The doubles, decorated in soft pastels, have a marble entry, a refrigerator, a safe, and a lanai wide enough for you to sit and enjoy the views. The suites are even more luxurious: Club suites have either a king-size bed or two doubles, a refrigerator, microwave, coffeemaker, and wet bar. Executive suites have two double beds and a kitchen with a microwave and full refrigerator; the executive king suites add a separate living room and bedroom. Every room comes with voice mail, as well as fax and modem hookups. The beach is about 4 or 5 blocks away, a 10 to 15 minute walk. There is a sandwich/coffee shop,

Cappuccino's, but the food is nothing to brag about, plus they allow smoking in the tiny restaurant creating a very unappetizing atmosphere.

MODERATE

Aston Island Colony. 445 Seaside Ave. (at Ala Wai Blvd.), Honolulu, HI 96815. ☎ **800/ 92-ASTON** or 808/923-2345. Fax 808/921-7105 or 808/922-8785. 347 rms. A/C TV TEL. $95–$130 double; $105–$140 studio with kitchenette; $155–$200 one-bedroom suite with kitchen. Extra person $18. Ask about the "Mix 7" rates, where you stay 7 or more consecutive nights with Aston and get 20%–30% off rates. AE, CB, DC, DISC, JCB, MC, V. Parking $8. TheBUS: 19 or 20.

This elegant hotel combines the spaciousness of a condominium property with the amenities of a hotel. All of the units have refrigerators, coffeemakers, private lanais, daily maid service, and can sleep up to four. The studio units have kitchenettes, and the one bedrooms, which can sleep up to five, have full kitchens. And the views are spectacular: either the jagged mountains and lush valleys, well-known Diamond Head, or the shimmering Pacific Ocean. The only caveat is the minuscule bathrooms: Our bathroom was so small that the door didn't clear the toilet; it doesn't sound like a big deal, but it was annoying to have to maneuver around a tiny bathroom with a door that only opened partway. The tub/shower combo was also cramped. The hotel has a pool, sundeck, restaurant, jet spa, and sauna. Access via car (always tricky on Waikiki's one-way streets) is very convenient from Ala Wai Boulevard.

✪ **Royal Kuhio.** 2240 Kuhio Ave. (between Royal Hawaiian Ave. and Seaside Ave.), ℅ Paradise Mgmt., 50 S. Beretania St., Suite C207, Honolulu, HI 96813. ☎ **800/367-5205** or 808/ 538-7145. Fax 808/533-4621. 389 units. A/C TV TEL. $95–$120 apt for 4. Extra person $15. MC, V. Free parking. TheBUS: 19 or 20.

Families take note: This is one of the best deals in Waikiki. All of the units in this high-rise condo are privately owned, and some are owner-occupied. Paradise Management is just one of several companies handling apartments here, but their units— and their rates—are among the best. All have full kitchens, separate bedrooms, living area with TV and phones, and lanai. Since each unit is individually owned, they're all decorated and furnished differently. The complex has a pool, exercise room, sauna, self-service laundromat, sundeck, volleyball, billiards, basketball court, shuffleboard, and putting green. It's 2 blocks to Waikiki Beach, and everything else Waikiki has to offer is within walking distance. *Hot tips:* Ask for a corner unit (they're the nicest); and if you plan to go in February, be sure to book a year in advance (it's the condo's busiest month).

INEXPENSIVE

✪ **Coconut Plaza.** 450 Lewers St. (at Ala Wai Blvd.), Honolulu, HI 96815. ☎ **800/882-9696** or 808/923-8828. Fax 808/923-3473. 80 rms. A/C TV TEL. $87–$97 double; $97–$125 double with kitchenette; $155 suite with kitchenette. Rates include continental breakfast. Extra person $12. AE, JCB, MC, V. Parking $7. TheBUS: 19 or 20.

This small hotel is an island of integrity in a sea of tourist schlock. Calling itself a "studio apartment boutique hotel," Coconut Plaza offers a few perks that are rare in Waikiki: complimentary continental breakfast, and the kind of personalized service that only a small hotel can offer. The recently renovated hotel has a tropical plantation feel, with big, airy rooms, terra-cotta tile, and lots of greenery. The island-style rooms have been recently redecorated in rattan and earth tones; all have a private lanai, TV, ceramic-tile bath, and daily maid service. The majority of the rooms have kitchenettes—with minifridge, microwave, countertop range, coffeemaker, and a complete set of cooking utensils—and most have views of the Ala Wai Canal and the mountains. There's an outdoor pool, a sundeck, exercise equipment, and a tour desk on the property; Ala Wai Golf Course is just across the canal, and the beach is 4 blocks away.

Holiday Surf Apartments. 2303 Ala Wai Blvd. (at Nohonani St.), Honolulu, HI 96815. ☎ **808/923-8488.** Fax 808/923-1475. 34 rms. A/C TV TEL. $75–$95 studio double; $85–$105 one-bedroom double (Frommer's readers are entitled to a 20% discount). Extra person $3. CB, DC, DISC, MC, V. Parking $4 (complimentary for Frommer's readers). TheBUS: 19 or 20.

This family-operated business has been catering to budget travelers for decades by offering nothing more than good value: clean, comfortable, inexpensive accommodations. All the rooms in this six-story building have complete kitchens, air-conditioning, TV with cable, phones, and small lanais. The studios comfortably accommodate two people, the one-bedrooms have a separate bedroom and can sleep up to five. All the units have views of the mountains, Ala Wai Canal, and the Ala Wai Golf course. Vending machines, laundry facilities, and covered parking are on the property. Here's a tip for getting even more bang for the buck: If you book six days between April 1 and December 15, you get the seventh night free.

Ilima Hotel. 445 Nohonani St. (at Ala Wai Blvd.), Honolulu, HI 96815. ☎ **800/801-9366** or 808/923-1877. Fax 808/924-8371. E-mail: mail@ilima.com. Web page: http://www.pete.com/ilima. 99 units. A/C TV TEL. $86–$127 double; $132–$166 one-bedroom (sleeps up to 3); $175–$229 two-bedroom for 4; $267–$279 three-bedroom for 6. Extra person $8. Discounted rates available for seniors. AE, CB, DC, DISC, JCB, MC, V. Limited free parking, or $8 parking across the street. TheBUS: 19 or 20.

The Teruya Brothers, owners of Hawaii's Times Supermarket, wanted to offer comfortable accommodations that Hawaii residents could afford, and they've succeeded with the Ilima. One of Hawaii's small, well-located condo-style hotels, the 17-story pale pink Ilima (named for the native orange flower used in royal leis) offers value for your money: Rooms are huge, the location (2 blocks to Waikiki Beach, near the International Marketplace and the Royal Hawaiian Shopping Center) is great, and prices are low. A tasteful koa-wood lobby lined with works by Hawaiian artists greets you upon arrival. There's a 24-hour front desk, daily maid service, free local phone calls (a nice plus), and a full kitchen in every unit; all the couches fold out into beds, making this a particularly good deal for families. Some of the beds are waveless water beds. There's a heated pool, three sundecks, a dry sauna, and an Italian restaurant on-site. Sorry, there's no ocean view—what you get is great value instead.

Outrigger Surf. 2280 Kuhio Ave. (at Nohonani St.), Honolulu, HI 96815. ☎ **800/ OUTRIGGER** or 808/922-5777. Fax 800/622-4852 or 808/921-3677. E-mail: reservations@outrigger.com. Web page: http://www.outrigger.com. 251 rms (with showers only). A/C TV TEL. $78–$98 double with kitchenette; $125 triple studio with kitchenette. Extra person $15. AE, CB, DC, DISC, JCB, MC, V. Parking $8. TheBUS: 19 or 20.

The Outrigger chain makes sure that it has a hotel to suit every budget and every need; this one has kitchenettes—with a two-burner stove, oven, refrigerator, coffeemaker, and cooking utensils—in every room. The guest rooms, pool deck, and lobby went through extensive renovations in 1995, and the rooms were outfitted with new bedspreads, chairs, lamp shades, refurbished furniture, new TVs, and new fridges. The Surf is centrally located, across the street from the Kuhio Mall and 2 blocks from the beach; restaurants and nightlife are also within walking distance, and there's an activity desk on-site.

Outrigger West. 2330 Kuhio Ave. (between Nahua and Walina sts.), Honolulu, HI 96815. ☎ **800/OUTRIGGER** or 808/922-5022. Fax 800/622-4852 or 808/924-6414. E-mail: reservations@outrigger.com. Web page: http://www.outrigger.com. 663 rms (with shower only). A/C TV TEL. $85–$110 double; $95–$115 double with kitchenette; $145 one-bedroom with kitchenette; $250 two-bedroom with kitchenette (sleeps up to 6). Extra person $15. AE, CB, DC, DISC, JCB, MC, V. Parking $8. TheBUS: 19 or 20.

On the upside, this Outrigger hotel has lots of guest services and facilities, including lounge, pool, laundry, kitchenettes, room service, lots of shops (including a pharmacy), and two restaurants (a deli and a Mexican restaurant). The downside is that it's located on a very busy and very noisy part of Kuhio Avenue. The rooms (redone in 1995 in beige and pale blue) all have refrigerators and coffeemakers; the units with kitchenettes also have a two-burner stove/oven and cooking utensils. Waikiki Beach is 2 blocks away, and restaurants, shopping, and nightlife are all within a 5- to 10-minute walk.

Marine Surf. 364 Seaside Ave. (at Kuhio Ave.), Honolulu, HI 96815. ☎ **888/456-SURF** or 808/923-0277. Fax 808/926-5915. 110 units. A/C TV TEL. $80–$103 double; $150–$175 one-bedroom penthouse suite double. Extra person $10. CB, DC, DISC, MC, V. Parking $5. TheBUS: 19 or 20.

Located in the heart of Waikiki, this high-rise is part privately owned condo units and part spacious studio apartments—only the studios are available for rent. Each one has a complete kitchen (refrigerator, stove/oven, toaster, coffeepot, and utensils), phone, two extralong double beds, TV, and a small lanai. The price difference depends on the view. *Hot tip:* The best views are from floors 17 to 22 ($90 in the summer and fall, $95 midsummer and $103 in the winter). Located just a half-block from Kuhio Mall and the International Market Place, the hotel is just about 1¹/₂ blocks from the beach. Facilities include tour desk, pool, coin-operated laundry on every floor, and an Italian restaurant in the lobby.

A Gay-Friendly Hotel

Hotel Honolulu. 376 Kaiolu St. (near Kuhio Ave., across from the metered parking lot), Honolulu, HI 96815. ☎ **800/426-2776** or 808/926-2766. Fax 808/922-3326. E-mail: hotelhnl@lava.net. Web page: http://www.lava.net/~hotelhnl/. 24 units (with shower only). Low season $69–$115 double. High season $79–$119 double. Extra person $10. 4-night minimum during Christmas season. AE, CB, DC, DISC, JCB, MC, V. Parking $5. TheBUS: 19 or 20.

This old 1940s low-rise apartment complex was renovated into a hotel in 1983—and it has truly become an "oasis in time." The three-story building is a tribute to the Art Deco age, but outfitted with the modern conveniences. You enter through an atrium with carefully tended tropical plants, including a beautiful orchid collection, and singing birds. The hotel offers two types of accommodations in the main building: deluxe studios (with sitting area and queen bed) and one-bedroom suites (with living room including a sofa sleeper). All rooms have kitchenettes, phones, air-conditioning, and lanais. Each suite is designed in a different theme: safari, Art Deco, bamboo, Rangoon, Hollywood, samurai, Norma Jean, and so on. Even if you don't stay here, come by for a tour of these uniquely decorated rooms.

The Bamboo Lanai building is a two-story wing for budget-minded travelers: standard studios with a queen bed, small kitchenettes (with stove and refrigerator), air-conditioning, and lanai. *A strong warning:* There is a nightclub behind these rooms—and a hot nightclub indeed, with loud music until 1:30am.

Although the hotel caters to gay men and women, everyone is welcome to enjoy the accommodations here. On-site amenities include complimentary coffee in the lobby all day, complimentary use of beach mats and towels, and use of the rooftop garden sundeck, which is great for working on your tan or for an evening barbecue and cocktails. From the hotel, it's about a 7-minute walk to the beach and about 2 minutes to Honolulu's top gay clubs. Hotel Honolulu also offers airport pick-up for $25 round-trip.

BUDGET

⊙ **Patrick Winston's Waikiki Condos** (formerly Patrick Winston's Hawaiian King Rentals). 417 Nohonani St. (between Kuhio Ave. and Ala Wai Blvd.), Honolulu, HI 96815. ☎ **800/545-1948** or 808/924-3332. Fax 808/924-3332. E-mail: hawnking@jav.com. 11 one-bedroom apts (with shower only). A/C TV TEL. Low season, $65–$99 double. High season, $79–$119 double. Extra person $10. 4-night minimum. AE, DC, DISC, MC, V. Parking $7. TheBUS: 19 or 20.

For a luxurious experience with a hefty dose of old-fashioned aloha, we recommend Patrick Winston's rentals. When this five-story condominium hotel was built in 1981, Winston bought one unit; he has since acquired 10 more, spent some $200,000 on refurbishment, and put his elegant suites on the market at budget prices. Located on a quiet side street, Winston's units are actually a hotel within a hotel: He owns, runs, cleans, renovates, and services all of his units himself—and he makes sure no guest leaves unhappy. Staying here is like having a personal concierge; Patrick will even give you a wake-up call. He wants to make sure that his guests enjoy Hawaii, and he's got lots of terrific tips on where to eat, where to shop, and how to get the most for your money.

Three types of units are available: one-bedroom suites, junior business suites (these are on the ground floor), and corporate business suites. All have sofa beds, separate bedrooms, lanais with breakfast table and chairs, air-conditioning and ceiling fans, TV (VCRs available on request), phone, and full kitchens; most have a washer and dryer. All are individually decorated, from the Blue Hawaiian suite (done in all blues) to the Mount Fuji suite (done in Asian style). There's an on-site cocktail lounge and a tropical courtyard with a pool. Waikiki Beach is just 2 blocks away, shopping is just a half-block away, and restaurants are within a 5- to 10-minute walk.

Warning: make sure that you ask for Patrick Winston's units or the front desk at the Hawaiian King Hotel may put you in their unit, which may not be quite as elegant (or as cheap) at Patrick's units.

WAIKIKI: DIAMOND HEAD END

You'll find all of these hotels between Ala Wai Boulevard and the ocean, and between Kaiulani Street (1 block Diamond Head from the International Marketplace) in the Ewa direction and the world-famous Diamond Head itself.

VERY EXPENSIVE

Hyatt Regency Waikiki. 2424 Kalakaua Ave. (at Kaiulani St., across the street from the beach), Honolulu, HI 96815. ☎ **800/233-1234** or 808/923-1234. Fax 808/923-7839. 1,230 rms, 11 suites. A/C MINIBAR TV TEL. $215–$375 double; $375 Regency Club; $450 Regency Club ocean; $550–$700 suite; $1,100–$1,500 penthouse; $1,700–$3,000 Ambassador or Presidential two-bedroom suite. Extra person $25 rm, $45 Regency Club. Children under 19 free in parents' room with existing bedding. AE, CB, DC, DISC, JCB, MC, V. Valet parking $10; self-parking $8. TheBUS: 19 or 20.

This is one of Waikiki's biggest hotels, a $100-million project, covering nearly a block and sporting two 40-story towers, it sits just across the street from the Diamond Head end of Waikiki Beach. The lobby, located above the ground-level shops, is up the escalator on the second floor. It's huge, decorated in koa and wrapped around an atrium that rises from the ground level to the top of the 40 floors. The registration desk is on the ocean side of the building with floor-to-ceiling windows taking in the ocean view and jungle plants; a few brilliantly colored parrots add to the decor. You will either love or hate these parrots as you wait in the sometimes-long lines to register. The sound of their constant squawking echoing off the 40-story towers gave us a headache, especially when mixed with the cigarette smoking of other guests in the line.

A $10-million investment in 1996 refurbished all the rooms with new curtains, drapes, carpets, and bedspreads. Every room has a coffeemaker; however, the coffee is not free—even though you are paying a minimum of $215 a night—the Hyatt charges $3 per package of coffee. Other amenities such as hair dryers, bathrobes, irons and ironing boards are complimentary. The deluxe ocean-view rooms overlooking Waikiki Beach are fabulous, but can be noisy (traffic on Kalakaua is constant). For a few dollars more, well, actually for more than a few dollars, you can upgrade to the Regency Club floors, the rooms are nicer (and the coffee is free). The club entitles you to an expedited check-in at a special desk (bypassing the song of the parrots and the secondary cigarette smoke), and entry to the Regency Club, which serves complimentary continental breakfast in the morning, pupus in the afternoon, and concierge service all day. Regency Club members also have access to the private rooftop sundeck and Jacuzzi. World-famous Waikiki is directly across the street, but guests can also swim and sun at the third-floor pool and enjoy poolside drinks at the Elegant Dive Bar.

Dining/Entertainment: The hotel has four restaurants and five cocktail lounges, including the Terrace Grille, an indoor-outdoor restaurant overlooking the ocean, serving breakfast and lunch; Musashi, a Japanese restaurant, serving Japanese breakfast and Teppanyaki or Teishoku dinners along with a sushi bar; Harry's Bar, located in the atrium and featuring Hawaiian and Polynesian entertainment; Ciao Mein for creative Chinese and Italian cuisine served family-style; and the Colony Seafood and Steak House for steaks, fresh seafood, salad, and dessert bars. Texas Rock 'N Roll Sushi Bar is Hyatt's latest addition, a combination of country-western and rock-and-roll music with Tex cuisine and sushi.

Services: Concierge, business services (including typing, personal computer rental, stock news, notary public), Camp Hyatt for kids, room service, daily maid service.

Facilities: Beach across the street, swimming pool, and shops.

EXPENSIVE

Aston at the Waikiki Banyan. 201 Ohua Ave. (on the mauka and Diamond Head side of Ohua Ave. at Kuhio Ave.), Honolulu, HI 96815. ☎ **808/922-0555,** or 800/922-7866 from the U.S. mainland and Canada. Fax 808/922-8785. 307 one-bedroom apts. A/C TV TEL. $155–$215 one-bedroom. Seniors 50 and older get 25% off regular rates, and the 7th night free, depending on availability. Extra person $18. Ask about the "Mix 7" rates, where you stay 7 or more consecutive nights with Aston and get 20%–30% off rates. AE, CB, DC, DISC, JCB, MC, V. Parking $5. TheBUS: 19 or 20.

Your first introduction to this two-tower, 38-story condominium complex is through the open-air lobby with impressive lacquer wall artwork, which was hand-carved and hand-painted in Hong Kong. All of the units in this condominium are one-bedrooms and offer the homey comforts of a condominium apartment combined with the attentions of a hotel—daily maid service, bell service, front desk, and much more, including an enormous sixth-floor recreation deck complete with pool, tennis court, sauna, barbecue areas, snack bar, and a children's play area—a great boon for families.

The units have full kitchens (refrigerator, stove with oven, microwave, rice cooker, toaster, coffeemaker and utensils), a comfortably furnished living room (with sofa bed), large lanai, and separate bedroom with two double beds or a king bed. The bedroom is separated from the living room by sliding doors, which can be opened up to make the apartment one big unit. The unit we stayed in had an old-fashioned air conditioner in the wall, but it did the job and we could control the temperature. The units open out to a fairly good-sized lanai with chairs and a small table. There is a partial ocean view, with some buildings blocking the way.

Dining: Snack bar on sixth floor.
Services: Daily maid service, activities desk, fax services, and sundry store.
Facilities: Pool, sauna, tennis, barbecue, and children's play area.

✪ **Aston Waikiki Beachside Hotel.** 2452 Kalakaua Ave. (mauka side of street between Uluniu and Liliuokalani aves.), Honolulu, HI 96815. ☎ **800/922-7866** or 808/931-2100. Fax 808/922-2129. 79 rms. A/C TV TEL. $180 standard rm; $195 superior rm; $259 partial ocean view; $280–$310 oceanfront; $295–$375 junior suites. Rates include continental breakfast. Maximum occupancy 2 adults per room. Seniors 50 and older get 25% off rates and 7th night free, depending on availability. Ask about the "Mix 7" rates, where you stay 7 or more consecutive nights with Aston and get 20%–30% off rates. AE, CB, DC, DISC, JCB, MC, V. Parking $10 at nearby hotel. TheBUS: 19 or 20.

This is an intimate luxury boutique hotel right across the street from Waikiki Beach. You step off busy Kalakaua Avenue into a marble-filled lobby with classical music wafting in the background, sprays of flowers everywhere, and a soothing Italian fountain. There is a feeling of elegance and charm throughout the hotel. The staff is attentive to every detail. The rooms are tiny, but tastefully decorated with works of art and antiques (including hand-painted Oriental screens and 18th-century furniture). Each room has its own air-conditioning system, refrigerator, complimentary safe, complimentary daily newspaper, and two phones.

There is no restaurant on the property but a complimentary continental breakfast is served daily in the lobby. On Saturday and Sunday a high tea service, on antique china, is presented in the lobby and courtyard in the afternoons.

Services: Concierge service, twice-daily maid service, morning newspaper, and same-day laundry and dry cleaning.

Colony Surf. 2885 Kalakaua Ave. (on the ocean side of the street between the Waikiki Aquarium and Outrigger Canoe Club, across the street from Kapiolani Park), Honolulu, HI 96815. ☎ **888/924-SURF** or 808/924-3111. Fax 808/923-2249. 75 rms. A/C TV TEL. West Building with full kitchens, $175–$240 studio, $285–$425 ocean-view studio; East Building, $225–$275 rm. MC, V. Free parking. TheBUS: 19 or 20.

As we went to press several rooms in the Colony Surf, an elegant condominium fronting its own white-sand beach in the quieter Diamond Head section of town, and the entire building next door, had been sold and both buildings were undergoing extensive renovations. Scheduled to reopen in Fall 1997, the Colony Surf was getting a complete makeover from its 1960s decor.

The West Building is the Colony Surf condominium, where rental units are mixed with full-time residential studio apartments. The units are all large (1,000 square feet): Studios come complete with a kitchen at one end (with 1990s appliances), two double beds or one giant king bed, and views of Waikiki or Diamond Head that are worth every penny of the cost. The bathrooms are large with showers, no tubs. The East Building is back off the beach with rooms of about 500 square feet and views of Diamond Head. Each room has a small refrigerator, coffeemaker, hair dryer, and safe. The bathrooms have showers only, no tubs. Both buildings have access to the small private sandy beach in front of the Colony Surf (great swimming here). Complimentary beach chairs and towels are provided.

If you are craving peace and quiet, away from the crowds of Waikiki, but close enough (about a 10-minute walk) to enjoy the shops and restaurants, this is a perfect location. The surrounding buildings are mainly residential condominiums: Kapiolani Park is across the street, and the Waikiki Aquarium is just a few steps away.

Dining/Entertainment: Michel's is an award-winning, seaside French/European restaurant in the West building.
Services: Free local calls.

Pacific Beach Hotel. 2490 Kalakaua Ave. (at Liliuokalani St., across the street from the beach), Honolulu, HI 96815. ☎ **800/367-6060** or 808/922-1233. Fax 808/922-8061. 830 rms. A/C TV TEL. $160–$260 double rm; $450–$700 suite. Extra person $25. Children under 18 free with existing bedding. AE, CB, DC, DISC, JCB, MC, V. Parking $7. TheBUS: 19 or 20.

The Pacific Beach has a unique feature, unmatched by any hotel in Hawaii: a three-story, 280,000-gallon indoor oceanarium. Some 52-feet long and 32-feet wide this oversized aquarium is the focal point of the hotel. Viewed from the lobby and several restaurants, this is something you definitely should stop by and see, even if you don't stay here (there are fish feedings six times a day for the more than 70 different species ranging from the 2-inch cleaner wrasse to the 4-foot Hawaiian stingray).

The hotel consists of two towers, the Beach Tower, built in 1969 and the Oceanarium Tower, built in 1979. The front desk to this complex is located off the entrance on Liliuokalani Street, right by the giant oceanarium. Every room has a lanai, full bath with tub and shower, refrigerator, and coffeemaker. No-smoking rooms are available. You can get a room with a city, mountain, or ocean view. The ocean-view rooms increase in price with each floor. The deluxe ocean-view rooms begin on the 10th floor and above (worth the extra money for the panoramic views).

Dining/Entertainment: The hotel has three restaurants and lounges: the Oceanarium Restaurant for casual, family dining; Neptune, for continental fare; and Shogun, a Japanese steak and seafood restaurant with sushi bar.

Services: Room service.

Facilities: Two professionally designed tennis courts, swimming pool, 24-hour health club, whirlpool spa, 17 shops.

MODERATE

✪ **Diamond Head Bed & Breakfast.** Noela Dr. (at Paki Ave., off Diamond Head Rd.), Honolulu. Reservations ℅ Hawaii's Best Bed & Breakfasts, P.O. Box 563, Kamuela, HI 96743. ☎ **800/262-9912** or 808/885-4550. Fax 808/885-0559. E-mail: bestbnb@aloha.net. 2 rms, 1 cottage. TV TEL. $100 double rm; $125 cottage (all units include large breakfast). Extra person $25. 2-night minimum. DISC. Free parking. TheBUS: 2.

Hostess Joanne and her longtime family housekeeper Sumiko offer a quiet, relaxing place to stay on the far side of Kapiolani Park, away from the hustle and bustle of Waikiki. Staying here is like venturing back in time to about 50 years ago, when *kamaaina* (native-born) families built huge houses with airy rooms opening outward, via sliding wooden-screen doors, to big lanais and tropical gardens. The house is filled with family heirlooms and Joanne's artwork. One room features the beyond king-size bed that once belonged to Princess Ruth, a member of the royal family; you'll feel like royalty sleeping in this giant carved koa bed. Other conveniences in the large room include a refrigerator, a TV, and a bathroom (big enough to dance in) with an old-fashioned tub. Off the bedroom you'll find a large lanai facing the greenery of Diamond Head. The other room in the house has two double koa beds, a lanai overlooking Waikiki through sweet-smelling plumeria trees, a TV, refrigerator, and another large bathroom. A separate building houses antique-filled Grandpa's Apartment, featuring a separate bedroom, a TV, phone, refrigerator, and a view of Diamond Head from the bed. Sumiko, who speaks fluent Japanese, whips up a hearty breakfast, which may include fish if they're biting.

✪ **The New Otani Kaimana Beach Hotel.** 2863 Kalakaua Ave. (ocean side of the street, Diamond Head side of the Waikiki Aquarium and the old Natatorium War Memorial, across the street from Kapiolani Park), Honolulu, HI 96815. ☎ **800/35-OTANI** or 808/923-1555. Fax 808/922-9404. E-mail: kaimana@pixi.net. Web page: http://www.kaimana.com/. 94 rms, 30 suites. A/C MINIBAR TV TEL. $110–$250 double; $170–$220 junior suite; $280–$600 suite. Diamond Head Wing: $150 park-view studio; $200 one-bedroom. $10 higher in all categories

Dec 20–Mar 31. Extra person $15. AE, CB, DC, DISC, JCB, MC, V. Parking $6. TheBUS: 19 or 20.

This is one of Waikiki's best-kept secrets: a boutique hotel just outside of Waikiki nestled right on the beach, at the foot of Diamond Head, with Kapiolani Park just across the street. The airy lobby opens to the open-air Hau Tree Lanai restaurant, under the same banyan tree that sheltered Robert Louis Stevenson a century ago. Stevenson's description of the beach fronting the hotel, Sans Souci, holds true today: "If anyone desires lovely scenery, pure air, clear sea water, good food and heavenly sunsets, I recommend him cordially to the Sans Souci."

The hotel has two buildings: on the Waikiki side the rooms open to an atrium courtyard and on the Diamond Head side they feature kitchenettes. The rooms are compact, but tastefully decorated in pale pastels and open out to large lanais with ocean, park, or Diamond Head views. Since the hotel overlooks Kapiolani Park, guests have easy access to such activities as golf, tennis, kite flying, jogging, and bicycling. Kayaking and snorkeling are available at the beach. The hotel also arranges for visitors to climb to the top of Diamond Head Crater and welcomes them to the Diamond Head Climbers' Hui when they've completed their hike.

Dining/Entertainment: The Hau Tree Lanai is a delightful beachfront restaurant, one of the most romantic spots in Hawaii (see the restaurant's listing in chapter 7). Miyako Restaurant offers gourmet Japanese dining with an ocean view. The beachfront ✪ **Sunset Lanai Lounge** is great for cocktails.

✪ **Prince Kuhio, A Royal Outrigger Hotel.** 2500 Kuhio Ave. (on the Diamond Head, mauka side of Kuhio at Liliuokalani Ave.), Honolulu, HI 96815. ☎ **800/OUTRIGGER** or 808/922-0811. Fax 800/622-4852. E-mail: reservations@outrigger.com. Web page: http://www.outrigger.com/. 625 rms. A/C MINIBAR TV TEL. $125–$180 double; $165–$205 Voyager Club; $350–$580 Voyager Club suite. Extra person $25. Children under 18 free in parents' room with existing bedding. Seniors 50 and older get 20% off and members of AARP get 25% off. Free rent-a-car when booking at rack rates. Maximum of 4 persons per room. AE, CB, DC, DISC, JCB, MC, V. Parking $8. TheBUS: 19 or 20.

The Prince Kuhio is one of the best hotels in the Outrigger chain, which is famous for providing comfortable accommodations at reasonable prices. The second-floor lobby, with its marble floors, chandelier, handwoven rugs, and artful decor, offers a hint of what to expect from your accommodations. Completely renovated in 1997, the 37-story Prince Kuhio is in the center of the Waikiki shopping scene, and only a few blocks from Waikiki Beach and the Honolulu Zoo.

Two levels of rooms are offered: The regular guest rooms with a king or two double beds, refrigerators, black-out drapes, coffeemaker, and lanais; and the rooms on the Voyagers Club floors (the top four floors), where guests find views to die for, and have use of a private lounge that serves continental breakfast and complimentary pupus in the evening. Guests staying on the Voyagers Club floors also have complimentary privileges at the Outrigger Beach Club & Fitness Center. Eight floors in the complex are designated as no-smoking, and 24 rooms are available for the disabled. Guests with children may or may not be happy to learn that all the rooms come equipped with Nintendo.

Dining/Entertainment: The complex has two restaurants, a snack bar, and two bars. Restaurants include Trellisses, set in a casual garden atmosphere serving breakfast, lunch, and dinner; and Shanghai Garden Chinese Seafood Restaurant. Snacks are available at the cocktail bar near the pool area. Cupid's Lobby Bar has Hawaiian entertainment every night.

Services: Room service 6am to 10pm, business center, coin-operated laundry facilities, nightly turndown service, complimentary in-room coffee, and hospitality room for late check-outs.

Facilities: Heated pool, voice mail in English, Japanese, Korean, and German, shops, and vending machines.

Queen Kapiolani Hotel. 150 Kapahulu Ave. (at Cartwright St., across from Kapiolani Park), Honolulu, HI 96815. ☎ **800/367-5004** or 808/922-1941. Fax 800/477-2329 or 808/ 922-2694. 315 rms. A/C TV TEL. $104–$151 double; $151–$167 studio with kitchenette; $239–$372 one-bedroom suite with kitchenette (sleeps up to 4). Extra person $17. AE, CB, DC, DISC, JCB, MC, V. Parking $7. TheBUS: 19 or 20.

Named for Queen Kapiolani (1834–1899), the wife of Hawaii's last king, David Kalakaua (1836–1891), this hotel harkens back to the days of the Hawaiian monarchs. The 19th-century flavor of the hotel reflects those grand days with 10-foot chandeliers in the main dining room and a full-size portrait of the queen in the lobby. The plush decor, however, doesn't extend up to the budget rooms, which are quite small. You'll have a view of the shoreline through louvered windows, a small refrigerator, coffeemaker, phone, and TV. The location is great: Just across the street from Kapiolani Park (which King Kalakaua gave to the people of Hawaii in 1877 and named after his beloved wife), a half-block to the beach, and within walking distance of the Honolulu Zoo, the Waikik Aquarium, and the activities of Waikiki. A large swimming pool and sundeck are on the third floor.

Waikiki Resort Hotel. 2460 Koa Ave. (on the mauka, Ewa side of Koa Ave., at Liliuokalani Ave.), Honolulu, HI 96815. ☎ **800/367-5116** or 808/922-4911. Fax 808/922-9468. 291 rms, 5 suites. A/C TV TEL. $105–$145 double; $145–$155 kitchenette; $315–$470 penthouse suite. Extra person $15. Children under 17 free in parents' room with existing bedding. AE, DISC, JCB, MC, V. Parking $5. TheBUS: 19 or 20.

One block from the beach and on a quiet street is the 19-story Waikiki Resort Hotel offering quality rooms at budget prices. Owned by Korean Air, the recently renovated hotel has a huge lobby, with entrances on both Koa and Liliuokalani avenues. A stained-glass mural of the ocean dominates one side of the marble lobby. Front desk personnel are fluent in English, Korean, and Japanese. The rooms have carved wooden doors and are decorated in tropical-pattern drapes and bedspreads. All rooms have refrigerators, lanais, safes, a TV, and either two double beds or a king bed. The higher the floor, the better the view and the more expensive the room. If you are on a budget, consider getting a kitchenette, which are corner units and have great views.

The Waikiki Resort also offers some excellent package deals such as the room-and-breakfast buffet for $115 to $125; a room and car for $115 to $125; and a room, car, and breakfast for $125 to $135. The hotel also offers free transportation to the airport on departure.

Dining/Entertainment: The Ilima Cafe features breakfast buffet and lunch and dinner daily. The Camellia Restaurant is one of Waikiki's few Korean restaurants. The hotel has two lounges: the poolside Orchid Lounge and the Club Ohsama, which features dancing nightly.

Facilities: Freshwater pool, sundry and gift shops, activities desk, and laundry.

INEXPENSIVE

Waikiki Sand Villa. 2375 Ala Wai Blvd. (entrance is on Kanekapolei Ave. on the makai, Diamond Head side of the street), Honolulu, HI 96815. ☎ **800/247-1903** or 808/922-4744. Fax 808/923-2541. E-mail: wsv@aloha.net. Web page: http://www.planet-hawaii.com/sand/. 220 rms, 12 studios. A/C TV TEL. $70–$114 double; $129–$144 kitchenette studios. Extra person $15. Children under 12 free in parents' room with existing bedding. AE, CB, DC, DISC, JCB, MC, V. Parking $5. TheBUS: 19 or 20.

Budget travelers take note of this very affordable hotel, located on the quieter side of Waikiki, across the street from the Ala Wai Canal, where a continental breakfast is served poolside every morning. The 10-story tower has medium-sized rooms, most with a double bed plus a single bed (convenient for families), lanai, refrigerator, and safe. Another plus for families is the Nintendo in every room (available at $6.20 an hour). Other facilities include: laundry, hospitality room for late check-out (complete with showers), and luggage storage area.

The three-story Pualeilani building features studio apartments with kitchenettes (refrigerator, stove, and microwave), situated adjacent to the pool. The 70-foot pool has its own island in the middle and an adjoining whirlpool spa. A scuba diving operation is also located on the premises.

BUDGET

Edmunds Hotel Apartments. 2411 Ala Wai Blvd. (at Kaiulani St.), Honolulu, Hi 96815. ☎ 808/923-8381. 8 studios (with shower only). TV. $40 single; $45 double. Additional person $10. No credit cards. No parking. TheBUS: 19 or 20.

This small, modest place isn't for everyone, but students and travelers on a tight budget will be delighted to find these clean and neat studios. Don't expect color-coordinated interiors—don't even expect a phone. These are basic studios with a bed, bath, TV, and a small kitchenette equipped with stove, refrigerator, toaster, and pots and pans. There's no air-conditioning, and leaving the windows wide open means even more noise from the constantly bustling Ala Wai Boulevard. But with rates this low, you won't mind investing in some earplugs.

Hostelling International—Waikiki. 2417 Prince Edward St. (between Kaiulani and Uluniu sts.), Honolulu, HI 96815. ☎ **808-926-8313.** Fax 808/922-3798. 50 beds with shared bath (showers only), 4 studios with private baths (showers only). $16 bed for Hostelling International members; $19 bed for nonmembers; $40 double studio for Hostelling International members; $46 double studio for nonmembers. AE, MC, V. Parking $5. TheBUS: 19 or 20.

A couple of blocks from the beach, a safe, clean alternative is available for the budget traveler. Housed in a converted apartment building, this hostel features the option of male and female dorm rooms (four beds to a room with a shared bath) or private studio (sleeps two, with private bath). The common areas include an immaculately clean full kitchen and a lounge area with TV and VCR; the covered patio area is great for lounging, and there's an adjacent, complimentary locked storage area. Laundry facilities are available. There are no lock-out hours; guests are given their own entry keys. The staff is friendly, the guests tend to be a young international crowd, and the price is easy on the wallet.

Royal Grove Hotel. 151 Uluniu Ave. (between Prince Edward and Kuhio aves.), Honolulu, HI 96815. ☎ **808/923-7691.** Fax 808/922-7508. 85 units. A/C TV TEL. $42.50 double (no A/C); $75 one-bedroom (no A/C); $57 standard double; $75 standard one-bedroom; $75 deluxe double; $85 deluxe condo double. Extra person $10. AE, DC, MC, V. No parking available. TheBUS: 19 or 20.

You can't miss the Royal Grove—it's bright pink. Among Waikiki's canyons of corporate-owned high-rises, it's also a rarity in another way: The Royal Grove is a small family-owned hotel. What you get here is old-fashioned aloha in old-fashioned, cozy accommodations. For years, Frommer's readers have written us about the aloha spirit of the Fong family: They love the potluck dinners and get-togethers the Fongs have organized so their guests can get to know one other. And you can't do better for the price—this has to be *the* bargain of Waikiki: For $42.50 (about the same price a couple would pay to stay in a private room at the hostel in Waikiki) you get a clean room in the older Mauka wing, with a double bed or two twins, television, and a kitchenette with refrigerator and stove. We suggest that you spend a few dollars more and go for an air-conditioned room ($57) to help drown out the street noise. Even the most expensive room, a one-bedroom suite with three beds, air-conditioning, kitchenette, television, and lanai, at $85, is half the price of similar accommodations elsewhere. The hotel is built around a courtyard pool, but the beach is just a 3-minute walk away. All of Waikiki's attractions are within walking distance, including the Honolulu Zoo, Kapiolani Park, and Waikiki Aquarium. There's a coin-operated laundry and a tour desk on-site. *Hot tip:* Book 7 nights or more from April to November, and get a discount on the already low rates.

Month-Long Stay

Waikiki Lei Apartments. 241 Kaiulani Ave. (between Cleghorn and Tusitala sts., 1 block from Kuhio Ave.), Honolulu, HI 96815. ☎/fax **808/923-6656**. 20 studios. TV. $700–$800 per month double. 30-night minimum. No credit cards. No parking available. TheBUS: 19 or 20.

If you plan to be on Oahu for a month, these fully furnished studio apartments work out to be quite a deal—just $23 to $25 a day. Built in 1967, the building has been well maintained through the years and offers clean, comfortable budget apartments on a long-term basis. It's located in a residential neighborhood comprised of apartment and condo buildings, 3 blocks from the beach and 1 block from the bus stop. Don't expect the interiors to look like something from *Architectural Digest*—or even to have matching furnishings—but all the apartments have full kitchens (with everything you need to cook three meals a day), bath, two twin beds, dresser, television, dining-room table and chairs, towels, and bed linen; a coin-operated laundry is on-site.

2 Honolulu Beyond Waikiki

ALA MOANA

MODERATE

Ala Moana Hotel. 410 Atkinson Dr. (at Kona St., next to Ala Moana Shopping Center), Honolulu, HI 96814. ☎ **800/367-6025** or 808/955-4811. Fax 808/944-2974. 1,169 rms. A/C TV TEL. $110–$195 double; from $230 suite. Extra person $20. AE, CB, DC, DISC, JCB, MC, V. Parking $8. TheBUS: 19 or 20.

This hotel is big—36 stories with 1,169 rooms make it feel like a metropolis. It's proximity to Waikiki, the financial and business district of Honolulu, and Hawaii's largest mall, Ala Moana Shopping Center, makes it a popular spot for out-of state visitors and locals alike. Lots of Asian tourists choose the Ala Moana Hotel, probably because the management does an excellent job of making sure the foreign guests feel welcome by providing a bilingual staff and translators. Shoppers, mostly from neighboring islands, also make up a good percentage of the guests (especially in December). The rooms vary in size according to price: The budget rooms are on the smaller side, with two double beds, refrigerator, safe, phones with voice mail and computer jacks. As a full-service hotel, the Ala Moana offers everything: concierge, room service, valet, laundry, valet parking, a sundeck and pool, games room, and more; with four restaurants in the complex and a night club, some guests rarely venture off-property.

INEXPENSIVE

Pagoda Hotel. 1525 Rycroft St. (between Keeaumoku and Kaheka sts.), Honolulu, HI 96814. ☎ **800/367-6060** or 808/923-4511. Fax 808/922-8061. 361 rms. A/C TV TEL. $85–$95 double; $110 double one-bedroom (sleeps up to 4); $135 double one-bedroom (sleeps up to 6); $135 double two-bedroom (sleeps up to 5). Extra person $15. AE, DC, DISC, MC, V. Parking $3. TheBUS: 5 or 6.

The Pagoda Hotel is where local residents from other islands stay when they come to Honolulu. Close to shopping and downtown, the Pagoda has been serving Hawaii's island community for decades. All rooms have a full bath, television, air-conditioning, phone, and refrigerator; the studios and one and two bedrooms also have kitchenettes. The property features two swimming pools, shops, self-service or valet laundry, and three different restaurants. There's easy access to Waikiki via TheBUS—the nearest stop is just a half-block away.

BUDGET

Central Branch YMCA. 401 Atkinson Dr. (at Ala Moana Blvd., across from Ala Moana Shopping Center), Honolulu, HI 96814. ☎ **808/941-3344.** 114 rms. TEL. $29 single with shared bath (men only); $40 double with shared bath (men only); $36.40 single with private bath; $51.50 double with private bath. AE, DC, JCB, MC, V. Free parking 6pm–6am; during the day, free parking at Ala Moana Shopping Center across the street. TheBUS: 6, 8, or 20.

For those that can't afford Waikiki's prices, the Central Y is a good alternative; it's ultracheap, and just a short bus ride from Waikiki. Women are welcome here, but in the rooms with private baths only. The rooms are small and furnished in monkish style: bed, desk, phone, and shower—no air-conditioning, no phone. There's a common room with TV, and self-service laundry. Guests also have use of all the Y's facilities—sauna, outdoor pool, gym, handball courts, and other athletic facilities—at no additional charge. Meals are available at the low-cost restaurant in the building.

DOWNTOWN
EXPENSIVE

✪ **Executive Centre Hotel.** 1088 Bishop St. (Ewa side of Bishop St., on makai corner of S. Hotel St.), Honolulu, HI 96813. ☎ **800/949-EXEC** or 808/539-3000. Fax 808/523-1088. 114 all-suite rms. A/C MINIBAR TV TEL. $140 city/mountain-view suite; $155 ocean-view suite; $180 city/mountain-view Executive Suite; $195 ocean-view Executive Suite. Rates include continental breakfast. AE, CB, DC, DISC, JCB, MC, V. Parking $10. TheBUS: 1, 2, 3, 9, 12.

Located in the heart of downtown, this is the perfect hotel for the business traveler. Not only is it close to the business and financial center of Honolulu, but the staff goes out of their way to make sure that every need is met, including a 24-hour business center with staff. The rooms occupy the top 10 floors of a 40-story multiuse, glass-walled tower so that each room boasts unobstructed views of the city, the mountains, or the Honolulu harbor waterfront. Each room is large enough to qualify as a minisuite with three phones and private voice mail, safe, whirlpool bath, hair dryer, iron and ironing board, and coffeemaker. The executive suites feature full kitchens, washer/dryer, and VCR. All guests awaken to a complimentary breakfast, and local newspaper outside their door. Free local phone calls make this hotel a huge plus for the business traveler. Coin-operated laundry facilities, same-day laundry, and dry-cleaning services are available. Guests can also take advantage of the 24-hour fitness center (with 20-meter swimming pool).

Dining/Entertainment: Andrew's Restaurant, which moved from Ward Center to this downtown location, offers breakfast, lunch, and dinner.

Services: The Business Services Center provides a full range of office and secretarial services: personal and laptop computers with a variety of word processing programs, printers, copy machines, typewriters, and more. Free daily newspaper and local phone calls; concierge service.

Facilities: A 20-meter outdoor swimming pool and Jacuzzi with sundeck; fitness center with free weights, aerobic equipment, men's and women's saunas. Small- to medium-sized rooms for business meetings and gatherings are available, as well as two corporate-style boardrooms.

NEAR DOWNTOWN HONOLULU

Fernhurst YWCA. 1566 Wilder Ave. (at Punahou Ave.), Honolulu, HI 96822. ☎ **808/941-2231.** Fax 808/949-0266. 100 rms (all with shared bath). TEL. $30 private single for nonmembers; $25 per person shared room for nonmembers; $28 private single for members; $20 per person shared room for members. Rates include breakfast and dinner Mon–Fri. After a stay of 3 nights, you must join the YWCA ($30 per year). Men not accepted. MC, V. Parking $2.50. TheBUS: 4 or 5.

This Y, located in a quiet residential area, offers accommodations for women only. Resembling a 1950s dorm, each room has two beds, two dressers, and a phone; the bathroom is shared with the adjacent room. Extremely safe (only residents are allowed in the dorm area) and budget-priced (breakfast and dinner, Monday through Friday included in the cost), this is a good alternative for female travelers. Guests have use of all the facilities: swimming pool, laundry room, lounge area, piano, typewriters, TV, and sewing machine. Nearby bus routes will get you anywhere you want to go on Oahu.

Nuuanu YMCA. 1441 Pali Hwy. (at Vineyard St.), Honolulu, HI 96813. ☎ **808/536-3556.** Fax 808/533-1286. 70 rms (some with shared bath; showers only). TEL. $29 single with shared bath; $36 single with private bath. Women and children not accepted. AE, MC, V. Free parking. TheBUS: 1, 2, 4, 6.

This isn't as extravagant as a Waikiki hotel, but budget travelers will welcome the $29 nightly rate—they'll also love the fact that buses stop right in front of the building. This modern facility offers accommodations for single men only. The rooms feature a single bed, desk, and dresser. Only two units have private baths, so book early. Guests have use of all facilities: fitness center, pool, gym, weight room, cardiovascular workout room, martial arts center, and aerobic classes. Other services include a sauna, self-service laundromat, two tennis courts (lit for night play), jogging path, video games, and microwave. There's also a cafeteria on the property, which is open 6am to 6pm. *Hot tip:* Request a room that doesn't face the Pali Highway (too noisy).

✪ **Prospect House.** Prospect St. (at Iolani St.), Honolulu. C/o Hawaii's Best Bed & Breakfasts, P.O. Box 563, Kamuela, HI 96743. ☎ **800/262-9912** or 808/885-4550. Fax 808/885-0559. E-mail: bestbnb@aloha.net. Two-bedroom apt. A/C TV TEL. $85 double. Rate includes continental breakfast. Extra person $25. 2-night minimum. DISC. Free parking. TheBUS: 4 or 6.

On a quiet residential street near Punchbowl, the Prospect House has a two-bedroom apartment with a spectacular view of Honolulu and the Pacific. The apartment has its own private entrance, outside deck, and hot tub with city view; there's even a small breakfast nook outside where you can sit and watch the city wake up as you sip your morning coffee. Inside, the cozy apartment features a living room/dining room with efficiency kitchen (microwave, toaster, blender, coffeemaker) and two bedrooms, a queen bed in one and two twins in the other. Extra touches that make this B&B a standout are well-stocked floor-to-ceiling bookshelves, Oriental rugs on the parquet floors, a comfortable sofa, and a koa rocking chair; in addition, plush bathrobes hang in the closet, and plants are everywhere. To top it all off, the location is great: 15 minutes from the airport and Waikiki, and just minutes from Honolulu's attractions.

A GAY-FRIENDLY INN

The Mango House. 2087 Iholena St. (at Judd St., in Nuuanu), Honolulu, HI 96817. ☎ **800-77-MANGO** or 808/595-6682. Fax 808/595-6682. E-mail: mango@pixi.com. 2 rms (one with shared bath), 1 cottage. $63 single; $73–$85 double (includes continental breakfast); $99 cottage double (no breakfast with cottage). Extra person $10–$15. 3-night minimum (Nov 23–Jan 6, 5-night minimum). AE, DISC, MC, V. Free parking. TheBUS: 4.

Innkeepers Tracey and Marga (who also consider themselves bread makers and tour desk staffers) offer rooms in their house as well as a separate romantic cottage. The house, in Nuuanu, a quiet residential neighborhood, is up two flights of stairs (you can work off the desserts from that luau just walking up and down). From the

Bed-&-Breakfast Reservation Agencies

For a more intimate experience, try staying in a bed-&-breakfast. Accommodations on Oahu calling themselves "bed-&-breakfast" vary from a room in a house (sometimes with a shared bath) to a vacation rental in a private cottage. Breakfast can be anything from coffee, pastries, and fruit to a home-cooked gourmet meal with just-caught fresh fish.

If you don't want to go through the hassle of calling around and trying to match your dream accommodation to what is available, use a bed-&-breakfast booking agency. We recommend the following:

Bed & Breakfast Hawaii, P.O. Box 449, Kapaa, HI 96746. ☎ **800/733-1632** or 808/822-7771. Fax 808/822-2723. Offers a range of different accommodations (from vacation homes to bed-&-breakfast units), starting at $65 a night on Oahu.

✪ **Hawaii's Best Bed & Breakfast,** P.O. Box 563, Kamuela, HI 96743. ☎ **800/ 262-9912** or 808/885-4550. Fax 808/885-0559. E-mail: bestbnb.@aloha.net. Operated by Barbara Campbell, who did the marketing for the luxury Kona Village Resort for decades, they choose only the creme de la creme of bed-&-breakfasts across the state. Rates on Oahu begin at $85 a night.

Three Bears' Hawaii Reservations, 72-1001 Puukala, Kailua-Kona, HI 96740. ☎ **800/765-0480** or 808/325-7563. Fax 800/765-0480 or 808/325-7563. E-mail: three.bears@pobox.com. The Stockels, who run a bed-and-breakfast on the Big Island, also book accommodations on Oahu. They have the extra advantage of speaking fluent German and French. Their units start at $70 a night.

Volcano Reservations, P.O. Box 998, Volcano, HI 96785. ☎ **800/736-7140** or 808/967-8216. Fax 800/577-1849. E-mail: bchawaii@aol.com. Yes, it says Volcano, but they book across the state. Brian and Lisha Crawford, owners of the Big Island's exquisite Chalet Kilauea, have a discriminating reservation service for accommodations statewide, starting at $45 for a double and up.

living room, and as you sip your morning coffee at the dining table, you'll have a panoramic view of Honolulu, Punchbowl Crater, and the ocean. The view from the bedrooms, of leafy mango and lychee trees, isn't too shabby, either. You'll wake to the sound of birds singing: a guest wrote, "Were those bird calls I kept hearing on tape?" Nope—it's the real thing. The two uniquely decorated rooms get plenty of breeze from the trade winds. One has a queen bed and shares a bath adorned with seashells from around the world; the other has a king bed and private bath and Jacuzzi. The Mango Cottage has a living room with a queen sofa sleeper, a bedroom with a queen bed, television, phone, full kitchen, and air-conditioning. A washer and dryer are available for use.

Located 15 minutes from the airport, 15 minutes from Waikiki, and 20 minutes from the Windward Coast, this is a great central location from which to explore Oahu. Tracey and Marga love providing tips on things to do, where to eat, and what's happening in the local gay community. "About 90% of our guests are gay," Tracey told us. "But we welcome everyone with a sense of humor." Gay or straight, guests leave Mango House happy.

NEAR HONOLULU INTERNATIONAL AIRPORT

If you have a long layover between flights, a delayed flight, or a long period of time between your noon check-out and your flight, consider the services of the **Honolulu Airport Mini-Hotel** (☎ 808/836-3044; fax 808/834-8986). It's the perfect answer to a traveler's dilemma. The clean, comfortable single rooms come with nothing more than a bed, a nightstand, and a private shower. They provide a wake-up call if you need it, there's always coffee brewing to get you going, and if you have something that needs refrigeration (medication or flowers to bring home), the management is happy to help out. Rates are $33 for 8 hours (additional hours $5 each); you can rent showers only for $8.25. There are only 17 rooms, so book in advance. The hotel does not provide transportation to the terminal, but it's just a short walk away.

MODERATE

Best Western—The Plaza Hotel. 3253 N. Nimitz Hwy. (at Paiea St.), Honolulu, HI 96819. ☎ **800/800-4683** or 808/836-3636. Fax 808/834-7406. Web page: http://www.bestwestern. com/thisco/bw/. 274 rms. A/C TV TEL. $97–$108 double. Extra person $20. AE, DC, DISC, JCB, MC, V. Free parking. Free shuttle van to and from airport. TheBUS: 19 or 20.

If you've got a flight that arrives late or leaves early, this is a good place to spend the night. The rooms are fairly standard, with television, phone, refrigerator, and, if requested, a microwave. Other conveniences include room service, a pool for a quick dip, coin-operated laundry for that last-minute wash, a restaurant, and free shuttle service to the airport (less than 5 minutes away).

Holiday Inn Airport. 3401 N. Nimitz Hwy. (Rodgers St.), Honolulu, HI 96819. ☎ **800/ 800-3477** or 808/833-0661. Fax 808/833-1738. 308 rms. A/C TV TEL. $102–$122 double. Extra person $20. AE, DISC, MC, V. Free parking. Free shuttle to and from the airport. TheBUS: 19 or 20.

You'll get the same level of service and quality that you've come to expect from the dependable Holiday Inn chain at this location, just minutes from the airport via a free shuttle. Two four-story buildings wrap around an outdoor swimming pool and garden; there's also a restaurant and lounge with entertainment on-site. There are noise problems here, though; the walls seem thin. If you don't have a lot of luggage, ask for a room well away from the elevator (late at night, lively guests tend to get louder). No-smoking and wheelchair-accessible rooms are available.

INEXPENSIVE

Pacific Marina Inn. 2628 Waiwai Loop (at Lagoon Dr.), Honolulu, HI 96819. ☎ **800/ 367-5004** or 808/836-1131. Fax 800/477-2329 or 808/833-0851. 119 rms. A/C TV TEL. $83 double; $99 suite triple; $99 quad for 4. Extra person $17. AE, CB, DC, DISC, MC, V. Free parking. Free shuttle to and from airport. TheBUS: 19 or 20.

Lots of airline crew members stay at this convenient airport hotel, just minutes to the airport via free shuttle. The Pacific Marina is a clean, affordable hotel featuring standard rooms with TV, phone, and showers. Facilities include swimming pool, sundeck, two restaurants, and karaoke fun in the evening. Next door is Keehi Lagoon Park, with free tennis courts and picnic areas.

MANOA
MODERATE

✪ **Manoa Valley Inn.** 2001 Vancouver Dr. (at University Ave.), Honolulu, HI 96822. ☎ **800/ 535-0085** or 808/947-6019. Fax 800/633-5085 or 808/946-6168. E-mail: marc@ marcresorts.com. 8 rms (3 with shared bath; 5 with private bath). TV TEL. $99–$120 double with shared bath; $140–$190 double with private bath (shower only). Rates include continental breakfast and evening wine service. AE, DC, JCB, MC, V. Free parking. TheBUS: 4 or 6.

It's completely off the tourist trail and far from the beach, but that doesn't stop travelers from heading to this historic 1915 Carpenter Gothic home, on a quiet residential street near the University of Hawaii. Saved from demolition by Rick Ralston (the

Red Adair of historic renovation in Hawaii) in 1978, this eight-room Manoa land-mark—it's on the National Register of Historic Places—offers a glimpse into the lifestyles of the rich and famous in early Honolulu.

Those who prefer to avoid resorts find the eclectically furnished inn refreshing. Each room has its own unique decor, and have been named for a prominent figure in Hawaii's history: The John Guild suite, for instance, has a turn-of-the-century parlor with antiques and old-fashioned rose wallpaper; the adjoining bedroom has a king-size koa bed, and the bath features an old-style tub as well as a separate modern shower. The three top-floor rooms share a full bath, and the others have private baths. All have phones, and some have safes.

A genteel ambiance pervades the place. Guests regularly gather in the parlor to listen to the Victrola or play the nickelodeon. There's also a billiard room with an antique billiard table, a piano in the living room, and croquet set up in the backyard. As the sun sets, complimentary wine and cheese are served on the quiet veranda. The innkeepers ask that children staying here be at least 14 years old.

BUDGET

Bed & Breakfast Manoa & Hillside Cottage. 2651 Terrace Dr. (at Manoa Rd.), Honolulu, HI 96822. ☎ **808/988-6333.** Fax 808/988-5240. E-mail: mgm@aloha.net. 3 rms (some with shared shower), 1 cottage. TV TEL. $60 single; $70 double. Rates include continental breakfast. Extra person in room $10. $120 cottage double, $140 cottage triple. Extra person in cottage $15. 3-night minimum. No credit cards. Free parking. TheBUS: 5.

Hosts Geoffrey Paterson, an architect originally from England, and Maureen McDonough, a writer and native of New Zealand, share their gorgeous home on the hills of Manoa, located 15 minutes from the airport and a 10-minute drive from Waikiki. The rooms (have either a king or queen bed) are located upstairs; each has its own TV, radio, and phone, but only one room has a private bathroom. Breakfast is served on the huge deck that overlooks Manoa Valley, with Diamond Head and Waikiki in the distance.

The downstairs cottage features an indoor-outdoor living room with the same great views, as well as a quaint bedroom built into the hillside. The cottage can actually sleep as many as seven people: Additional accommodations are a king bed on the sleeping porch and a sleeper sofa in the living room. Breakfast isn't included in rates for cottage guests.

Hostelling International—Honolulu. 2323-A Seaview Ave. (at University Ave.), Honolulu, HI 96822. ☎ **808/946-0591.** Fax 808/946-5904. 43 beds (with shared bath, shower only), 2 studios. $12.50 dorm beds; $35 studio double, $47.50 studio triple. AE, MC, V. Free limited parking. TheBUS: 4 or 6.

A block from the University of Hawaii you'll find this cheap alternative place to stay. Tucked into the crowded residential community of Manoa is this spotless oasis surrounded by plants, picnic tables, and the sound of dozens of languages being spoken. Mrs. Akau makes sure that guests are happy and that the house rules are met. The rooms are dormitory style, with three to four beds in each room with a shared bath. She will happily arrange the beds so a party of two to four can share the same room (she charges an additional $10 per room for this service). Guests also have use of a full kitchen and a recently renovated common room with TV, VCR, stereo, and games. The facility is locked between noon and 4pm daily.

Off-street parking is extremely limited and street parking is unheard of in this neighborhood, so think twice about staying here if you rent a car. A nearby bus stop gives you access to Waikiki and the rest of Oahu.

TO THE EAST: KAHALA

✪ **Kahala Mandarin Oriental Hawaii** (formerly Kahala Hilton). 5000 Kahala Ave. (Kealaolu Ave.), Honolulu, HI 96816 ☎ **800/367-2525** or 808/739-8888. Fax 808/739-8800. E-mail: mohnl@aol.com. Web page: http://www.mohnl.com/. 370 rms, 32 suites. A/C MINIBAR TV TEL. $260–$635 double rms; $600–$2,950 suites. Extra person $80. Children 17 and under free when staying with parents. AE, CB, DC, DISC, JCB, MC, V. Parking $12.

In March 1996, after $75 million in renovations, the Kahala Mandarin Oriental Hawaii opened to much fanfare. Since 1964, when Conrad Hilton first opened the hotel as a place for rest and relaxation far from the crowds of Waikiki, the Kahala has always been rated one of Hawaii's premiere hotels. A venerable who's who of celebrities have stayed at the hotel, including every president since Richard Nixon, a host of rock stars from the Rolling Stones to the Beach Boys and a range of actors from John Wayne to Bette Midler. The new ownership by the Mandarin Oriental chain, renown for their excellence of service, coupled with the massive renovations, took this Grande Dame of hotels to a new level. The Mandarin has retained the traditional feeling of an earlier time in Hawaii, which defined the Kahala for a generation, and has combined it with exotic Asian touches, creating a resort hotel for the 21st century, but with the grace and elegance of a softer, gentler time. The most noticeable change was moving both dining rooms to give them oceanfront vistas.

All of the guest rooms have been totally remodeled with replicas of 19th-century mahogany furniture, teak parquet floors with hand-loomed Tibetan rugs, overstuffed chairs, canopy beds covered with soft throw pillows, and artwork by local artists decorating the grass-cloth wall covering. Views from the floor-to-ceiling sliding glass doors are of the ocean, Diamond Head, and Koko Head. Some of the more modern conveniences in the rooms include two-line phones, computer and fax connections, 27-inch TV, and Super Nintendo. The large bathrooms include vintage furnishings such as a freestanding mahogany vanity sink with porcelain handle faucets. The flooring is white Italian ceramic tiles with terra-cotta. In addition to the separate freestanding glass-shower is a large soaking tub. Each room has a "his" and "her" dressing area, plush bathrobes and slippers, hair dryer, and illuminated makeup mirror.

Located 10 minutes (driving) from Waikiki, in one of Oahu's most prestigious residential areas, the Kahala Mandarin Oriental provides an otherworldly experience: one of beauty, peace, and serenity. The lush tropical grounds include an 800-foot crescent shaped beach, a swimming pool and a 26,000-square-foot lagoon, home to two bottle-nosed dolphins, sea turtles, and tropical fish.

Dining/Entertainment: Hoku's, the main dining room of the hotel, has a new multilevel layout so every table has an ocean view, and features Pacific and European cuisine for lunch and dinner. Plumeria Beach Café serves both creative and traditional breakfast, and lunch and dinner items in a casual, open-air setting; their specialty is Sunday brunch. The Poolside Snack Bar has casual outdoor dining for lunch. The Plumeria Bar offers tropical drinks in an oceanfront setting. The Lobby Lounge serves drinks with nightly entertainment.

Services: 24-hour room service, valet and self-parking, nightly turndown, in-room safe, fax and modem connections, free scuba lesson in pool, baby-sitting, concierge, dolphin education program, foreign exchange facilities, Hawaiian cultural program, massage, multilingual personnel, and shuttle service to Waikiki and major shopping centers.

Facilities: Beach; swimming pool; gardens with man-made waterfall, lagoons, and islet; fitness center with steam rooms, dry sauna, outdoor Jacuzzis, Stairmasters, treadmills, weight room; Kahala Keiki Club for children; business center; shops; no-smoking rooms; and banquet and meeting rooms.

HAWAII KAI

J&B's Haven. 780 Ainapo St. (at Pepeekeo St., off Hawaii Kai Dr.), Hawaii Kai. Reservations: P.O. Box 25907, Honolulu, HI 96825. ☎ **808/396-9462.** E-mail: babe@hits.net. 2 rms (one with shower only). TV TEL. $65–$70 double. Rates include continental breakfast. Extra person $10. 2-night minimum. No credit cards. Free parking. TheBUS: 1.

Englishwomen Joan and Barbara Webb have had a successful bed-and-breakfast on Oahu since 1982. Both Joan, who moved to Hawaii in 1981, and her daughter Barbara, who has been living here since 1970, are very knowledgeable about Oahu's attractions and love meeting new people and introducing them to the Hawaii they love. In 1996, they moved to this beautiful house in Hawaii Kai, just 15 minutes east of Waikiki (on the other side of Diamond Head) and close to Hanauma Bay, Sandy Beach, and Sea Life Park, as well as within easy reach of three shopping centers with excellent restaurants. There are two rooms in the house: the upstairs master bedroom, with private bath, king bed, television, minirefrigerator, and ceiling fan; and the private room downstairs (the only room on that floor) with a queen bed, television and VCR, refrigerator, microwave, and a small dining table and chairs for two. The room is large enough to sleep four if two of you don't mind sleeping on futons on the floor.

PEARL CITY

✪ **Rainbow Inn.** 98–1049 Mahola Place (off Kaonohi St., 2 miles from Kamehameha Hwy.), Pearl Ridge, HI. ☎/fax **808/488-7525.** E-mail: 102766.1237@compuserve.com. 1 apt. A/C TV TEL. $65 double. Rates include refrigerator stocked with breakfast items. Extra person $10. 3-night minimum. No credit cards. Free parking. TheBUS: 20, 50, 51, or 52.

This private tropical-garden studio, downstairs from the home of retired military officer Gene Smith and his wife Betty, has panoramic views of Pearl Harbor, the entire south coast of Oahu, and the Waianae and Koolau mountains. A large deck and full-sized pool is just outside the apartment's door; inside, the apartment features a double bed, TV, phone, washer/dryer, and kitchen. The Smiths are happy to lend their guests any beach and picnic equipment they might need—ice chest, beach mats and chairs, even wine glasses. Located close to Pearl Ridge Shopping Center, Rainbow Inn is freeway-close to all of Oahu's attractions, yet far enough way to provide you with lots of peace and quiet. And at $65 a night, this is one of Oahu's best bed-and-breakfast deals. *Hot tip:* Reserve early—bargains like this book up fast.

3 The Windward Coast

KAILUA

Pat O'Malley of **Pat's Kailua Beach Properties,** 204 S. Kalaheo Ave., Kailua, HI 96734 (☎ **808/261-1653** or 808/262-4128; fax 808/261-0893), books a wide range of houses and cottages on or near Kailua Beach, from a million-dollar beachfront estate to studio cottages on or close to the water. Rates start at $65 a day for a studio cottage near the beach and go up to $400 per day for a multimillion dollar home right on the beach. All units are fully furnished, with everything from cooking and dining utensils, to telephone and TV, even washer and dryers.

MODERATE

✪ **Ingrid's.** Pauku St. (across from Enchanted Lakes School), Kailua. c/o Hawaii's Best Bed & Breakfasts, P.O. Box 563, Kamuela, HI 96743. ☎ **800/262-9912** or 808/885-4550.

Fax 808/885-0559. E-mail: bestbnb@aloha.net. 1 apt. TV TEL. $110 double. Rate includes continental breakfast. Extra person $15. 2-night minimum. DISC. Free parking. TheBUS: 52, 55, or 56.

Ingrid has impeccable taste. Upstairs, past the Japanese garden and through a private entrance, is the cute one-bedroom apartment that she keeps immaculate. Decorated in modern Japanese style, this place is straight out of a magazine: The pristine white walls and cabinets are accented with such dramatic touches as black tile on the counter top, black-and-white shoji doors, and a black Oriental screen behind a king bed dressed in white quilts and red, red, red throw pillows. The tiled bathroom is done in complementary gray and has a luxurious soaking tub. The kitchenette includes a dishwasher, refrigerator, microwave, and coffeemaker. A huge tiled deck extends out from the apartment, and a small alcove is off the bedroom for a third person or a reading area. Fresh flowers are everywhere.

The place is gorgeous, but the best part is Ingrid (who isn't Swedish, but Portuguese). A former advertising sales manager for a local TV station, Ingrid is one of the friendliest and most helpful people you'll meet in Hawaii. People return year after year because of her welcoming warmth; she frequently becomes lifelong friends with former guests.

INEXPENSIVE

Schrader's Windward Marine Resort. 47–039 Lihikai Dr. (off Kamehameha Hwy.), Kaneohe, HI 96744. ☎ **800/735-5711** or 808/239-5711. Fax 808/239-6658. 19 units. A/C TV TEL. $70–$117 one-bedroom double; $110–$150 two-bedroom double; $160–$210 three-bedroom. Rates include continental breakfast. Extra person $7.50. 2-night minimum. AE, DC, DISC, JCB, MC, V. Free parking. TheBUS: 52, 55, or 56.

This older cottage-style motel is nestled in a tranquil, tropical setting on Kaneohe Bay, only a 30-minute drive from Waikiki. Despite the name, the ambiance here is more motel than resort, but Schrader's offers a good alternative for families. Many of the guests are military families visiting nearby Kaneohe Marine Corps base. Cottages have kitchenettes with refrigerator and microwave, TV, and phones. Prices are based on the views; depending on how much you're willing to pay, you can look out over Kahuluu fish pond, the Koolau Mountains, or Kaneohe Bay. Lots of water sports are available at an additional cost. *Hot tip:* When booking, ask for a unit with a lanai; that way, you'll end up with at least a partial view of the bay.

BUDGET

Fairway View Bed & Breakfast. 515 Paumakua Place, Kailua, HI 96734. ☎ **808/263-6439** or 808/262-0485. 2 rms (with shared bath). $45–$55 double. Rates include continental breakfast. 3-night minimum. No credit cards. Free parking. TheBUS: 52, 55, or 56. Follow Pali Hwy. to Kuulei Rd.; in Kailua, turn right on Kawailoa Rd. and cross bridge; turn right on Alalala (past Lanikai Elementary School) and left on Paumakua Place.

Hostess Louise "Weezie" Wooden calls her bed-and-breakfast a "homestay," because after staying with her and her husband, Neal (a retired naval aviator and communicator), it'll feel just like home to you. Located right on the second fairway of the Mid-Pacific Golf Course and just a half-mile from Kailua Beach, Fairway View offers comfortable accommodations at a budget price. The two color-coordinated guest rooms share a large bathroom with tub and shower: One features a queen bed, koa furniture, a small TV, and a minirefrigerator; the other has white wicker twin beds, koa-framed Hawaiian art, and a minifridge. Most of the action, including breakfast, takes place in the family room, which has a spectacular view of the golf course and the Koolau Mountains in the background. Guests also congregate on the adjacent covered lanai (smokers can light up out here). "It's fun meeting the different people," Weezie told us. "And it gives me a great excuse to continue to upgrade our home."

J&B's Place. 57 Pilipu Place (at Kalaheo Dr.), Kailua. Reservations: 602 Kailua Rd., no. 102, Kailua, HI 96734. ☎ **808/262-2302** or 808/262-9530. Fax 808/262-2305 or 808/262-1387. E-mail: realest@aloha.net. 2 units. A/C TV TEL. $65 one-bedroom double; extra person $10; 3-night minimum. $100 two-bedroom double; extra person $20; 7-night minimum. No credit cards. Free parking. TheBUS: 52, 55, or 56.

This isn't a B&B—it's a true vacation rental. Bill and Jeanne Hailer have two separate units on their property that they rent out. The two-story, two-bedroom apartment (with queen bed in the master bedroom and two twins in the second bedroom) is about 1,000 square feet and can easily sleep six with the futon couch. Full kitchen, TV, VCR, hot tub, and barbecue add to the amenities for this affordable family unit. The one-bedroom unit is a little oddly laid out, with a long hallway with rooms branching off, but it works. All the comforts are here, too: a separate bedroom with double bed, a kitchenette (with microwave, hot plate, coffeemaker, and fridge), dining room, and living room with TV, and VCR. Kailua Beach is just 200 yards away.

✪ Lanikai Bed & Breakfast. 1277 Mokulua Dr. (between Onekea and A'ala drs., Lanikai), Kailua, HI 96734. ☎ **800/258-7895** or 808/261-1059. Fax 808/261-7355. E-mail: hi4rent@ aloha.net. 1 studio, 1 apt. TV TEL. $65 studio double, $85 apt. Rates include breakfast items in refrigerator. Extra person $10–$20. 3-night minimum. MC, V. Free parking. TheBUS: 52, 55, or 56.

This old-time bed-and-breakfast, a *kamaaina* (native-born) home that reflects the Hawaii of yesteryear, is now into its second generation. For years Mahina and Homer Maxey ran this large, comfortable island-style residence. Today their son, Rick, and his wife Nini are the hosts. The recently renovated 1,000-square-foot upstairs apartment is decorated in old Hawaii bungalow–style. With a king bed in the bedroom, separate den, large living/dining room, and big bathroom, it easily accommodates four. It has all the modern conveniences—TV, VCR, and kitchenette—and oversized windows let you enjoy wonderful views. Or, you can follow the ginger- and ti-lined path to a 540-square-foot honeymooner's delight, with queen bed and sitting area with TV, VCR, and kitchenette. Rick and Nini carry on the family tradition of hospitality by stocking the units with breakfast fixings (muffins, juice, fruit, coffee, tea) and all the beach equipment you'll need (towels, mats, chairs, coolers, water jugs). Picture-perfect white-sand Lanikai Beach access is across the street, bus routes are close by, and a 2¹/₂-mile biking-walking loop is just outside.

Manu Mele Bed & Breakfast. 153 Kailuana Place (at Kalaheo Dr.), Kailua, HI 96734. ☎ /fax **808/262-0016.** 2 rms (with shower only). TV TEL. $65–$75 double. Rates include continental breakfast items in refrigerator for 3 mornings. 2-night minimum. No credit cards. Free parking. TheBUS: 52, 55, or 56.

Just a few minutes walk from Kailua Bay is Manu Mele ("bird song"), a vacation rental with two separate units around the garden and swimming pool. The largest unit, the Hibiscus Room, features a king bed and large bathroom with double vanity. The smaller Pikake Room has a queen bed and full bath. Both rooms have tile floors, a nice mix of antiques and modern furniture, Laura Ashley linens, and a TV, microwave, coffeemaker, and refrigerator in the custom wall unit. Hostess Carol Isaacs, originally from England, has been running Manu Mele for more than a decade; she loves helping travelers plan their visit to Oahu. She stocks the refrigerators with three days of muffins, fruit, and coffee to get her visitors started.

Papaya Paradise. 395 Auwinala Rd. (at Wanaao Rd.), Enchanted Lake, Kailua, HI 96734. ☎ /fax **808/261-0316.** 2 rms (with shower only). A/C TV TEL. $70 double. Rate includes continental breakfast. Extra person $15. 3-night minimum. No credit cards. Free parking. TheBUS: 52, 55, or 56. Take Pali Hwy. into Kailua; turn right on Kailua Rd., which becomes Wanaao Rd.; turn right on Auwinala Rd.

As their daughter Jona Williams, who runs Kailua Tradewinds next door, put it: "My dad is a character; I think people come here because they love his sense of humor." What is Bob Martz's sense of humor? Well, this should give you an idea: He has a collection of old tea kettles hanging like Christmas ornaments from a tree in the backyard; accompanying it is his collection of figurines, which guests have sent from all over the world—not just standard-issue patio and garden figures, but small dinosaurs, raccoons, gnomes, alligators, and more. But it's not just Bob's offbeat sense of humor that wins guests over to this Enchanted Lake B&B; they love the excellent accommodations and good breakfasts as well. The two units have private entrances and are furnished in tropical rattan and wicker; they each come with two beds, ceiling fan, A/C, and TV, and open onto a 20×40-foot pool and Jacuzzi surrounded by tropical plants, fruit trees, flowers, and Bob's aforementioned collections. A refrigerator, microwave, and library on Hawaiiana and Hawaii attractions are also available for guests' use.

Bob and his wife Jeanette love sitting on the poolside lanai at breakfast, sharing stories with their guests (Bob has many, many stories). Visitors include a large number of German tourists and, of course, people with a sense of humor—who like tea.

✪ **Sharon's Serenity.** 127 Kakahiaka St. (Mahelani St.), Kailua, HI. 96734. ☎ **800/914-2271,** 808/263-3634, or 808/262-5621. 2 rms. TV TEL. $60–$75 double. Rates include continental breakfast. Extra person $10. 3-night minimum. No credit cards. Free parking. TheBUS: 52, 55, or 56.

What a setting: In the backyard, beyond the pool and deck and the grassy lawn, runs the slow-moving water of a canal, framed by the greens of the Mid Pacific Golf Course and the lush Koolau Range in the distance. This place is serenity to the max. Hostess Sharon Price has a warm, welcoming attitude that makes you feel at home. And what a home it is—a huge living area with three large couches, a giant kitchen, and two guest rooms to chose from: one with pool view and a king bed as well as a twin, the other with a queen bed in a more romantic ambiance. Kailua Beach is just a couple of blocks away, but the atmosphere is so relaxing here that sometimes guests want to just stay home. Sharon has an adorably chubby Bichon Frise who loves everyone, plus two indoor-outdoor cats.

✪ **Sheffield House.** 131 Kuulei Rd. (at Kalaheo Dr.), Kailua, HI 96734. ☎/fax **808/262-0721.** E-mail: sheffieldhouse@poi.net. Web page: http://www.poi.net/~sheffieldhouse. 1 studio (with shower only), 1 apt. TV. $55 double studio; $80 double apt. Rates include continental breakfast. Extra person $10. 3-night minimum. No credit cards. Free parking. TheBUS: 52, 55, or 56.

Unlike at many other B&Bs, children are welcome here. Architect Paul Sheffield and his landscape-architect wife, Rachel, have three kids who aren't shy about making new friends and including younger guests in their fun. "With every booking, my kids always ask me, 'Do they have children?'" Rachel said. "When I say yes, they're thrilled." The yard is set up for children: jungle gym, swing set, a tire swing, and toys for children. The Sheffields have two units, a one-bedroom and a studio (which is fully wheelchair-accessible), each with a private entry through elaborately landscaped tropical gardens. Both are equipped with a refrigerator, microwave, toaster oven, and coffeemaker.

KANEOHE
INEXPENSIVE

A 5-Star Bed & Breakfast. 44–491 Kaneohe Bay Dr. (by Kaneohe Yacht Club, on the ocean side of Kaneohe Bay Dr.), Kaneohe, HI 96744. ☎ **800/235-5214** or 808/235-8235. Fax 808/247-6116. 3 rms (2 with shared bath). TV. $75–$85 double. Rates include continental breakfast. 3-night minimum. No credit cards. Free parking. TheBUS: 52, 55, or 56.

An interior decorator has definitely molded this luxury house near the Kaneohe Yacht Club: Parquet floors, Japanese shoji doors, and creamy white furniture give this waterfront home a tropical-Asian feeling. Two bedrooms (one with twin beds and one with a queen) share a gorgeous marble bathroom—with marble shower—that looks out onto a tropical garden. The master suite (with its less extravagant private bath) has a view of the swimming pool, the Koolau Range, and the yacht club. The rooms sit back off the street and are generally pretty quiet. Hostess Sherri gives her guests the run of the house—including kitchen privileges—and acts as concierge, tour guide, and reservationist. She serves a continental breakfast on the pool deck or in the formal dining room, depending on what her guests prefer. A large pool with cabana is the featured entertainment. Shopping and restaurants are nearby, and Waikiki and Honolulu are just a 20- to 30-minute drive away.

BUDGET

Alii Bluffs Windward Bed & Breakfast. 46–251 Ikiiki St. (off Kamehameha Hwy.), Kaneohe, HI 96744. ☎/fax **800/235-1151** or 808/235-1124. 2 rms. $55–$65 double. Rates include continental breakfast. 3-night minimum. No credit cards. Free parking. TheBUS: 52, 55, or 56.

Realtor Donald Munro and artist L. (De) de Chambs, who moved here from New York (where they had a fashion design business and an art gallery), have been welcoming travelers from around the globe into their home for a decade. Located on a quiet residential street, this traditional bed-and-breakfast is filled with antiques and collectibles from their former gallery as well as de Chambs's original art. The guest wing has two rooms, one with a double bed and adjacent bath, the other with two extralong twins and a bath across the hall. The yard blooms with tropical plants, and the view of Kaneohe Bay from the pool area is breathtaking.

Donald, originally from Scotland, where his mother ran a bed-and-breakfast, wants to make it clear, "We are not like so many places on the island—a vacation rental posing as a B&B, with a couple of muffins in the fridge." Lots of extras make this B&B stand out from the crowd, including daily maid service, a large breakfast served on the poolside lanai, afternoon tea, and hair dryers and sewing kits in the bathroom—they'll even lend you anything you need for the beach.

✪ **Hulakai Hale.** 44-002 Hulakai Place (off Kaneohe Bay Dr.), Kaneohe, HI 96744. ☎ **808/235-6754.** 2 rms. TV. $55–$65. Rates include continental breakfast. Extra person $15. 3-night minimum. No credit cards. Free parking. TheBUS: 52, 55, or 56.

Hulakai Hale ("house of the dancing waters") sits right on Kaneohe Bay, with picture-postcard views in every direction; the view from the swimming pool deck, of the bay and the yacht club next door, is worth the price alone. You could lounge around the pool all day in the comfortable deck chairs and be happy just watching the birds soar overhead or billowing sails dance in the wind. Located at the end of a private road, Hulakai Hale is well away from traffic, but just minutes from the restaurants and shops of Kaneohe. Each of the two well-furnished units has a small fridge, microwave, coffeemaker, full bath, and a private outdoor entrance, and come stocked with beach mats, towels, and cooler; one room has a king bed, the other a queen. Breakfast (tropical juice, fresh fruit, a variety of breads, cereal, coffee, and tea) is served every morning on the pool deck or in the formal dining area. Hosts Ditty and Tom Pico have a wonderful sense of humor, and do everything they can to make sure you have the time of your life.

4 The North Shore

Team Real Estate, 66–134 Kamahameha Hwy., Suite 1, Haleiwa, HI 96712 (☎ **800/982-8602** or 808/637-3507; fax 808/637-8881), E-mail luckyc@ibm.net.

URL: http://www.teamrealestate.com, manages vacation rentals on the North Shore. The units range from affordable cottages to oceanfront homes. The rates start at $95 per night and go up to $250 per night. A minimum stay of 1 week is required for some properties, but shorter stays are available.

EXPENSIVE

✪ **Turtle Bay Hilton Golf and Tennis Resort.** P.O. Box 187 (Kuilima Dr., off Kamehameha Hwy. [Hwy. 83]), Kahuku, HI 96731. ☎ **800/HILTONS** or 808/293-8811. Fax 808/293-1286. Web page: http://www.hilton.com/. 485 rms, cottages, and suites. A/C TV TEL. $155–$255 double, $285–$600 cabana. $400–$1,500 suite. Extra person $25. Children of any age free in parents' room. AE, CB, DC, DISC, ER, JCB, MC, V. Parking $3. TheBUS: 52 or 55.

An hour's drive from Waikiki and eons away from that tourist Mecca is this luxurious oceanfront resort in a country setting. Sitting on 808 acres, this is a resort loaded with activities: 27 holes of golf, 10 tennis courts and 5 miles of shoreline with secluded white-sand coves. Choose from the spacious guest rooms, suites, or oceanside cabanas—all have oceanfront views.

The resort was built on Kalaeokaunu Point ("point of the alter"), where ancient Hawaiians built a small alter to the fish gods. The remains of that alter are now at the bishop Museum, but it is easy to see why the Hawaiians considered this holy ground. Next to the point is Kuilima Cove, one of the safest swimming beaches on the North Shore due to the large reef off shore. The feeling of old Hawaii is carried through to the guest rooms, which are decorated in Polynesian decor. Each room has a private lanai, tub or shower, all the amenities—and a great view of the ocean.

Dining/Entertainment: The Palm Terrace, overlooking the pool and Turtle Bay, is known for fabulous buffets. Sunday champagne brunch at the Sea Tide Room is a favorite. For fine dining overlooking Turtle Bay, there's the Cove, featuring continental and local cuisine and an excellent wine list. There's live entertainment nightly, plus drinks and dancing, at the Bay View Lounge. The "Hang Ten Lounge" is the place for poolside or sunset cocktails.

Services: Room service, concierge desk, many shops (including a branch of Liberty House), daily craft demonstrations, children's program, sightseeing programs, and guided nature and Hawaiian reef walks.

Facilities: Ocean-view, championship 27-hole golf course designed by Arnold Palmer Management Company, 10 Plexipave-court tennis complex, horseback riding, fitness center, idyllic beach, two swimming pools, snorkeling, scuba diving, and windsurfing.

INEXPENSIVE

Ke Iki Hale. 59–579 Ke Iki Rd. (off Kamehameha Hwy.), Haleiwa, HI 96712. ☎ **800/ 377-4030** or 808/638-8229. 11 rms, 5 one-bedrooms, 3 two-bedrooms. $85 double; $132– $174 one- and two-bedroom units. Extra person $15. 2-night minimum. MC, V. Free parking. TheBUS: 52 or 55.

This collection of rustic one- and two-bedroom duplex cottages has a divine location: snuggled on 1¹/₂ acres with its own 200-foot stretch of beach between two legendary surf spots—Waimea Bay, where the winter waves can climb to 30 feet or more, and Banzai Pipeline, where experts shoot perfect tubes. These winter waves are rough stuff; us regular folks can only venture in to swim in the flat summer seas. But there's a large lava reef nearby with tide pools to explore, and on the other side, Shark's Cove, a relatively protected snorkeling area.

The North Shore doesn't have many places for visitors to stay; Ke Iki Hale is a good choice for those who enjoy the beach. It's not for everyone, though. Kitchens, barbecues, hammocks, and laundry facilities provide some of the comforts of home. The furnishings are modest but clean, homey, and comfortable. The one-bedrooms have two single beds in the living room, two beds in the separate bedroom, and a full kitchen. Nearby are tennis courts and a jogging path. The downside is that the units are subject to constant salt spray, which adds to their very evident deterioration. And none have a TV or phones (there's a pay phone in the parking lot). *Hot tip:* Don't stay in one of the noisy streetside units; instead, spring for one closer to the water.

✪ Santa's By the Sea. Ke Waena Rd. (off Kamehameha Hwy.), Haleiwa. ℅ Hawaii's Best Bed & Breakfasts, P.O. Box 563, Kamuela, HI 96743. ☎ **800/262-9912** or 808/885-4550. Fax 808/885-0559. E-mail: bestbnb@aloha.net. 1 apt with shower only. TV TEL. $99 double. Rate includes breakfast items in refrigerator. Extra person $5. 2-night minimum. Free parking. TheBUS: 52 or 55.

This certainly must be where Santa Claus comes to vacation, and for good reason: St. Nick knows a bargain when he sees it. The location, price, and style make this place a must-stay if you plan to see the North Shore. It's one of the few North Shore B&Bs right on the beach—and not just any beach, but the famous Banzai Pipeline. You can go from your bed to the sand in less than 30 seconds to watch the sun rise over the Pacific. Hosts Gary and Cyndie renovated this vacation hideaway into an impeccable one-bedroom unit with finely crafted woodwork, bay windows, and a collection of unique Santa figurines and one-of-a-kind Christmas items that Cyndie has assembled over the years; it may sound schlocky, but somehow it gives the apartment a country charm. Honeymooners take note: There's lots of privacy here. The unit has its own entrance; a living room with TV, VCR, and stereo; and a full kitchen with everything a cook would need and an adjacent dining room. Fruit, cereals, bread, coffee, tea, and juice are provided on the first morning to get you started.

Santa's also features a covered gazebo for non-sun-worshipers, a moss-rock outdoor shower (with hot water), and a tranquil setting that would cost you four times as much if this were a hotel rather than a privately run B&B. The only sound you'll hear is the waves gently lapping on the beach in summer, or thundering onto the shore in winter.

Ulu Wehu Bed & Breakfast. 59–416 Alapio Rd. (off Pupukea Rd.), Haleiwa, HI 96712. ☎/fax **808/638-8161.** Studio bunkhouse (with outside electric toilet and shower), 2 rms in cottage (with shared bath). TV. $85 double studio bunkhouse, $90–$100 cottage double. Rates include continental breakfast. Extra person $15. No credit cards. Free parking. TheBUS: 52 or 55.

Set above the North Shore's famous beaches is Ulu Wehu, a working plant nursery/flower and fruit farm/bed-and-breakfast. Two different types of accommodations are available. The plantation-style bunkhouse is a tiny separate building with a double bed in an antique metal frame, a kitchenette with a small refrigerator and microwave, TV/VCR, and phone; outside is an electric toilet and outdoor shower with painted fish on the walls, and in the orchids you'll find an old-fashioned bathtub. If this all sounds a little too close to nature for you, there's also a two-bedroom cottage with shared bath, living area with a sofa-bed and TV/VCR, and a full kitchen; one bedroom has a queen bed and the other has a double (you can rent one bedroom or the entire cottage).

Also on the property—in addition to the gorgeous plants—is a 75-foot lap pool, a large video library, a firepit for bonfires, a horseshoe pit, and sports equipment for rent; there's also an outdoor shower to wash off the sand when you return from the beach. It's a 10-minute drive to the shops and restaurants of Haleiwa, and just minutes to the North Shore's beaches and hiking and mountainbiking trails. The only caveat is the long hike uphill—to 900 feet—from the closest bus stop.

BUDGET

Backpackers Vacation Inns. 59–788 Kamehameha Hwy., Haleiwa, HI 96712. ☎ **808/ 638-7838.** Fax 808/638-7515. E-mail: backpackers@aloha.net. Web page: http:// www.backpackers-hawaii.com. 20 rms, 12 studios, 4 cabins. TV. $45–$55 dorm single with shared bath; $75–$95 private double with shared bath; $75–$95 oceanfront studio; $100–$135 oceanview cabins. MC, V. Free parking. TheBUS: 52 or 55.

With two locations—on Waimea Bay and just across from Three Tables at Pupukea Beach—Backpackers has something for just about every budget traveler. For the back-packing set, they offer inexpensive, basic accommodations in hostel-type facilities consisting of four bunks to a room with a shared bath. There's a common living room with TV and kitchen. For a bit more money, private rooms are available. For families, we recommend the recently renovated oceanfront studios and ocean-view cabins. The one-room studios are the best deal: They're right on the beach, and fea-ture a big, airy room with terra-cotta tile floors, two double beds, kitchen, and TV. *Hot tip:* If you're booking an oceanfront studio, ask for one on the second floor for a better view. The swimming, snorkeling, and diving here are excellent in summer; in the winter, this is a great place to sit on the beach and watch the pros ride the wild waves.

North Shore Villa. 59–575 Makana Rd. (off Pupukea Rd., in the Sunset Hills subdivision), Haleiwa, HI. 96712. ☎/fax **808/638-1185.** E-mail: gingone@lava.net. 1 apt. A/C TV TEL. $75 double. Rate includes fruit basket and baked goods upon arrival. Extra person $10. 5-night mini-mum. No credit cards. Free parking. TheBUS: 52 or 55.

Located in the North Shore's Pupukea area, in the hills behind the famous surfing spots, is this studio apartment, which can sleep up to four in its one large room. The studio has a queen bed, a double-sized fold-out futon couch, stove, refrigerator, and its own private entrance. Other amenities include TV, VCR, A/C, and lanai with barbecue. Hosts Dr. Michael Young (a chiropractor) and his wife, Ginger Suriano, leave a fruit basket and baked goods in the apartment to welcome you; they also pro-vide beach towels and mats (the beach is just 5 minutes away). The only drawback is that the unit is a long, long walk uphill from the nearest bus stop.

Rodeway Inn Hukilau Resort. 55–109 Laniloa St. (off Kamehameha Hwy., near the Polynesian Cultural Center), Laie, HI 96762. ☎ **800/526-4562** or 808/293-9282. Fax 808/ 293-8115. E-mail: rodeway@aloha.net. 48 rms. A/C TV TEL. $69–$99 double. Rates include continental breakfast. Extra person $10. Children under 18 stay free. AE, DISC, JCB, MC, V. Free parking. TheBUS: 52 or 55.

If you plan to see the Polynesian Cultural Center, you might want to stay at this Rodeway, which is within walking distance. The two-story, plantation-style hotel is a small, intimate property, also within walking distance of Brigham Young Uni-versity Hawaii and the Mormon Temple. The rooms are standard, with two double beds, TV, phone, A/C, fridge, coffeemaker on request, and full bath. A continen-tal breakfast with bagels, muffins, fresh fruit, juice, and coffee is included in the price. Access to a secluded white-sand beach is just across the street. Other ameni-ties include a pool and sundeck, self-service Laundromat, tour desk, and free local calls.

☼ Thomsen's Bed & Breakfast. 59–420 Kamehameha Hwy. (6 miles from Haleiwa, near Ehukai Beach), Haleiwa, HI 96712. ☎ **808/638-7947.** Fax 808/638-7694. 1 studio (with shower only). TV TEL. $65 double. Rate includes fruit bowl on arrival. Extra person $5. 3-night minimum. No credit cards. Free parking. TheBUS: 52 or 55.

In the bed-and-breakfast business since 1989, Thomsen's is one of the great values of the North Shore. On a one-acre lot in the country you'll find this quaint studio upstairs above the garage. The airy one-room apartment has a king bed (which can be made into two twins), dining area, kitchenette (with large refrigerator), wicker furniture (including a sleeper sofa), and TV, plus its own private entrance and big deck with views of the majestic Koolau Range. Washer and dryer are available for your use. Located just across the street from the world-famous Banzai Pipeline beach, Thomsen's has an outdoor shower to wash off the sand when you return from the beach.

5 Leeward Oahu: The Waianae Coast

✪ **Ihilani Resort & Spa.** At Ko Olina Resort, 92–1001 Olani St., Kapolei, HI 96707. ☎ **800/ 626-4446** or 808/679-0070. Fax 808/679-0080. 387 rms, 42 suites. A/C MINIBAR TV TEL. $285–$575 double rms; $800–$5,000 suite. Extra person $35. Children under 18 free in parents' room with existing bedding. AE, CB, DC, JCB, MC, V. Free parking. No bus service. To get here from the Honolulu International Airport: Take H-1 west toward Pearl City/Ewa Beach. Stay on H-1 until it becomes Hwy. 93 (Farrington Hwy.). Look for the exit sign for Ihilani Resort. Exit road is Alinui Dr., which goes into the Ko Olina Resort. Turn right on Olani Place, which ends at the hotel.

In December 1993, some 17 miles and 25 minutes west of Honolulu International Airport—and worlds away from the tourist scene of Waikiki—the first hotel in the 640-acre Ko Olina Resort community opened to much speculation. It was so far from Waikiki and Honolulu, who would want go all the way out to Kapolei, critics charged. Lots of people, it turns out. The Ihilani, featuring a luxury spa and fitness center, tennis and golf at Ko Olina, has been well-booked ever since. Located in the quiet of Oahu's west (leeward) coast, Ihilani (which means "heavenly splendor") is nestled between the Pacific Ocean and first of four man-made beach lagoons.

Currently the only hotel on the Ko Olina property, the Ihilani rises some 15 stories along the virgin coastline. Entry to the lobby is through a glass-dome atrium with verdant plants hanging from each floor. It's hard to get a bad room here—some 85% of guest rooms enjoy lagoon or ocean views. The luxuriously appointed rooms are larger than most (680 square feet), with huge lanais, complete with extremely comfortable cushioned teak furniture (chaise lounge, chairs, and table). The rooms also feature a state-of-the-art comfort control system panel (to operate the ceiling fans, air-conditioning, lights, etc.) built into the phone, three telephones, compact disc player, minibar and an in-room safe. Luxurious marble bathrooms have deep-soaking tubs, separate glass-enclosed showers, hair dryers, Yukata robes, and many more amenities.

Dining/Entertainment: Extraordinary cuisine, using the freshest ingredients from neighboring farms and waters, is found in all three Ihilani restaurants. At Azul, the dinner-only restaurant, guests are seated on an intimate terrace overlooking the ocean, and dine on Mediterranean-inspired cuisine. There's open-air dining on light tropical fare all day long at the informal poolside Naupaka Restaurant. A low-fat, low-calorie menu is served at The Spa Café. Talented island artists provide entertainment and music to dance by in the resort's two lounges.

Services: Full-service concierge, 24-hour room service, daily newspaper, business services, transportation to Waikiki and Ala Moana Shopping Center. Keiki Beach-comber Club is a year-round program for toddlers to teens, housed in its own ground-floor facility, with a wide variety of outdoor adventures and indoor learning activities. It has its own Computer Learning Center, a 125-gallon fish tank, an outdoor performance space, an evening lounge for teen-themed parties, and more. Special meals are served and children can spend the day or a half-day.

Facilities: Championship 18-hole Ko Olina Golf Course, designed by Ted Robinson and recognized as one of Hawaii's premier golf course; a tennis club with pro shop; shopping arcade; 3-mile coastal fitness trail; two pools; and a stretch of four white-sand beaches for ocean activities.

The world-class Ihilani Spa offers just about everything to enhance one's health, fitness, and well-being, including hydrotherapies such as Thalasso treatments with sea water and seaweeds, Swiss showers, Grand Jets, Vichy showers, and Roman pools. Shiatsu, Swedish, and Hawaiian Lomi Lomi massages are offered, as well as herbal bodywraps. Complete fitness and relaxation programs can be designed for each guest. For us, the Spa alone would be reason enough to leave home and come to Oahu.

6 Oahu's Campgrounds & Wilderness Cabins

Camping is a year-round experience on Oahu thanks to the balmy weather. There is, however, a wet (winter) and dry (summer) season. You should be prepared for rain year-round. You also need to be ready for insects (have a good repellent for mosquitoes), water purification (boiling, filtration, or iodine crystals), and sun protection (sunscreen, a hat, and a long sleeve shirt).

If you don't plan to bring your own camping equipment, you can rent equipment at **Omar the Tent Man,** 94-158 Leoole St., Waipahu, HI 96797 (☎ **808/677-8775**), or **The Bike Shop,** at 1149 S. King St. (☎ **808/595-0588**) and the Windward City Shopping Center (☎ **808/235-8722**). Both also have equipment for sale.

Oahu is the only Hawaiian island with a public transportation system that serves the entire Island (see "Getting Around" in chapter 5 for details). However, one problem with getting to a camping site on the TheBus is that luggage larger than you can hold on your lap or place under your seat, is forbidden. Metal-frame packs are not permitted on TheBUS. Drivers do use discretion, but be forewarned.

The best places to camp on Oahu are listed below. You can locate them on the map entitled "Beaches & Outdoor Activities on Oahu" in chapter 8.

HONOLULU
SAND ISLAND STATE RECREATION AREA

Believe it or not, there is a campground in Honolulu. In this case located just south of the Honolulu Harbor on a waterfront park. Don't be put off by the heavy industrial area you have to drive through to reach this 102-acre park with grassy lawns, ironwood trees, and sandy beaches. Campers have great views of the entire Honolulu coastline all the way to Waikiki, better than some of the guests in the $400-a-night hotel rooms in Waikiki. In addition to the scenic beauty, the most popular activity here is shoreline fishing, especially along the west shore of Sand Island. Swimming is an option, but watch out for the rocks along the shoreline bottom, and the water quality is occasionally questionable.

The park is also in an excellent location to enjoy the attractions in Honolulu, it is just 15 minutes from Waikiki or Pearl Harbor.

Tent camping only in this beach park. There are picnic tables (some under small covered shelters), rest rooms with cold showers only, and potable water. You'll need a permit; applications are accepted no earlier than 30 days in advance. Write to the **Department of Land and Natural Resources,** State Parks Division, P.O. Box 621, Honolulu, HI 96809 (☎ **808/587-0300**). Permits are limited to a 5-day stay in every 30-day period. The park is closed on Wednesdays and

Thursdays for maintenance. The gates close at 6:45pm in the fall and winter (from the weekend after Labor Day until March 31) and 7:45pm in the spring and summer (April 1 to Friday after Labor Day). The gates do not open until 7am the next morning; cars cannot enter or leave during that period. TheBUS 19 stops at Nimitz Highway and Puuhale Road, just over a mile walk to the park entrance.

To get there from the Honolulu International Airport take Nimitz Highway toward Honolulu and Waikiki. Turn right at the Sand Island Access Road (Hwy. 64) and follow it to the end of the road and the park entrance.

CENTRAL OAHU
KEAIWA HEIAU STATE RECREATION AREA

Located at the southern end of central Oahu, above Halawa Heights, this 385-acre wooded park offers a cool mountain camp with hiking trails and picnic facilities. This area, in the foothills of the Koolaus, is filled with eucalyptus, ironwood, and Norfolk pines. The remains of the *heiau ho'ola* (temple of treating the sick) are on the grounds, and specimens of Hawaiian medicinal plants are on display. An excellent 5-mile hiking trail, the Aiea loop, offers magnificent Pearl Harbor and mountain views. There's tent camping only; campers have the choice of flat, open grassy areas or slightly sloping areas with shade trees. Facilities include picnic tables, rest rooms with cold showers, outdoor grills, a dishwashing area, a covered pavilion, drinking water, and a public phone. Supplies are available in Aiea, 2 miles away.

You'll need a permit; applications are accepted no earlier than 30 days in advance. Write to the Department of Land and Natural Resources, State Parks Division, P.O. Box 621, Honolulu, HI 96809 (☎ **808/587-0300**). Permits are limited to a 5-day stay in every 30-day period. The park is closed on Wednesdays and Thursdays for maintenance. The gates close at 6:45pm in the fall and winter (from the weekend after Labor Day until March 31) and 7:45pm in the spring and summer (April 1 to Friday after Labor Day). The gates do not open until 7am the next morning; cars cannot enter or leave during that period.

To get here from Waikiki, take the H-1 Freeway to Highway 78 and exit at Aiea (Exit 13A). Follow Moanalua Road to Aiea Heights Drive and turn right; the park entrance is at the end of the road. There is no bus service to this area.

WINDWARD
HOOMALUHIA BOTANICAL GARDENS

This relatively unknown windward-side camping area, outside of Kaneohe, is a find. Hoomaluhia means "peace and tranquility," an apt description of this 400-acre botanical garden. In this lush garden setting with rare plants and craggy cliffs in the background, it's hard to believe that you're just a half-hour from downtown Honolulu. The gardens are laid out in areas devoted to the plants specific to tropical America, native Hawaii, Polynesia, India–Sri Lanka, and Africa. A 32-acre lake sits in the middle of the scenic park (no swimming or boating is allowed, though), and there are numerous hiking trails. The Visitors Center can suggest a host of activities, ranging from guided walks to demonstrations of ancient Hawaiian plant use. The facilities for this tent-camp area include rest rooms, cold showers, dishwashing stations, picnic tables, grills, and water. A public phone is available at the Visitors Center, and shopping and gas are available in Kaneohe, 1 mile away.

Permits are free, but you're only allowed to stay 4 nights per month. Camping is permitted Friday to Monday nights only. For information, contact **Hoomaluhia Botanical Gardens,** 45-680 Luluku Rd., (at Kamehameha Hwy.), Kaneohe, HI 96744 (☎ **808/233-7323**). The gate is locked at 4pm, it is open again from 5:30

to 6:30pm, then closed for the night after that. The gates open again at 9am. TheBus no. 55 (Circle Island) stops 4 miles from the park entrance. To get there from Waikiki, take H-1 to the Pali Highway (Hi. 61); turn left on Kamehameha Hwy. (Hi. 83); at the fourth light, turn left on Luluku Road.

KUALOA REGIONAL PARK

Located on a peninsula on Kaneohe Bay, this park has a spectacular setting. The gold-sand beach is excellent for snorkeling, and fishing can be rewarding (see "Beaches," in chapter 8, for details). There are two campgrounds: Campground A—in a wooded area with a sandy beach and palm, ironwoods, kamani, and monkeypod trees—is mainly used for groups, but has a few sites for families, except during the summer (June through August), when the Department of Parks and Recreation conducts a children's camping program here. Campground B is on the main beach; it has fewer shade trees, but a great view of Mokolii Island. Facilities at both sites include rest rooms, showers, picnic tables, drinking fountains, and a public phone. Campground A also has sinks for dishwashing, a volleyball court, and a kitchen building. Gas and groceries are available in Kaaawa, 2 1/2 miles away. The gate hours at Kualoa Regional Park are 7am to 8pm; if you're not back to the park by 8pm, you're locked out for the night.

Permits are free, but limited to 5 days (no camping on Wednesday and Thursday). Contact the **Honolulu Department of Parks and Recreation,** 650 S. King St., Honolulu, HI 96713 (☎ **808/523-4525**), for information and permits. Kualoa Regional Park is located in the 49-600 area of Kamehameha Hwy., across from Mokolii Island. To get there, take the Likelike Hwy. (Hi. 63); after the Wilson Tunnel, get in the right lane and turn off on Kahakili Hwy. (Hi. 83). Or, you can take TheBUS no. 55.

KAHANA BAY BEACH PARK

Under Tahiti-like cliffs, with a beautiful, gold-sand crescent beach framed by pine-needle casuarina trees, Kahana Bay Beach Park is a place of serene beauty. You can swim, bodysurf, fish, hike, and picnic, or just sit and listen to the trade winds whistle through the beach pines.

Tent and vehicle camping only are allowed at this oceanside oasis. Facilities include rest rooms, picnic tables, drinking water, public phones, and a boat-launching ramp. Do note that the rest rooms are located at the north end of the beach, far away from the camping area, and there are no showers. There's no fee for camping, but you must get a permit, which is also free; the limit is 5 nights. You can obtain a permit at the **State Parks Division,** P.O. Box 621, Honolulu, HI 96809 (☎ **808/587-0300**).

Kahana Bay Beach Park is located in the 52-222 block of Kamehameha Hwy. (Hi. 83) in Kahana. To get there from Waikiki, take the H-1 west to the Likelike Highway (Hi. 63). Continue north on the Likelike, through the Wilson Tunnel, turning left on Hi. 83; Kahana Bay is 13 miles down the road on the right. You can also get there via TheBUS no. 55.

WAIMANALO BAY STATE RECREATION AREA

Just outside the town of Waimanalo is one of the most beautiful beachfront camping grounds on Oahu: steep verdant cliffs in the background, a view of Rabbit Island off shore, and miles of white-sand beach complete the picture of Waimanalo Bay State Recreation Area. This campground is close to Sea Life Park, and relatively close to Hanauma Bay, Makapuu, and Sandy Beach.

Ocean activities abound: great swimming offshore, good surfing for beginners and plentiful fishing grounds. There is tent camping only at the 12 campsites, which assures plenty of privacy. The campsites are all in the open grassy lawn between the ironwood trees and the shoreline in numbered slots. Each campsite has its own picnic table, barbecue grill, and garbage can. Other facilities in the area include a central rest room with showers, water fountains, and a dishwashing sink. A public telephone is located by the caretaker's house.

You'll need a permit; applications are accepted no earlier than 30 days in advance. Write to the **Department of Land and Natural Resources,** State Parks Division, P.O. Box 621, Honolulu, HI 96809 (☎ **808/587-0300**). Permits are limited to a 5-day stay in every 30-day period. The park is closed on Wednesdays and Thursdays for maintenance. The gates close at 6:45pm in the fall and winter (from the weekend after Labor Day until March 31) and 7:45pm in the spring and summer (April 1 to Friday after Labor Day). The gates do not open until 7am the next morning; cars cannot enter or leave during that period. TheBUS 57 stops on Kalanianaole Highway (Hwy. 72), about a mile walking distance to the park entrance.

To get there from Honolulu take the H-1 Freeway east until it ends. Continue on Highway 72 (the Kalanianaole Highway) into Waimanalo. Turn right on Whiteman Road and then right again on Walker Road, which leads to the park entrance.

THE NORTH SHORE
MALAEKAHANA BAY STATE RECREATION AREA

One of the most beautiful beach camping areas in the state, with a mile-long gold-sand beach (see "Beaches," in chapter 8, for details), is this site on Oahu's Windward Coast. There are two areas for tent camping. Facilities include picnic tables, rest rooms, showers, sinks, drinking water, and a phone. Permits are free, but limited to 5 nights and may be obtained at any state parks office, including the **State Parks Division,** P.O. Box 621, Honolulu, HI 96809 (☎ **808/587-0300**).

The recreation area is located on Kamehameha Hwy. (Hi. 83) between Laie and Kahuku. To get there, take the H-2 Freeway to Hi. 99 to Hi. 83 (both roads are called Kamehameha Hwy.); continue on Hi. 83 just past Kahuku. Or take TheBUS: 55.

For your safety, the park gate is closed between 6:45pm and 7am; vehicles cannot enter or exit during those hours. Groceries and gas are available in Laie and Kahuku, less than a mile away.

CAMP MOKULEIA

A quiet, isolated beach on Oahu's North Shore, 4 miles from Kaena Point, is the centerpiece of a 9-acre campground that's a great getaway. Camping is available on the beach or in a grassy, wooded area. Activities include swimming, surfing, shore fishing, and beachcombing.

Facilities include tent camping, cabins, and lodge accommodations. The tent-camping site has portable chemical toilets, a water spigot, and outdoor showers; there are no picnic tables or barbecue grills, so come prepared. The cabins have bunk beds and can sleep up to 14 people in the small cabins and 22 in the large cabins. The lodge facilities include rooms with and without a private bath. The cabins are $140 per night for the 14-bed cabin and $180 per night for the 22-bed cabin. The rooms at the lodge are $50 to $55 for a shared bath and $60 to $65 for a private bath. Many groups use the camp, but it's still a very peaceful place. The tent area is separated from the buildings—but you can use all the facilities if you opt for it—and there's a real sense of privacy. Tent camping is $8 per adult, per night and $4 for children ages 6 to 17 years per night (children 5 and under stay free). Reservations for permits are needed; contact **Camp Mokuleia,** 68–729 Farrington Hwy., Waialua, HI 96791 (☎ **808/637-6241**; fax 808/637-5505).

Camp Mokuleia is located on Farrington Hwy., west of Haleiwa. To get there from Waikiki, take the H-1 to the H-2 exit; stay on H-2 until the end. Where the road forks, bear left to Waialua on Hi. 803, which turns into Hi. 930, to Kaena Point. Look for the green fence on the right, where a small sign at the driveway reads CAMP MOKULEIA, EPISCOPAL CHURCH OF HAWAII.

7

Dining

by Jocelyn Fujii

Oahu's dining scene falls into several categories: Waikiki restaurants, chef-owned glamour restaurants, neighborhood eateries, fast-food joints, ethnic restaurants, and restaurants and food courts in shopping malls. One of Honolulu's greatest assets is the range of restaurants in all categories, and one of Honolulu's greatest paradoxes is the fact that even in this sluggish economy, you can hardly get a table at Alan Wong's Restaurant or Sam Choy's new crabhouse. Even for a culinary late bloomer like Honolulu, dining is a top priority—not only for pleasure, but also because Hawaii has one of the highest percentages of working mothers in the nation.

All the better for our chefs. Chefs once trained and celebrated in Hawaii's top resorts are moving into their own spheres beyond hotel properties and walk-in traffic, creating their own destinations and loyal clientele who are willing to find them in unexpected neighborhoods and urban niches. Chefs such as Alan Wong, Jean-Marie Josselin, Sam Choy, and Roy Yamaguchi are spreading their empires across the major islands of Hawaii. People have stopped counting their restaurants—at last count, five Roy's Restaurants in Hawaii, four of Josselin's A Pacific Cafes, three Sam Choy's, with a Maui-opening imminent—because they are blazing across the landscape like Indy 500 racers. Their restaurants are worth renting a car to find, because, like the plate-lunch palaces for casual dining on the run, they offer an authentic Hawaii experience.

The recommendations below will lead you to the few noteworthy hotel dining rooms, neighborhood hangouts worth finding, ethnic winners, and isolated marvels in all corners of the island.

Chain Restaurants   It's hard to spend more than $5 at the **Ba-le Sandwich Shops,** whose French and Vietnamese specialties such as pho (the noodle soup that's a national ritual in Vietnam), croissants as good as the espresso, and wonderful taro/tapioca desserts have won an islandwide following. Their sandwiches, on freshly made, crusty baguettes are inexpensive and tasty. Hard work, low prices, and delectable offerings have made Ba-le a roaring success. Recommended: shrimp rolls in translucent rice paper, tofu sandwiches, seafood pho, lemongrass chicken with garlic shrimp, lemongrass and vegetarian sandwiches on fresh French bread or croissants. Branches are in Ala Moana Center (☎ **808/944-4752**); at 333 Ward Ave. (☎ **808/591-0935**); in Kahala Mall, 4211 Waialae Ave. (☎ **808/735-6889**);

in Manoa Marketplace, 2855 E. Manoa Rd. (☎ **808/988-1407**); and in Chinatown at 150 N. King St. (☎ **808/521-3973**).

With branches in Kaimuki, Kailua, Kaneohe, Wahiawa, and Kaneohe, the high-profile **Boston's North End Pizza Bakery** (corporate ☎ **808/263-2253**) chain has an enthusiastic following among pizza lovers, and not just because it boasts "Hawaii's largest slice." Boston's reasonable prices and hefty sizes (19 in. and 3 lb.!) add extra value, and fans swear by the sauces and toppings. Since the Waikiki location closed, they've added a Kapolei/Makakilo site.

And try topping **Zippy's Restaurants,** at last count 17 of them on Oahu alone (call ☎ **808/955-6622** for the one nearest you). Some are better than others (the Vineyard and Makiki branches are faves, and the McCully one sometimes smells like stale cigarette smoke), but all feature cheap, tasty chili (regular and vegetarian), fabulous fresh-mushroom omelets swimming in garlic, respectable saimin, surprisingly decent specials, and burgers, sandwiches, salads, and American fare that is likable if not predictable. At Zippy's you may find local politicos discussing important issues in the next booth, or your next-door neighbor after the Little League game.

The streets of Waikiki are lined with famous fast-food joints from Denny's to McDonald's, from Burger King to Jack in the Box. Oahu also has most of the familiar sit-down chain restaurants and pubs. In Waikiki, the local **Hard Rock Cafe** resides at 1837 Kapiolani Blvd. (☎ **808/955-7383**), while **Planet Hollywood Honolulu** is nearby at 2155 Kalakaua Ave. (☎ **808/924-7877**). On downtown's Restaurant Row, several popular newcomers have appeared for those unwilling to spring for the high-ticket **Ruth's Chris Steak House,** 500 Ala Moana Blvd. ☎ **808/599-3860.** In Kahala Mall, you can savor the famous **Starbucks** (☎ **808/737-0283**) coffee near Star Market, or tuck into the flavor-of-the-month toppings offered by the local branch of **California Pizza Kitchen,** 4211 Waialae Ave. (☎ **808/737-9446**). On the North Shore, the **Chart House Haleiwa,** 66-011 Kamehameha Hwy. (☎ **808/637-8005**), has a fine view of the harbor from outdoor tables to complement its fresh fish and prime rib.

Food Courts   Several shopping centers have food courts where you can grab a quick and cheap meal on the run. The largest is the Makai Court in **Ala Moana Shopping Center,** at Ala Moana Blvd. and Atkinson Dr. (☎ **808/946-2811**). There are 17 different types of cookery in this busy, noisy complex on the ground floor of the rambling mall. Our favorites: Tsuruya Noodles (the Tenzaru is excellent), Sbarro's pizza, Poi Bowl (Hawaiian plates), and the Thirst Aid Station with its smoothies and fresh fruit juices. Korean, Italian, Thai, Chinese, and other ethnic foods, as well as health foods, are also available. Open Monday to Saturday from 9:30am to 9pm, Sunday from 10am to 5pm.

1 Waikiki

VERY EXPENSIVE

✪ **La Mer.** In the Halekulani, 2199 Kalia Rd. ☎ **808/923-2311.** Reservations recommended. Main courses $37–$43. Prix fixe $85–$105. AE, CB, DC, JCB, MC, V. Daily 6–10pm. Jackets required for men. NEOCLASSIC FRENCH.

Honolulu's most elegant and expensive dining takes place in this second-floor, open-sided oceanside room with views of Diamond Head and the sunset between palm fronds. Southern French influences meld seamlessly with the fresh island ingredients that La Mer has always celebrated. The offerings of Michelin award–winning chef Yves Garnier include a flawless foie gras sautéed with apples and a French sweet-sour sauce; fillet of *kumu* (goatfish, a delicacy) in a rosemary salt crust; the bouillabaisse, a La Mer signature now served out of puff pastry; a thyme-marinated rack of lamb that is redolent with garlic and thyme. Lovers of seafood will find it hard to choose between the *onaga* fillet, cooked crisp on the skin, the dover sole, *moano* (another type of goatfish), salmon steamed in lettuce, and the several fish entrees in delicate preparations. Top it off with the Gallic splendors of the cheese tray, served with walnut bread, or the Symphony of La Mer (almond tart, crème brûlée, mousse of three chocolates). Frightfully expensive though it is, La Mer is in a class of its own in Honolulu.

EXPENSIVE

Acqua. In Hawaiian Regent Hotel, 2552 Kalakaua Ave. ☎ **808/924-0123.** Reservations recommended. Main courses $11.95–$44.95. Prix fixe $24.95. AE, DC, DISC, JCB, MC, V. Sun–Thurs 6–9:30pm, Fri–Sat 6–10:30pm. STEAK/SEAFOOD.

Acqua seems to have found an even keel with its current menu of pasta, seafood, and steak—everything from a $15.95 paella to a $44.95 Maine lobster. At $19.95, grilled guava-barbecued prawns and fresh Island fish are a friendly choice. Meat lovers will love the rack of lamb (half order for $19.95), roasted chicken ($16.95), and 10 steak house selections, while seafood lovers have ample choices, too. The dining is casual, around an open kitchen, and the Thursday-through-Saturday evening live entertainment features prominent names in island music.

Bali by the Sea. In Hilton Hawaiian Village, 2005 Kalia Rd. ☎ **808/941-2254.** Reservations recommended. Dinner main courses $26.50–$29.50. Prix fixe $39.50. AE, DC, JCB, MC, V. Mon–Fri 7am–10am and 11am–2pm; Mon–Sat 6–9:30pm. CONTINENTAL/PACIFIC RIM.

Bali by the Sea is one of Waikiki's most memorable oceanfront dining rooms—pale and full of light, with a white grand piano at the entrance and sweeping views of the ocean. Some diners call it stuffy; others, supremely elegant. The menu includes lunchtime offerings that score high on the culinary scale: taro and crab cakes with green papaya salad; salmon baked in rice paper; Scottish smoked salmon clubhouse sandwich; and, for extravagant lunchers without time or waistline considerations, macadamia-nut herb-crusted lamb and a number of seafood and pasta dishes. Dinner inches upward in scale and extravagance, with the herb-crusted lamb still popular, and the kiawe opakapaka (with shiitake, asparagus risotto, and tobiko!) the prevailing choice among seafood lovers. The substantial, sophisticated appetizer menu, with the likes of grilled eggplant napoleon, coriander-flavored lobster tartar, escargots strudel, and eggplant Napoleon, make the Bali a plausible choice for glamorous grazers as well.

Caffelatte. 339 Saratoga Rd. ☎ **808/924-1414.** Reservations recommended. Prix fixe $35. MC, V. Wed–Mon 6:30pm to closing. NORTHERN ITALIAN.

Owner/chef Laura Magni makes everything from scratch and to order; you wouldn't catch her near a microwave oven. As a result, you won't find a better bruschetta, pasta carbonara, marinara, or risotto in Honolulu. Because of her generations-old recipes and long hours of simmering soups and sauces, the menu is built on solidly good, uncompromising basics. The prix-fixe–only dinner consists of appetizer or salad, soup (usually fish, lentil, or vegetable, and always good), and the entree, which could be a porcini risotto, or homemade ravioli, or any of the five veal selections (for an additional $5). While fans swear by the food quality, the lack of parking and the inflexibility of the prix fixe format are problematic, not to mention the price, which could end up being a bit steep for pasta in a dining room this casual. Still, purists swear by Laura's cooking.

Waikiki Dining

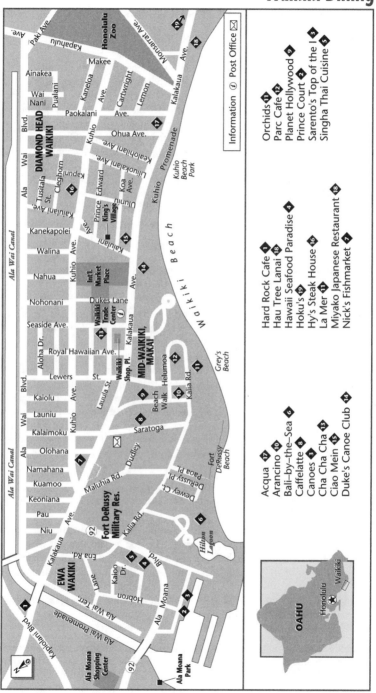

Information ⓘ   Post Office ⌧

Orchids **11**
Parc Cafe **12**
Planet Hollywood **9**
Prince Court **2**
Sarento's Top of the I **3**
Singha Thai Cuisine **5**

Hard Rock Cafe **1**
Hau Tree Lanai **18**
Hawaii Seafood Paradise **4**
Hoku's **12**
Hy's Steak House **16**
La Mer **11**
Miyako Japanese Restaurant **13**
Nick's Fishmarket **7**

Acqua **17**
Arancino **10**
Bali-by-the-Sea **6**
Caffelatte **8**
Canoes **9**
Cha Cha Cha **13**
Ciao Mein **15**
Duke's Canoe Club **14**

OAHU

Honolulu

Waikiki

1-07068

Hau Tree Lanai. In New Otani Kaimana Beach Hotel, 2863 Kalakaua Ave. ☎ **808/921-7066.** Reservations recommended. Breakfast $7.50–$13.50, lunch $9.50–$14.10, dinner main courses $22.50–$29.50. AE, CB, DC, DISC, JCB, MC, V. Daily 7–11am and 5:30–9pm; Mon–Sat 11:30am–2pm, Sun 12–2pm. Late lunch in the open-air bar, daily 2–4pm. AMERICAN/ISLAND.

The centerpiece of this terrace on the sand is an ancient hau tree that provides shade and charm for diners, most of whom are busy observing the diverse parade of well-oiled beachgoing bodies at Sans Souci Beach, which to locals is the most cherished strip of urban Honolulu. The view of the ocean, the sunset, the Waianae mountains, and the historic architecture of the saltwater pool called the Natatorium is gorgeous, as much a part of the dining experience as the food itself. Breakfast here is a must: salmon Florentine, served on spinach and a fresh-baked scone; a scrumptious smoked-salmon omelet; poi pancakes; eggs Benedict; an $8.50 continental breakfast. At lunch, regulars swear by the $13.50 fresh mahimahi and Oriental chicken salad, and at dinner, a selection of fresh moonfish, red snapper, opakapaka, ahi, and meats (garlic-lemon pepper chicken, filet mignon, lamb chops) offer a diverse and pleasant selection. Just mauka of the tree-shaded terrace is the cocktail lounge, where savvy sunset watchers gather for appetizers and cocktails while local performers play acoustic or pedal-steel guitar.

Hy's Steak House. 2440 Kuhio Ave. ☎ **808/922-5555.** Reservations recommended. Main courses $15.50–$36. AE, CB, DC, DISC, MC, V. Daily 6–10pm. AMERICAN.

Call it old-fashioned or call it a survivor, but there's no denying that Hy's has demonstrated admirable staying power through nouvelle, vegetarian, and light Hawaii Regional Cuisine. And their prices have escalated too. This dark and clubby steak house still scores high among carnivores and even offers a grilled vegetable platter for carniphobes, a relief for the arteries on a menu of chateaubriand, beef Wellington, shrimp scampi, and other fruits de mer and terre. "The Only" is its classic best, a New York strip steak, kiawe-grilled and served with a mysterious signature sauce. Garlic lovers swear by the Garlic Steak Diane, a richly endowed rib eye with sliced mushrooms, but the good-as-gold filet mignon needs no embellishment. For an appetizer, you can order Thai-style scallops, buttery escargots, or wonderful salads—an excellent Caesar, warm spinach, and seafood-and-avocado. Hy's is a great choice for steak lovers with bottomless pocketbooks, or for those tiring of Hawaii Regional Cuisine.

Miyako Japanese Restaurant. In New Otani Kaimana Beach Hotel, 2863 Kalakaua Ave. ☎ **808/923-4739.** Reservations recommended. Main courses $30–$40. AE, DC, DISC, JCB, MC, V. Daily 6–9:30pm. JAPANESE.

Ikebana arrangements accent the dining room, and servers in gorgeous kimonos bustle to bring you brisk, courteous service. The food presentation is flawless: lacquer trays, precious sake cups, esthetically arranged morsels reminiscent of imperial dining in Kyoto. Offerings include make-your-own sushi hand-rolls (temaki) from a tray of vegetables, mountain yam, crab, king clam, sashimi, nori, and salmon roe; prearranged kaiseki dinners ($60); and several combinations of tempura, sashimi, shrimp, fresh lobster, soup, and pickled vegetables. This is a pretty room on the second floor of the hotel, with the Waikiki skyline glittering in the distance.

Nicholas Nickolas. In Ala Moana Hotel, 410 Atkinson Dr. ☎ **808/955-4466.** Reservations recommended. Main courses $19–$42. AE, CB, DC, DISC, MC, V. Daily 5:30–11:30pm. AMERICAN/CONTINENTAL/SEAFOOD.

Take the express elevator at the Ala Moana Hotel to the 36th floor, where the newly renovated circular dining room reveals the city in a mountain-to-sea panorama. The menu is spare and to the point, strong on appetizers and seafood: crab cakes (a best-seller), the signature Cajun-seared ahi, specialties prime rib, veal Oskar, and farm-raised catfish. Blackened onaga has always been a house specialty, seared in Cajun spices and baked. You'll dine at tables along the edge of the dining room, or at cozy booths along the interior, and when dinner's over, the dancing begins with live music Sunday to Thursday from 9:30pm to 3am, Friday and Saturday from 10pm to 4am. Ask about the appetizer menu, available daily from 5pm to 2:30am. There's a dress code in effect for men here: collared shirt, slacks, and shoes.

Nick's Fishmarket. In Waikiki Gateway Hotel, 2070 Kalakaua Ave. ☎ **808/955-6333.** Reservations recommended. Main courses $20–$55. AE, CB, DC, DISC, JCB, MC, V. Sun–Thurs 5:30–10pm, including cafe menu; Fri–Sat 5:30–11pm, cafe menu 5:30pm–midnight. SEAFOOD.

With its extensive menu and lobster specialties, Nick's will always be the restaurant for seafood lovers with upscale tastes. Call it old-fashioned; it still has a following among celebrities and others who are used to the clubby, macho ambiance and may even find it refreshing in these days of bustling open kitchens and noisy, lively dining rooms. The menu is an awesome flexing of Neptunian muscle. Appetizers include a cold platter, salmon cakes, and an ounce of Beluga caviar (the latter at a hefty $120). The entrees include chicken, rack of lamb (very popular), and a few obligatory pasta dishes. The Hawaiian fresh fish selection reeks of authority: several kinds of ahi, mahimahi, broadbill swordfish, ono, salmon, and snappers—whatever is fresh on the auction block. But the true bonanza is the luxury lobster: whether it's slipper, rock, spiny, or Maine, the selection is the best we've seen. The chef's specials change weekly.

Orchids. In the Halekulani, 2199 Kalia Rd. ☎ **808/923-2311.** Reservations recommended. Main courses $25–$39. Prix fixe $44.50 and $58. AE, CB, DC, JCB, MC, V. Daily 7:30–11am, 11:30am–2pm, and 6–10pm; Sun brunch 9:30am–2:30pm. INDO-PACIFIC.

The stunning oceanside ambiance of this Honolulu landmark hasn't changed, but its menu has, and new chef Wayne Hirabayashi has added his touch to Orchids. Prices have gone up, and the offerings are no longer Pacific Rim, or Pacific Edge, or Euro-anything. After several recent theme changes, it's now Indo-Pacific. So, while viewing Diamond Head over crisp, blindingly white linens, or over flickering candlelight, you can sample steamed onaga Oriental style, miso-marinated swordfish, lemongrass-cashew chicken, Dungeness crab cakes, and curried duck puffs, Orchids specialties all. For lighter fare, the grilled fish of the day is safe and satisfying, and the Kula tomato–Maui onion salad is a perennial favorite. Regardless, it's imperative you save room for the ginger crème brûlée or warm apple tart.

Prince Court. In Hawaii Prince Hotel, 100 Holomoana St. ☎ **808/956-1111.** Reservations recommended. Main courses $18–$38. Prix fixe $44.50. AE, CB, JCB, MC, V. Daily 6–10:30am and 6–9:30pm; Mon–Fri 11:30am–2pm, Sun brunch 11am–1pm. HAWAII REGIONAL.

The gorgeous view of the boat harbor is an asset any time of the day or night, particularly at sunset, or on Friday nights when fireworks light up the skies from Waikiki shores. For $36, diners can sample a lavish seafood buffet Friday and Saturday nights, or order off an à la carte menu appealing to both seafood and steak lovers. For a proponent of Hawaii Regional Cuisine, Prince Court offers stunningly simple (and satisfying) grilled and roasted meats: rack of lamb, prime rib of beef, and a perfectly done, buttery-tender New York steak with wild mushrooms and Maui onions. Solid seafood hits include the seafood Napoleon (opakapaka, mahimahi, and salmon on fresh hearts of palm and shiitake mushrooms), pepper-seared salmon, and the wok-charred ahi with creamy wasabi. Thanks to chef Gary Strehl, Prince Court has remained the one true thing among the changeable elements of the Hawaii Prince.

Sarento's Top of the I. In Ilikai Hotel Nikko Waikiki, 1777 Ala Moana Blvd. ☎ **808/ 949-3811.** Reservations recommended. Main courses $16–$41. AE, JCB, MC, V. Sun–Thurs 5:30–10:30pm, Fri–Sat 5:30–11pm. ITALIAN.

The ride up the glass elevator is an event in itself, but Sarento's is not all show. Diners rave about the romantic view of the city, the pizza baked in a wood-burning oven, the Caesar salad, the frutti de mare that's rich but engaging, and the sautéed scallops with porcini mushrooms and garlic butter. The shrimp pesto pizza is also a success. On the lighter side, the blackened sashimi and smoked salmon Italiano are both safe bets, as are any of the cold appetizers.

MODERATE

Arancino. 255 Beach Walk. ☎ **808/923-5557.** Main courses $6.50–$14.50. AE, JCB, MC, V. Daily 11am–9:30pm. ITALIAN.

When jaded Honolulu residents venture into Waikiki for dinner, it had better be good. And for the price, Arancino is worth the hunt. Here's what you'll find: a cheerful cafe of Monet-yellow walls and tile floors, located on a side street; respectable pastas and risotto and fabulous red pepper salsa and rock-salt focaccia; we-try-harder service; and reasonable prices. The shredded-radicchio risotto (risotto changes daily) for $8.50 is notable; the steamed mussels, $4.50, come seasoned assertively; the gorgonzola-asparagus pizza, $7.50, is unconventional and zesty; and heaven forbid you should miss out on the $14.50 lobster linguine if it's on the menu. Arancino is frequently filled, and its intimate, convivial atmosphere of fairy lights on potted trees, Italian posters, and dangling strands of garlic make it all the more enjoyable.

Canoes. In Ilikai Hotel Nikko Waikiki, 1777 Ala Moana Blvd. ☎ **808/949-3811.** Reservations recommended. Main courses $11–$33. AE, DISC, MC, V. Daily 6am–2pm and 5:30–10pm. Fri– Sun buffet, with last seating at 9:30pm. CONTINENTAL/SEAFOOD.

If you're in the mood for a theme buffet, Canoes has perfected the genre with inexpensive monthly appetizer spreads and regular weekend dinner buffets. Including the popular Friday Hawaiian lunch buffet, they're offered in the Ilikai's informal alfresco dining room. With its lomi salmon, poi, kalua pig, lau lau, chicken long rice, barbecued fish, and haupia cake, the Hawaiian feast offers visitors a chance to sample what is usually laid out at a luau, minus the beachfront location and fire-dancing. On Saturday the buffet is strictly seafood, and on Sunday, family fare (roast beef, ham, mahimahi with Maui onions, fried chicken) takes over the dining room. Buffet lovers, take note: For $5 the first Sunday afternoon of each month, an Oriental appetizer selection features fresh island veggies and dips, Korean barbecue chicken wings, egg rolls, and other finger foods, with similar offerings the second Sunday of the month. Every third Sunday, say olé to the Mexican buffet, and the fourth Sunday, to Italian specialties such as pasta and pizza. Save room for the Bubbie's ice cream and deep-fried Hawaiian coconut pudding, two local favorites.

Ciao Mein. In Hyatt Regency Waikiki, 2424 Kalakaua Ave. ☎ **808/923-2426.** Reservations recommended. Main courses $8–$25. Prix fixe $26–$36. AE, CB, DC, DISC, JCB, MC, V. Daily 6–10pm; Sun brunch 10am–2pm. ITALIAN/CHINESE.

The cross-cultural connection seemed gimmicky at first, but Ciao Mein has pulled it off in a large, pleasing dining room with efficient service, surprisingly good Chinese food (especially for a hotel restaurant), and award-winning menu items that make this a haven for noodle lovers. If you're feeling extravagant, the honey-walnut shrimp, with snap peas and honey-glazed walnuts, is worth every penny of its $21.50 price. The crisp fried noodles with chicken and lobster is hailed by fans and equaled in aplomb by the award-winning bell-pepper-and-sausage penne. And few Honolulu festival-goers will forget the spicy wok-fried Szechuan eggplant, $6.75, that won accolades and helped put Ciao Mein on Honolulu's culinary map.

✪ **Duke's Canoe Club.** 2335 Kalakaua Ave., Outrigger Waikiki Hotel. ☎ **808/922-2268.** Reservations recommended for dinner. Main courses $15.95–$23. AE, DC, MC, V. Daily 7am–1am. STEAK/SEAFOOD.

Named after fabled surfer Duke Kahanamoku, this casual, upbeat oceanfront hotspot buzzes with diners and Hawaiian music lovers throughout the day, some of them wandering in from the beach, where they overheard slack-key guitar riffs that were too good to resist. Open-air dining gives a front-row view to the sunset—this is what dining in Waikiki should be. The dinner fare is steak and seafood, with high marks for the prime rib and several preparations on the daily fresh catch. The average dinner, including salad bar, is usually under $20, a good value for Waikiki. Duke's also serves breakfast and lunch (fresh fish sandwiches are a lunchtime staple), and at sunset turns into Waikiki's nexus for Hawaiian music at its ocean bar. (See also chapter 11, "Oahu After Dark.")

✪ **Hawaii Seafood Paradise.** 1830 Ala Moana Blvd. ☎ **808/946-4514.** Reservations recommended. Main courses $7–$32. AE, JCB, DC, MC, V. Daily 6:30am–3am. CHINESE/SEAFOOD.

You can dine as simply or as lavishly as you choose in this quirky, unpretentious restaurant that serves nine kinds of roast duck (I'd stake my life on the Peking duck); peerless shrimp fried rice; many selections of chicken, noodles, and seafood; sizzling platters; an impressive selection of abalone and clam dishes; and "hotpot" casseroles with everything from lamb to lobster and fish. Top quality in the more than 200 Cantonese and Szechuan selections make this a mecca for Chinese food aficionados, including those speaking their native dialects—a sure sign of good Chinese food. A few of the best items on the menu are written in Chinese with no English translation, so don't be afraid to ask questions. There are Thai selections as well, among them the spicy, delectable Tom Yum soup with prawns, a hint of coconut, and lemongrass—rich but irresistible.

✪ **Parc Cafe.** In the Waikiki Parc Hotel, 2233 Helumoa Rd. ☎ **808/921-7272.** Reservations recommended. Buffets $11.50–$24.50. Mon–Sat 6:30–10am and 11:30am–2pm, Sun 6:30–9:30am and 11am–2pm; daily 5:30–9:30pm. BUFFETS/BRUNCH.

Even the most dedicated buffet-bashers are won over by the high quality and moderate prices of the Halekulani's sister hotel. The Waikiki Parc may not be on the beach, but its restaurant has made a name for itself as Honolulu's top spot for buffets. Regulars flock to the dining room for the Wednesday and Friday Hawaiian luncheon buffet, the finest such spread around: lau lau, lomi salmon, kalua pig, Oriental-style steamed fresh catch, mashed Molokai potatoes, Kauai taro au gratin, and dozens of salads. Chafing dishes notwithstanding, this is gourmet fare using fresh, fine ingredients. The seafood soup is always good, and the squid luau, with coconut milk, taro tops, and a brilliant smattering of tomatoes, is arguably the best in Hawaii. A carving station serves up rotisserie chicken and prime rib on Monday through Thursday nights and prime rib and seafood on Friday through Sunday nights. The popular seafood dinner offers sashimi, poke, and oysters on the half shell; crab legs and fresh catch; made-to-order pastas; charbroiled eggplant; tofu, watercress, and Peking duck salad; and many other selections, including smashing desserts. The $11.50 breakfast buffet is offered Monday through Saturday. All in all, one of Waikiki's top values.

✪ **Singha Thai Cuisine.** Canterbury Place, 1910 Ala Moana Blvd., ☎ **808/941-2898.** Reservations recommended. Main courses $7–$22. AE, CB, DC, DISC, JCB, MC, V. Mon–Fri 11am–11pm, nightly 4–11pm. THAI.

The Royal Thai dancers arch their graceful, boneless fingers nightly in classical Thai dance on the small center stage, but you may be too busy tucking into your Thai chili fresh fish or blackened ahi summer rolls to notice. Indeed, the flavors and sights are rich here. Imaginative combination dinners and the use of local organic ingredients are among the special touches of this Thai-Hawaiian fusion restaurant at the Ala Moana end of Waikiki. Complete dinners for two to five cover many tastes and are an ideal way for the uninitiated to sample this cuisine, as well as the elements of Hawaii Regional Cuisine that have considerable influence on the chef. Some highlights on a diverse menu: local fresh catch with Thai chili and light black-bean sauce; red, green, yellow, and vegetarian curries; spicy Thai eggplant; ginseng chicken soup; and many seafood dishes. Such extensive use of fresh fish (mahimahi, ono, ahi, opakapaka, onaga, and uku) in traditional Thai preparations is unusual for a Thai restaurant. Curry puffs (shrimp, pork, and vegetables in puff pastry), chicken and shrimp sate, fresh ahi tempura (very Japanese), blackened ahi summer rolls (very Hawaii Regional), fresh ahi katsu (dusted in rice flour, rolled in dried seaweed, and seared—wonderful!), Alaskan king crab cakes (flavored with lemongrass and cilantro), and naked squid salad are among the many curiosities of the menu that have received acceptance. The entertainment and indoor-outdoor dining add to this first-class dining experience.

INEXPENSIVE

Cha Cha Cha. 342 Seaside Ave. ☎ **808/923-7797.** Complete dinners $7–$9. MC, V. Daily 11:30am–midnight. MEXICAN/CARIBBEAN.

This is a happy and happening place. Upbeat service, steel drum music on weekends, Bob Marley on the airwaves, green burritos, great food—and the best margaritas in town. Nothing wimpy about the flavors here; the lime, coconut, and Caribbean spices make Cha Cha more than plain ole Mex, adding zing to the fresh fish and shrimp ceviche, the jerk-chicken breast, ceviche tostada, Cuban black-bean soup, and a savory assortment of inexpensive treats, most of them under $8 (tacos under $4). We love the vegetarian black-bean burritos, red chili tortilla shells, toe-curling salsas, and spinach tortillas. The temperatures rise from there, with red chilies, jalapenos, and lively Caribbean spices perking up the pork, chicken, and beef dishes. Finally, jumpstart the sweet tooth with coconut custard, Jamaican rum flan, and piña-colada ice cream pie—extraordinary desserts all.

There's another branch with the same prices in Hawaii Kai Town Centre (☎ **808/ 395-7797**). It's open Sunday to Thursday from 11am to 9pm, Friday and Saturday from 11am to 10pm. Free Waikiki delivery offered, and steel-drum Caribbean music from 6 to 8pm Thursday and Friday.

2 Honolulu Beyond Waikiki

ALA MOANA

EXPENSIVE

✪ **A Pacific Cafe Oahu.** At Ward Centre, 1200 Ala Moana Blvd. ☎ **808/593-0035.** Reservations recommended. Lunch $8–$15, dinner main courses $16–$28, 4-course Pacific Rim sampling, $34.50. AE, DC, DISC, MC, V. Mon–Fri 11:30am–2pm; Sun–Thurs 5:30–9pm, Fri–Sat 5:30–9:30pm. HAWAII REGIONAL CUISINE.

The appetizer bar rates its own kitchen in the elevated part of the dining room, and the appetizers deserve it. Chef-owner Jean-Marie Josselin is known for his innovative starters (firecracker salmon rolls, tiger-eye ahi sushi, tempura, seared crab cake) and his imaginative hand with fresh Island produce and seafood. (On Kauai, most of it is grown in his own garden.) A Pacific Cafe Oahu is his fourth in Hawaii, following 8 years of international accolades at A Pacific Cafe on Kauai and, more recently, A Pacific Cafe on Maui and The Beach House in Poipu, Kauai. A triathlete, Josselin lost 40 pounds while managing and cooking for his four restaurants on three islands, which accounts for his recent addition to the menu: light cuisine. Roasted tomato and Tuscan bean soup, oven-baked salmon with sweet Thai dip, potato terrine with fresh herbs and mushrooms, whole roasted artichoke with spinach and roasted tomato—less fat, more to love. Not that the regular menu is flawed: We swear by the seared sea scallops in Japanese pear Riesling broth, the ahi poke, and the inevitable triumph of the evening, the sesame and garlic-crisped mahimahi, a signature dish in all of his restaurants.

☼ **Akasaka.** 1646B Kona St. ☎ **808/942-4466.** Reservations recommended. Main courses $10–$19. AE, DC, DISC, MC, V. Mon–Sat 11am–2:30pm and 5pm–2am. JAPANESE.

Tiny, busy, casual, and occasionally smoky, with a tatami room for small groups, Akasaka wins top scores for sushi, sizzling tofu and scallops, miso-clam soup, and the overall quality and integrity of its Japanese cuisine. The zesty, spicy tuna hand-roll (temaki) is the best in town, and many claim the California roll, scallop roll with flying fish roe, and hamachi also occupy the top of the sushi heap. During soft-shell crab season, lovers of these delicacies can order them in sushi, a treat that looks prehistoric but tastes wonderful. Fresh ingredients at the sushi bar (the hamachi is never less than buttery-fresh) make this a good bet for topnotch Japanese, with lunch and dinner specials that can help take the bite out of the bill. À la carte sushi here is wonderful, but be aware that, like all sushi bars, the bill can sneak up on you.

MODERATE

Bernard's Deli. 1200 Ala Moana Blvd., Ward Centre. ☎ **808/594-3353.** Mini plate lunches $5.99; most items under $8.99. AE, CB, DC, DISC, JCB, MC, V. Daily 7am–10pm. DELI.

From *New Yorker* magazines on the racks to Fifth Avenue signs to Little Italy posters on the wall, Bernard's Deli is all-out New York bagels and attitude. Seat yourself indoors or on the lanai and choose from among knishes, "New York's finest smoked nova lox," hot pastrami, Italian subs, kippered salmon salad, potato pancakes, blintzes, cold borscht with sour cream, all-beef kosher knockwurst, Hebrew National hot dogs, and tangy Hebrew National mustards. This may be the only place in the world that serves a plate lunch without rice. We haven't tried it, but we have tried the matzo ball soup, which tends to disappoint. Mini–plate lunch selections include several bests and "wursts": cabbage roll with potato pancake, grilled knockwurst with baked beans and sauerkraut, and grilled bratwurst or grilled bockwurst with German potato salad and red cabbage.

Cafe Sistina. 1314 S. King St. ☎ **808/596-0061.** Reservations recommended for dinner. Main courses $12–$13. AE, DC, MC, V. Mon–Fri 11am–2pm; Sun–Mon 5:30–9:30pm, Tues–Thurs 5:30–10pm, Fri–Sat 5:30–10:30pm. NORTHERN ITALIAN.

Chef/owner Sergio Mitrotti displays his multiple talents on the walls, where his Sistine Chapel redux and pope's portraits in the alcove amuse and delight in an otherwise industrially stylized room. His talents abound in the kitchen, too, in the steaming platters of homemade pasta. The extensive list of specials on the board offer great possibilities (roasted red peppers, asparagus pasta), but otherwise, the frutti de mare, linguine puttanesca, and rich smoked salmon-artichoke fettuccine are touted by regulars.

Honolulu Area Dining

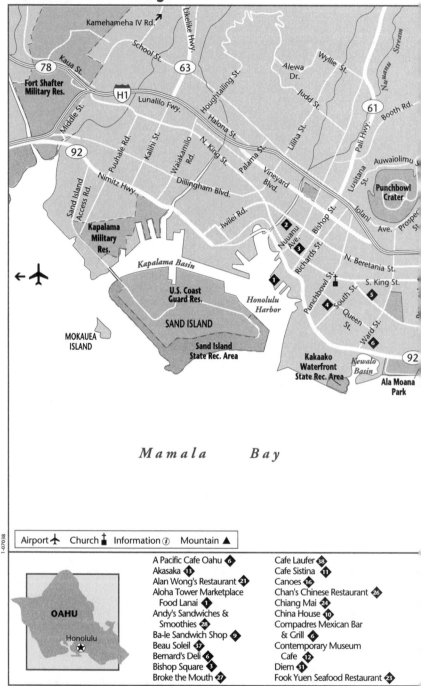

Airport ✈ Church 🕇 Information ⓘ Mountain ▲

144

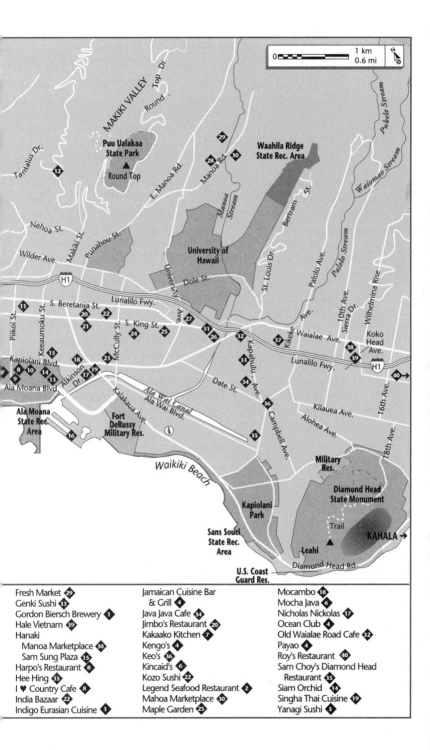

Fresh Market 29
Genki Sushi 33
Gordon Biersch Brewery 1
Hale Vietnam 39
Hanaki
  Manoa Marketplace 30
  Sam Sung Plaza 15
Harpo's Restaurant 8
Hee Hing 35
I ♥ Country Cafe 8
India Bazaar 22
Indigo Eurasian Cuisine 3

Jamaican Cuisine Bar
  & Grill 4
Java Java Cafe 34
Jimbo's Restaurant 20
Kakaako Kitchen 7
Kengo's 4
Keo's 36
Kincaid's 6
Kozo Sushi 22
Legend Seafood Restaurant 2
Mahoa Marketplace 30
Maple Garden 25

Mocambo 18
Mocha Java 6
Nicholas Nickolas 17
Ocean Club 4
Old Waialae Road Cafe 32
Payao 4
Roy's Restaurant 40
Sam Choy's Diamond Head
  Restaurant 35
Siam Orchid 14
Singha Thai Cuisine 19
Yanagi Sushi 5

China House. 1349 Kapiolani Blvd. ☎ **808/949-6622.** Reservations recommended for large parties. Main courses $6.50–$28. AE, MC, V. Mon–Fri 10am–10pm, Sat–Sun 9am–10pm. CHINESE.

Cavernous and noisy and synonymous with dim sum, China House is a beehive of activity: servers pushing carts with bamboo steamers and trays of exotic delicacies, the clatter of plastic chopsticks, brusque service, much craning of necks and raising of voices to hear above the din. But this is one of Honolulu's major purveyors of the dainty Chinese delectables, with a selection (37 choices!) that includes some surprises: mochi-rice chicken pouch, spinach-and-scallop dim sum, pan-fried turnip cake, and fresh scallop roll, as well as the more commonly known varieties. There are more than 100 items on the rest of the menu, including some that we think are overpriced. On a menu that charges $28 for shark's-fin soup with crabmeat and $20 for sautéed scallops in a taro nest, enjoy the dim sum but beware the market-priced items.

Compadres Mexican Bar & Grill. 1200 Ala Moana Blvd., Ward Centre. ☎ **808/591-8307.** Reservations recommended. Main courses $7.99–$12.99. DC, JCB, MC, V. Mon–Thurs 11am–11pm, Fri–Sat 11am–midnight, Sun 11am–10pm. Bar closes Sun–Thurs 12:30–1am, Fri–Sat 1:30–2am.

Cigar smoke notwithstanding, they make the best margaritas in town, served in a festive, light-filled atmosphere with one wall of glass windows looking out toward Ala Moana Park. Tequila festivals, Cinco de Mayo, fund-raisers, live entertainment on Thursdays and Fridays, and parties galore make it an all-around good deal. Oh yes, the food—from chimichangas to enchilada platters to the simple pleasures of guacamole and nachos, no complaints. At Compadres, huevos rancheros are a must any time of the day, and the locally smoked "lomi lomi" salmon in a large spinach tortilla is a twist to a south-of-the-border classic. Eight different types of enchiladas; steak, chicken, and fish combination plates; fajitas; carnitas; and notable nachos are among the major attractions at this festive eatery, where the back-bar margarita (Gold tequila, Grand Marnier, fresh lime, sweet-and-sour, and orange juice) is a libation of great renown.

INEXPENSIVE

Hanaki. Sam Sung Plaza #101, 655 Keeaumoku St. ☎ **808/955-1347.** 2752 Woodlawn Drive, Manoa Marketplace, ☎ 808/988-1551. Reservations recommended for groups. Main courses $5.25–$14; Kaiseki $17.50–$20. AE, JCB, MC, V. Daily 11am–2pm and 5–10pm. JAPANESE.

Noodleheads love Hanaki for its nabeyaki, udon, and other slurpy specialties, in savory broths with various accompaniments of fresh vegetables, shiitake, shrimp tempura, and chicken. At lunch, in the Keeaumoku Street location, the inexpensive bentos move quickly, and at dinner, the sushi bar at the new Manoa location is the best deal in town. Hanaki's recent expansion (enlarging the Keeaumoku St. location and adding a new restaurant in Manoa Marketplace) has met with resounding approval—try getting in at either location on a Friday night. The reckless order fried gyoza (dumplings); we love the shiitake mushroom udon and the shiitake donburi, with the tasty black mushrooms and eggs served over hot rice. Tempura udon (with shrimp and vegetables esthetically arranged over the thick, steaming noodles) and the teishoku (combination) dinners of three or four choices are elegant and affordable—you'll forget you're in a modest eatery without tablecloths.

Harpo's Restaurant. In Ala Moana Plaza, 451 Piikoi St. ☎ **808/591-0040.** Reservations not accepted. Pizzas $18.50–$28 for large; pasta $6.50–$9.95. MC, V. Daily 10:30am–10pm. PIZZA.

This is for those who love thick-crust pan pizzas that can feed a family without breaking the bank. Two of the six Oahu locations (this one and the one at 477 Kapahulu

🏠 Family-Friendly Restaurants

Honolulu is constantly battling its image as an expensive destination. It's true that accommodations on Oahu are pricey, but the abundance of ethnic restaurants (born of burgeoning new ethnic populations) and the high percentage of working mothers in Hawaii paint an entirely different scenario for dining. Even with a sluggish economy, residents eat out—because they're busy, because they want to, and because many popular ethnic traditions aren't so easy to duplicate at home. What makes a good family restaurant in Hawaii? More than the presence of high chairs, we think it's friendliness, affordability, and menu choices that take into consideration the tastes and preferences of more than one generation. Not including the usual fast-food burger joints that are prosaically popular with the kids, here are some suggestions for family-friendly eateries in Honolulu. (There are fuller descriptions where each restaurant is listed geographically.)

Genki Sushi (900 Kapahulu Ave., ☎ 808/735-8889) is part entertainment, part assertiveness training, and part culinary pleasure. Kids love to lunge for their favorites among the freshly made, individually wrapped sushis that parade by on conveyor belts, and the slower ones who miss the first time around get a chance on the next revolution. Sit with your family around the curvy counters and empty your plates without emptying your pocketbook. *(See p. 157.)*

Our observation is that Blockbuster Video outlets are often adjacent to places kids and teenagers love. And because they may mean less cooking, these places are popular among parents, too. Adjacent to Ala Moana Center, Honolulu's busiest Blockbuster is smack dab next to **Harpo's Pizza** (451 Piikoi St., Ala Moana Plaza, ☎ 808/591-0040) and **I ♥ Country Cafe** (same address, ☎ 808/596-8108), two eateries that bridge the gaps of several generations. Harpo's serves more than a dozen different toppings on thick-crust pizza, as well as sandwiches and pastas, with a few tables for dining and dashing. Next door, I ♥ Country Cafe offers everything from meat loaf to shoyu chicken, burgers, vegetarian dishes, and stir-frys, for take-out or dining in. *(See p. 148.)*

At the gateway to Waikiki, **Hawaii Seafood Paradise** (1830 Ala Moana Blvd., ☎ 808/946-4514) is open late (until 3am) but is popular for the pre-curfew set, too. Families love to sit at the circular tables and order the works from a menu of more than 200 items—enough to please several dynasties and more than a few generations. Excellent fried rice, noodle dishes, sizzling platters, soups, lemon chicken, several selections of duck, and many other delicacies are among Paradise's offerings. *(See p. 141.)*

On the outskirts of Honolulu, **Swiss Inn** (5730 Kalanianaole Hi. Niu Valley Shopping Center, ☎ 808/377-5447) is another family favorite—not just for its children's-portion spaghetti for $4, but also because they serve European-style frankfurters, with Swiss potato salad or French fries, for $5.50. Parents and children can feel much more elegant dining here than at a sandwich shop, and they don't have to dress up. Martin and Jeanie Wyss have always welcomed families with a combination of good value, pleasing service, and good food, including a cheese fondue for those too young to consider cholesterol. *(See p. 160.)*

Finally we arrive at **Zippy's,** the mecca of chili and saimin. There are nearly two dozen of them on Oahu alone (call ☎ 808/955-6622 for the one nearest you). All locations feature cheap, tasty chili, burgers, sandwiches, salads, and all-day American fare that is popular among parents and kids. Tasty vegetarian chili and meatless, smoky Boca Burgers are among the healthy choices for vegetarians.

Ave.) have tables and a full menu of sandwiches, pasta, and pizza, including at least 14 varieties of toppings for the individual, medium, and large pizzas. Among them: Thai chicken, grilled eggplant, artichoke pesto, the Gourmet (everything from their homemade Italian sausage to pepperoni and olives), and prosciutto tomato. Pizza by the slice goes for $1.85; a hunger-buster for diners in a rush.

I ♥ Country Cafe. In Ala Moana Plaza, 451 Piikoi St. ☎ **808/596-8108.** Main courses $5–$8.50. MC, V. Mon–Sat 10:30am–9pm, Sun 10:30am–8pm. INTERNATIONAL.

Give yourself time to peruse the lengthy list of specials posted on the menu board, as well as the prodigious printed menu. Stand in line at the counter, place your order and pay, and find a Formica-top table or wait about 10 minutes for your take-out order to appear in a Styrofoam plate heaping with salad and other accompaniments. The selection is mind-boggling: nine types of cheese steaks, including vegetarian tofu; garlic mahimahi; spinach-stuffed ravioli; Cajun meat loaf; Thai curries; various stir-frys; shoyu chicken; vegetarian or eggplant lasagna; and a long list of other choices spanning many cultures and tastes. Take a good look at the diners and notice that the menu appeals equally to bodybuilders and hedonists. Favorites include the lasagna, oven-roasted chicken Dijon, and the Cajun-style ahi.

Kakaako Kitchen. 1216 Waimanu St. ☎ **808/596-7488.** Main courses $5.75–$8.50. Mon–Fri 6:30am–2pm, Sat 7am–2pm. No credit cards. GOURMET PLATE LUNCHES.

Island-style chicken linguine is the headliner in this industrial-style kitchen near Ala Moana Center, where the owners of 3660 On the Rise, a popular Kaimuki restaurant, have turned their attentions to elevating the local tradition called a plate lunch. Vegetarian specials, homemade veggie burgers, homestyle pot roast, shrimp curry, fresh catch, mahimahi sandwich on taro roll, burgers, ahi steak, and "mixed plate" with two entrees are becoming the lunch of choice among office workers in the Ala Moana–Kakaako area. At breakfast, omelets, scones, and fried rice fly out of the open kitchen. Although much of the business is takeout, there are tables for casual dining in a high-ceiling, warehouselike room.

Kincaid's. In Ward Warehouse, 1050 Ala Moana Blvd. ☎ **808/591-2005.** Reservations recommended. Lunch $8.95–$15.95; dinner main courses $8.95–$29.95. AE, DC, JCB, MC, V. Daily 11:15am–10pm (later for pupus). SEAFOOD.

Kincaid's is always winning surveys for one thing or another—best place for a business lunch, best seafood restaurant—because it manages to please wide-ranging tastes and pocketbooks. Brisk service, a pleasing harbor view, and an extensive seafood menu keep the large dining room full. Great fresh fish sandwiches, seafood chowders and French onion soups, kiawe-grilled salmon with thyme butter, fresh mahimahi with key-lime butter, herbed chicken breast, and garlic prawns are among Kincaid's highlights. Steaks are big here too, and so is the mushroom garden burger—but we love the romaine-and-blue-cheese salad and the open-faced, rich, and reckless Dungeness crab and artichoke sandwich. You might want to pace yourself to save room for the signature dessert, the original burnt crème—sinfully rich and custardy, with a glazed sugar topping. Kincaid's is a popular happy-hour rendezvous, with beer for $2.25 and appetizers (sautéed mushrooms, potatoes stuffed with cheese and spinach, sashimi) that may carry the evening.

Mocambo. 1718 Kapiolani Blvd. ☎ **808/945-7999.** Reservations recommended. Lunch $6.50–$11.50, dinner main courses $8–$15. AE, DC, DISC, JCB, MC, V. Mon–Fri 11:30am–2:30pm; daily 6–10pm. ITALIAN

Here's what you get at this new, very hip, split-level, often smoky trattoria: linguine, fettuccine, spaghetti, or penne in many preparations, with tiger shrimp, Italian sausage, herbs, cheeses, fresh mushroom, smoked salmon, fresh clams, fresh octopus, and spicy tomato sauces—all in all, some 20 choices in red, olive-oil, white-wine, or cream sauces. Located at the entrance to Waikiki where the Convention Center is being constructed, Mocambo offers reasonable prices and respectable fare, such as soup-sandwich combos ($8) that are popular at lunch and four choices of pasta prepared five different ways: basilico (basil, anchovy, roasted garlic, and chili pepper); Bolognese (sausage, beef, and pork); arrabbiata (garlic, basil, and oregano in tomato sauce; carbonara (Italian bacon, egg, and cheese); pepperoncino (roasted garlic and chili pepper in olive oil). The fresh homemade lasagna, cannelloni, and very tasty ravioli are a solid hit, and so are the baked mussel appetizer and fresh squid grilled with julienned vegetables. If asparagus is in season, have the chef prepare it with parmesan—it's marvelous that something so simple could be so sumptuous. (We'd love Mocambo so much more if they made it a no-smoking dining room.)

Mocha Java. 1200 Ala Moana Blvd., Ward Centre. ☎ **808/591-9023.** Most items under $7.95. MC, V. Mon–Sat 8am–9pm, Sun 8am–4pm. COFFEE HOUSE/CRÊPERIE.

This tiny cafe is a Honolulu staple with a gaggle of loyal followers, who love the spinach-lemon crêpes and the eight types of veggie burgers, as well as the Java Jolt double espresso and light-and-tasty tofu scramble. Light, wholesome fare is the order of the day: breakfast crêpes and omelets; sandwiches, salads, burritos, and crêpe specials for lunch and dinner; fresh fruit smoothies; homemade soups; and many other choices. The eclectic menu includes stir-frys, Mexican salads and burritos, curried crêpes—nothing fancy, but you'll want to return, even for a plain old garden burger. Located across from a chocolate shop in the Ward Centre and surrounded as it is by boutiques, Mocha Java has a coffee bar that's great for quick pick-me-ups with its earth-shattering coffee shakes.

Siam Orchid. 1517 Kapiolani Blvd. ☎ **808/955-6161.** Reservations recommended. Main courses $6.95–$12.95. AE, JCB, DC, DISC, MC. V. Mon–Sat 11am–2pm; daily 5:30–9:30pm. THAI.

A Honolulu favorite for more than 12 years, Siam Orchid recently moved to a larger, more visible location on Kapiolani Boulevard, and fans happily followed. Just around the corner from its previous location and still a stone's throw from Ala Moana Center, the restaurant serves its well-known Tom Yum spicy shrimp soup; fiery Thai garlic shrimp; "evil tofu" with Thai basil; and a panang vegetable curry with tofu, one of a dozen great offerings for vegetarians. Noodle lovers may consider the Pad Thai fried noodles with shrimp, while curry lovers will be pleased with the extensive selection of chicken, beef, pork, shrimp, and vegetables in a rich, nutty panang sauce or in traditional red, green, and yellow versions. The new restaurant is decorated with fresh orchid plants and Thai artworks hanging on peach-colored walls, and there's ample free parking both mauka and makai of the dining room.

ALOHA TOWER MARKETPLACE

✪ **Gordon Biersch Brewery Restaurant.** In Aloha Tower Marketplace, 1 Aloha Tower Dr. ☎ **808/599-4877.** Reservations recommended. Main courses $8–$20. AE, CB, DC, DISC, JCB, MC, V. Sun–Wed 11am–10pm, Thurs–Sat 11am–11pm. NEW AMERICAN/PACIFIC RIM.

German-style lagers brewed on the premises, including the new Pilsner, would be enough of a draw, but the food is the main attraction at Honolulu's liveliest after-work rendezvous. The lanai bar and the brewery bar, open until 1am, are the brightest spot in the Aloha Tower Marketplace, always teeming with downtown types who think that suds are swell as they nosh on vegetarian potstickers with a sambal-soy dipping sauce, grilled Asian New York steak in an Asian version of ratatouille (with star anise and hoisin), grilled chicken pizza with basil pesto, baby-back ribs, the famous garlic fries, and any number of American classics with deft cross-cultural touches. Live music on weekends is an additional draw.

DOWNTOWN

Bishop Square. 1001 Bishop St., corner of Bishop and King sts., Downtown. VARIED.

Downtowners love the informal walk-in cafes lining one side of this attractive square in the middle of the business district, where free entertainment is offered every Friday during lunch hour. The popular **Che Pasta** is a stalwart of the square, chic enough for business meetings and not too formal (or expensive) for a spontaneous rendezvous over pasta and minestrone soup. Next to Che Pasta are the inexpensive fast-food eateries into which busy professionals duck for lunch on the run: **Jack in the Box, Kyotaru** (sushi and bento take-out), **Yummy's Korean Bar-B-Q, Harpo's Pizza, Heidi's** (soups, salads, baked goods, pasta), and the ever-comforting **Cookie Corner.** Some operations open for breakfast and lunch; others for lunch, but most of them close when the business offices empty.

Indigo Eurasian Cuisine. 1211 Nuuanu Ave. ☎ **808/521-2900.** Reservations recommended. Lunch $5.50–$15.50, dinner main dishes $12–$18.50. AE, DC, DISC, JCB, MC, V. Tues–Fri 11:30am–2pm and 5:30–9:30pm, Sat 5:30–9:30pm; for theater events, half-hour earlier to accommodate theatergoers. EURASIAN.

Hardwood floors, red brick, wicker, high ceilings, and an overall feeling of informal luxe make this a pleasing atmosphere. Dine indoors or in a garden setting on potstickers, pizza, pasta and Asian-style noodles, crab cakes, bouillabaisse, grilled and wok-charred fresh fish, and entrees that range from lilikoi-glazed baby-back ribs to Mongolian lamb chops and Maui free-range New York steak. The clever names of the dishes (China Seas Scallops, Thousand Loved Crab Cakes, Grilled Dragon Fire Shrimp Brochettes, etc.) grab the attention, and the food presentation holds it.

Jamaican Cuisine Bar & Grill. 500 Ala Moana Blvd., Restaurant Row. ☎ **808/521-5855.** Reservations recommended. Lunch $7–$13.50, dinner $10.50–$15.50. AE, CB, JCB, DC, DISC, MC, V. Mon–Sat 11am–10pm, Sun 3–10pm. Fri–Sat, live reggae music until 2am. JAMAICAN.

Live reggae music, assertive Jamaican curries and jerk specialties, Jamaican Blue Mountain coffee, Appleton rum, and Red Stripe beer are part of the many-flavored Caribbean festival drawing new fans to Restaurant Row. Come here when you're up to here with blandness and your taste buds are clamoring for a jump-start. The Jamaican home cooking includes curries (chicken, shrimp, goat, and lobster), plum chicken, fried plantains, the deep-fried corn cakes called festival, and the Jamaican specialty called jerk—pork or chicken soaked in a marinade of 18 herbs and spices, then grilled. Owners Clarence Allen and Verna Malcolm say they've turned down the heat a bit since they moved from the thick of Waikiki to this sleek downtown center, but they still have plenty of fans. Seafood, stewed chicken, Jamaican-style roast beef, and Marley's vegetable medley cater to all tastes, and there's Scotch Bonnet pepper sauce for the chiliphiles. On weekends, live reggae bands loosen up the Row and the partying continues into the night.

Note: For this and other Restaurant Row eateries, keep in mind that Restaurant Row, which features several hot new restaurants, offers free validated parking in the evenings.

Kengo's. 500 Ala Moana Blvd., Restaurant Row. ☎ **808/533-0039.** Reservations recommended. Lunch buffet, $10.95 adults, $6.95 children; dinner buffet, $22.95 adults, $9.95 children. AE, DC, DISC, MC, V. Daily 11am–2pm and 5:30–9:30pm. LOCAL BUFFET.

Look for the queue and you'll know it's Kengo's, the place that pleases kids, parents, and grandparents, who line up for the prime rib and seafood buffet, the salad and fresh fruit bar, the sushi bar with sashimi and poke, and the dessert bar with soft-frozen yogurt. The dinner buffet isn't cheap, but for crab legs and sashimi, it's a value for those with unabashed appetites. Kengo's is known for its salad bar of local favorites, everything from kimchee to seaweed salads and local fruit in season.

✪ **Legend Seafood Restaurant.** In the Chinese Cultural Plaza, 100 N. Beretania St. ☎ **808/532-1868.** Reservations recommended. Most items under $15. AE, DC, MC, V. Mon, Tues, Thurs, Fri 10:30am–2pm and 5:30–10pm; Sat–Sun 8am–2pm and 5:30–10pm. DIM SUM/SEAFOOD.

It's like dining in Hong Kong here, with a clientele poring over Chinese newspapers, and the clicking of teapot to teacup punctuating animated conversations in Chinese. Excellent dim sum comes in bamboo steamers that beckon from carts. Although you must often wave madly to catch the server's eye, and then point to what you want, the system is efficient—and a small price to pay for the mouthwatering dim sum. Among our favorites: deep-fried taro puffs and prawn dumplings, shrimp dim sum, vegetable dumplings, and the open-faced seafood with shiitake, scallop, and a tofu product called aburage. Dim sum is only served at lunch, but at dinner the seafood shines.

✪ **Ocean Club.** 500 Ala Moana Blvd., Restaurant Row. ☎ **808/526-9888.** Reservations recommended. All items $4.95–$8.95 ($1.95–$4.95 during happy hour). AE, DISC, MC, V. Tues–Thurs 4:30pm–2am, Fri–Sat 4:30pm–3am. SEAFOOD.

Honolulu's newest sensation could be listed as a restaurant or a nightclub, but we list it here because it is so much more than a drinks-only joint. Brilliantly and masterfully executed, Ocean Club is a sleek, chic new magnet that has redefined happy hour with its extended hours of slashed prices, excellent appetizers-only seafood menu, and ultracool ambience of fake mahimahi and frosted glass dangling from the ceiling in a quasi-fifties-retro mood. Galvanized steel counters, mahogany bars lined with shoyu bottles, linoleum-tile floors, and oddly attractive pillars resembling pahu (Hawaiian drums) are a wonderfully eclectic mix. Add deejays in bowling shirts and cat-eyed eyeglasses playing the Kingston Trio—this is a fabuloso time warp. The menu of appetizers lives up to its "ultimate cocktail hour" claim, especially from 4:30pm to 8pm nightly, when great seafood is slashed to half-price and the upbeat mood starts spiraling. A happy-hour sampling: $4.95 for two huge lobster claws; $2.95 for a toothsome spinach and artichoke dip, served with tortilla chips, salsa, and sour cream; $3.95 for Pacific crab dip; $2.95 for ahi tacos; $1.95 for fresh ahi poke; $3.95 for fresh, good-quality sashimi; $1 each for an oyster, shrimp, or crab shooter; $3.95 for coconut shrimp; and other delectables. The night we discovered Ocean Club, we canceled our dinner reservation at a nearby restaurant; we just couldn't bear to leave. *Caveat:* the decibels build as the evening wears on, and the crowed gets thicker and younger.

Payao. 500 Ala Moana Blvd., Restaurant Row. ☎ **808/5211-3511.** Reservations recommended for dinner. Lunch special $7.95, dinner main courses $6.95–$11.95. AE, DC, DISC, JCB, MC, V. Mon–Sat 11am–2:30pm; daily 5–10pm. THAI.

The owners of "the home of sticky rice," the recently expanded Chiang Mai restaurant in the neighborhood called McCully, opened their uptown version with their familiar Thai specialties, among them green chicken curry rich with coconut milk and tangy spices; the Tom Yum soups (chicken, shrimp, fish, and seafood combo); the peanut-rich satay chicken; and the stir-fried eggplant redolent with basil and garlic.

Payao's Thai noodle dishes (curried, in black-bean sauce, and with vegetables) are a good bet, as is the popular new lemongrass chicken. With its few tables indoors and 30 seats in open-air terrace-style dining, Payao brings a pleasant new option to Restaurant Row.

Yanagi Sushi. 762 Kapiolani Blvd. ☎ **808/597-1525.** Reservations recommended. Main courses $8–$33, complete dinners $11.50–$18.50. AE, CB, DC, JCB, MC, V. Daily 11am–2pm; Mon–Sat 5:30pm–2am, Sun 5:30–10pm. JAPANESE.

The hostess usually acts as if she's having a bad hair day, but never mind, we love the late-night hours, the sushi bar with its fresh ingredients and well-trained chefs, and the extensive choices in the combination lunches and dinners. But we also love the à la carte Japanese menu, which covers everything from *chazuke* (rice with tea, salmon, seaweed, and other condiments; a comfort food) to shabu shabu and other steaming earthenware-pot dishes. Nosh on noodles or complete dinners with choices of sashimi, shrimp tempura, broiled salmon, New York steak, and other possibilities. Nearly 20 different types of sashimi, consistently crisp tempura, and one of the town's finer spicy ahi hand-rolled sushis make Yanagi worth remembering. There are tables at the sushi bar, in an adjoining dining room, and in two small private rooms.

MANOA VALLEY/MOILIILI/MAKIKI
EXPENSIVE

۞ Alan Wong's Restaurant. 1857 S. King St., 5th Floor. ☎ **808/949-2526.** Reservations recommended. Main courses $15–$30, 5-course chef's tasting $65. AE, MC, V. Daily 5–10pm. HAWAII REGIONAL.

Renowned for his innovative flavors at the Mauna Lani Bay Hotel's Canoe House on the Big Island, Alan Wong achieved instant success when he chucked the resort world for a neighborhood in Honolulu that is neither glamorous nor particularly convenient. A brilliant chef with staying power who has influenced the direction of regional cuisine, he owns what many consider the foremost Honolulu restaurant. The 90-seat room has a glassed-in terrace and open kitchen, accented with stylish floral arrangements, minimalist avant-garde lighting, and curly-koa wall panels, with many touches of Hawaiiana. Abandon all restraint and try as many items as you can from the nightly changing menu. Recommended: crispy ahi lumpia, fresh "day boat" scallops (in season) with caramelized onions and chili saffron sauce, seared pepper ahi, grilled lamp chops, potato- and crab-crusted mahimahi. It is an awesome menu that changes with the seasonal availability of ingredients. Wong's flavors shine with Asian lemongrass, sweet-sour, garlic, wasabi, and other sensuous ingredients deftly melded with the fresh seafood and produce of the islands. The California roll is a triumph, made with salmon roe, wasabi, and Kona lobster instead of rice, served warm. But don't get attached, because the menu changes daily.

MODERATE

Chan's Chinese Restaurant. 2600 S. King St. ☎ **808/949-1188.** Reservations recommended for large groups. Main courses $6–$13.50. AE, MC, V. Sun–Thurs 10:30am–midnight. CANTONESE/NORTHERN CHINESE.

Chan's opens early and closes late, doesn't oversalt its food, and serves noodles, seafood, and dim sum that are reasonable and tasty. The dim sum is reliable, other dishes less so: some dishes can be overly greasy like the worst Chinese food, but others shine. (Also, we have learned to ignore the decor.) The dim sum arrives in bamboo steamers in wrappers so translucent you can clearly see the fillings. The clams in black-bean sauce are succulent, drenched in the savory sauce, peppered with heaps of fresh scallions. You can order everything from roast duck to elegant taro nest dishes with five different fillings that please vegetarians, beef eaters, and seafood lovers. We recommend the spinach garlic and the boneless chicken with black-bean sauce and fine, soft noodles.

Chiang Mai. 2239 S. King St. ☎ **808/941-1151.** Reservations suggested for dinner. Main courses $7.95–$12.95. AE, DC, DISC, JCB, MC, V. Mon–Fri 11am–2pm; daily 5:30–10pm. THAI.

The predecessor to sister restaurant Payao on Restaurant Row, Chiang Mai was one of Honolulu's early Thai restaurants, and has retained a stalwart following despite fierce competition. Recently expanded to accommodate 100, Chiang Mai made sticky rice famous, serving it in bamboo steamers to accompany excellent red, green, and yellow curries, the signature Cornish game hen in lemongrass and spices, and a garlic-infused green papaya salad marinated in tamarind sauce. Spicy shrimp soup, eggplant with basil and tofu, and the vegetarian green curry are some time-honored favorites. *Note:* the vegetarian menu is superb.

Contemporary Museum Cafe. In The Contemporary Museum, 2411 Makiki Heights Dr. ☎ **808/523-3362.** Reservations recommended. Main courses $8–$11. MC, V. Tues–Sat 10am–3pm, Sun noon–3pm. PACIFIC RIM/MEDITERRANEAN.

The surroundings are an integral part of the dining experience, because this tiny lunchtime cafe is part of a must-see art museum nestled on the slopes of Tantalus, amid carefully cultivated Oriental gardens, a breathtaking view of Diamond Head, and priceless contemporary art displayed indoors and outdoors. The cafe's menu is limited to sandwiches, soups, salads, and appetizers, so it's best to keep your expectations in check. What is offered, however, does the job well, and chances are you won't leave disappointed, especially if you crown the meal with the flourless chocolate cake. In between, consider the grilled eggplant sandwich, or the baked Brie and Indonesian mushrooms, or the oven-roasted turkey breast sandwich. The ubiquitous garden burger is given a taste twist with a homemade barbecue sauce, and the house-smoked mahimahi with Caesar dressing and a tower of greens is the choice for fish lovers.

Diem. 2633 S. King St. ☎ **808/941-8657.** Reservations recommended for dinner. Main courses $6–$10. AE, DISC, JCB, MC, V. Daily 10am–10pm. VIETNAMESE.

We love Diem for its Royal Seafood Noodle Soup, the best pho in town; its roll-up appetizers (fish, shrimp, beef, seafood); its spicy fried rice, vegetarian or with shrimp or chicken; and its lemongrass fish, chicken, seafood, and vegetarian dishes. Crisp flavors and fresh ingredients are the Diem trademark. Curries also score high on this menu of simple delights, catering as much to tofu-loving vegetarians as to beef and pork enthusiasts. The tiny eatery in the university area has earned its following by word of mouth, and spreads the taste treats with a thriving catering business.

Fook Yuen Seafood Restaurant. 1960 Kapiolani Blvd., Ste 200. ☎ **808/973-0168.** Reservations recommended. Mon–Sat lunch buffet $8.50; Sun brunch $12.95; main courses $8.50–$36. AE, DC, DISC, JCB, MC, V. Daily 11am–2pm and 5:30pm–3am. CANTONESE.

Tables fill up quickly at this popular Hong Kong–style Cantonese restaurant, where the happy rumble of chopsticks resounds over platters heaped with Dungeness crab, sizzling king prawns, and urns of exotic soups (shark's fin, bird's nest, dried scallop, fish maw with crab meat). There are nearly 140 items on this extensive menu, most of them seafood (live Maine lobster, live Dungeness crab, steamed fresh fish, shrimp Szechuan-style, sautéed king clam, sautéed seabass). Some of these items are market priced by season, and can be expensive—but the menu choices are vast enough to make Fook Yuen a strong recommendation for all but the tightest budgets. The "sizzling platters" come crackling with king prawns, oysters, scallops, beef, and chicken, served with tasty accompaniments (satay, Szechuan, black-bean sauces). The house specialty, sautéed king prawns with honey glazed walnuts, is a major attraction.

Maple Garden. 909 Isenberg St. ☎ **808/941-6641.** Main courses $5–$29.50. AE, JCB, MC, V. Daily 11am–2pm and 5:30–10:30pm. SZECHUAN.

In addition to the Peking duck, which must be ordered a day in advance and which has earned its reputation, there are many specialties for which Maple Garden is known. The Chinaman's Hat, a version of mu shui pork, is always good, and you can order it vegetarian as well. Other hits: braised scallops with Chinese mushroooms, spicy garlic eggplant, diced chicken with chili, prawns in chili sauce. The more sub-dued can try the vegetarian selections (sautéed spinach or crisp string beans), or any of the dozens of seafood entrees—everything from sea cucumbers to lobster with black-bean sauce and braised salmon. An ever-expanding visual feast adorns the din-ing room walls, covered with noted artist John Young's original drawings, sketches, and murals.

Shipley's Alehouse and Grill. 2756 Woodlawn Drive, Manoa Marketplace. ☎ **808/988-5555.** Reservations recommended. Main courses $10–$20. AE, DC, DISC, MC, V. Mon–Fri 11:30am–10pm, Sat–Sun 4pm–10pm. Bar open until midnight, 2am on weekends. AMERICAN.

If you're curious about the Kona Lilikoi, Wild Irish Rogue, Taddy Porter, Black Butte Porter, Spaten Optimator, Oatmeal Stout, and 80 other beers from the breweries of the world, ship off to Shipley's. Sunday night jam sessions with top Hawaiian per-formers (Bla and Cyril Pahinui, Ledward Kaapana, Dennis Kamakahi, and others) add to the convivial atmosphere in the split-level, high-beamed room, and the food is hearty-gregarious-American stuff, friendly all the way. Best loved are the fresh mahimahi beer-batter fish and chips ($9), the beer-battered onion rings, cajun-style ($5.50), and the clam chowder. Top of the line is the cedar-roasted salmon entree ($17), fresh farm-raised salmon the Shipleys roast themselves, served with grilled pears and asparagus, spinach mashed potatoes, and a lemon-caper-butter sauce. Others on a long list of favorites: northwest nachos, grilled catch sandwich, and the crisp calamari, all the better to accompany that frosty mug of Obsidian Stout or Steelhead Pale.

INEXPENSIVE

Andy's Sandwiches & Smoothies. 2904 E. Manoa Rd., opposite Manoa Marketplace. ☎ **808/988-6161.** Most items under $5. MC, V. Mon–Thurs 7am–6pm, Fri 7am–5pm, Sun 7am–12:30pm. HEALTH FOOD.

It started as a health food restaurant, expanded into a juice bar, and today is a neigh-borhood fixture for fresh-baked bread, healthy breakfasts and lunches (its mango muffins are famous), and homemade vegetarian fare. Andy's is a roadside stop that always carries fresh papayas, sandwiches, and healthy snacks for folks on the run.

Broke the Mouth. Puck's Alley, 1023 University Ave., Moiliili. ☎ **808/955-5599.** Plate lunches $4–$6. Mon 9am–8pm, Tues–Sat 9am–9pm. HEALTH FOOD/PLATE LUNCHES.

A forward-looking Big Island farmer developed the concept and the menu around the Hilo Farmers Market, so everything here is healthy, vegetarian, and inexpensive. Best bets: Mamo plate lunch, with greens, pesto pasta, or Hawaiian potato salad; the meatless hot dog and a slice of taro/coconut pudding, for $5; the salad of taro, sweet potato, and veggies with macadamia nut dressing, and the sweet potato/basil pesto manapua.

Fresh Market. 2972 E. Manoa Rd. ☎ **808/988-5919.** Most items under $8.50. No credit cards. Mon–Fri 7am–5pm, Sat–Sun 7am–4pm. HEALTH FOOD.

What began as Manoa's brightest corner produce stand is now the tiniest of cafes, with a small coffee bar, a good selection of local produce, limited health foods, and a small deli for takeout or dining at one of the few tables in the house. Manoa residents swear by the breakfasts here (pancakes made with purple Okinawan sweet potato), and the lunch specials, notably the smoked turkey and ahi frittata with hearty country fries, are worth a trip to Manoa Valley. Vegetarian chili and soup are always available in large pots in the corner, and they're good.

Island Manapua Factory. 2752 Woodlawn Dr., Manoa Marketplace. ☎ **808/988-5441.** Most items under $6.45. No credit cards. Mon–Fri 8:30am–8pm, Sat 8:30am–7pm, Sun 8:30am–5pm. CHINESE.

If you belong to the count-your-calories-or-die club, don't come here. This is a greasy spoon, but it does have its place in a world where fast and cheap are occasional necessities. There was a time when take-out counters like Island Manapua ruled Honolulu, in the days before everything went gourmet, including the humble plate lunch. Well, Island Manapua still serves old-fashioned Chinese food, and it's greasy but good. There's always a long line at lunch for the dim sum and manapua (45 cents to $2.25 each) and the prodigious noodle dishes (chow mein, gon lau mein, rice noodles, gau gee mein, cake noodles, and many other types). We ask them to hold the MSG and go easy on the oil for the made-to-order menu items, and they accommodate when possible. Daily plate lunch specials stream out of the kitchen for $3.95 to $5.45 for one to three choices. There are also rice plates, vegetarian selections, and oven-roasted pork, duck, and chicken.

India Bazaar. Old Stadium Sq., 2320 S. King St. ☎ **808/949-4840.** Main courses $5.75–$6.75. No credit cards. Daily 11am–9pm. INDIAN.

Spicy curries, crispy papadams, moist chapatis, and the full range of Indian delicacies are served from a counter where you point and choose. The vegetables are overcooked in the Indian fashion, but this is acceptable for a take-out curry house. A few tables are scattered about a room filled with the scent of spices; one wall is lined with exotic chutneys and Indian condiments for home cooking. The vegetarian thali is a favorite. The spiced Indian rice comes with your choice of three vegetable curries and other choices: lentil, cauliflower, eggplant, tofu/peas, potato, spinach/lentil, garbanzo beans, okra, and other selections. Chicken tandoori (with two vegetable curries) and shrimp thali appeal to nonvegetarians.

✪ Jimbo's Restaurant. 1936 S. King St. ☎ **808/947-2211.** Reservations not accepted. Main courses $4.50–$11. CB, JCB, MC, V. Wed–Mon 11am–3pm; Wed–Thurs and Sun–Mon 5–10pm, Fri–Sat 5–11pm. JAPANESE.

Jimbo's is tiny, fewer than a dozen tables, and there is such demand for its sublime fare that there's often a wait for a table. It's worth it. A must for any noodle lover, Jimbo's serves homemade udon noodles in a marvelously smoky homemade broth, then tops the works with shrimp tempura, chicken, egg-and-vegetable, seaweed, roasted mochi, and a variety of other accompaniments. The Zouni, with chicken, vegetables, and mochi rice roasted to a toasty flavor, is one of life's great pleasures. Cold noodles, stir-fried noodles, donburi steamed rice dishes with assorted toppings, Japanese-style curries, and combination dinners served on trays are among Jimbo's many attractions. The earthenware pot of noodles, shiitake mushrooms, vegetables, and udon, with a platter of tempura on the side, is the top-of-the-line combo, a designer dish at an affordable price.

Kozo Sushi. 2334 S. King St. ☎ **808/973-5666.** Most items under $3.50; party plates $15–$24. No credit cards. Mon–Sat 9am–7pm, Sun 9am–6pm. SUSHI.

Into the pricey, floating world of expensive sushi houses came Kozo—fast, affordable, take-out sushi that isn't Kyoto quality, but is more than respectable, and extremely popular. Kozo's combination platters turn up apace at pot luck functions and large gatherings, but individual sushi can also be ordered: California roll, unagi roll, salmon and shrimp, and dozens of other choices, including the newest addition, the odd hybrid called BLT maki. There are four other locations in Honolulu.

Old Waialae Road Cafe. 2820 S. King St. ☎ **808/951-7779.** Reservations not accepted. Main courses $5–$8. No credit cards. Mon–Fri 11am–9pm, Sat–Sun 8am–9pm. LOCAL/PLATE LUNCH.

Two enterprising women resurrected a fading pillar in the plate lunch world and infused it with new ideas and a gourmet touch without losing any of its "local" quality. There are a few tables outdoors, but mostly it's a stylish take-out stand that serves an ahi plate, kimchee burgers, a sliced chicken breast pasta with Waimanalo gourmet greens, and a familiar list of local favorites. Items from the old menu board inside, a holdover from the old Ted's Drive-In, are still offered, but there's an excellent Hawaiian plate lunch now, spinach lasagna with polenta, garlic bread, and greens, and an impressive selection of daily changing specials. Weekend breakfasts are notable: everything from huevos rancheros and banana French toast to a handsome tofu scramble with Maui onions and many vegetables.

KAIMUKI/KAPAHULU
EXPENSIVE

☉ Sam Choy's Diamond Head Restaurant. 449 Kapahulu Ave. ☎ **808/732-8645.** Reservations required. Main courses $19–$30. AE, DC, MC, V. Mon–Thurs 5:30–9:30pm, Fri–Sun 5–10pm; Sun brunch 10:30am–1pm. HAWAII REGIONAL.

You'll know you're in the right place if you see exiting diners clutching their Styrofoam bundles, or with eyes glazed over from a surfeit of osso bucco, a Choy specialty. Leftovers are de rigueur at any Sam Choy's operation, where the servings are almost embarrassingly gargantuan. But don't take it personally: Choy is known for his humongous servings. The master of poke, Choy serves several of the best versions invented, among them a white fish (ono, opakapaka) drizzled with hot oil and topped with chopped herbs and condiments. The ti-leaf steamed seafood laulau is a signature dish, though we miss the traditional taro greens on top. Heartily recommended are the Brie wontons, the teriyaki-style rib-eye steak, the no-fat steamed fish with ginger and shiitake mushrooms, and his Kapakahi mashed potatoes—the best. The entrees are served with salad and soup, which doubles the generosity and makes each meal more than most single diners can consume.

3660 On the Rise. 3660 Waialae Ave. ☎ **808/737-1177.** Reservations required. Main courses $17.50–$24.50. AE, DC, MC, V. Tues–Thurs 5:30–9:30pm, Fri–Sat 5:30–10pm, Sun 5:30–9pm. EUROPEAN/ISLAND.

This is a busy, noisy restaurant with a menu that has retained only tried-and-true favorites, ranging from the basics like roasted chicken and rack of lamb to exotic touches such as ti-leaf–wrapped seafood in a tomato-butter sauce. Our favorites: the ahi katsu, wrapped in nori and deep-fried rare, an excellent appetizer; Caesar salad; and the opakapaka simmered in Chinese black-bean broth.

MODERATE

Beau Soleil. 3184 Waialae Ave. ☎ **808/732-0967.** Reservations recommended. Prix fixe, $20–$27. AE, DC, DISC, MC, V. Mon–Thurs 6–9pm, Fri–Sat 6–10pm. CONTEMPORARY MEDITERRANEAN.

The ambiance scores high (cobalt vases on the table, painted pink exterior, window boxes, and innlike atmosphere), and the food, though not riveting, is pleasant and affordable. There are three nightly specials and no printed menu, but they make a sincere effort to please vegetarians and fish lovers as well as carnivores. Neighborhood diners come to this charmingly appointed restaurant for eggplant terrine or fresh swordfish with couscous pilaf.

Genki Sushi. 900 Kapahulu Ave. ☎ **808/735-8889.** Individual sushi $1.20 and up per order. AE, DC, DISC, JCB, MC, V. Take-out counter, Sun–Thurs 11am–9pm, Fri–Sat 11am–10pm. Dining room closed Mon–Fri 3–5pm. SUSHI.

Fun! Crowded! Entertaining! Take your place in line for a seat at one of the U-shaped counters at which conveyor belts parade by with freshly made sushi, usually two pieces per color-coded plate, priced inexpensively. The dizzying variety is entertaining, adventuresome, and full of possibilities: spicy tuna topped with scallions, ahi, scallops with mayonnaise, Canadian roll (like California roll, except with salmon), sea urchin, flavored octopus, sweet shrimp, surfclam, corn, tuna salad, and so on. Genki starts with a Japanese culinary tradition and takes liberties with it, so purists miss out on some fun. By the end of the meal, the piled-high plates are tallied up by color and presto, your bill appears, much smaller than the pleasure. Brilliant combination platters stream across the take-out counter, $7.40 to $38.60.

Keo's. 625 Kapahulu Ave. ☎ **808/737-8240.** Reservations recommended. Main courses $8–$15; set dinners for 2 to 10 people, $22 per person. AE, JCB, DC, DISC, MC, V. Daily 5–10:30pm. THAI.

Keo's at one time was the only game in town, but competition from newer and smaller Thai restaurants has dulled his star considerably. Still, there are pluses: the food is tasty, the room is always busy, and the herbs, vegetables, fruits, and many of the spices used are grown without pesticides on a North Shore farm. The large banana stalks and dangling heliconias bring a strong dose of elegant country into this popular urban restaurant. Orchids are ubiquitous. Service is brisk, the mango daiquiris are legendary, and the Evil Jungle Prince, eggplant with basil and tofu, and green curry with seafood remain notable.

INEXPENSIVE

Bueno Nalo. 3045 Monsarrat Ave. ☎ **808/735-8818.** Most items under $9.95. MC, V. Daily 11am–10pm. MEXICAN.

Ole for Bueno Nalo and its sizzling fajitas, hearty combination platters, and famous chimichangas. There are two tables outside, six tables indoors, and a brisk take-out business among those who like its simple Mexican fare and adjoining juice bar. (Diamond Head–area joggers fuel their exercise on this place.) The super veggie burrito, mahimahi burrito, chicken chimichangas, and Mexican pizzas compete for your attention with Bueno's famous wraps (chicken, vegetarian, and a special of the day).

Cafe Laufer. 3565 Waialae Ave. ☎ **808/735-7717.** Most items under $7. AE, DC, JCB, MC, V. Sun–Mon and Wed–Thurs 8am–10pm, Fri–Sat 8am–11pm. COFFEE SHOP.

Unlike the coffee shops that lean toward the bohemian, Laufer is airy, cheerful, and a bit frilly—lots of pink and ruffles. But the pastries are the real thing: apple scones, linzer tortes, fruit flans, decadent chocolate mousses, and carrot cakes to accompany the lattes and espresso. Lunch fans drop in for simple soups and deli sandwiches on fresh-baked breads; biscotti for their coffee break; or a hearty loaf of seven-grain, rye, pumpernickel (the best), or French for breaking bread tomorrow. Solid hits: the $6.95 Chinese chicken salad, the $7.95 mesclun salad with mango-infused honey-mustard dressing, and the special Saturday night desserts such as the made-to-order soufflés—fresh lemon or strawberry, chocolate, Grand Marnier, and other fantasy flavors.

Hale Vietnam. 1140 12th Ave. ☎ **808/735-7581.** Reservations recommended for groups. Main courses $4.50–$16. DISC, MC, V. Mon–Sat 11am–10pm, Sun 11am–9pm. VIETNAMESE.

Duck into this house of pho and brave the no-frills service for the steaming noodle soups, the house specialty. The stock is simmered and skimmed for many hours and is accompanied with noodles, beef, chicken, and a platter of bean sprouts and fresh herbs. Approach the green chilis with caution; they may be the ones with the over-the-top scoville units. Although we love the chicken soup and shrimp vermicelli as well as the seafood pho and imperial rolls, caution is advised because this restaurant, like most other Vietnamese eateries, uses MSG.

Hee Hing Restaurant. 449 Kapahulu Ave. ☎ **808/735-5544** or 808/734-8474. Reservations required for parties of 5 or more. Main courses $5–$22. AE, DISC, MC, V. Mon–Thurs and Sun 10:30am–9:30pm, Fri–Sat 10:30am–10:30pm. CANTONESE.

Word is that quality has declined since its recent expansion, but it remains a local institution for multigeneration local families at retirement and anniversary parties. Weighty cargoes of drunken prawns, boneless crisp duck, crackling chicken, 15 types of rice soup, and fresh Dungeness crab in black-bean sauce rotate on the lazy Susans. Complete multicourse, family-style dinners can be prearranged affordably and generously. Best of all, Hee Hing's offerings are free of MSG.

Java Java Cafe. 760 Kapahulu Ave. ☎ **808/732-2670.** Most items under $6. No credit cards. Mon–Sat 10am–midnight, Sun 6pm–midnight. COFFEE HOUSE.

Quite the Kapahulu hangout, Java Java is the classic coffee house where aspiring playwrights and students reading Nietzsche mingle over coffee, drinks, salads, and sandwiches. The coffees outnumber all other items on the menu. Sandwiches (garden burgers, cumin chicken salad, tuna), bagels, Belgian waffles, salads (tuna/tomato, Greek, cumin/chicken), and fresh fruit smoothies appeal to diners from early morning to the late evening hours. Italian cream sodas are a hit, and the milky Thai tea competes with the Zombie, mochaccino, iced chocolate-mint latte, and dozens of specialty and iced coffees much loved by javanistas. New attractions: homemade granitas and the heavily hedonistic cookies 'n cream and peanut butter espresso shakes. Music, plays, poetry, coffee, and decent food draw customers of all ages, from the teens to mid-seventies.

3 East of Honolulu & Waikiki

KAHALA
VERY EXPENSIVE

Hoku's. In Kahala Mandarin Oriental Hotel, 5000 Kahala Ave. ☎ **808/739-8777.** Reservations recommended. Main courses $16.95–$34.95. AE, CB, DC, DISC, JCB, MC, V. Daily 11:30am–2:30pm and 5:30–10:30pm; Sun brunch 11:30am–2:30pm. PACIFIC/EUROPEAN.

The fine dining room of the Kahala Mandarin is less formal than its predecessor, the Maile Restaurant of the erstwhile Kahala Hilton, but it retains its elegance despite its newfound informality. The ocean view, open kitchen, and astonishing bamboo floor are stellar touches in the dining room. Many proclaim this the finest cuisine they've encountered in years, others say it's overrated. Reflecting its cross-cultural influences, the kitchen is equipped with a *kiawe* grill, an Indian tandoori oven for its chicken and naan bread, and Szechuan woks for the prawn, lobster, tofu, and other stir-fried specialties. The deep-fried whole Island fresh fish, served for two with a choice from three sauces, is luxuriously Oriental ($32.50 per person), while the grilled pepper-crusted rare tuna ($29.95) is a reliable best. Both are signature dishes, as are the braised beef shoulder ($26.95) and bouillabaisse ($28.95). All entrees are served with homemade bread baked in the wood-fired pizza oven, while the naan bread, hot from the Tandoori oven, comes with a melt-in-your-mouth smoked salmon–pineapple-horseradish-dill spread. At the upper end of the appetizer selections ($6.75 to $14.95), the chef's daily seafood sampler is a cool way to start the feast.

EXPENSIVE TO MODERATE

۞ Kahala Moon Cafe. 4614 Kilauea Ave. ☎ **808/732-7777.** Reservations recommended. Main courses $15–$24. AE, MC, V. Tues–Fri 11am–2pm and 5:30–9:30pm, Fri–Sat 5:30–10pm, Sun 5:30–9:30pm. HAWAII REGIONAL.

Stylish without being pretentious, with designer flowers in large pots accenting the windowless room, Kahala Moon is a top choice for lunch and great value for a special-occasion dinner. It isn't cheap, but many other restaurants of this ilk charge far more for far less pleasure. We love the sake-steamed clams and lemon-herb–crusted crab cakes. Add the whole-leaf Caesar salad, another favorite, and you have a light and satisfying meal. At dinner, the grilled lamb chops with caramelized onions, roasted potatoes, and sherry-coriander-lemon butter are among Honolulu's finest, and the sautéed salmon with wild mushroom stuffing is a salmon-lover's dream. Save room for the mango bread pudding or lemongrass crème brûlée, ambrosia to the final spoonful.

MODERATE

The Patisserie. 4211 Waialae Ave., Kahala Mall. ☎ **808/735-4402.** Deli sandwiches $3.75–$4.75; complete dinners $13.50–$17. MC, V. Dinner service Tues–Sat 5:30–8:30pm; deli service Mon–Sat 7am–9pm, Sun 7am–5pm. GERMAN.

In its bakery setting with eight tables and a gleaming deli counter, the complete dinners are a pleasant surprise, more elegant than the casual mall surroundings would indicate and kind to the pocketbook, too. The Patisserie sells everything from deluxe wedding cakes and European breads to inexpensive deli sandwiches (tuna, egg salad, pastrami, black forest ham) and 10 types of complete dinners. The Tuesday to Saturday dinners include sauerbraten, osso bucco, veal ribs, baked pork tenderloin, braised lamb shank, and a particularly memorable sautéed chicken breast in a Marsala-mushroom sauce, served with linguine. A fish dinner is offered every Friday, and the German dinners are schnitzel heaven: Wienerschnitzel, rahm schnitzel, pepper schnitzel, and potato pancakes with sour cream and applesauce. Served with garden salad and rolls, the dinners are a terrific value if you're willing to go without the candlelight and roses.

INEXPENSIVE

۞ Olive Tree Cafe. 4614 Kilauea Ave., next to Kahala Mall. ☎ **808/737-0303.** Reservations not accepted. Main courses $5–$10. No credit cards. Mon–Fri 5–11pm, Sat–Sun 11am–10pm. GREEK/MEDITERRANEAN.

Olive Tree fans are continually amazed at the delights from this tiny open kitchen at bargain prices. With umbrellas over tables on the sidewalk, a few seats indoors, and the best Greek food in Hawaii, this informal cafe is one of the top values in town. The tabouli salad is generously greened with herbs and mint; the falafel, hummus, and taramasalata—a pink caviar spread with pita—are a pleasurable launch to a meal that just keeps getting better. The soup changes by the day (egg-lemon, lentil-vegetable, pumpkin, sherry-eggplant, fish), and the superb souvlakis (kebabs in pita bread) range from fresh fish to chicken and lean New Zealand lamb, enhanced with a yogurt-dill sauce. You'll order at the counter from a neon menu that includes the daily specials: lamb shank in tomato and herbs, lemon chicken, spanakopita, a stuffed eggplant called imambayaldi. Located next door to Kahala Mall (where you can buy your own libations), Olive Tree is BYOB, which means a large group can dine like sultans for a song, and take in a movie next door, too.

NIU VALLEY

Cliquo. 5730 Kalanianaole Hwy., Niu Valley Shopping Center. ☎ **808/377-8854.** Reservations recommended. Main courses $16–$29. Prix fixe $27. AE, DC, DISC, JCB, MC, V. Mon–Sat 5:30–9pm. FRENCH.

Chef Yves Menoret has a glowing reputation in Honolulu as the man who established the erstwhile Bagwell's and Bali by the Sea before opening his own very *intime* dining room 2 years ago. His solidly French offerings are prepared with care and Old World meticulousness, particularly the flaky opakapaka with watercress and ginger beurre blanc ($24); seared foie gras with leek and yukon potato ($29); and the vol au vent, the buttery escargots in clouds of leeks and garlic. The medley of lobster with wild mushrooms and the lobster medaillion salad come in two sizes, a plus. On such a spare, selective, and elegant menu, the prix fixe selections soar. (One night the prix fixe menu included asparagus with wild mushrooms, tournedos of filet mignon in a light cabernet sauce or fresh opakapaka with a puree of organic pumpkin, and macadamia chocolate mousse or fresh fruit granite—all for an affordable $27.) Menoret's following grows.

Swiss Inn. 5730 Kalanianaole Hwy., Niu Valley Shopping Center. ☎ **808/377-5447.** Reservations recommended. Complete dinners $14–$21. AE, CB, DC, DISC, JCB, MC, V. Wed–Sun 6pm–closing; Sun brunch 10:30am–1pm. CONTINENTAL.

Martin and Jeanie Wyss have been welcoming families for more than 15 years to their cordial "chalet" in suburban Honolulu. The quintessential neighborhood restaurant, Swiss Inn offers terrific values with no compromise in quality: Wienerschnitzel, $16; New York steak, $21; scallops Madagascar, $19.25; baked chicken, $14. The complete dinners include soup, salad, vegetables, and coffee or tea. Families have always been welcome at Swiss Inn, and when the kids grow up, they bring their friends and families, too. It is always full. Specialties include the veal dishes and the fresh fish, usually mahimahi or onaga, in a lemon-butter-caper sauce, and at Thanksgiving and holidays, the home-cooked turkey dinner, just the way mom made it.

HAWAII KAI

✪ **Roy's Restaurant.** 6600 Kalanianaole Hwy. ☎ **808/396-7697.** Reservations recommended. Main courses $9–$25. AE, JCB, MC, V. Daily 5:30–9:15pm. EUROPEAN/ASIAN.

He built in Hawaii Kai, and diners came—in droves. Roy Yamaguchi's flagship Hawaii restaurant was the first of what is now a chain of 13 throughout Hawaii, Asia, and the Pacific—but don't count on that figure, because his dining empire grows faster than we can count. A prolific winner of culinary awards, Yamaguchi devised a winning formula—open kitchen, fresh ingredients, ethnic touches, and a good dose of nostalgia mingling with European techniques. The menu changes nightly, but you can generally count on individual pizzas; a varied appetizer menu (summer rolls, blackened ahi, hibachi-style salmon); a small pasta selection; and entrees such as lemongrass-roasted chicken, garlic-mustard short ribs, mustard-crusted lamb shanks, hibachi-style salmon in ponzu sauce, and several types of fresh catch prepared at least five different ways. Roy's is also renowned for its high-decibel–style of dining, so full and so noisy you'll have to join in the fracas to be heard. But the food quality, service, impeccable timing, and eclectic, well-priced wine list are impressive.

4 The Windward Coast

✪ **Ahi's Restaurant.** 59146 Kamehameha Hwy., Punaluu. ☎ **808/293-5650.** Reservations for 8 or more. Main courses $6–$11.95. No credit cards. Mon–Sat 11am–9pm. AMERICAN/LOCAL.

Fans were devastated two years ago to hear that Ahi's had burned down, but the good news is that Ahi's has reopened, at the site of the old Paniolo Cafe on the main highway in Punaluu. Ahi Logan and his three-generation family business have breathed new life into this former biker bar, bringing their fabulous shrimp dishes and generous aloha to the windward side. Ahi's is a quaint roadside oasis with a large grassy parking lot, abundant foliage all around, split-level indoor dining, and an airy, screened-in room (for larger parties) that is a charming throwback to pre-resort, pre-marble, pre-plastic Hawaii. A rolling green lawn and towering trees rim the wooden structure; from food to ambiance to clientele, it is informal and comfortably rural. The shrimp, the menu highlight, comes fresh, plump, and served four ways (cocktail, scampi, tempura, and deep-fried), and the mahimahi and fresh fish specials have retained the old magic. Come here when you're hungering for the taste of real Hawaii that resorts long ago abandoned.

Assaggio Italian Restaurant. 354 Ulunui St., Kailua. ☎ **808/261-2772.** Reservations recommended. Lunch main courses $3.90–$9.90, dinner main courses $8–$18. AE, DC, DISC, MC, V. Mon–Fri 11:30am–2:30pm; daily 5–10pm. ITALIAN.

You may not want to make the half-hour trip over the Pali for dinner here, but it's nice to know about Assaggio if you happen to be visiting the Windward Coast. Affordable prices, attentive service, and some winning items have won Assaggio loyal fans throughout the years in the changeable Kailua environment. The best-selling homemade hot antipasto has jumbo shrimp, fresh clams, mussels, and calamari in a sauce of cayenne pepper, white wine, and garlic. You can choose linguine, fettuccine, or ziti with 10 different sauces in small or regular portions, or any of nine chicken pastas (the chicken Assaggio, with garlic, peppers, and mushrooms, is especially flavorful). Especially impressive is the extensive list of seafood pastas and other combinations, including the plain, wonderful garlic/olive oil sauté. The homemade tiramisu and zabaglione are local legends. At lunch, lighter fare, such as ziti, Caesar salad, and sandwiches, prevails.

There's another branch in Hawaii Kai at 7192 Kalanianaole Hwy. (☎ **808/396-0756**).

Brent's Restaurant & Delicatessen. 629-A Kailua Rd. ☎ **808/262-8588.** Most items under $15. MC, V. Tues–Sat 7am–9pm, Sun 7am–8pm. KOSHER DELI.

Finally, a kosher deli with real cheese blintzes, cream cheese and shrimp omelets, and some spirited cultural digressions, such as pesto poached eggs and an artichoke-laced frittata. And bagels galore, with baked salmon, sturgeon-and-cream cheese, or any number of accompaniments to compete with the New York–style pastrami and hot corned-beef sandwiches on Brent's abundant menu.

Baci Bistro. 30 Aulike St., Kailua. ☎ **808/262-7555.** Reservations recommended for dinner. Main courses $12.95–$19.95. MC, V. Mon–Fri 11:30am–2pm; daily 5:30–10pm. ITALIAN.

Baci fans have been hoping for a reappearance since Waikiki closed, and then Kaimuki, and presto: Baci opened its doors in Kailua where Solana used to be, a pleasingly casual indoor-outdoor dining room in which hip Kailuans can nosh on homemade gnocchi, fresh-made raviolis, and squid-ink fettuccine with scallops and saffron sauce—on their side of the Pali! Baci fans also tout the charcoaled shrimp with lime and feta cheese ($9.95), veal Baci (the signature scaloppini with artichoke hearts, sundried tomatoes, capers, and wine, for $18.95), and the fresh raviolis with lamb, lobster, or combinations of fresh seafood. The lunch and dinner menus include salads, hot and cold appetizers (they're famous for their bruschetta), risottos, homemade pastas, and veal, seafood, and chicken entrees. The lighter lunch fare includes inexpensive sandwiches.

Bueno Nalo. 41–865 Kalanianaole Hwy., Waimanalo. ☎ **808/259-7186.** Combination plates $9.95; main courses $4.25–$8.25. MC, V. Daily 11:30am–9pm. MEXICAN.

Now in two locations (the newer location is in the Kapahulu-Diamond Head area, see the listing under "Honolulu Beyond Waikiki"), this popular, serape-draped roadside eatery serves stick-to-your ribs Mexican fare that hits the spot after bodysurfing and swimming at Waimanalo Beach. Friendly service, modest surroundings, and familiar south-of-the-border basics suit the laid-back, rubber-slipper ambiance of Waimanalo, a favorite windward Oahu hamlet. Tuck into the chicken chimichangas, fajitas, Bueno burritos, or Mexican pizzas, but beware the fried foods. There may be more bloat than bueno after the chili rellenos, and you may need a flotation device (or a siesta!) when you head back to the surf.

Masa and Joyce Fish Market. 47–388 Hui Iwa St., Temple Valley Shopping Center in Haiku, across from the Valley of the Temples. Hawaiian plate lunches $5.95–$7.50; Japanese *okazu* items under $1.25. MC, V. Mon–Thurs 8am–6pm, Fri–Sat 8am–6:30pm, Sun 8am–5pm. HAWAIIAN/JAPANESE.

Located between Pizza Hut and Subway, in the culinary desert of a suburban shopping center, Masa and Joyce is a breath of fresh air: real food! It offers Hawaiian and Japanese food, point-and-pick *okazu* style from counters. Most of the business is takeout, but you can eat at one of the two unadorned tables near the counters. Local folks love this place for its homestyle cooking: chicken hekka, sushi, fried noodles, various patties and tempuras, and wonderful Hawaiian plate lunches—lau lau (taro tops, pork, and fish steamed in ti-leaves), lomi salmon, kalua pork, poi, chicken long rice, and, for a dollar more, excellent ahi poke with fresh seaweed. An adjoining fish counter proffers a selection of fresh seafood and prepared items for happy-hour at home. Great prices, too—the Hawaiian plate lunches are under $7.50, a steal. **Masa & Joyce 2** is the second location (45-582 Kamehameha Hi. in Kaneohe, ☎ **808/ 235-6129**), similarly centered around the Japanese okazu, sushi, and Hawaiian plates—$6.25 for the lau lau plate, $7.50 for the kalua plate. Most items in the *okazu* counter are under $1.50—and no MSG is used.

Waimanalo Fish Market. 41–1537 Kalanianaole Hwy., Waimanalo Center. ☎ **808/ 259-8008.** Plate lunches $3.95–$6.50; Hawaiian plates $5.75–$8.25. No credit cards. Sat–Tues 8am–5pm, Wed–Fri 8am–7pm. HAWAIIAN.

Although they offer the usual plate lunch and sandwich offerings, Hawaiian food is the reason to come here. Rita Akeo makes everything from scratch, including the poi, made from top-quality lehua taro. The Hawaiian plates come in various combinations: kalua pork, lau lau, lomi salmon, fried fish, $7.50; with teriyaki chicken, $7.95; with squid luau, lomi salmon, kalua pig, and haupia (coconut pudding), $8.25, and so on. You can take it out or choose to dine in the no-frills room, but wherever you are, this is as good as Hawaiian food gets. (We especially favor the squid luau and lau lau with the homemade poi.)

5 The North Shore

Cafe Haleiwa. 66–460 Kamehameha Hwy., Haleiwa. ☎ **808/637-5516.** Reservations not accepted. Main courses $5.50–$10.50. AE, MC, V. Mon–Sat 7am–3pm, Sun 7am–2pm. MEXICAN/LOCAL.

Cafe Haleiwa, at the Wahiawa entrance to Haleiwa, has made some changes since its concrete floors sagged and cracked (we liked it then, too), but it has retained its stature as the breakfast joint of surfers, urban gentry with weekend country homes, reclusive artists, and anyone who loves mahimahi plate lunches and homemade Mexican food. It's a wake-up-and-hit-the-beach kind of place serving generous burritos and omelets with names like Off the Wall, Off the Lip, and Breakfast in a Barrel. Surf pictures line the walls, and the ambiance is Formica-style casual. You can order a mahimahi plate lunch with home fries, rice, or beans. Spicy chicken tacos; fish tacos with grilled mahi, tomatoes, lime, and cilantro; and burritos, tostadas, and combination plates will make it hard for you to stick to a veggie or chicken sandwich. But they serve those too—tuna salad, mahimahi, burgers, steak sandwiches—made with individual attention and grilled onions on request. Our favorite breakfast is the truly epic huevos rancheros, smothered with cheese and salsa.

Coffee Gallery. In North Shore Marketplace, 66–250 Kamehameha Hwy., Haleiwa. ☎ **808/637-5355.** Reservations not accepted. Most items under $6. AE, DISC, MC, V. Mon–Fri 6am–9pm, Sat–Sun 7am–9pm. COFFEE HOUSE/VEGETARIAN.

On the other side of town from Kua Aina (see below) and its meat-lover's cuisine, this indoor-outdoor coffee house has carved a firm niche in the hearts of Haleiwa's health-conscious diners, vegetarians, and coffee lovers. The lemon squares here are famous (its recipe was printed, by popular request, in the local newspaper), and the granola is made with premium Big Island honey. There are tofu burritos with fresh spinach and roasted garlic tomato sauce, bagels galore, salads and pastas, and a spicy three-bean vegetarian chili served with rennetless cheddar cheese. The vegan soup is served with fresh-baked whole-wheat French bread. Spinach pesto, vegetarian enchiladas, tempeh and garden burgers, hummus platters, and many pages of healthy enticements make this one of Haleiwa's heavenly stops, as inexpensive as it is thoughtful.

✪ Jameson's by the Sea. 62–540 Kamehameha Hwy., Haleiwa. ☎ **808/637-4336.** Reservations recommended. Downstairs lunch menu $7–$12; main courses $13–$39 in upstairs dining room. AE, DC, DISC, JCB, MC, V. Downstairs, daily 11am–5pm; pub menu Mon–Tues 5–9pm, Sat–Sun 11am–9pm. Upstairs, Wed–Sun 5–9pm. SEAFOOD.

The roadside watering hole across the street from the ocean is always full with fun-loving north shore types or rubbernecking tourists agog with the beauty of the area. It's a happy place; duck in for cocktails, sashimi, and salmon pâté, or for other hot and cold appetizers, salads, and sandwiches throughout the day. Especially popular are the Jameson's vegetarian and curried chicken salads, the grilled crab and shrimp sandwich (pardon the mayonnaise) on sourdough bread, and the fresh fish sandwich of the day, grilled plain and simple. Upstairs, the much pricier dining room opens 5 nights a week for the usual surf-and-turf choices: fresh opakapaka, ulua (Hawaiian jack fish), and mahimahi; scallops in lemon butter and capers; and lobster tail, New York steak, and filet mignon. Jameson's and the nearby Chart House are similarly cast as North Shore standbys that have stuck to their generic formulas, without apology, for years.

Kua Aina. 66–214 Kamehameha Hwy., Haleiwa. ☎ **808/637-6067.** Most items under $6. No credit cards. Daily 11am–8pm. AMERICAN.

"What's the name of that famous sandwich shop on the north shore?" We hear that often. Kua Aina is as much a part of the north shore ritual as a Ke Iki Beach sunset. Recent renovations haven't cut down on the long lines at this tiny north shore bee-hive, because demand still outpaces the kitchen for the French fries and grilled ham-burgers and mahimahi sandwiches. Because the few tables on the streetside porch fill early, customers often pick up their burgers and head for the beach. Kua Aina's thin and spindly french fries are renowned islandwide and are the perfect accompaniment to its legendary burgers. Fat, moist, and homemade, the burgers can be ordered with avocado, bacon, and many other accompaniments in addition to its tower of sprouts and greens. Also recommended are the roast beef and fresh fish sandwiches, tried-and-true and totally satisfying. In this neck of the woods, it's not a picnic unless it's Kua Aina, which sets the pace for many a north shore outing.

North Shore Pizza Company. In North Shore Marketplace, 66–250 Kamehameha Hwy., Haleiwa. ☎ **808/637-2782.** Main courses and pizzas $7–$21. AE, MC, V. Mon–Fri 4–9pm, Fri 4–10pm, Sat–Sun 11am–10pm. PIZZA.

Pizza delivery in Haleiwa is more than a convenience, it's a damn good idea. People like to stay put after they've driven an hour from town to get home, and who wants to hop in the car when there's a sunset to be ogled? North Shore Pizza isn't cheap, but it's reliable, delicious, and it won't cause arguments with the kids. The same people who opened trendy Portofino and who introduced Zorro's Pizza to Hawaii also make and deliver the pizzas, calzones, focaccia sandwiches, and pastas from a small but dynamic menu fashioned by chefs from Milan and Florence. The 16-inch New York–style pizzas are named after North Shore surf spots and are topped with fresh island produce such as Maui onions, North Shore basil, Portuguese sausage, and, for pizza heretics, Hawaiian pineapple. The Kaena Point, with barbecue chicken, Maui onions, fresh tomatoes, and cilantro, is a nontraditional good bet. Healthy eaters will notice the Healthy Italian, a calzone with grilled zucchini, eggplant, peppers, mushrooms, onions, and marinara sauce.

Paradise Found Cafe. 66–443 Kamehameha Hwy., Haleiwa. ☎ **808/637-4540.** Most items under $6.75. No credit cards. Mon–Sat 9am–6:30pm, Sun 10am–6pm. VEGETARIAN.

This is one of the many reasons we love Haleiwa: nondeprivation vegetarian food! A tiny cafe behind the Celestial Natural foods, Paradise Found takes looking for, but it's a charming way to begin a North Shore sojourn. You can buy a bowl of vegetarian chili and rice for about $3, and for very little more, a hummus dip with pita and cucumber. It's as good as the baba gannoujh, the veggie burgers (with cheese and avocado, a winner), the chapati wraps, quesadilla, and any of the fresh fruit smoothies that have fueled many a beachlover's day. The mix of Mexican favorites (quesadilla with chili and avocado) and Middle-Eastern samplings is a solid success at this tiny corner of the health food store.

Portofino. In North Shore Marketplace, 66–250 Kamehameha Hwy., Haleiwa. ☎ **808/637-7678.** Reservations recommended. Main courses $6.25–$18. AE, MC, V. Sun–Thurs 8am–10pm, Fri–Sat 8am–11pm. NORTHERN ITALIAN.

The North Shore's newest and most attractive restaurant has terra-cotta tile floors, columns and arches, and hand-painted murals that bring a splendid scene of Portofino into the airy room. Although the decibel level can get high, it's a cordial environment in which to enjoy the aromas and creations emanating from the wood-burning oven and open kitchen. Chefs from Italy have devised a menu of homemade pastas, focaccia, calzones, sandwiches, oven-baked fish, and wood-fired pizzas, as well as everyday comforts such as chicken, meat loaf, and roasted-garlic mashed potatoes.

Fun in the Surf & Sun

by Jeanette Foster

Visions of hotels lining the shores of Waikiki Beach and canyons of tall buildings in downtown Honolulu have caused people to pass judgment on Oahu. Oahu, however, is much more than an urban, concrete jungle or a tropical Disneyland blighted by overdevelopment; it's also a haven for the nature lover and outdoor enthusiast. With year-round air temperatures in the upper 70s, ocean temperatures in the mid- to high 70s, and miles of verdant and unspoiled landscape, Oahu is perfect for outdoor activities of all kinds including hiking, golf, tennis, biking, and horseback riding. The island's waters, though, are where the majority of both residents and visitors head for relaxation, rejuvenation, and recreation. Locals don't think of their island or state boundaries as ending at land's edge—rather, they extend beyond the reefs, well out into the ocean.

1 Beaches

Oahu has more than 130 beaches of every conceivable description, from legendary white-sand stretches to secluded rocky bays. Waikiki, of course, is the best known of Oahu's beaches, but there are many others—some more beautiful, all less crowded. What follows is a selection of the finest of Oahu's beaches, carefully chosen to suit every need, taste, and interest, from the sunbather in repose to the most ardent diver.

A note of caution: Keep in mind—wherever you are on Oahu—that you're in an urban area. Never leave valuables in your car. Thefts do occur at Oahu's beaches, and locked cars are no deterrent.

WAIKIKI BEACH

The name of the world-famous 2-mile stretch means "spouting water," probably referring to the duck ponds that once occupied this former swamp land. A crescent-shaped beach of imported sand on Oahu's south shore, Waikiki extends—interrupted periodically by sea walls, rock groins, and a yacht harbor—from the Ala Wai Canal to the foot of Mount Leahi (better known as Diamond Head). Hawaii's most popular beach, Waikiki is always crowded with tourists. You can experience nearly every type of ocean activity here: One of the best places on Oahu for swimming, Waikiki also offers both board- and bodysurfing, outrigger canoeing, diving, sailing, snorkeling, and pole fishing. Every imaginable type of marine equipment and toy is available for rent. The many hotels that line the beach

Beaches & Outdoor Activities on Oahu

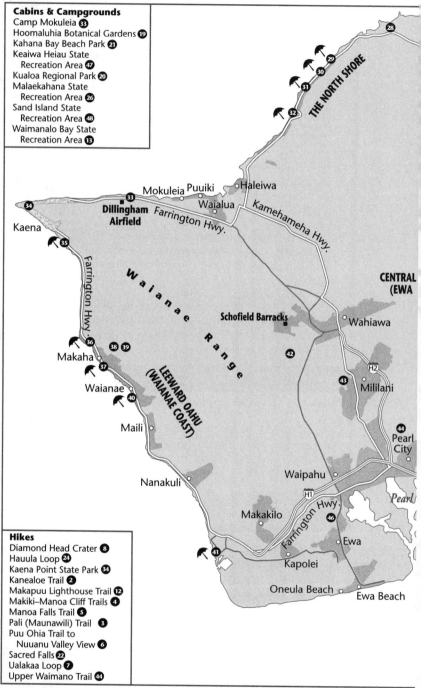

Cabins & Campgrounds
Camp Mokuleia ③③
Hoomaluhia Botanical Gardens ⑲
Kahana Bay Beach Park ㉑
Keaiwa Heiau State
  Recreation Area ㊼
Kualoa Regional Park ⑳
Malaekahana State
  Recreation Area ㉖
Sand Island State
  Recreation Area ㊽
Waimanalo Bay State
  Recreation Area ⑬

THE NORTH SHORE

Mokuleia Puuiki Haleiwa

Waialua

Kamehameha Hwy.

Kaena

Dillingham
Airfield

Farrington Hwy.

Farrington Hwy.

W a i a n a e

R a n g e

CENTRAL
(EWA

Schofield Barracks

Wahiawa

LEEWARD OAHU
(WAIANAE COAST)

Makaha

Waianae

Maili

Mililani

H2

Nanakuli

Pearl
City

Waipahu

Pearl

Makakilo

H1

Farrington Hwy.

Ewa

Kapolei

Oneula Beach

Ewa Beach

Hikes
Diamond Head Crater ⑧
Hauula Loop ㉔
Kaena Point State Park ㉞
Kanealoe Trail ②
Makapuu Lighthouse Trail ⑫
Makiki–Manoa Cliff Trails ④
Manoa Falls Trail ⑤
Pali (Maunawili) Trail ③
Puu Ohia Trail to
  Nuuanu Valley View ⑥
Sacred Falls ㉒
Ualakaa Loop ⑦
Upper Waimano Trail ㊹

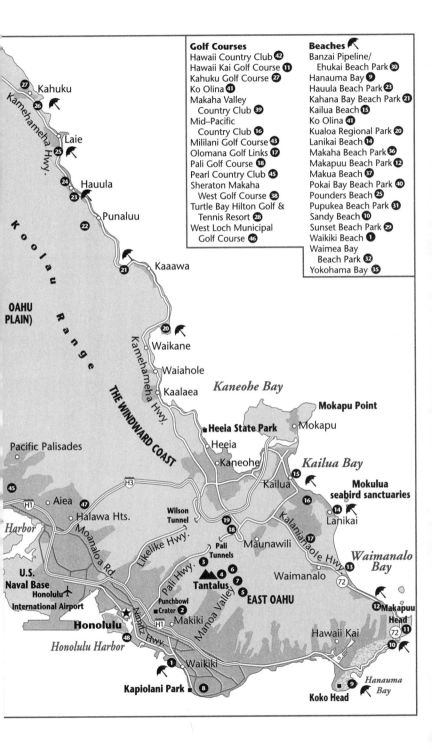

Golf Courses
Hawaii Country Club **42**
Hawaii Kai Golf Course **11**
Kahuku Golf Course **27**
Ko Olina **41**
Makaha Valley
  Country Club **39**
Mid–Pacific
  Country Club **16**
Mililani Golf Course **43**
Olomana Golf Links **17**
Pali Golf Course **18**
Pearl Country Club **45**
Sheraton Makaha
  West Golf Course **38**
Turtle Bay Hilton Golf &
  Tennis Resort **28**
West Loch Municipal
  Golf Course **46**

Beaches
Banzai Pipeline/
  Ehukai Beach Park **30**
Hanauma Bay **9**
Hauula Beach Park **23**
Kahana Bay Beach Park **21**
Kailua Beach **15**
Ko Olina **41**
Kualoa Regional Park **20**
Lanikai Beach **14**
Makaha Beach Park **36**
Makapuu Beach Park **12**
Makua Beach **37**
Pokai Bay Beach Park **40**
Pounders Beach **25**
Pupukea Beach Park **31**
Sandy Beach **10**
Sunset Beach Park **29**
Waikiki Beach **1**
Waimea Bay
  Beach Park **32**
Yokohama Bay **35**

Kamehameha Hwy.

27 Kahuku
26
25 Laie
24 Hauula
23
22 Punaluu

K o o l a u   R a n g e

**OAHU
PLAIN)**

21 Kaaawa

20 Waikane

Waiahole

Kaalaea

Kaneohe Bay

Kamehameha Hwy.

Mokapu Point

Heeia State Park ● Mokapu

Heeia

Kaneohe

THE WINDWARD COAST

Kailua Bay

15 Kailua

Pacific Palisades

H3

**Mokulua
seabird sanctuaries**

45

H1 ● Aiea **47**

Halawa Hts.

16

14 Lanikai

Harbor

Moanalua Rd.

**Wilson
Tunnel**

Likelike Hwy.

19
18 Maunawili

17

Kalanianaole Hwy.

*Waimanalo
Bay*

**Pali
Tunnels**

3

6

7

5

Pali Hwy.

Tantalus

Waimanalo

13

72

**U.S.
Naval Base**

Honolulu ✈

International Airport

Punchbowl
■ **Crater 2**

Makiki

Manoa Valley

EAST OAHU

12 Makapuu
Head

Nimitz Hwy.

H1

★

Honolulu

48

Honolulu Harbor

1 Waikiki

Kapiolani Park ■ **8**

Hawaii Kai

72

11

10

9 *Hanauma
Bay*

Koko Head

167

offer an array of food and drink. The best place to park is around Kapiolani Park. Facilities on the beach include showers, lifeguards, public rest rooms, and picnic pavilions at the Queen's Surf end of the beach (near the park).

✪ HANAUMA BAY

Formerly a playground for Hawaiian royalty, this beautiful bay is now a Marine Life Conservation District and the most popular snorkeling spot on Oahu for both visitors and residents. The enclosed 2,000-foot beach just east of Koko Head fronts a pristine bay, which is actually a volcanic crater open to the ocean on one side. Hanauma's shallow shoreline waters and bountiful marine life are both a blessing and a curse; the number of visitors to the bay is so overwhelming that some fear that the ecology of the marine preserve is in danger. Because of the existing threat, the government has restricted both parking and access by commercial operators. Since Hanauma Bay is a conservation district, taking anything from the ocean is prohibited. Facilities include parking, rest rooms, a picnic pavilion, grass volleyball court, lifeguard, barbecues, picnic tables, and a food concession.

If you're driving, take Kalanianaole Highway to Koko Head Regional Park. To avoid the crowds and ensure yourself a parking space, go early on a weekday morning. Or, take TheBUS no. 22 to escape the parking problem. The Hanauma Bay Shuttle runs from Waikiki to Hanauma Bay every half hour from 8:45am to 1pm; you can catch it at the Ala Moana Hotel, the Ilikai Hotel, or at any city bus stop on the route. It returns every hour on the hour from noon to 4pm. The park closes every day at 6pm. The park is closed on Wednesdays until noon for maintenance. Visitors can enter after noon.

SANDY BEACH

Also part of Koko Head Regional Park, Sandy Beach is one of the best bodysurfing beaches on Oahu. Unless you're experienced, though, you might be restricted to watching the expert bodysurfers and boogie boarders ride the waves and the chiseled bodies strut up and down the shore. This 1,200-foot-long beach is pounded by waves nearly all year long. The steep, quick drop-off underwater adds to the intensity of the waves and produces a strong, forceful backwash. The backwash is especially dangerous for children and weak swimmers. (The lifeguards here make more rescues in a year than those stationed at any other beach except nearby Makapuu.) Visitors unfamiliar with the beach and its dangers—and fooled by the experienced bodysurfers who make wave-riding look so easy—all too often find themselves overwhelmed by the waves. As a result, the lifeguards have developed a flag system that warns you of the surf's danger level: Green means safe, yellow caution, and red indicates very dangerous water conditions. Be sure to check the flags before you dive in. Facilities include rest rooms and parking. The best times to avoid the crowds are weekdays; the best times to watch top bodysurfers are weekends. TheBUS no. 22 (Kuhio) will get you to Sandy Beach from Waikiki.

MAKAPUU BEACH PARK

At the base of the Koolau Mountains on Oahu's easternmost point is Makapuu Beach Park, the most famous bodysurfing beach in Hawaii. Movie fans will recognize this classically beautiful 1,000-foot-long white-sand beach, bordered by the stark black cliff of Makapuu Point, as a location for the famous Burt Lancaster-Deborah Kerr love scene in *From Here to Eternity*. Picturesque Rabbit Island lies just off the coast. During the summer months the ocean can be as gentle as a backyard pool, making swimming and diving a breeze; but extremely dangerous currents and surf can be present from September through April, when the pounding waves erode the beach and expose rocks and boulders in the shorebreak area. Because these conditions are ideal for expert bodysurfers, board surfing is prohibited by state law. Small boards, 3 feet or less with no skeg (bottom fin), are permitted. Facilities include rest rooms, lifeguard, barbecue grills, picnic tables, and parking. To get to Makapuu, follow Kalanianaole Highway toward Waimanalo. TheBUS no. 57 or 58 (Sea Life Park) will get you to there from Waikiki.

✪ LANIKAI BEACH

Hidden by the residential area of Mokulua Drive on the windward side of the island, Lanikai is a beautiful mile-long beach that's safe for swimming and—with the prevailing trade winds—excellent for sailing and windsurfing. The fine, hard-packed sand along the shoreline is perfect for jogging. Offshore, the two tiny islands called the Mokuluas (which are sea-bird sanctuaries) are easily reachable by kayak. Because Lanikai is off the main roads, undeveloped, without facilities, and surrounded by residential homes, it's less crowded than other beaches on the windward side. It's the perfect place to claim a remote, isolated spot for a morning of swimming and relaxation. Sun-worshipers should arrive in the morning, as the Koolaus' shadow will block your access to the rays in the afternoon. From Waikiki, take TheBUS no. 56 or 57 (Kailua), then transfer to the shuttle bus.

✪ KAILUA BEACH PARK

A 30-acre public park located on the east end of Kailua Bay, Kailua Beach Park is a broad, grassy area with picnic tables, a public boat ramp, rest rooms, a pavilion, a volleyball court, and food stands. The wide, sandy beach area is popular for diving, swimming, sailing, snorkeling, and board- and windsurfing. In fact, the dependable winds make this one of the more popular windsurfing areas on Oahu. The water conditions are generally safe, but parents should keep an eye on young children, who are often attracted to the brackish water pond in the middle of the park. The seemingly shallow pond has deep holes and has been the site of several drownings. The park gets extremely crowded with local families on weekends; the best time to come is during the week. To get to Kailua Beach Park, take the Kalanianaole Highway or the Pali Highway to Kailua Road, which loops around to Kawailoa Road. Parking is available. From Waikiki, take TheBUS no. 56 or 57 (Kailua) into Kailua, then take the no. 70 shuttle.

KUALOA REGIONAL PARK

In ancient Hawaii this was a very sacred spot, and today the park is listed in the National Register of Historic Places. Hawaiian chiefs brought their infant children here to be raised and trained as rulers. When canoes passed offshore, sails were lowered in recognition of the sacredness of Kualoa. It is easy to see why this was considered a sacred place: The curtain of the Koolau Mountains provides a spectacular backdrop for this broad grassy park bordered by a white-sand beach, with the islet Mokolii (popularly known as Chinaman's Hat) in the distance. The offshore waters are shallow and safe for swimming year-round; they're also excellent for kayaking and fishing. Lifeguards are on duty, and picnic and camping areas are available. Since both residents and visitors frequent this huge beach park, it's better to go on a weekday. The park is located on the Kamehameha Highway in Kauloa; you can take TheBUS no. 55 (Circle Island) to get there.

✪ KAHANA BAY BEACH PARK

This white-sand, crescent-shaped beach is backed by a huge, jungle-cloaked valley with dramatic, jagged cliffs, and protected by ironwood and *kamani* trees. The bay's calm water and shallow, sandy bottom make it a safe swimming area for children. The bay is famous for the *akule* (big-eyed scad), which come in seasonally. Other fish often taken here include *papio* and goatfish. The surrounding park has picnic areas, camping, and hiking trails, and the wide sand-bottom channel that runs through the park and out to Kahana Bay is one of the largest on Oahu—it's perfect for kayakers. Visitors and residents alike come to this relaxing beach, so weekdays are best. The beach park is located on Kamehameha Highway in Kahana; if you like, take TheBUS no. 55 (Circle Island) to get there.

HAUULA BEACH PARK

The town of Hauula and nearby Hauula Beach Park were named after the *hau* trees that used to be abundant in the area. Although less plentiful now, hau blooms every morning with a bright yellow flower during July and August. The yellow flowers change color as the day progresses, until they are a reddish gold by dusk and dark red by night, when they fall to the ground. The cycle is repeated the next day.

Hauula Beach Park is straight and narrow, about 1,000-feet long, fronting Kamehameha Highway, and shaded by kamani and ironwood trees. An offshore reef protects the waters off the beach, however, the shallow and rocky bottom make the area unsafe for swimming. Snorkeling is good along the edge of the coral reef, and fishing for papio and goatfish can be productive. There are picnic and camping facilities. Weekends tend to be more crowded here, too. TheBUS no. 55 (Circle Island) will get you to Hauula Beach.

POUNDERS BEACH

Because of its easy accessibility and its great bodysurfing waves, Pounders is a popular weekend beach. The beach used to be called Pahumoa, after a local fisherman who arranged the local *hukilau* (the catching of fish in a net) and made sure that the elderly living in the area received a portion of the catch. The name change occurred in the 1950s, when a group of students at the Church College of the Pacific (now Brigham Young University—Hawaii) called the beach "Pounders" after the crushing shorebreak that provided brief but spectacular bodysurfing rides; the nickname stuck.

Pounders is a wide beach, extending a quarter mile between two points. At the west end of the beach, next to the old landing, the waters usually are calm and safe for swimming; at the opposite end, near the limestone cliffs, there's a shorebreak that can be dangerous for inexperienced bodysurfers. The bottom here drops off abruptly, causing strong rip currents. Fishermen catch moi, oio, and papio here. Favored by local residents, the weekends and after school hours are the busiest time for this beach; weekday mornings are the quietest. Park on Kamehameha Highway in Kailua, or take TheBUS no. 55 (Circle Island) to get here.

✪ MALAEKAHANA STATE RECREATIONAL AREA

According to Hawaiian legend, a beautiful young princess, Laieikawai, was hidden here to guard her from mortal men. But word of her beauty got out, and many princes tried to woo her. Like the princess, public access to this beautiful, long (over a mile), curving, sandy beach was once restricted; wealthy families used the area for private beach homes. The state has since reclaimed the land, turning it into a recreational area with picnic spots and camping. TheBUS no. 55 (Circle Island) takes you right to the park. As you enter through the main gate off Kamehameha Highway, 2 miles north of the Polynesian Cultural Center, you'll come upon the wooded beach park area; it's excellent for picnicking, shore activities, and swimming. There's no lifeguard here, but the inshore waters are protected from the ocean swells most of the year, making the area safe for swimming.

Mokauauia (Goat) Island, which lies just offshore, is a state bird refuge. You can wade out to the island at low tide to visit secluded Mokauauia Beach, on the island's leeward shore. Surprisingly, very few visitors come to Malaekahana Beach, one of the best on Oahu—it's a true find.

☼ SUNSET BEACH PARK

Surfers around the world know this famous site for the spectacular winter surf—the waves can be huge, thundering peaks reach 15 to 20 feet. Oddly enough, this surfing site wasn't really "discovered" until the 1940s; before that, surfers preferred Makaha on the leeward side of the island. During the winter surf season, September to April, swimming is very dangerous here, due to the alongshore currents and powerful rip currents. The "Sunset rip" has been the site of numerous rescues, and has carried numerous surfboards out to sea. The only safe time to swim at Sunset is during the calm summer months. Sunset also features a huge sandy beach adjacent to the street. This is a great place to people watch, but don't go too near the water when the lifeguards have posted the red warning flags. One of the most popular beaches on the island, Sunset attracts local surfers, sunbathing beauties, and visitors wanting to get a glimpse of this world-famous surf spot. To avoid the crowds, go during midweek. On the other hand, if people watching is what you want, try Saturdays and Sundays. Located right on Kamehameha Highway in Paumalu, TheBUS no. 52 (Circle Island) will get you there if you would rather not drive.

BANZAI PIPELINE/EHUKAI BEACH PARK

These are actually three separate areas, but since the sandy beach is continuous with only one sign, EHUKAI BEACH PARK, most people think of it as one beach park. Located near Pupukea, the actual Ehukai Beach Park is 1 acre of grass with a parking lot. The long, broad, white-sand beach is known for its winter surfing action. Swimming is good during the spring and summer months, but currents and waves prohibit safe swimming in the winter. The surf in front of Ehukai Beach Park is excellent for body and board surfers.

The park also provides access to Pipeline and Banzai. Pipeline is actually about 100 yards to the left of Ehukai Beach Park. When the winter surf rolls in and hits the shallow coral shelf, the waves that quickly form are steep—so steep, in fact, that the crest of the wave falls forward, forming a near-perfect tube, or "pipeline." Surfers tried for years to master Pipeline; many wiped out, suffering lacerations and broken bones on the shallow reef. The first surfer to ride Pipeline successfully was Phil Edwards in the early 1960s. Even today, Pipeline still causes injuries and a few fatalities.

Just west of Pipeline is the area surfers call "Banzai Beach." The Japanese word *banzai* means "10,000 years"; it's given as a toast or as a battle charge, meaning "go for it." In the late 1950s, filmmaker Bruce Brown was shooting one of the first surf movies ever made, *Surf Safari*, when he saw a bodysurfer ride a huge wave. Brown yelled: "Banzai!" and the name stuck. In the winter, this is a very popular beach with surfers, surf fans, curious residents, and visitors; it's less crowded in the summer months. Again, access is via Ehukai Beach Park, located off Kamehameha Highway on Ke Nui Road in Pupukea. TheBUS no. 52 (Circle Island) will drop you on the highway.

PUPUKEA BEACH PARK

This 80-acre beach park is a Marine Life Conservation District; as such, it has strict rules about the taking of marine life, sand, coral, shells, and rocks. There are two major swimming areas in the Marine Life Conservation District: **Shark's Cove** and **Three Tables.** Don't worry: Shark's Cove, near the northern end, is *not* named for an abundance of sharks that call this home (in fact, it's relatively uncommon to see a shark here); rather, it's a popular snorkeling and dive site. Diving is best outside the cove, where caves promise interesting night diving. During the calm summer months, this is a popular dive site both day and night.

At the southern end of the Marine Life Conservation District is Three Tables, which is named for the three flat sections of reef visible at low tide. Snorkeling is good around these tables where the water is about 15 feet deep. Diving outside the tables, where the water is 30 to 45 feet deep, is excellent—there are many ledges, arches, lava tubes, and a variety of marine life. Swimming, diving, and snorkeling are best from May to October, when the water is calm; nevertheless, watch out for surges. In the winter, when currents form and waves roll in, this area is very dangerous, even in the tidepools, and there is no lifeguard present. Summers find this Marine Life Conservation District brimming with visitors weekdays and weekends; this is a very popular site for local dive operators to take their clients. In the winter, it's nearly empty during the week. It's located right on Kamehameha Highway in Pupukea; there's a very small parking lot. TheBUS no. 52 (Circle Island) stops at the park.

✪ WAIMEA BAY BEACH PARK

Despite what the Beach Boys' croon in their hit song (why-a-MEE-ah), the name of this famous surfing beach is pronounced why-MAY-ah. Waimea Bay is known in the surfing circuit as the home of some of the biggest ridable surfing waves in the world. During the winter—October to April—huge, pounding waves come rolling in, creating strong rip currents. Even expert surfers think twice when confronted with 30-foot waves. When the surf's up, it seems like everyone on Oahu drives out on Kamehameha Highway to Waimea to get a look at the monstrous waves and those who ride them. It's hard to believe that during the summer this same bay is glassy and calm, a great place for swimming, snorkeling, and diving. Since this beach is popular with local residents, weekdays are best. From Waikiki, take The BUS no. 52 (Circle Island) to get to Waimea Bay Beach Park.

YOKOHAMA BAY

At the end of the paved Farrington Highway on the Waianae coast, this area abuts the 853-acre Kaena Point State Park, a remote and wild coastline preserve offering picnicking, hiking, swimming, and surfing. Also known as Keawalua Beach and Puau Beach, Yokohama got its name from the Japanese immigrants, originally from Yokohama, who traveled to this bay to fish. This is the last sandy stretch of shore on the northwestern coast of Oahu. There's a fairly wide beach between two rocky points. When the surf is calm (mainly during the summer) this is a good area for snorkeling, diving, swimming, and shore fishing. When the surf's up, the board and bodysurfers are out. Surfing can be dangerous here. There are no lifeguards, no facilities, and no bus service to this beach.

MAKAHA BEACH PARK

Makaha means "fierce" or "savage," but many people think the name refers to the giant surf and dangerous rip currents, shorebreaks, and backwashes that occur from October through April. The word actually alludes to a community of robbers who lived in the Makaha Valley and would threaten anyone who walked through. Today Makaha still may not be the safest place for visitors to roam, but when the surf's up at Makaha Beach it's spectacular. This is the original home of Hawaii's big-wave surfing championship: When the north or west swells run during the winter, monstrous waves pound the beach here. During the summer months, the waters are perfectly safe for swimming. To get to Makaha Beach from Waikiki, take TheBUS no. 51

(Makaha). You'll not find many visitors here; there's some sentiment in the local community that there are plenty of beaches for visitors and this beach should be reserved for local residents. Chances are good that no one will bother you, but you might want to respect these feelings and stop at another beach for swimming.

MAKUA BEACH

Visitors rarely sojourn to this long, gently curving sandy beach—known for its diving, fishing, swimming, and limited bodysurfing. Makua was a movie star in the 1960s, when it was used in the movie *Hawaii.* Swimming is good here during the calm summer months, but when the big swells roll in, so do turbulent and dangerous currents. The eastern end of the beach is popular for catching moi. The area off the Makua Cave has the best snorkeling. But be warned: There is no lifeguard here. Mostly local residents use this beach, which really never gets crowded. Located on Farrington Highway past Makaha Beach; there is no bus service.

✪ POKAI BAY BEACH PARK

This wonderful beach, off the beaten path for most visitors, offers excellent swimming year-round, even when the rest of the Waianae shoreline is getting battered by heavy surf. A protected bay, the waters inside are calm enough for children and offer excellent snorkeling. The swimming area is marked by buoys. The Waianae area does have something of a provincial reputation for being xenophobic; however, local residents want the same thing most people want, guests who come with respect for local customs, conscious of being good stewards of the land, and with appreciation of the local resources—do what the natives do, pick up your garbage, don't play loud music, and be courteous and friendly. On weekdays, you can practically have the area to yourself. The beach park is located on Waianae Valley Road, off Farrington Highway. TheBUS no. 51 will drop you off on the highway, and you can walk the block to the park.

KO OLINA

The developer of the 640-acre Ko Olina Resort has created four white-sand lagoons to make the rocky shoreline more attractive. Only two of these man-made lagoons are currently open. The northernmost lagoon, located adjacent to the Ihilani Resort and Spa, is the best. The nearly circular lagoon, with calm, shallow waters and a powdery white-sand beach bordered by a broad, grassy lawn, is the most attractive of the four lagoons. Lifeguards and rest rooms are on the site, and the amenities and restaurants of the hotel are steps away. The other lagoon that's open right now is located three lagoons away from the Ihilani Hotel. There's plenty of public parking, a lifeguard station, and rest rooms. This scenic, calm lagoon is mainly used by local residents, but it doesn't have quite the ambiance of the lagoon next to the hotel (only part of which is used by hotel guests). Located off H-1 in Kapolei, there is no local bus service to Ko Olina; the closest bus stop is on Farrington Highway, more than 4 miles away.

2 Hitting the Water

Every type of water activity is pursued on Oahu, from professional surfers braving giant winter waves on the North Shore to recreational water-skiers enjoying the calm waters of Hawaii Kai. You can kayak from Lanikai Beach to the Mokulua Islands or float above Waikiki on a parasail as a speedboat tows you blissfully through the air. If you have something of an adventurous spirit, you might scuba dive the walls of the Kahuna Canyon, swim with clouds of *ta'ape* (butterfly fish), or view an occasional shark from the comfort of a passenger submarine. Whatever water recreation you might be interested in, whether you're a beginner or an expert, you can find it on Oahu.

BODYBOARDING (BOOGIE BOARDING) & BODYSURFING

Bodysurfing—riding waves without a board, becoming one with the rolling water—is immensely popular in Hawaii. Some bodysurfers just rely on their outstretched hands (or hands at their sides) to ride the waves. Others use handboards (flat, paddlelike gloves). An excellent beach at which to learn bodysurfing is Kailua. The best beaches for experts are Makapuu and Sandy Beach.

For additional maneuverability, try a boogie or bodyboard (also known as belly boards or paipo boards). These 3-foot-long vehicles, which support the upper part of your body, are easy to carry and are very maneuverable in the water. The same open-heel fins that are used in bodysurfing are used in bodyboarding. The best place to learn boogie boarding is in the calm waters of Waikiki or Kailua Beach, under the careful watch of the lifeguards. The consistently gentle waves and generally placid conditions allow beginners to practice under ideal conditions. Once you get the feel of boogie boarding and are ready to test your skills against more aggressive waves, check out those at Point Panic (by Kewalo Basin) or Makapuu. When the waves are right, advanced boogie boarders will relish the challenge at Sandy Beach or Banzai Beach.

Good places to learn to bodyboard are in the small waves of Waikiki Beach, Kailua Beach, and Bellows Field Beach Park, off Kalanianole Hwy. (Hi. 72) in Waimanalo, which is open to the public on weekends (from noon on Friday to midnight on Sunday and holidays); to get to Bellows Field, turn toward the ocean on Hughs Road, then right on Tinker Road, which takes you right to the park.

You can rent boogie boards for as little at $20 a day from **Surf & Sea,** 62-595 Kamehameha Hwy., Haleiwa (☎ **808/637-9887;** fax 808/637-3008); **Aloha Beach Service,** Sheraton Moana Surfrider Hotel, 2365 Kalakaua Ave., Waikiki (☎ **808/922-3111**); and at all Local Motion locations: 1714 Kapiolani Blvd., Honolulu (☎ **808/955-7873**), Koko Marina Shopping Center (☎ **808/396-7873**), Windward Mall, Kaneohe (☎ **808/263-7873**), and Pearl Kai Center, Aiea (☎ **808/486-7873**). These outfitters will rent you the fins you need as well.

OCEAN KAYAKING

Gliding along the ocean, with only the sound of your paddle dipping into the water to disturb your peace, is what kayaking is all about. A popular sport on Oahu, there are several kayak clubs that have regularly scheduled outings and can provide visitors with useful information. Contact: **Hui Waa Kaukahi,** P.O. Box 88143, Honolulu, HI 96744; **Kanaka Ikaika,** P.O. Box 438, Kaneohe, HI 96744; and **Women's Kayak Club of Hawaii,** P.O. Box 438, Kaneohe, HI 96744.

First-timers should go to the North Shore's **Waimea Falls Park,** 59-864 Kamehameha Hwy. (☎ **808/638-8511;** E-mail kayak@lava.net), where kayak lessons, including equipment, are $15 per person. The kayaking takes place along the Waimea River; you'll paddle out to the golden sands of Waimea Bay, where you can rest or swim. TheBUS no. 52 will get you there.

For a guided kayaking tour, call **Kayak Oahu Adventure,** with locations on the North Shore, at 59-864 Kamehameha Hwy. (Waimea Park), Haleiwa 96712 (☎ **808/638-8189**) and in Waikiki at the New Otani Kaimana Beach Hotel, 2863 Kalakaua Avenue (at the Diamond Head end of Waikiki, across from the Kapiolani Park), Honolulu, HI 96815 (☎ **808/923-0539**). The tours of the North Shore, available from May to October, consist of 1- to 3-hour guided tours, starting at

Waimea Falls, where the kayaks are launched through the estuary and paddled out to the bay. Snorkeling is available on the 2- and 3-hour tours. Rates are $35 for the 1-hour tour, $50 for the 2-hour tour, and $75 for the 3-hour tour (children under 6 years old are free). All equipment (including reef-walking shoes, mask, fin and snorkel) is provided.

The Waikiki tours are available year-round and consist of a 2-hour guided tour (for $50), starting at the beach in front of the New Otani Kaimana Beach Hotel and continue to Diamond Head Marine Life Sanctuary, where everyone jumps into the water for snorkeling. If the conditions are right, kayakers get to experience wave riding on the way back.

After you have gotten your paddle wet, and want to explore on your own, Kayak Oahu Adventure also has rentals: single kayaks are $15 an hour, $25 for half-day, and $45 for full-day; two-person kayaks are $20 an hour, $35 for half-day, and $55 full-day. Other kayak equipment rentals are available at: **Prime Time Sports,** Fort DeRussy Beach, Waikiki (☎ **808/949-8952**); or **Karel's Fiberglass,** 789 Kailua Rd., Kailua (☎ **808/261-8424;** TheBUS: 56 or 57).

A wonderful adventure is to rent a kayak, arrive at Lanikai Beach just as the sun is appearing, and paddle across the emerald lagoon to the pyramid-shaped islands off the beach called Mokulua—it's an experience you won't forget.

PARASAILING

This ocean adventure sport is something of a cross between skydiving and waterskiing. You sail through the air, suspended under a large parachute attached by a tow line to a speedboat. The best deal we could find comes from Hawaii's original parasail company, **Aloha Parasail,** (☎ **808/521-2446**). They take you over the Waikiki and Ala Moana coastlines; the cost is $41 for a 10-minute "flight" (as they call it). Participants must weigh at least 100 pounds. They also provide free pick-up service. Or, try **Sea Breeze Parasailing,** Koko Marina (☎ **808/396-0100**), the largest parasail business on the island, which picks up passengers at the Koko Marina in their boat and takes them out to Maunalua Bay for the "flight," at the cost of $49 for 8 minutes. They will take children weighing 65 pounds or more (but no special rate for children). The third company we recommend is **Hawaiian Parasail,** 24 Sand Access Rd., by the Honolulu International Airport (☎ **808/847-6229**). Their trips are $40 for 6 minutes, which includes pick-up at Waikiki hotels. Children weighing 70 pounds or more can "fly." *Hot tip:* Book directly with the parasail company and save money; if you book through an activities center, you'll also pay their commission.

SAILING

From a 2-hour sunset sail to a day-long adventure on the waves, Oahu offers a variety of sailing activities, including lessons—picture yourself at the helm! **Honolulu Sailing Co.,** Pier 2, Honolulu Harbor (☎ **800/829-0114** or 808/239-3900; fax 808/239-9718), has been in the business for nearly 2 decades, providing everything from weddings at sea to honeymoon cruises, sailing/snorkeling sails, private lessons, and exclusive charters. The fleet ranges from 36- to 70-foot yachts. Charters start at $50 per person and lessons start at $125 per person per day. To get to Pier 2, take TheBUS no 19, 20, or 47 (this way, you won't have to worry about parking).

SEA CRUISES

A funny thing happens to people when they come to Hawaii: Maybe it's the salt air, the warm tropical nights, or the blue Hawaiian moonlight, but otherwise rational people who have never set foot on a boat in their life suddenly want to go out to sea.

You can go to sea on a "booze cruise" with a thousand loud, rum-soaked strangers, or you can sail on one of three special yachts: one for landlubbers and two for more experienced sailors.

Navatek I. c/o Royal Hawaiian Cruises Ltd. ☎ **800/852-4183** or 808/848-6360.

You've never been on a boat, you don't want to be on a boat, you are being dragged aboard a boat to see the sunset you can see perfectly well from your hotel lanai. Why are you boarding this weird-looking boat? It guarantees that you'll be "seasick-free," that's why. The 140-foot long *Navatek I* isn't even called a boat; it's actually a SWATH (Small Waterplane Area Twin Hull) vessel. That means the ship's super-structure—the part you ride on—rests on twin torpedolike hulls that cut through the water so you don't bob like a cork and spill your Mai Tai. It's the smoothest ride on Mamala Bay. In fact, *Navatek I* is the only dinner cruise ship to receive U.S. Coast Guard certification to travel beyond Diamond Head.

Dinner cruises leave Pier 6 (across from the Hawaii Maritime Museum) 7 nights a week. The best deal, however, is the lunch cruise (from noon to 2pm), with a full buffet lunch, live Hawaiian music, and a great view of Oahu offshore for $47 adults, $28.50 kids. During whale season (January to March), a naturalist is on board, informing the passengers about the whales. If you have your heart set on seeing the city lights of Honolulu, the best bet is to take the Skyline Dinner cruise, which runs nightly from 8:15pm to 10:15pm and costs $75 for a three-course gourmet dinner in a romantic, candlelit setting with a great jazz band. Upstairs, on the same cruise, an upscale dinner is served (four courses for $125). There's an even more expensive dinner cruise at 5:30pm (except during the winter, January to April, when it leaves at 5pm to get in whale watching before the sun sets) that lasts until 7:30pm; it's $147 for adults, $115 for kids 2 to 11, and features top local entertainers and gourmet meals.

To get to the pier, take TheBUS no. 8, 19, 20, 55, 56, or 57, or the Waikiki Trolly to stop no. 7. If you drive, parking in the Aloha Tower lot is validated, so you pay only $3.

Leahi. ☎ **808/922-5665.**

You're a sailor and you want the real thing. Come fly aboard the *Leahi,* the green-sailed, aluminum-hulled 45-foot racing catamaran skippered by George Howland Parsons III, an ex–Pearl Harbor submariner and descendant of a New Bedford whaler who called on Lahaina in the late 1700s. Parsons's sleek 48-passenger catamaran is the best choice for authentic experience and price. One-hour sightseeing tours sail five times daily; it's $16 for adults, $6 for kids 7 to 14; those under 6 ride free. The sunset sail, which lasts from 5pm to 6:30pm, is $24 adults, including three drinks ($20 for no-alcohol passengers); $12 for children. You board the *Leahi* on the beach in front of the Sheraton Waikiki, 2255 Kalakaua Ave.; to get there, take TheBUS no. 19 or 20. Repeat guests receive discounts.

Captain Bob's Adventure Cruises. ☎ **808/942-5077.**

See the majestic Windward Coast the way it should be seen—from a boat. Captain Bob will take you on a 4-hour, lazy-day sail of Kaneohe Bay aboard his 42-foot cata-maran. It skims across the almost always calm water above the shallow coral reef, lands at Ahu o Laka—a disappearing sandbar—and takes you past two small islands and to snorkel spots full of tropical fish and, sometimes, turtles. The color of the water alone is worth the price. It's $69 for adults, $59 kids 13 to 17, $49 for those 12 and under, including an all-you-can-eat lunch barbecue with hamburgers and the works. A shuttle will pick you up at your Waikiki hotel between 9am and 9:30am and return you there at about 4pm, which is a lot quicker than taking TheBUS (no. 55 or 56). No cruises on Sundays and holidays.

✪ SCUBA DIVING

Oahu is a wonderful place to scuba dive, especially for those interested in wreck-diving. One of the more famous wrecks in Hawaii is the ✪ *Mahi,* a 185-foot former mine sweeper easily accessible just south of Waianae. Abundant marine life makes this a great place to shoot photos—schools of lemon butterfly fish and taape are so comfortable with divers and photographers that they practically pose. Eagle rays, green sea turtles, manta rays, and white-tipped sharks occasionally cruise by, and eels peer from the wreck.

For non-wreck-diving, one of the best dive spots in the summer is ✪ **Kahuna Canyon.** In Hawaiian, Kahuna translates as priest, wise man, or sorcerer. This massive amphitheater, located near Mokuleia, is a perfect example of something a sorcerer might conjure up: Walls rising from the ocean floor create the illusion of an underwater Grand Canyon. Inside the amphitheater, crabs, octopi, and slipper and spiny lobsters abound (be aware that taking them in the summer is illegal), and giant trevally, parrot fish, and unicorn fish congregate. Outside the amphitheater, you're likely to see the occasional shark in the distance.

Oahu's best dives are offshore, so your best bet is to book a two-tank dive from a dive boat. **Aloha Dive Shop,** Koko Marina, (☎ **808/395-5922**), has been showing divers the waters off Oahu since 1970. Although they offer a range of dives from people who have never donned scuba gear to experts, they specialize in the newly certified or the "rusty divers." Instructors go along as dive masters on the dives off the south shore around Koko Head. They take divers to a turtle preserve, guaranteeing that you will be so comfortable and so thrilled with the turtles that you will forget any fears you made have had. The two-tank, two-location dives are $85 for everything, including free pick-up at Waikiki hotels. Just bring your swimsuit and towel and they'll supply everything else.

Hawaii's oldest and largest dive shop is **Aaron's Dive Shop,** 602 Kailua Rd., Kailua (☎ **808/262-2333**). Aaron's offers boat and beach dive excursions off the coast of Oahu. The boat dive is $90 per person; it includes two tanks and all gear and transportation from the Kailua shop or their Pearl City location. The beach dive off the North Shore in summer and Waianae Coast in winter is the same price as a boat dive, including all gear and transportation, so Aaron's recommends the boat dive.

SNORKELING

You don't need to take courses to enjoy snorkeling—all you need is a mask, fins, and a snorkel. A word of advice on snorkeling equipment: Many tour operators provide equipment for free, but if your equipment doesn't fit you, it's all but worthless. There's nothing worse than having a snorkeling trip ruined by a leaky mask. The mask should stick to your face, without the strap, when you inhale (make sure all hair is away from the mask—men with moustaches often have leakages in that area). You might want to make the investment (about $15 a week) and rent snorkel gear that fits. If you wear eyeglasses, you should be able to rent a suitable prescription mask for an extra charge. Fins should fit comfortably and float (you are snorkeling, not swimming great distances, so monstrous fins are not necessarily better, unless you're a swimmer in training).

Some of the best snorkeling on Oahu is at the underwater park at Hanauma Bay. It's crowded and sometimes it seems there are more people than fish, but Hanauma has clear, warm, protected waters and an abundance of friendly reef fish—including

Moorish idols, scores of butterfly fish, damsel fish, and wrasses. Hanauma Bay has two reefs, an inner and an outer—the first for novices, the other for experts. The inner reef is calm and shallow (less than 10 ft.); in some places you can just wade in and put your face in the water. Go early; it's packed by 10am, and closed on Wednesdays. It's easy to get to get to Hanauma Bay; for details, see "Beaches," above.

Tommy's Tours, 444 Niu St., in Waikiki (☎ **808/944-8828**) offers a range of snorkel tours to Haunama Bay that include transportation from your hotel, snorkeling equipment and instruction starting from $18 for a half day ($15 for children) to $28 for a full day ($25 for children). Tommy's also offers a shuttle bus service from your hotel to Haunama Bay for $12 round-trip.

The braver snorkelers among us may want to head to ✪ **Shark's Cove,** on the North Shore just off Kamehameha Highway, between Haleiwa and Pupukea. Sounds risky, we know, but we've never seen nor heard of any sharks in this cove, and in summer this big, lava-edged pool is one of Oahu's best snorkel spots. Waves splash over the natural lava grotto and cascade like waterfalls into the pool full of tropical fish. There are deep-sea caves to explore to the right of the cove.

Snorkel rentals are available at most dive shops and beach activity centers, including **Aloha Dive Shop,** Koko Marine Shopping Center (☎ **808/395-5922**), the closest dive shop to the underwater park at Hanauma Bay; **Snorkel Bob's,** also on the way to Hanauma Bay at 700 Kapahulu Ave., Honolulu (☎ **808/735-7944**); and **Haleiwa Surf Center,** 66-167 Haleiwa Rd., Haleiwa (☎ **808/637-5051**), which also teaches snorkeling and offers guided snorkeling tours.

SPORTFISHING

The waters surrounding Hawaii are known the world over as one of the best places for big game sportfishing. The largest blue marlin ever captured on rod and reel anywhere on the planet was landed on a charter boat operated by Captain Cornelius Choy off Oahu. The monstrous fish weighed in at 1,805 pounds! No saltwater fishing license is required in Hawaii.

In addition to marlin (which, unlike other places, are caught in all 12 months of the year in Hawaii), you can try for sailfish, swordfish, various tunas, rainbow runner, mahimahi, wahoo, barracuda, trevally, bonefish, and various snappers, groupers, and other bottom fish. Some 28 current world fishing records were set in Hawaii for marlin, swordfish, tuna, rainbow runner, and trevally.

Charter boats can be contacted through most activities' desks or by walking the docks and talking with the captains; the latter method also allows you to make sure that they do the type of fishing you're interested in—fishing styles can range from bottom fishing to trolling for big game fish. Charter fishing-boats range both in size—from small 24-foot open skiffs to luxurious 50-foot-plus yachts—and in price, from a low of less than $50 per person to "share" a boat with other anglers to more than $800 a day to book an entire luxury sportfishing yacht on an exclusive basis.

Kewalo Basin, located between the Honolulu International Airport and Waikiki, is the main location for charter fishing-boats on Oahu. Top sportfishing boats from Kewalo Basin include the **Aukai Island Charters** (☎ 808/593-9455), *Fish Hawk* (☎ 808/596-8338), **Kono Fishing Charters** (☎ 808/536-7472), **Kuu Huapala** (☎ 808/596-0918), *Maggie Joe* (☎ 808/591-8888), and *Mary I* **Sportfishing** (☎ 808/596-2998). From Waikiki, take Kalakaua *ewa* (west) beyond Ala Moana Shopping Center; Kewalo Basin is on the left, across from Ward Centre. Look for charter boats all in a row in their slips; on lucky days, the captains display the catch of the day in the afternoon. You can also take TheBUS no. 19 or 20 (Airport).

Impressions

The boldness and address with which we saw them perform these difficult and dangerous maneuvers was altogether astonishing.
—Capt. James Cook's observations of Hawaiian surfers

SUBMARINE DIVING

Here's your chance to play Jules Verne and experience the underwater world in the comfort of a submarine. It'll take you on a 2-hour ride 60 feet below the surface. The entire trip is narrated, and professional divers feed the tropical fish just outside the sub so you can get a better look at them. Subs leave from Hilton Hawaiian Village Pier. The cost is $89 for adults, $39 for kids 12 and younger; call **Atlantis Submarines** at ☎ **800/548-6262** or 808/973-9811 to reserve.

Voyager Submarines Hawaii, 1085 Ala Moana Blvd., Honolulu (☎ 808/592-7850), also offers tours of the deep. Passengers board a 90-foot catamaran at Kewalo Basin for a 6-minute ride, with views of Waikiki and Diamond Head, to the submarine moored offshore. As the submarine descends to Kewalo Reef, an ancient lava flow 80 feet beneath the surface, passengers can see the underwater world through 30-inch-wide viewports or via the color video monitors at each seat. For the next 35 minutes, the submarine explores the reef. The first stop is Trumpetfish Cove, a lava outcropping with cauliflower coral and flittering tropical reef fish. Next stop: Urchin Hill, covered with hundreds of red spiny urchins. The sub then begins its trip across the face of the reef, passing volcanic rocks and boulders, clouds of reef fish, colorful corals and, occasionally, dolphins. The 73-foot sub weighs 99 tons and is certified by the U.S. Coast Guard to dive to 150 feet. Price (which includes round-trip bus transfers from Waikiki) is $89 for adults and $29 for children 12 and under. Children must be at least 30 inches tall to board the submarine.

SURFING

In the summertime, when the water is warm and there's a soft breeze in the air, the south swell comes up. It's surf season in Waikiki, the best place to learn how to surf on Oahu. At last count, Oahu had more than 100 surf sites—this is the place to be when the waves are happening. Winter in Hawaii also means waves—monstrous waves—on the North Shore. These are not the gentle swells of summer, lapping lazily on the shore. These mountains of water, 20-plus feet tall, explode when they collapse on the beach and the ground rumbles.

Surfing is the sport Hawaii has given to the world. The ancient origins of surfing in Hawaii can be seen in carved petroglyphs and in ancient chants traced back to the 15th century. The Hawaiians looked upon surfing not only as a sport (a betting sport, at that, with spectators wagering property on their favorite wave rider), but also as a religious experience. The Hawaiian word for surfing, *he'e nalu,* can be translated literally to mean wave sliding, but a more poetic translation—and one favored by surfers—summons up a metaphor of a newborn baby slipping from a terrifying, roaring, surging saltwater womb.

While you're on Oahu, don't pass up the opportunity to learn to surf, go early to **Aloha Beach Service,** next to the Sheraton Moana Surfrider Hotel, 2365 Kalakaua Ave., in Waikiki (☎ 808/922-3111). The beach boys offer surfing lessons for $25 an hour; board rentals are $8 for an hour and $12 for 2 hours. You must know how to swim. **Surf & Sea,** 62-595 Kamehameha Hwy., Haleiwa (☎ 808/637-9887) offers surfing lessons for $65 for 2 hours or $150 all day, equipment included.

Surfboards are also available for rent (expect to pay about $5 to $10 an hour and $18 to $25 for the day) at **Local Motion,** 1714 Kapiolani Blvd., Honolulu (☎ 808/955-7873); **Plant Surf,** 412 Nahua, Waikiki (☎ 808/926-2060); or **Surf & Sea,** 62-595 Kamehameha Hwy., Haleiwa (☎ 808/637-9887).

More experienced surfers should drop in on any surf shop around Oahu, or call the **Surf News Network Surfline** at ☎ 808/596-SURF or 808/836-1952 to get the latest surf conditions. A good spot for advanced surfers is The Cliffs, at the base of Diamond Head. The 4- to 6-foot waves churn here, allowing high-performance surfing—and the view of Diamond Head is great.

During the months of November and December, the world championship of surfing, the Triple Crown, is held in Hawaii, a three-event series that concludes the year-long Association of Surfing Professional's World Tour. Even if you've never given surfing much thought, this event is exciting—it's the Super Bowl of surfing; more than 60 surfing competitions held throughout the world lead up to this event. Some $2.5 million in prize money is given away to the men and women, the greatest surfers in the world, who can best the monstrous waves.

If you're in Hawaii in the winter and want to see the serious surfers catch the really big waves, bring your binoculars and grab a front-row seat on the beach near Kalalua Point. To get there from Waikiki, take the H-1 toward the North Shore, veering off at H-2, which becomes Kamehameha Highway (Hi. 83). Keep going to the funky surf town of Haleiwa and Waimea Bay; the big waves will be on your left, just past Pupukea Beach Park.

SWIMMING

For a quiet, peaceful place to swim, **Malaekahana Bay,** near Kahuku, is one of the best Oahu beaches. This mile-long, white-sand, crescent-shaped beach is about a 90-minute drive and a million miles from the crowds at Waikiki. To get there, take Kamehameha Highway past Laie and follow the signs to Malaekahana State Recreational Area. Or, take TheBUS no. 52 (Circle Island). Another good swimming beach is **Lanikai:** Secluded and calm, this beach is great for families. From Waikiki, take TheBUS no. 56 or 57 (Kailua), then transfer to the shuttle bus. (See also "Beaches," above.)

WATERSKIING

Believe it or not, there's waterskiing on Oahu. To learn to water-ski, or to just go out and have a good time, call the oldest water ski company in Hawaii, **Suyderhoud Water Ski Center,** Koko Marina Shopping Center (☎ 808/395-3773; TheBUS: 58). Lessons and boat rental are $49 for a half-hour lesson and $98 for an hour, including the boat and all equipment rental (maximum of five people).

WHALE WATCHING

From December to April, 45-foot humpback whales—Hawaii's most impressive visitors—come to spend the winter. They make the journey from Alaska to calve and mate in Hawaii's calm, warm waters. Once nearly hunted to extinction, humpback whales are now protected by federal law. The mammals may not be approached by any individual or watercraft within 100 yards.

Whales can frequently be seen off the island on calm days. If you spot the familiar spout of water—a sign the mammal is exhaling—there's a good chance that you'll see the whale on the surface. If you're in a car, please pull over, as numerous accidents have occurred when visitors try to spot whales and drive at the same time.

The *Navatek II,* the so-called "seasick-free" boat (see "Sea Cruises," above), is the only tourist vessel that ventures into the often choppy waters off Koko Head, where the whales cruise to and from Maui. In whale season (roughly January to April), whale-watching cruises depart from Pier 6, on the Diamond Head side of Aloha Tower Marketplace, at 8:30am, and return at 11am. The cost is $39 adults, $24 kids 2 to 11, and includes a breakfast buffet, Hawaiian entertainment, and commentary by a naturalist. The luncheon cruises and sunset cruise (see "Sea Cruises," above) also offer whale watching in season. Call **Hawaiian Cruises Ltd.** (☎ **800/852-4183** or 808/848-6360) to reserve. You can get to the pier via TheBUS no. 8, 19, 20, 55, 56, or 57.

WINDSURFING

This is another ocean activity that combines two sports: sailing and surfing. Windsurfers stand on a surfboard that has a sail attached to it, thus bringing the wind and the waves together in a ride that enthusiasts claim is a real adrenalin rush. Windward Oahu's Kailua Beach Park is the home of champion and pioneer windsurfer Robbie Naish; it's also the best place to learn to windsurf. The oldest and most established windsurfing business in Hawaii is **Naish Windsurfing Hawaii,** 155-C Hamakua Dr., Kailua (☎ **808/261-3539**). The company offers everything: sales, rentals, instruction, repair, and free advice on where to go when the wind and waves are happening. Lessons start at $55 private lesson for one, $75 for two; equipment rental is $25 for a half day and $30 for a full day. The **Kailua Sailboard Co.,** 130 Kailua Dr., across the street from the Kailua Beach Park (☎ **808/262-2555**), offers 3-hour small group lessons $39 each, and also offers rentals. To get to Kailua Beach Park take TheBUS no 56, 57, or 58 and shuttle no. 70.

Windsurfer-wannabes on the North Shore can contact **North Shore Windsurf School,** 59-452 Makana Rd. (Kamehameha Hwy.), Haleiwa (☎ **808/638-8198;** fax 808/638-5532), TheBUS: 52. Experts give 2¹/₂-hour lessons in a protected area on the North Shore for $35. Some people can get up and sail away in one lesson, but it usually takes about three lessons to be sailing over the waves. Another place on the North Shore for lessons ($65 for 2 hours and $150 for the day) and equipment rental is **Surf & Sea,** 62-595 Kamehameha Hwy., Haleiwa (☎ **808/637-9887**). TheBUS: 52.

3 Nature Hikes

Everyone thinks Oahu is just one big urban island, so they're always surprised to discover that the great outdoors is less than an hour away from downtown Honolulu. The island's 33 major trails take you across razor-thin ridge backs and deep into waterfall valleys.

Check out Stuart Ball's *The Hikers Guide to Oahu* (Honolulu: University of Hawaii Press, 1993) before you go. For a free Oahu Recreation Map, listing all 33 trails, write to the **Department of Land and Natural Resources,** 1151 Punchbowl St., Room 130, Honolulu, HI 96813 (☎ **808/587-0300**). They'll also send you free topographic trail maps on request and issue camping permits. Another good source of information is the Hiking/Camping Information Packet from **Hawaii Geographic Maps and Books,** 49 S. Hotel St., Suite 218, Honolulu, HI 96813 (☎ **808/ 538-3952**), for a cost of $7 (postage included). Also be sure to get a copy of *Hiking on Oahu: The Official Guide,* a hiking safety guide that includes instructions on hiking preparation, safety procedures, emergency phone numbers, and necessary equipment. The brochure was created in response to the frequent disappearance of hikers and the deaths of two police officers and a firefighter who were searching for lost hikers. For a copy of the brochure, contact Erin Lau, Trails and Access Manager, **City and County of Honolulu** (☎ **808/973-9782**); the **Hawaii Nature Center,**

2131 Makiki Heights Dr. (☎ **808/955-0100**); or **The Bike Shop,** 1149 S. King St. (☎ **808/596-0588**).

The **Hawaiian Trail and Mountain Club,** P.O. Box 2238, Honolulu, HI 96804, offers regularly scheduled hikes on Oahu. You bring your own lunch and drinking water, and meet up with the club at the Iolani Palace to join them on a hike. They also have an information packet on hiking and camping in Hawaii, as well as a schedule of all upcoming hikes; send $1.25, plus a legal-sized, self-addressed, stamped envelope to the address above.

The **Sierra Club,** P.O. Box 2577, Honolulu, HI 96803, also offers regularly scheduled hikes on which they welcome visitors. The **Hawaii Nature Center,** 2131 Makiki Heights Dr. (☎ **808/955-0100;** open Monday through Friday, from 8am to 4:30pm) is another organization that offers organized hikes, as well as "Sunday Adventures" for children.

Reece Olayvar, who was born and raised in Hawaii, conducts guided hikes for novices and families around Oahu in her **Hike Hawaii,** 91-261 Hanapouli Circle, Unit W, Ewa Beach, HI 96706 (☎ **808/683-3967**). Her hikes include her knowledge of Hawaiian plants (including their uses in medicine and cooking), history of the region (with any Hawaiian myths), talks on the birds and wildlife you will see, and her special interest in looking for endangered species. She provides everything for her half-day and full-day hikes, including transportation from your hotel, water, raingear, and lunch for full-day hikes. The cost is $65 for a full day and $50 for a half day (which includes a snack).

HONOLULU AREA
✪ DIAMOND HEAD CRATER

Everyone can make this easy walk to the summit of Hawaii's most famous landmark. Kids love the top of the 760-foot volcanic cone, where they have 360° views of Oahu up the leeward coast from Waikiki. The 1.4-mile round-trip will take about an hour.

Diamond Head was created by a volcanic explosion about a half-million years ago. The Hawaiians called the crater Leahi (meaning the brow of the ahi, or tuna, referring to the shape of the crater). Diamond Head was considered a sacred spot; King Kamehameha offered human sacrifices at a *heiau* (temple) on the western slope. It wasn't until the 19th century that Mount Leahi got its current name: A group of sailors found what they thought were diamonds in the crater; it turned out they really only found worthless calcite crystals, but the Diamond Head moniker stuck.

Before you begin your adventure hiking to the top of the crater, gather a flashlight (you walk through several dark tunnels), binoculars (for better viewing at the top), water, and your camera. Go early, before the noonday sun starts beating down. Start your hike to the summit of Diamond Head at Monsarrat and 18th avenues on the crater's inland (or mauka) side. To get there, take TheBUS no. 58 from the Ala Moana Shopping Center or drive to the intersection of Diamond Head Road and 18th Avenue. Follow the road through the tunnel (which is closed from 6pm to 6am) and park in the lot. The trailhead starts in the parking lot and proceeds along a paved walkway (with handrails) as it climbs up the slope. You'll pass old World War I and

Factoid

Amelia Earhart was the first woman to fly solo from Hawaii to the U.S. mainland in 1935. A plaque on Diamond Head Road memorializes her 12-hour, 50-minute flight from Honolulu to Oakland, California.

II pillboxes, gun emplacements, and tunnels built as part of the Pacific defense network. Several steps take you up to the top observation post on Point Leahi. The views are indescribable.

KANEALOLE TRAIL

This is the starting place for some of Oahu's best hiking trails; miles of trails converge through the Makiki Valley–Tantalus–Round Top–Nuuanu Valley area. To get a general feel for the hikes in the region, take this 1 1/2-mile round-trip moderate hike, which climbs some 500 feet and takes less than an hour. If you are more intrigued, stop at the **Hawaii Nature Center,** located by the trailhead at 2131 Makiki Heights Dr. (☎ 808/955-0100; open Monday to Friday, from 8am to 4:30pm), where you will find information on the environmental and conservation needs of Hawaii, displays on plants and animals, hands-on type exhibits, and numerous maps and pamphlets about this hiking area. They also sponsor organized hikes on weekends.

After stopping at the Hawaii Nature Center, continue up the path, which wanders under the protection of kukui and lush vines. The road gets smaller and smaller until it's just a footpath. Along this narrow path, look for the tall, bushy grasslike plant, called Job's Tears. While it's considered a weed in Hawaii, this is no ordinary grass; it can grow up to 5-feet high and produces a grey, tear-shaped seed. The trail continues through an abandoned valley where there once was a thriving Hawaiian community. Occasionally you'll spot the remains of stone walls and even a few coffee plants; Makiki Valley supported a coffee plantation in the last century. When you meet the Makiki Valley Trail, you can retrace your steps, or choose from the dozens of trails in the area.

To get there, take McCully Avenue north out of Waikiki; cross over the H-1 Freeway and turn left on Wilder Avenue. Make a right turn on Makiki Street and continue until the road forks at the park. Take the left fork past the Makiki Pumping Station; the road is now called Makiki Heights Drive. Follow it up to the hairpin turn and make a right onto the small spur road that goes into Makiki Valley; park just beyond the green trailers that house the Hawaii Nature Center. If you are taking the bus, it's a little trickier: From Waikiki, take TheBUS no. 8, 19, 20, or 58 to the Ala Moana Shopping Center and transfer to TheBUS no. 17. Tell your driver where you're going, and he'll let you off near the spur road just off Makiki Heights Drive; you'll have to walk the rest of the way.

✪ MAKIKI–MANOA CLIFF TRAILS

From rain forests to ridgetop views, this somewhat strenuous loop trail is one you'll never forget. The hike is just over 6 miles, gains 1,260 feet in elevation, and takes about 3 hours. This trail is part of the labyrinth of trails found in this area (see "Kanealole Trail," above).

The trail starts by the rest rooms of the Hawaii Nature Center. Look for the paved path that crosses Kanealole Stream via a footbridge (Maunalaha Trail). Stay on the trail, following it up the hill into the forest, where you'll pass bananas, Norfolk and Cook island pines, ti plants, even a few taro patches. Cross over Moleka Stream and look for the four-way junction with the Makiki Valley and Ualakaa trails; turn right on the Makiki Valley Trail. This takes you through a dense forest, past a giant banyan tree, and then joins with the Moleka Trail. Turn left on the Moleka Trail—now you're in the rain forest: ancient guava trees reach overhead, maiden hair ferns cling to rocks, tiny white-flowered begonias crop up.

Further on, the kukui and koa give way to a bamboo-filled forest, which opens up to a parking lot on Round Top Drive at the end of the Moleka Trail. Cross Round Top Drive to the Manoa Cliffs Trail, which emerges on Tantalus Drive. Turn right on Tantalus and walk about 100 yards down the street to the Nahuina Trail on the left side of Tantalus. As you walk downhill, you'll have breathtaking views of downtown Honolulu. At the junction of Kanealole Trail, turn right and continue back to where you started.

To get there follow the directions for the Kanealole Trail (see above).

✪ MANOA FALLS TRAIL

This easy, $^8/_{10}$ of a mile (one-way) hike is terrific for families; it takes less than an hour to reach idyllic Manoa Falls. The trailhead, marked by a footbridge, is at the end of Manoa Road, past Lyon Arboretum. The arboretum prefers that hikers do not use their lot, so the best place to park is in the residential area below the former Paradise Park; you can also get to the arboretum via TheBUS no. 5. The often-muddy trail follows Waihi Stream and meanders through the forest reserve past guava, mountain apple, and wild ginger. The forest is moist and humid and inhabited by giant bloodthirsty mosquitoes, so bring repellent.

PUU OHIA TRAIL TO NUUANU VALLEY VIEW

This moderate hike takes you through a rain forest, up to the top of Tantalus (Puu Ohia) cinder cone, and down through Pauoa Flats to view Nuuanu Valley. Plan about 2 hours for this $3^1/_2$-mile round-trip hike, which gains about 1,200 feet in altitude.

Park at the top of Round Top Drive at the turnout on the ocean side of the street. The Puu Ohia trailhead is located across the street from where you parked. As you head up (a series of switchbacks and, at the steepest, hand-cut stairs in the dirt) you pass night-blooming jasmine, ginger, Christmas berry, and avocado trees. After dense guava trees and bamboo, the vegetation parts for a magnificent view of Honolulu and Diamond Head. Just as quickly, as you continue along the trail, the bamboo once again obstructs the view. At the next junction stay on the main trail by bearing to the left; you'll pass through ginger, koa, and bamboo. At the next junction, bear left again, and climb up the steps around the trunk of an old koa tree. At the top is a paved road; turn right and walk downhill. The road leads to an old telephone relay station, then turns into a footpath. Passing through bamboo, koa, ti, and strawberry guava, turn left onto the Manoa Cliffs Trail. At the next junction, turn right on the Puu Ohia Trail, which leads to the Pauoa Flats and to the view of the Nuuanu Valley. Retrace your steps for your return.

No buses service this area. To get there, follow the directions given to the Kanealole Trail, above, but turn to the right at the park fork in Makiki Street. The fork to the right is Round Top Drive; drive to the top and park in the turnout on the ocean side.

UALAKAA LOOP

The same series of volcanic eruptions that produced Diamond Head and Koko Crater also produced the cinder cones of Round Top (Puu Ualakaa), Sugarloaf (Puu Kakea), and Tantalus (Puu Ohia). Puu, as you may have already guessed, means hill; these three hills overlook Honolulu and offer spectacular views. The easy Ualakaa Loop Trail is a half-hour hike of about a mile that traverses through woods, offering occasional panoramic views of Honolulu.

The loop trail, lined with impatiens, passes through more Norfolk Pines, palm trees, ironwoods, and Christmas berry trees. The once native forest now has many foreign intrusions—including all of the foregoing—as well as the ti, banana, banyan, guava, and mountain apple. At two points along the trail, you emerge on Round Top Drive; just walk about 100 feet to continue on the trail on the opposite side of the road. The loop will bring you back to where you started.

There's no bus service to this trailhead. Follow the directions for the Puu Ohia hike, above, but instead of driving to the top of Round Top Drive, turn off on the fourth major hairpin turn (look for it after a long stretch of panoramic straightaway). The turn will go through the gate of the Puu Ualakaa State Wayside Park. Continue a little more than four miles inside the park; look for a stand of Norfolk Pine trees and park there. The trailhead is on the right side of the Norfolk Pines. The park is open from 7am to 7:45pm from April 1 to Labor Day; after Labor Day, the park closes at 6:45pm.

PEARL CITY
UPPER WAIMANO TRAIL

This is a strenuous, 14-mile round-trip with an altitude gain of nearly 2,000 feet. But the rewards are worth it: magnificent views from the top of windward Oahu's Koolau Mountains, and a chance to see rare native Hawaiian plants. Plan a full day for this 8-hour hike.

Pick up the trailhead at the dirt path to the left of the gate, outside the fence surrounding the Waimano Home, above Pearl City. Follow the trail through swamp mahogany trees to the first junction; turn right at the junction to stay on the upper Waimano Trail. At the second junction, turn right again to stay on the upper trail. The Christmas berry becomes denser, but as you move up the mountain, koa, kukui, hau, mango, guava, mountain apple, and ginger start to appear. You'll know you are getting closer to the stream bed when the mosquitoes begin buzzing. Cross the stream bed and climb the switchbacks on the eucalyptus-covered ridge. More native plants begin to appear: ohia, uluhe, and koa. Just before you reach the crest of the next ridge, look for rarely seen plants like yellow-flowered *ohia lehua, kanawao* (a relative of the hydrangea), and mountain *naupaka*. The trail ends on the sometimes rainy—and nearly always windy—peak of the Koolaus, where you'll have views of Waihee Valley and the entire windward side from Kahaluu to Kaneohe Bay. It's very clear that this is the end of the trail; retrace your steps to the trailhead.

To get there from Waikiki, take the H-1 to the Pearl City exit (Exit 10) on Moanalua Road; head north and turn right on Waimano Home Road; follow it to the end, just over 22 miles. Park on the road. Or take TheBUS nos. 8, 19, 20, or 58 from Waikiki to the Ala Moana Shopping Center and transfer to TheBUS no. 53. Tell your driver where you are going and he will take you as far as he can on Waimano Home Road; you'll have to walk the rest of the way to the trailhead (about 1 1/2 miles).

EAST OAHU
MAKAPUU LIGHTHOUSE TRAIL

You've seen this famous old lighthouse on episodes of "Magnum P.I." and "Hawaii Five-O." No longer manned by the Coast Guard (it's fully automated now), the lighthouse is the goal of hikers who challenge a precipitous cliff trail to gain an airy perch over the Windward Coast, Manana (Rabbit) Island, and the azure Pacific. It's about a 45-minute, mile-long hike from Kalanianaole Highway (Hi. 72), along a paved road that begins across from Hawaii Kai Executive Golf Course and winds around the 646-foot-high sea bluff to the lighthouse lookout.

To get to the trailhead from Waikiki, take Kalanianaole Highway (Hi. 72) past Hanauma Bay and Sandy Beach to Makapuu Head, the southeastern tip of the island; you can also take TheBUS no. 57–58. Look for a sign that says NO VEHICLES ALLOWED on a gate to the right, a few hundred yards past the entrance to the golf course. The trail isn't marked, but it's fairly obvious: Just follow the abandoned road that leads gradually uphill to a trail that wraps around Makapuu Point. It's a little precarious, but anyone in reasonably good shape can handle it.

Blow hole alert: When the south swell is running, usually in summer, there are a couple of blow holes on the south side of Makapuu Head that put the famous Halona Blow Hole to shame.

WINDWARD OAHU
HAUULA LOOP

For one of the best views of the coast and the ocean, follow the Hauula Loop Trail on the windward side of the island. It's an easy, 2¹/₂-mile loop on a well-maintained path that passes through a whispering ironwood forest and a grove of tall Norfolk pines. The trip takes about 3 hours and gains some 600 feet in elevation.

To get to the trail, take TheBUS no. 55 or follow Hi. 83 to Hauula Beach Park. Turn toward the mountains on Hauula Homestead Road; when the road forks to the left at Maakua Road, park on the side of the road. Walk along Maakua Road to the wide, grassy trail that begins the hike into the mountains. The climb is fairly steep for about 300 yards, but continues on to easier-on-the-calves switchbacks as you go up the ridge. Look down as you climb: You'll spot wildflowers and mushrooms among the matted needles. The trail continues up, crossing Waipilopilo Gulch, where you'll see several forms of native plant life. Eventually you reach the top of the ridge, where the views are spectacular.

Although the Division of Forestry permits camping along the trail, it's difficult to find a place to pitch a tent on the steep slopes and in the dense forest growth. There are a few places along the ridge, however, that are wide enough for a tent. Contact the **Division of Forestry and Wildlife,** 1151 Punchbowl St., Honolulu, HI 96813 (☎ 808/587-0166) for information on camping permits.

PALI (MAUNAWILI) TRAIL

For a million-dollar view of the Windward Coast, take this easy 11-mile (one-way) foothill trail. The trailhead is about 6 miles from downtown Honolulu, on the windward side of the Nuuanu Pali Tunnels, at the scenic lookout just beyond the hairpin turn of the Pali Highway (Hi. 61). Just as you begin the turn, look for the SCENIC OVERLOOK sign, slow down, and pull off the highway into the parking lot (sorry, no bus service available).

The mostly flat, well-marked, easy-to-moderate trail goes through the forest on the lower slopes of the 3,000-foot Koolau Mountain range and ends up in the backyard of the coastal Hawaiian village of Waimanalo. Go halfway to get the view and return to your car, or have someone meet you in 'Nalo.

✪ SACRED FALLS

It's easy to see why this place was given the name "Sacred": Clear, cold water, originating from the top of the Koolau Mountains, descends down the Kaluanui Stream and cascades over Sacred Falls into a deep, boulder-strewn pool. The hike to this awe-inspiring waterfall passes under guava and mountain apple trees and through a fern-filled narrow canyon that parallels the stream bed.

A few words of warning before you grab your hiking boots: First, do not attempt this hike in wet weather. In fact, the State Parks Division closes the falls if there's a danger of flash floods. This is no idle warning—in 1987, five hikers attempting to reach the falls died in three separate incidents when the normally babbling stream was flooded; in October 1993, a Boy Scout troop had to be rescued by helicopter during a flash flood. Second, go in a group—there have been a few muggings along the 2.2-mile trail in recent years.

The best time to take this hike is in the morning, when the light is good. Be prepared with rain gear and insect repellent. The easy 4.4-mile round-trip will take about 2 to 3 hours. To get to the trail, drive north on the Kamehameha Highway (Hi. 83) to the turnoff for Sacred Falls State Park, or take TheBUS no. 55. The trail begins at the parking lot and heads for the mountains, paralleling the Kaluanui Stream. About a mile into the trail is a grassy area with emergency warning equipment inside a cyclone fence; the trailhead is to the left of the fence. The beginning is a bit rough—the trail is muddy and passes under tangled branches and through a tunnel of Christmas berry. About a half-mile beyond the trailhead, you'll cross the Kaluanui Stream; if the water is high or muddy, don't cross—you could become trapped in the canyon during a flash flood. As you continue up the trail, the canyon becomes increasingly narrow, with steep walls on either side. Be on the lookout for falling rocks. At the end of the trail are the majestic falls and an extremely cold pool, home to spidery Malaysian prawns.

LEEWARD OAHU
KAENA POINT

At the remote western tip of Oahu lie the dry, barren lands of Kaena Point State Park: 853 acres of wild wind- and surf-battered coastline with jagged sea cliffs, deep gulches, sand dunes, endangered plant life. Kaena means "red-hot" or "glowing" in Hawaiian; the name refers to the brilliant sunsets visible from the point.

Kaena is steeped in numerous legends. A popular one involves the demigod Maui: Maui had a famous hook that he used to raise islands from the sea. He decided that he wanted to bring the islands of Oahu and Kauai closer together, so one day he threw his hook across the Kauai Channel and snagged the island of Kauai (which actually is visible from Kaena Point on clear days). Using all his might, Maui was only able to pull loose a huge boulder, which fell into the waters very close to the present lighthouse at Kaena. The rock is still called Pohaku o Kauai (the rock from Kauai). Like Black Rock in Kaanapali on Maui, Kaena is thought of as the point on Oahu from which souls depart.

To start the hike, take the clearly marked trail from the parking lot of the Makua–Kaena Point State Park. The moderate, 5-mile round-trip hike to the point will take a couple of hours. The trail along the cliff passes tide pools abundant in marine life and rugged protrusions of lava reaching out to the turbulent sea; seabirds circle overhead. There are no sandy beaches and the water is almost always turbulent. During the winter months, when a big north swell is running, the waves at Kaena are the biggest in the state, averaging heights of 30 to 40 feet. Even when the water appears calm, offshore currents are powerful, so don't plan to swim. Go early in the morning to see the school of porpoises that frequent the area just offshore.

To get to the trailhead from Honolulu or Waikiki, take the H-1 freeway west to its end; continue on Hi. 93 past Makaha and follow Hi. 930 to the end of the road. There's no bus service.

4 Great Golf

Oahu has nearly three dozen golf courses, ranging from bare-bones municipal courses to exclusive country club courses with membership fees at six figures a year. However, it is possible to play some top-notch golf in Hawaii without having to take out a second mortgage on your home. Golfers unfamiliar with Hawaii's golf courses will be dazzled by the spectacular view of the shimmering ocean and the majestic mountains. They also will come to know that the windward golf courses play much different than the leeward courses. On the windward side, the prevailing winds blow from the ocean to shore and the grain direction of the greens tends to run the same way—from the ocean to the mountains. Leeward golf courses have the opposite tendency, the winds usually blow from the mountains to the ocean and the grain direction on the greens matches. Below are a variety of courses, with greens fees—cart costs included—and notes on scenic views, challenges, and a taste of what golfing in paradise is like.

Some hot tips on beating the crowds and saving money: Oahu's golf courses tend to be crowded, so we suggest that you go midweek if you can. Also, most island courses have twilight rates that offer you substantial discounts if you're willing to tee off in the afternoon, usually between 1pm and 3pm; we've included them in the listings below where applicable.

Transportation note: TheBUS does not allow golf bags onboard, so if you want to use it to get to a course, you're going to have to rent clubs at the course. If you want to bring your own clubs, you'll have to seek alternative transportation.

For last minute and discount tee times, call **Stand-by Golf** (from Hawaii call ☎ **888/645-BOOK,** from the mainland call 808/322-BOOK), which offers discounted and guaranteed tee times for same day or next day golfing. You can call up to 11pm, Hawaii Standard Time, to book one of the seven semiprivate and resort courses they handle and get a guaranteed tee time for the next day at a 10% to 40% discount. Or you can call from 6am to 11am to get a same-day tee time.

EAST OAHU

Hawaii Kai Golf Course. 8902 Kalanianaole Hwy., Honolulu, HI 96825. ☎ **808/395-2358.** From Waikiki, go east on H-1, past Hawaii Kai; the course is immediately past Sandy Beach on the left. TheBUS: 58.

Actually, this is two golf courses in one: the par-72, 6,222-yard **Hawaii Kai Championship Golf Course** and the par-3 **Hawaii Kai Executive Golf Course.** Both are located between Sandy Beach and Makapuu Point on the island's eastern tip. The Championship course is moderately challenging, with scenic vistas and twilight rates of only $50—half the regular greens fees of $100—if you're willing to tee off between 1pm and 2:30pm weekdays). The course is forgiving to high-handicap golfers, although it does have a few surprises. The Executive Golf course is fun for beginners and those just getting back in the game. It has lots of hills and valleys, but no water hazards and only a few sand traps. Rates for this par-3 course are a mere $37, with twilight rates (after 4pm) for just $6. Lockers are available.

THE NORTH SHORE

✪ **Kahuku Golf Course.** P. O. Box 417, Kahuku, HI 96731. ☎ **808/293-5842.** From Waikiki take the H-1 west to H-2; follow H-2 through Wahiawa and Schofield Barracks to Kamehameha Hwy. (Hi. 99, then Hi. 83); follow it to Kahuku. TheBUS: 55.

We admit that this nine-hole budget golf course is a bit funky: Except for a few pull carts that disappear with the first handful of golfers, there are no facilities: no club rentals, no club house. But playing here, amongst the scenic beauty of this oceanside course and the tranquillity of the North Shore, is quite an experience nonetheless. Duffers will love the ease of this recreational course, and weight watchers will be happy to walk the gently sloping greens. Don't forget to bring your camera for the views (especially at holes 3, 4, 7, and 8, which are right on the ocean). No reservations are taken; tee times are doled out on a first-come, first-served basis—with plenty of retirees happy to sit and wait. The competition is fierce for early tee times. Bring your own clubs and call ahead to check the weather. The cost for this experience? Just $20 for nine holes.

✪ Turtle Bay Hilton Golf & Tennis Resort. P.O. Box 187, Kahuku, HI 96731. ☎ **808/ 293-8574.** Take H-1 west past Pearl City; when the freeway splits, take H-1 and follow the signs to Haleiwa; at Haleiwa, take Hi. 83 to Turtle Bay Resort. TheBUS: 52 or 55.

Here's a chance to play one of Hawaii's top golf courses, located about an hour's drive from Waikiki, for just $55 for 18 holes. The budget course is the **George Fazio– designed 9-hole course**—the only one Fazio designed in Hawaii—which can be played twice for a regulation par-71, 6,200 yard course. The course has two sets of tees, one designed for men and one for women, so you can get a slightly different play if you decided to tackle 18 holes. Larry Keil, pro at Turtle Bay, says that people like the Fazio course because it's more of a forgiving resort course, without the water hazards and bunkers of the more challenging and expensive Links Course, below. "A lot of visitors like the option to just play nine holes," he added. The sixth hole has two greens so you can play the hole as a par 3 or a par 4. The toughest hole has to be the par 3, 176-yard second hole, where you tee off across a lake with the normal tradewinds creating a mean cross wind; you have to clear the lake and land on the green and two putt to make par. The most scenic hole is the seventh, where the ocean is on your left; if you're lucky, you'll see whales cavorting in the winter months.

If you want to splurge ($125), you can play the 18-hole **Links at Kuilima,** designed by Arnold Palmer and Ed Seay—*Golf Digest* rated it the fourth best new resort course in 1994. Turtle Bay used to be labeled a "wind tunnel;" it still is one, but the casuarina (ironwood) trees have matured and dampened the wind somewhat. But Palmer and Seay never meant for golfers to get off too easy; this is a challenging course. The front nine holes, with rolling terrain, only a few trees, and lots of wind, play like a British Isles course. The back nine holes have narrower, tree-lined fairways and water. The course circles Punahoolapa Marsh, a protected wetland for endangered Hawaiian waterfowl.

Facilities include pro shop, driving range, putting and chipping green, and snack bar. Weekdays are best for tee times. Unfortunately, no twilight rates are available.

CENTRAL OAHU

Hawaii Country Club. 98-1211 Kunia Rd., Wahiawa, HI 96786 ☎ **808/621-5654.** From Waikiki take the H-1 freeway west for about 20 minutes. Turn off at the Kunia exit (Exit 5B) and follow it to the course. No bus service.

This public course, located in central Oahu in Wahiawa, is a modest course where golfers usually have no trouble getting a tee time. The 5,861-yard, par-71 course is not manicured like the resort courses, but it does offer fair play, with relatively inexpensive greens fees. Located in the middle of former sugar cane and pineapple fields, the greens and fairways tend to be a bit bumpy and there are a number of tall monkeypod and pine trees to shoot around, but the views of Pearl Harbor and Waikiki in the distance are spectacular. There are a few challenging holes, like the seventh (a 252-yard, par-4), which has a lake in the middle of the fairway and slim pickings on either side. With the wind usually blowing in your face, most golfers choose an iron to lay up short of the water and then pitch it over for par. Facilities include a driving range, practice greens, club rental pro shop, and restaurant. Green fees are easy on the budget: tee times from 6am to 11am are $25 weekdays and $37 on weekends (cart included); from 11am to 4pm the cost is $20 weekdays and $35 on weekends (with cart); and after 4pm the fees drop to $14 weekdays and $18 weekends.

Mililani Golf Club. 95-176 Kuahelani Ave., Mililani, HI 96789. ☎ **808/623-2222.** From Waikiki, take the H-1 west (toward Ewa), past Aloha Stadium; at the split in the freeway, turn off onto H-2. Exit at Mililani (Exit 5-B) onto Meheula Parkway; go to the third stoplight (about 2 miles from the exit) and make a right turn on to Kuahelani Ave. TheBUS: 52.

The bargain at this par-72, 6,455-yard public course is the twilight (after 1pm) rate on weekdays—only $42. Mililani, which opened in 1966, is the home of the Sports Shinko Rainbow Open, where Hawaii's top professionals compete. Located between the Koolau and Waianae mountain ranges on the Leilehua Plateau, this is one of Oahu's scenic courses, with views of mountains from every hole. Unfortunately, there are also lots of views of trees, especially eucalyptus, Norfolk pines, and coconut palms; it's a lesson in patience to stay on the fairways and away from the trees. The two signature holes, the par-4 no. 4 (a classic middle hole with water, flowers, and bunkers) and the par-3 no. 12 (a comfortable tee-shot over a ravine filled with tropical flowers, that jumps to the undulating green with bunkers on each side) are so scenic, you'll forgive the challenges they pose. If you can't make the budget twilight rates, expect to pay $84 on weekdays ($62 on weekdays after 11am), and $92 on weekends and holidays.

LEEWARD OAHU
JUST BEYOND PEARL HARBOR: AIEA

Pearl Country Club. 98-535 Kaonohi St., Aiea, HI 96701 ☎ **808/487-3802.** To get there from Waikiki take H-1 Freeway past Pearl Harbor to the Hi. 78 (Moanalua Freeway) exit (from the left hand lane, Hi. 78 becomes Hi. 99 [Kamehameha Hwy.]). Turn right on Kaonohi St. and drive up the hill to the course. TheBUS: 32 (stops at the Pearlridge Shopping Center, Kaonohi and Moanalua sts.; you will have to walk about a half a mile up hill from here).

Looking for a challenge? This popular public course, located just above Pearl City in Aiea, has all the challenges you can imagine. Sure, the 6,230-yard, par-72 looks harmless enough, and the views of Pearl Harbor and the USS *Arizona* Memorial are gorgeous; but around the fifth hole, you'll start to see what you're in for. That par-5, a blind 472-yard hole, doglegs quite seriously to the left (with a small margin of error between the tee and the steep out-of-bounds hillside on the entire left side of the fairway). A water hazard and a forest await your next two shots. Suddenly, this nice public course becomes not so nice. Oahu residents can't get enough of this course, so don't even try to get a tee time on weekends; stick to weekdays—Mondays are usually the best bet. Greens fees are $75, weekdays, including cart and $80 weekends with cart. Call ☎ **808/487-3802** at least a week in advance. Twilight rates are as follows: after 4pm, 9 holes for $25 (including cart) and on Wednesdays 18 holes after 3pm are $35 (including cart). Facilities include a driving range, practice greens, club rental, pro shop, and restaurant.

EWA BEACH

West Loch Municipal Golf Course. 91-1126 Olepekeupe Loop, Ewa Beach, HI 96706. ☎ **808/676-2210.** From Waikiki, take H-1 west to the Hi. 76 Exit; stay in the left lane and turn left at West Loch Estates, just opposite St. Francis Medical Center. To park, take 2 immediate right turns. TheBUS: 50.

This par-72, 6,615-yard course located just 30 minutes from Waikiki, in Ewa Beach, offers golfers a challenge at bargain rates. If you're willing to tee off between 1pm and 3:30pm, you'll pay twilight rates of only $23.50, vs. the normal green fees of $47. The challenges on this municipal course are water (lots of hazards), wind (constant trade winds), and narrow fairways. To help you out, the course features a "water" driving range (with a lake). After a few practice rounds on the driving range, you'll be ready to take on this unusual course, designed by Robin Nelson and Rodney Wright. The first hole starts in front of the clubhouse; the course then crosses a freeway for the next 10 holes and then goes back across the freeway for holes 12 to 18. In addition to the driving range, West Loch also has practice greens, a pro shop, and a restaurant. We suggest booking a week in advance to get the tee time you want.

KO OLINA

✪ **Ko Olina Golf Club.** 3733 Alii Dr., West Beach, HI 96707 ☎ **808/676-5300.** To get there from Waikiki, take H-1 freeway until it ends and becomes Hi. 93 (Farrington Hwy.), turn off at Ko Olina exit. Take exit road (Alinui Dr.) into Ko Olina Resort, and turn left on Alii Dr. to Club-house. No bus service.

Golf Digest named this 6,867-yard, par-72 course one of "America's Top 75 Resort Courses" in 1992. The Ted Robinson–designed course has rolling fairways and el-evated tee and water features. The signature hole—the 12th, a par-3—has an elevated tee that sits on a rock garden, with a cascading waterfall. Wait until you get to the 18th hole; you'll see and hear water all around you—seven pools begin on the right side of the fairway and slope down to a lake. A waterfall is on your left off the elevated green. You'll have no choice but to play the left and approach the green over the water.

There is a dress code for the course: Men are asked to wear shirts with a collar. Facilities include a driving range, locker rooms, Jacuzzi/steam rooms, and a restau-rant/bar. Lessons and twilight rates are available. This course is crowded all the time. Greens fees are $145. Twilight rates after 2:30pm are $65. Book in advance.

ON THE WAIANAE COAST

Makaha Valley Country Club. 84-627 Makaha Valley Rd., Waianae, HI 96792 ☎ **808/695-9578.** To get there from Waikiki, take H-1 west until it turns into Hi. 93, which will wind through the coastal towns of Nanakuli, Waianae, and Makaha. Turn right on Makaha Valley Rd. and follow it to the fork; turn right. TheBUS: 51 and Shuttle: 75.

This beautiful public course offers three tees to choose from, you probably will be able to play your handicap from the middle tee, so for a challenging game, you might want to go for the back tee, still a sporting par 69 for the 6,369 yards. The course presents a few challenges along the way: numerous trees and an abundance of water (especially on the third hole, which has a couple of small lakes right at a 90-degree dogleg, followed by a stand of trees). You might want to get an early tee time, as the afternoons in Makaha valley can get windy. The last hole is a doozie, a 494-yard, par 5 with two 90-degree turns to get up to the green. Greens fees are $55 weekdays (in-cluding cart) and $65 on weekend (with cart). Facilities include driving range, prac-tice greens, club rental, clubhouse with restaurant.

✪ **Sheraton Makaha Golf Club.** 84-626 Makaha Valley Rd., Waianae, HI 96792. ☎ **800/757-8060** or 808/695-9544. From Waikiki, take H-1 west until it turns into Hi. 93, which goes through Nanakuli, Waianae, and Makaha. Turn right on Makaha Valley Rd., and follow it to the fork; the course is on the left fork. TheBUS: 51 and Shuttle: 75.

The secret to playing this challenging course—recently named "The Best Golf Course on Oahu" by *Honolulu* magazine and ranked as one of Hawaii's top 10 by the read-ers of *Golfweek*—without going into debt is to book a tee time after noon on week-days, when greens fees drop to $90 for 18 holes. This golf course sits some 45 miles (or an hour's drive) west of Honolulu, in Makaha Valley. Designed by William Bell, the par-72, 7,091-yard course meanders toward the ocean before turning and head-ing into the valley. Sheer volcanic walls tower 1,500 feet above the course and swaying palm trees and neon bright bougainvillea surround it; an occasional peacock will even strut across the fairways. The beauty of the course might make it difficult to keep your mind on the game if it weren't for the 8 water hazards, 107 bunkers, and frequent and brisk winds. Facilities include a pro shop, bag storage, and a snack shop. This course is packed on weekends, so it's best to try weekdays. Standard greens fees for guests of Waikiki's Sheraton resorts (Sheraton Moana Surfrider, Royal Hawaiian, Sheraton Waikiki, and Princess Kaiulani) are $90 any time of day, and $160 for nonguests.

WINDWARD OAHU

Mid-Pacific Country Club. 266 Kaelepulu Dr., Kailua, HI 96734 ☎ **808/261-9765.** To get there from Waikiki, take the H-1 freeway to Pali Hwy. (Hi. 61) to Kailua. Pali Hwy. becomes Kailua Rd. in Kailua town and dead ends on Kalaheo Ave. Turn right and follow Kalaheo past Buzz's Steak House. At the stop sign just past Buzz's, turn left on to Alala St. At the second right, Kaelepule Dr., turn and that will take you into the Mid-Pacific Country Club. TheBUS: 57 (get off at Hele and Keolu in Kailua and walk just over a mile to the clubhouse).

This is a rare chance for nonmembers to play on a private course. The public is invited to play this par-72, 6,848-yard course on weekdays (most private golf clubs on Oahu do not allow non-members to play unless accompanied by a member). Don't pass up the opportunity to experience this challenging, unique course, located in the beachside community of Lanikai, on the windward side of the island. The first nine holes were designed by Seth Raynor and opened for play in 1928; 20 years later, the next nine opened. In 1981, William Bell brought the course up to date, but left the basic design alone. The most challenging hole is the fifth, a par-5, 517-yard dogleg left, bordered on the right by a tributary from Enchanted Lakes and by another small lake on the left. The green is on a narrow, 39-yard island in the tributary. *Hint:* use a mid- to long-iron (check the wind conditions). Regular players make the green in two—better two than one in the drink. Reservations are taken one day in advance only. Facilities include a driving range, practice greens, club rental, locker rooms, pro shop, and restaurant. Green fees $125 with cart; 9 holes $64.50 (with cart). No twilight rates.

✪ Olomana Golf Links. 41-1801 Kalanianaole Hwy., Waimanalo, HI 96795. ☎ **808/259-7926.** To get there from Waikiki, take H-1 freeway to the Pali Hwy. (Hi. 61). Turn right on Kalanianaole Hwy.; about 5 miles further, Olomana will be on the left. TheBUS: 57.

This is a gorgeous course located in Waimanalo, on the other side of the island from Waikiki. The low-handicap golfer may not find this course difficult, but the striking views of the craggy Koolau Mountain Ridge are worth the greens fees alone. The par-72, 6,326-yard course is very popular with local residents and visitors alike. The course starts off a bit hilly on the front nine, but flattens out by the back nine. The back nine have their own special surprises, including tricky water hazards. The first hole, a 384-yard, par-4 that tees downhill and approaches uphill, is definitely a warm-up. The next hole is a 160-yard, par-3 that starts from an elevated tee to an elevated green over a severely banked, V-shaped gully. Shoot long here—it's longer than you think—as short shots tend to roll all the way back down the fairway to the base of the gully. This course is very, very green; the rain gods bless it regularly with brief passing showers. You can tell the regular players here—they all carry umbrellas and wait patiently for the squalls to pass, then resume play. Reservations are a must. Greens fees are $90, including cart; twilight fees after 2:30pm Monday to Friday are $23 with cart and $13 without. Facilities include a driving range, practice greens, club rental, pro shop, and restaurant.

Pali Golf Course. 45-050 Kamehameha Hwy., Kaneohe, HI 96744. ☎ **808/296-7254.** To get there from Waikiki, take the H-1 freeway to the Pali Hwy. (Hi. 61). Turn left at Kamehameha Hwy. at the first traffic light after you are through the Pali Tunnels. The course is immediately on your left after you turn on Kamehameha Hwy. TheBUS: 55.

This beautiful municipal course sits on the windward side of the island near Kaneohe, just below the historical spot where King Kamehameha the Great won the battle to unite the islands of Hawaii. Built in 1953, this par-72, 6,494-yard course has no man-made traps, but it does have a small stream that meanders through the course. If you're off line on the ninth, you'll get to know the stream quite well. The course, designed by Willard G. Wilkinson, makes use of the natural terrain (hills and valleys that make up the majority of the 250 acres). The challenge of the course is the weather—whipping winds and frequent rain squalls. The views include Kaneohe Bay, the towns of Kailua and Kaneohe, and the verdant cliffs of the Koolau Mountains. Due to the frequent rains, you might want to pay for nine holes and then check out the weather before signing up for the next nine. Greens fees are $40, plus another $14 for an optional cart (which will carry two golfers); twilight rates after 2pm $20, walking only, no carts. Facilities include practice greens, club rental, locker rooms, and a restaurant.

5 Other Outdoor Activities

Oahu is a great place to fulfill all your outdoor needs, and even a dream or two: You can gallop on horseback over a white-sand beach at sunset or jump out of an airplane and parachute to the island's surface. You can play a game of tennis at dawn or watch international racing yachts cross the finish line at Diamond Head. Oahu even has an ice skating rink. The top professional football players can be seen at the annual Pro Bowl game in Honolulu, and top cowboys from across the country compete in a rodeo that draws people from all over the globe.

BICYCLING

For a guided bicycling adventure, try the Bike & Hike at **Kualoa Ranch,** P.O. Box 650, Kaaawa, HI 96730 (☎ **808/237-7321**). Mountain bike through the scenic Kaaawa Valley (seen in the movie *Jurassic Park*), on the 4,000-acre Kualoa Ranch, situated between Kaneohe Bay and the Koolau Mountain Range. The adventure takes place Monday to Friday at 11am (weather permitting); cost is $25 for adults and $20 for children ages 5 to 11. Thrill seekers will enjoy the hour and 45-minute downhill bike ride at **Waimea Valley,** Waimea Falls Park (☎ **808/638-8511**). The $55 fee includes park admission, rental of bike, and safety equipment. The guided downhill trips take place at 10:15am, 1:30pm, and 3:30pm daily. Minimum age is 16.

For those who prefer to venture out on their own, **Island Triathlon and Bike,** 569 Kapahulu Ave. (☎ **808/732-7227**), has mountain bike rentals—complete with lock, pump, repair kit, and helmet—for $25 the first day and $10 for each additional day. They're also in the know about upcoming bicycle events or interesting bike rides you can enjoy on your own. Other bicycle rental sources include **Diamond Head Rentals,** 2463 Kuhio Ave. (next to Kuhio Village Resort), Waikiki (☎ **808/923-0105**), and **Blue Sky Rentals and Sports Center,** 1920 Ala Moana (in the Inn on the Park, next to Kalia Rd.), Waikiki (☎ **808/947-0101**), which rents mountain bikes beginning at $15 a day; they also have tandem bikes for rent.

If you'd like to join in on some club rides, contact the **Hawaii Bicycle League,** P.O. Box 4403, Honolulu, HI 96812 (☎ **808/735-5756**), which offers rides every weekend, as well as several annual events. The league can also provide you with a schedule of upcoming rides, races, and outings.

○ GLIDING

Imagine soaring through silence on gossamerlike wings, with a panaramic view of Oahu. A ride on a glider is an unforgettable experience. Glider rides are available at Dillingham Air Field, in Mokuleia, on Oahu's North Shore. The glider is towed behind a plane; at the right altitude, the tow is dropped and you (and the glider pilot) are left to soar in the thermals. The best deal is to go with another person—the price drops to $60 each for the 20-minute ride. We recommend Mr. Bill at **Glider Rides**

(☎ 808/677-3404); he's been offering piloted glider rides since 1970. If Mr. Bill is booked, try **Soar Hawaii** (☎ 808/637-3147), which offers rides at the same price.

✪ HANG GLIDING

See things from a bird's eye view (literally) as you and your instructor float high above Oahu on a tandem hang glider. **North Shore Hang/Para Gliding,** at the Dillingham Air Field (☎ 808/637-3178), offers you an opportunity to try out this daredevil sport for $150. If you like it, they have lessons available.

HORSEBACK RIDING

Up into the valley of kings, riders on horseback go deep into Oahu's interior, which only a lucky few have ever seen. **Senator Fong's Plantation and Gardens,** 47-285 Pualma Rd. (just outside of Kahaluu, off Kamehameha Hwy.), Kaneohe, HI 96744 (☎ 808/239-6775; TheBUS:55 will drop you off at the highway, but it is over a mile walk uphill to Senator Fong's) has guided horseback rides through the botanical gardens and up into the rain forest. Tours range form 1-hour tours for $45 up to 4 hours for $115.

Take a ride on **Kualoa Ranch,** 49-560 Kamehameha Hwy. (Hwy. 93), Kaaawa, HI 96730 (☎ 800/231-7321 or 808/237-8515; TheBUS: 55), a 4,000-acre working cattle ranch that John Morgan, a scion of a sugar planter, turned into an outdoor playground. The ranch offers a number of different tours through their 4,000-acre property: 45-minute rides go for $25, 1¹/₂-hour rides for $40. You're required to wear long pants and closed-toe shoes.

You can gallop on the beach at the **Turtle Bay Hilton Golf and Tennis Resort,** 57-091 Kamehameha Hwy., Kahuku, HI 96731 (☎ 808/293-8811; TheBUS: 52 or 55), where 45-minute rides along sandy beaches with spectacular ocean views and through a forest of ironwood trees cost $30 for adults and $20 for children 9 to 12 (they must be at least 4 ft., 6 in.). Romantic evening rides take place on Friday and Saturday from 5pm to 6:30pm, and cost $60 per person. Advanced riders can sign up for a 40-minute trot and canter ride along Kawela Bay for $45. If you've dreamed of learning how to ride, the **Hilltop Equestrian Center,** 41-430 Waikupanaha St., Waimanalo, HI 96895 (☎ 808/259-8463; TheBUS: 57 or 58), will be happy to teach you. They offer lessons in either British or Western style from British Horse Society–accredited instructors for $40 per lesson, minimum of three lessons.

ROCK CLIMBING

Oahu has an indoor climbing center, **Climbers Paradise,** 214 Sand Island Rd., Honolulu, HI 96819 (☎ 808/842-ROCK), where you can scale walls up to 30 feet, traverse an elaborate boulder cave, and explore thousands of feet of man-made rock-like surfaces. Open to all ages, there are classes for this newest Olympic sport. Rates start at $25 for the day and include professional instruction and gear rental. Family discount rates are available. TheBUS: 19 or 20 will drop you off on Nimitz Highway and you will have to walk about about 2 blocks.

SKYDIVING

Everything you need to leap from a plane and float to earth can be obtained from **Blue Sky Rentals and Sports Center,** 1920 Ala Moana Blvd. (located on the ground floor of Inn on the Park, in Waikiki, on the corner of Ala Moana Blvd. and Ena Rd.), Honolulu, HI 96815 (☎ 808/947-0101), for $225 per jump (including suit, parachute, goggles, plane rental, lesson, etc.). For instructions, call **SkyDive Hawaii,** 68-760 Farrington Hwy., Waiawa, HI 96791 (☎ 808/637-9700), which has a seven-jump course for $1,000. If you want to try skydiving first to see if you like it, they also offer a tandem jump (where you're strapped to an expert who wears a chute big enough for the both of you) for $275. There's no doubt about it—this is the thrill of a lifetime. Other skydiving instruction centers at the Dillingham Airfield include **Pacific International Skydiving Center** (☎ 808/637-7472), **Parachutes Hawaii** (☎ 808/623-7076), and **Tandem Hawaii** (☎ 808/637-8544).

TENNIS

Oahu has 181 free public tennis courts. To get a complete list of all facilities, or information on upcoming tournaments, send a self-addressed, stamped envelope to **Department of Parks and Recreation,** Tennis Unit, 650 S. King St., Honolulu, HI 96813 (☎ 808/971-7150). The courts are available on a first-come, first-served basis; playing time is limited to 45 minutes.

If you're staying in Waikiki, the **Ilikai Sports Center** at the Ilikai Hotel, 1777 Ala Moana Blvd. (at Hobron Lane) (☎ 808/949-3811; TheBUS: 19 or 20), has six courts, equipment rental, lessons, and repair service. Courts are $7.50 per person per hour; lessons are $44 per hour. If you're on the other side of the island, the **Turtle Bay Hilton Golf and Tennis Resort,** 57-091 Kamehameha Hwy., Kahuku, HI 96731 (☎ 808/293-8811, ext. 24; TheBUS: 52 or 55), has 10 courts, 4 of which are lit for night play. You must make advance reservations for the night courts, as they're very popular. Court rates are $12 for the entire day. *Budget tip:* Book a court between noon and 4pm for half off. Equipment rental and lessons are available.

6 From the Sidelines: Spectator Sports

Don't expect the Chicago Bulls, the San Francisco 49ers, or the New York Yankees. Local people love these sports, and fill the public parks on weeknights and weekends to play them themselves. Although there aren't any major-league sports teams, there are some minor-league teams and a handful of professional exposition games played in Hawaii. Check the schedule at the 50,000-seat **Aloha Stadium,** located near Pearl Harbor (☎ 808/486-9300), where high school and University of Hawaii football games are also held. There are usually express buses that will take you to the stadium on game nights; they depart from Ala Moana Shopping Center (TheBUS no. 47–50 and 52) or from Monsarrat Avenue near Kapiolani Park (TheBUS no. 20). Call TheBUS at ☎ 808/848-5555 for times and fares.

The **Neal Blaisdell Center,** at Kapiolani Boulevard and Ward Avenue (☎ 808/521-2911), features a variety of sporting events such as professional boxing and Japanese sumo wrestling. In December, the Annual Rainbow Classic, a collegiate basketball invitational tournament, takes place at the Blaisdell. For bus information, call TheBUS at ☎ 808/848-5555.

With Hawaii's cowboy history, polo is a very popular sport, played every Sunday from March through August in Mokuleia or Waimanalo. Bring a picnic lunch and enjoy the game. Call ☎ 808/637-7656 for details on times and admission charges.

A sport you might not be familiar with is Hawaiian outrigger canoe racing, which is very big locally. Every weekend from Memorial Day to Labor Day canoe races are held around Oahu. The races are free and draw huge crowds. Check the local papers for information on the race schedule.

Motor-racing fans can enjoy their sport at **Hawaii Raceway Park,** 91-201 Malakole, in Campbell Industrial Park, in Ewa Beach next to the Barbers Point Naval Air Station (☎ 808/682-7139), on Friday and Saturday nights. No bus service.

Some of the other spectator sports that are scheduled during the year are detailed in the following calendar:

CALENDAR OF EVENTS: SPORTS

January

- **Women's World Bodyboarding Championship,** Banzai Pipeline, North Shore. Held in conjunction with the bodysurfing competition, this international event crowns the world champion and awards the largest purse, now more than $20,000, on the women's tour. Late January to mid-February. The meet will be held January 28–February 10 in 1998. Deadline for participants is January 18, 1998. Public is welcome. Call ☎ **808/638-1149;** http://www.aloha.net/~carolp; e-mail: carolp@aloha.net.

- **Morey World Bodyboard Championships,** Banzai Pipeline, depending on the surf conditions. First week in January. In 1998, the event will be held January 3–11. Participants must register by December 21, 1997. Free to the public. For more information call ☎ **808/396-2326.**

- ✪ **Ala Wai Challenge,** Ala Wai Park, Waikiki. Based on ancient Hawaiian sports, this all-day event features ancient games like *ulu maika* (bowling a round stone through pegs), *oo ihe* (spear throwing at an upright target), *moa pahee* (wooden torpedo slide through two pegs), *huki kaula* (tug of war), and a quarter-mile outrigger canoe race. Great place to hear Hawaiian music. Usually held on the third Sunday in January. Call ☎ **808/923-1802.**

- **NFL Pro Bowl Battle of the Gridiron,** Ihilani Resort & Spa. Kicking off the NFL Pro Bowl, a position and skills-oriented challenge between the best of the best in the National Football League. Usually held in late January or early February. In 1998, the game will be played on January 29. Call ☎ **808/521-4322** or 808/486-9300.

February

- ✪ **Buffalo's Big Board Surfing Classic,** Makaha. This is a colorful, old-style surfing competition—on long boards. Held during the first two weekends in February. Participants can just show up on the first weekend in February to enter. The event is free and open to the public. For information call ☎ **808/695-8934.**

- ✪ **NFL Pro Bowl,** Aloha Stadium. The National Football League's best pro players square off in this annual gridiron all-star game. First Sunday in February. Tickets go on sale the day after Labor Day and sell out quickly. Call ☎ **808/486-9300** for tickets and information.

- **The Great Aloha Run,** Honolulu. Thousands run 8.25 miles from Aloha Tower to Aloha Stadium. Always held on Presidents' Day (third Monday in February). Call ☎ **808/528-7388** for information and to preregister for the race (you can also sign up on race day).

March

- ✪ **Hawaii Challenge International Sportkite Championship,** Kapiolani Park. The longest running sportkite competition in the world. This event attracts the top kite pilots in the world. First weekend in March.

    The next weekend is the **International Kite Festival,** Sandy Beach. Here more than 130 competitors participate in such events as a kite ballet to Taiko drumming and the world's largest kite flying. Just show up on contest day to sign up for the event. First weekend in March. Call ☎ **808/735-9059.**

- **Outrigger Hotels Hawaiian Mountain Tour.** The world's top professional mountain bikers compete for a $70,000 purse in a 4-day, 5-stage race plus Downhill Mania and Dual Slalom. The event is open to all amateur classes too. Mid- to late March. The event will be held on March 12–15, 1998 at Kualoa

Ranch (49-560 Kamehameha Hwy., Kaneohe). Entry deadline is 2 weeks before the race. Call ☎ **808/521-4322.**

April

- **Hawaiian Highland Gathering,** Kapiolani Park, Waikiki. This gathering of the clans for Scottish games, competitions, food, dancing, and pipe bands is open to everyone. First weekend in April. Call ☎ **808/988-7872.**
- **Hawaiian Professional Rodeo.** In April, and again in August, cowboys compete in rodeo events in Waimanalo, which are rounded out with a barbecue, country music, and dancing in the dirt for a true Hawaiian *paniolo* experience. For information call ☎ **808/235-3691.**
- **Hawaiian Classic Senior Men's Ice Hockey Tournament.** Skating aces from Hawaii compete in this invitational tournament at the Ice Palace. Usually held the weekend after Easter. For information call ☎ **808/487-9921.**
- ✪ **Honolulu International Bed Race Festival,** Honolulu. This popular fund-raising event allows visitors a mini taste of Honolulu with food booths sponsored by local restaurants, live entertainment, a Keiki Carnival with games and rides, and a race through the streets of Honolulu with runners pushing beds to raise money for local charities. Usually held the third Saturday in April. Sit on the bleachers at Kapiolani Park for the best view. Call ☎ **808/735-6092.**

May

- ✪ **AT&T Dragon Boat Festival,** Ala Moana Beach, Honolulu. Teams from throughout Asia race in this festival. Late May. The best place to watch the races is on the bleachers that are set up in the park. Call ☎ **808/734-6900.**

July

- **Walter J. McFarlane Regatta and Surf Race,** Waikiki. An outrigger canoe regatta featuring 30 events. July 4. Call ☎ **808/261-6615** or 808/526-1969.
- **Hawaiian Open Ice Skating Competition.** Top skaters compete for honors in July at the Ice Palace. Date varies. For information call ☎ **808/487-9921.**

August

- **Duke Kahanamoku Beach Doubles Volleyball Championship,** Waikiki. First held in 1958, this is the oldest-running beach volleyball tournament in the state; currently hosted by the Outrigger Canoe Club. Championship-caliber men players can enter. Register at least 1 month in advance; fee is $20 per team. Mid-August. Call ☎ **808/923-1585.**
- ✪ **Kenwood Cup.** This international yacht race is held during July in even-numbered years only (1998, 2000, 2002, and so on). Sailors from the United States, Japan, Australia, New Zealand, Europe, and Hawaii participate in a series of races around the state. For information call ☎ **808/946-9061.**

September

- **Na Wahine O Ke Kai.** This invitational, 41-mile, open-ocean Hawaii outrigger canoe race from Hale O Lono, Molokai, to Duke Kahanamoku Beach, Waikiki, attracts international teams. Usually held the last weekend in September. For information call ☎ **808/262-7567.**
- **Outrigger Hotels Hawaiian Oceanfest,** various Oahu locations. A 2-week celebration of ocean sports includes the Hawaiian International Ocean Challenge featuring teams of the world's best professional lifeguards; Outrigger Waikiki Kings Race, an ocean iron-man race; Diamond Head Wahine Windsurfing Classic, the only all-women professional windsurfing competition; and Diamond Head Biathlon, a run/swim event. Great competitors, serious competition, a variety of

evening events, and more. Second through last week in September; winds up with the Armed Forces Family Festival on last Sunday in September. Entries on race day are accepted. Call ☎ 808/521-4322.

✪ **Waikiki Rough-Water Swim.** This popular 2.4-mile, open-ocean swim from Sans Souci Beach to Duke Kahanamoku Beach in Waikiki takes place on Labor Day. Early registration is encouraged, but they will take last-minute entries on race day. For information call ☎ **808/988-7788.**

October

- **Bankoh Molokai Hoe.** Top outrigger canoe teams from around the world compete in a 41-mile, open-ocean race from Molokai to Waikiki. Sunday before Columbus Day. For information call ☎ **808/261-6615.**

- **Hawaii International Rugby Tournament,** Kapiolani Park, Waikiki. Teams from around the world gather to compete in this exciting tournament. The event has a division for all players including Masters, Social, Championship, 7-side, 9-side, and touch. Second week in October. Call ☎ **808/926-5641.**

November

✪ **Triple Crown of Surfing.** The top surfing events held in Hawaii, these November to December competitions include the Pipeline Masters, the Hawaiian Pro, and the World Cup of Surfing. The world's best surfers compete for $250,000 in prize money. Generally held from mid-November to mid-to-late December. Participation is by invitation only. For information call ☎ **808/623-5024.**

December

- **Honolulu Marathon.** More than 20,000 runners descend on Honolulu for the 26.2-mile race in December. Second Sunday in December. Preregistration is recommended, but participants can sign up on race day. For information call ☎ **808/ 734-7200.**

✪ **Aloha Bowl,** Aloha Stadium. The winner of the PAC 10 will play the winner of the Big 12 in this nationally-televised collegiate football classic. Christmas Day. You can purchase tickets year round; a few are usually even available on game day. Tickets cost $22–$28. Call ☎ **808/947-4141.**

✪ **Rainbow Classic,** University of Hawaii, Manoa Valley. Eight of the best NCAA basketball teams compete at the Special Events Arena. Week after Christmas. Call ☎ **808/956-4481** for tickets (ticket packages for the tournament go on sale December 16; individual game tickets go on sale the day of the event); call ☎ 808/ 956-6501 for more information.

Seeing the Sights   **9**

by Jeanette Foster

In one day you can see and do more in Honolulu than you can in most places in a week. There's historical Honolulu to explore, from the Queen's Summer Palace to the bombing site that launched the U.S. into World War II. Wander through exotic gardens with gentle fragrances wafting through the air, meet brilliantly colored tropical fish, stand on the deck of a four-masted schooner that sailed 100 years ago, venture into haunted places where ghosts are said to roam, take in the spicy smells and sights of Chinatown, and participate in a host of cultural activities from flower lei making to hula dancing. Plus there's plenty of activities for the kids (and the kid at heart) to do!

You don't need a big budget to experience Honolulu's best activities. You don't really even need a car. TheBUS will get you where you need to go for $1, or you can hop on the moderately priced tours and trolleys. The only problem you may encounter is scheduling all the activities you want to enjoy during your vacation time.

1 Orientation & Adventure Tours

GUIDED SIGHTSEEING TOURS

If your time is limited, you might want to consider a guided tour: They're informative, entertaining, and you'll probably be surprised at how much you'll enjoy yourself. **E Noa Tours,** 1141 Waimanu St., Honolulu, HI 96814 (☎ **800/824-8804** or 808/591-2561, fax 808/591-9065, e-mail: enoa@pixi.com), offers a range of tours from circling the island to exploring historical Honolulu. Their 2-hour narrated tour of Honolulu and Waikiki is aboard an open-air trolley, and includes 20 stops from Waikiki to the Bishop Museum. It's a great way to get the "lay of the land," with the driver not only pointing out the historical sights, but also Honolulu's attractions, shopping locations, and restaurants. You can get on and off the trolley as needed (trolleys come along every 15 minutes). An all-day pass (from 8am to 4:30pm) costs $17 for adults, $5 for children under 11 years; a 5-day pass is $30 for adults and $10 for children.

Other E Noa tours include a "Circle Island" beach and waterfall tour ($49 adults, $37 children 6 to 12 years, and $31 children under 5), which stops at Diamond Head Crater, the Mormon Temple, Sunset Beach, Waimea Valley (admission is included in cost), Hanauma Bay, and various beach sites along the way. Shopping excursions, nightlife tours, and a Pearl Harbor historic tour are also available.

Polynesian Adventure Tours, 1049 Kikowaena Pl., Honolulu, HI 96819 (☎ 808/833-3000), also offers a range of guided tours from circling the island to shopping excursions. The all-day island tours start at $46 adults, $37 for children 6 to 12 years, $31 for children 4 to 5 years, $15 for children 3 years; the half-day scenic shore and rain forest tours are $23 for adults and $18 for children 3 to 11 years; and the half-day Arizona Memorial Excursion is $14 adults and $10 children 3 to 11 years.

GUIDED ECOTOURS

Local boy Darren Akau was chosen Hawaii's tour guide of the year in 1989, then set out on his own to show Hawaii to visitors his way. A day with Darren is a rare chance to explore the "real" Hawaii. He takes groups of eight or more on guided, active day-long outings, such as a hike to Manoa Falls for a splash in the waterfall pool, a beach picnic, or snorkeling and boogie boarding at very local Waimanalo Beach. Along the way, Darren discusses island ways and local customs, flora and fauna, history and culture, language and food, and more. The day starts at 7am, and usually ends at about 3:30pm. The cost is $75 for adults and $64 for kids, which includes lunch and hotel pickup and return. You should be in fairly good shape and be able to hike at least a half-mile in a rain forest, and feel at ease in gentle-to-moderate waves. Reservations are required at least a day in advance; call **Darren Akau's Hideaway Tours,** 41-127 Nalu St., Waimanalo, HI 96795 (☎ 808/259-9165).

WALKING TOURS

Honolulu TimeWalks (☎ 808/943-0371; fax 808/951-8878; http://www.aaim.com/TIMEWALK/Timewalks.html; e-mail: timewalk@pixi.com) features Glen Grant and his storytelling guides leading a variety of lively 2- to 3-hour walks through Waikiki, Chinatown, and other areas of Honolulu. Much of what they "show" you doesn't exist anymore, so they need to be clever—and you need to have some imagination—in order for you to get the picture. Guides appear in turn-of-the-century togs, and tell it like it was through lively anecdotes about King Kalakaua, Prince Kuhio, Robert Louis Stevenson, and Mark Twain.

The **Haunted Honolulu Walk/Trolley Tour** through supernatural Honolulu is offered every Tuesday from 7pm to 11pm for $30. Another spooky tour is the **Haunted Honolulu Walk,** a tour of the strange and unexplainable happenings around the capitol district, which takes place two Wednesdays a month from 6pm to 9pm; the cost is $8. History buffs will love the **Historic Honolulu Rediscovered: Heritage Trail Tour** of downtown Honolulu, which is offered Saturdays from 9am to noon for $10 adults, $8 children; it starts down by the Honolulu Harbor and ends up by Iolani Palace. Another historical tour is the **Revolution of 1893,** which relives the days of the overthrow of the Hawaiian monarchy, complete with actors in costume; it's offered one Thursday a month from 6pm to 8:30pm at $7 per person. The company also offers a **Mystical Chinatown Tour** one Saturday a month from 9am to 10:30am that explores Chinatown, its myths, folklore, foods, and cultural activities; the cost is $8.

Honolulu TimeWalks also offers a variety of storytelling and historical theater programs at the Waikiki Heritage Theatre and the International Market Place, as well as excursions around the island. Call for complete information and scheduling.

DOWNTOWN HONOLULU   The **Mission Houses Museum,** 553 S. King St. (at Kawaiahao St.), Honolulu, HI 96813 (☎ 808/531-0481; TheBUS: 2), offers a walking tour of historic downtown buildings on Thursday and Friday mornings.

A guide takes visitors through the capitol district, making stops at sites such as Iolani Palace, the Kamehameha Statue, the Royal Tomb, and James Kekela's grave. The tour starts at 9:30am at the museum and lasts until 12:30pm. The Mission Houses Museum also offers a **Women's History Walking Tour** one Saturday a month, which tells the stories of women of the Hawaiian *ali'i* (royalty). The fee for walking tours is $7 for adults, $4 for college students, $3 for kids 4 to 18, and includes the regular Mission Houses tour (see "Walking Tour: Historic Honolulu," below). Reserve a day ahead in person or by phone.

Kapiolani Community College has a unique series of walking tours into Hawaii's past, including visits to Honolulu's famous cemeteries, the almost-vanished "Little Tokyo" neighborhood, and many more fascinating destinations. Tours, which generally cost about $5, are for groups only, but you may be able to tag along. For information and reservations, call ☎ **808/734-9245.**

The Hawaii Geographic Society, ℅ Hawaii Geographic Maps and Books, 49 S. Hotel St. (P.O. Box 1698), Honolulu, HI 96808 (☎ **808/538-3952**), presents numerous interesting and unusual tours like "A Temple Tour," including Chinese, Japanese, Christian, and Jewish temples, cathedrals, and other houses of worship; an archaeology tour in and around downtown Honolulu; and others. Each is guided by an expert from the Hawaii Geographic Society and must have a minimum of three people. Cost is $10 per person.

The Society's brochure, "Historic Downtown Honolulu Walking Tour," is a fascinating self-guided tour of the 200-year-old city center. It's $3, including postage, from the address above.

CHINATOWN HISTORIC DISTRICT   In addition to the Chinatown walk offered by Honolulu TimeWalks (see above), two 3-hour guided tours of Chinatown are offered Tuesdays at 9:30am by the **Chinese Chamber of Commerce,** 42 N. King St. (at Smith St.), Honolulu, HI (☎ **808/533-3181;** TheBUS: 2). The cost is $5 per person; call to reserve.

The **Hawaii Heritage Center** (☎ **808/521-2749**) also conducts walking tours every Friday at 9:30am that focus on the history and culture of Chinatown. Tours begin at the Ramsay Gallery, 1128 Smith St. (at N. King St.; TheBUS: 2); the cost is $4 per person.

Also see our very own walking tour of Chinatown (see p. 214).

BEYOND HONOLULU   The **Moanalua Gardens Foundation,** 1352 Pineapple Pl., Honolulu, HI 96819 (☎ **808/839-5334**), offers a 4- to 5-hour guided walking tour of Kamananui Valley once a month, a chance to see what Hawaii looked like before the introduction of numerous alien plants. The cost is $3.

CULTURAL ACTIVITIES

More and more people are traveling to Hawaii not for the sun, the sand, and the shoreline, but for the Hawaiian culture. The best place to see and participate in this ancient culture is the Hawaiian Hall of the **Bishop Museum,** 1525 Bernice St., Honolulu, HI 96817 (☎ **808/847-3511**), TheBUS: 2. They offer a series of free classes in Hawaiian quilt making (Monday and Friday, 9am to 2pm), stone and bone carving (Tuesday, 9am to 2pm), lauhala weaving (Wednesday, 10am to 3pm), feather lei making (Thursday, 10am to 3pm), flower lei making (Saturday, 9am to 3pm), and coconut frond weaving (Sunday, 9am to 3pm).

Hawaiian quilt making also is taught at **Kwilts 'n Koa,** 1126 12th Ave. (between Harding and Waialae avenues in Kaimuki), Honolulu, HI, 96816 (☎ **808/ 735-2300**). Call for class information and times.

If you have ever wanted to learn the hula, the **Waikiki Community Center,** 310 Paoakalani Ave. (Ewa side of the street between Ala Wai Blvd. and Kuhio Ave.), Honolulu, HI 96815 (☎ **808/923-1802**), offers "drop-in" beginner hula classes every Friday night at 7pm; cost is $3.

2 Historic Honolulu

For just about as long as we can remember, the Eastman Kodak Company has been hosting the ✪ **Kodak Hula Show** at the Waikiki Band Shell in Kapiolani Park (TheBUS: 4, 8, 19, or 20). It's really more '50s nostalgia than ancient culture, but it's a good bit of fun any way you slice it. Shows begin at 10am every Tuesday, Wednesday, and Thursday, and last until 11:15am. Admission is free. The area seats 1,500 and you'll have a good view no matter where you sit. However, if you want to be front and center (the best spot for photo ops), Kodak suggests that you arrive around 9:15am. For more information, call ☎ **808/627-3300.** (See "Walking Tour: Kapiolani Park," below.)

For a more genuine Hawaiian hula experience, catch the hula *halau* that performs weekdays at 1pm at the Bishop Museum (see below).

✪ **Bishop Museum.** 1525 Bernice St., just off Kalihi St. (also known as Likelike Hwy.). ☎ **808/ 847-3511.** Fax 808/841-8968. Web page: http://www.bishop.hawaii.org/. Admission $8 adults, $7 children 6–17 and seniors. Daily 9am–5pm. TheBUS: 2.

This forbidding, four-story Romanesque structure (it looks like something out of a Charles Addams cartoon) holds safe the world's greatest collection of natural and cultural artifacts from Hawaii and the Pacific. The museum was founded by a Hawaiian princess, Bernice Pauahi, who collected priceless artifacts, and in her will instructed her husband, Charles Reed Bishop, to establish a Hawaiian museum "to enrich and delight" the people of Hawaii. The museum is now world-renowned, and home to Dr. Yoshihiko Sinoto, the last in a proud line of adventuring archaeologists who has explored more of the Pacific than Captain Cook, and traced Hawaii's history and culture through its fishhooks.

The Bishop is jam-packed with more than 20 million acquisitions—there are 12 million insect specimens alone—from ceremonial spears to calabashes to old photos of topless hula dancers. A visit here will give you a good basis for understanding Hawaiian life and culture. You'll see the great feathered capes of kings, the last grass shack in Hawaii, preindustrial Polynesian art, even the skeleton of a 50-foot sperm whale. There are seashells, koa-wood bowls, nose flutes, and Dr. Sinoto's major collection of fishhooks.

A hula *halau* performs weekdays, and various Hawaiian crafts like lei making, feather working, and quilting are demonstrated. *Tip:* The hula halau performs at 1pm, so be sure to be at the Museum to see it.

✪ **Hawaii Maritime Center.** Pier 7 (near Aloha Tower), Honolulu Harbor. ☎ **808/ 536-6373.** Admission $7.50 adults, $4.50 children 6–17. Daily 9am–5pm. TheBUS: 19, 20, 55, 56, or 57.

From the ancient journey of Polynesian voyagers to the nostalgic days of the *Lurline,* which once brought tourists from San Francisco on 4-day cruises, the story of Hawaii's rich maritime heritage is told with artifacts and exhibits at the Hawaii Maritime Center's Kalakaua Boat House, patterned after His Majesty King David Kalakaua's own canoe house.

Outside, the *Hokulea,* a double-hulled sailing canoe that in 1976 re-enacted the Polynesian voyage of discovery, is moored next to the *Falls of Clyde,* a four-masted schooner that once ran tea from China to the West Coast. Inside, the more than 30 exhibits include Matson cruise ships, which brought the first tourists to Waikiki; flying boats that delivered the mail; and the skeleton of a Pacific humpback whale that beached on Kahoolawe. The museum's open-air harborfront restaurant is a popular downtown lunch spot with its view of passing tugboats, sampans, and cargo and cruise ships.

Budget tip: Parking at or near the Aloha Tower is very expensive; we suggest that you take the bus instead.

✪ **Iolani Palace.** At S. King and Richards sts. ☎ **808/522-0832.** Admission $8 adults, $3 children 5–13. Guided tours conducted Wed–Sat 9am–2:15pm. Call ahead to reserve. You must be booked on a guided tour to enter the palace; children under 5 not permitted. TheBUS: 2.

This royal palace was built by King David Kalakaua, who spared no expense. The 4-year project, completed in 1882, cost $360,000—and nearly bankrupted the Hawaiian kingdom. The four-story Italian Renaissance palace, complete with Corinthian columns imported from San Francisco, was the first electrified building in Honolulu (it had electricity before the White House and Buckingham Palace). Royals lived here for 11 years, until Queen Liliuokalani was deposed, and the Hawaiian monarchy fell forever in a January 17, 1893 palace coup led by U.S. Marines at the demand of sugar planters and missionary descendants.

Cherished by latter-day royalists, the 10-room palace stands as a flamboyant architectural statement of the monarchy period. (Iolani, often identified as the only royal palace on American soil, actually shares that distinction with the Big Island's Hulihee Palace, which also served as a royal house.) Open to the public since 1970, Iolani Palace attracts 100,000 visitors a year in groups of 20, who must don denim booties to scoot across the royal floors. The 45-minute tour is well worth your time. Some areas are unfurnished, but the State Dining Room, Throne Room, King's Library, and Privy Council Chamber are complete. The two-story staircase is the largest koa-wood case on earth.

Kawaiahao Church. 957 Punchbowl St. (at King St.). ☎ **808/522-1333.** Free admission (small donations appreciated). Mon–Sat 8am–4pm; Sun services 10:30am. TheBUS: 2.

In 1842, Kawaiahao Church stood at last, the crowning achievement of missionaries and Hawaiians working together for the first time on a common project. Designed by Rev. Hiram Bingham and supervised by Kamehameha III, who ordered his people to help build it, the project took 5 years. Workers quarried 14,000 thousand-pound coral blocks from the offshore reefs and cut timber in the forests for the beams.

The proud stone church, complete with bell tower and colonial colonnade, was the first permanent Western house of worship in the islands. It became the church of the Hawaiian royalty and remains in use today by Hawaiians who conduct services in the Hawaiian language (which probably sets old Rev. Bingham spinning in his grave). Some fine portraits of Hawaiian royalty hang inside. Hawaiian-language services are conducted on Sundays at 10:30am.

Mission Houses Museum. 553 S. King St. (at Kawaiahao St.). ☎ **808/531-0481.** Fax 808/545-2280. Admission $6 adults, $5 seniors, $3 college students, $2 children. Tues–Sat 9am–4pm. TheBUS: 2.

The Mission Houses Museum tells the dramatic story of cultural change in 19th-century Hawaii. Here, American Protestant missionaries established their headquarters in 1820. Included in the complex are a visitors center and three historic mission buildings restored and refurnished to reflect the daily life and work of the missionaries.

Walking tours of historic downtown buildings are offered on Thursday and Friday mornings. For details, see "Orientation & Adventure Tours," above.

Honolulu Attractions

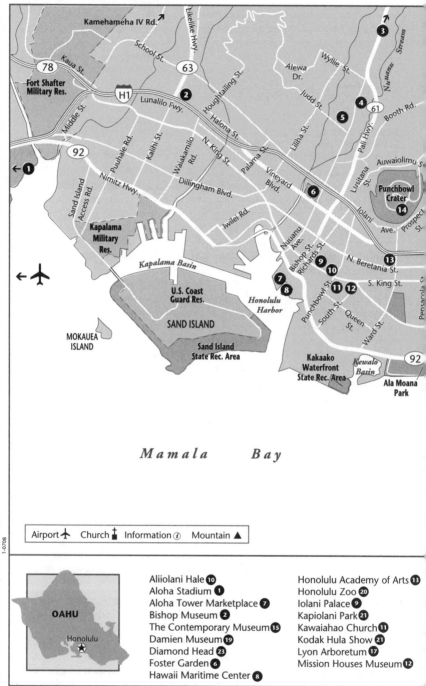

Airport ✈ Church ⛪ Information ⓘ Mountain ▲

204

0   1 km
     0.6 mi

MAKIKI VALLEY

Puu Ualakaa
State Park
16 ▲
Round Top

Waahila Ridge
State Rec. Area

Puu Ualakaa State Park

17

Tantalus Dr.

Round

Top Dr.

E. Manoa Rd.

Manoa Rd.

Manoa Stream

Waiomao Stream

Pukele Stream

15

Nehoa St.

Makiki St.

Punahou St.

University of
Hawaii

St. Louis Dr.

Bertram St.

Palolo Ave.

Palolo Stream

Wilder Ave.

H1

Lunalilo Fwy.

S. Beretania St.

Dole St.

University Ave.

10th Ave.

Sierra Dr.

Wilhelmina Rise

Piikoi St.

Keeaumoku St.

S. King St.

Kikeke

Waialae Ave.

Koko
Head
Ave.

Kapiolani Blvd.

McCully St.

Kapahulu Ave.

Lunalilo Fwy.

H1

Ala Moana Blvd.

Atkinson Dr.

Date St.

Kilauea Ave.

16th Ave.

Ala Moana
State Rec.
Area

Kalakaua Ave.

Ala Wai Canal
Ala Wai Blvd.

Campbell Ave.

Alohea Ave.

18th Ave.

Fort
DeRussy
Military Res.
18

ⓘ

19

Waikiki Beach

20

21
Kapiolani
Park

22

Sans Souci
State Rec.
Area

Military
Res.

Diamond Head
State Monument

Trail

23
Leahi ▲

KAHALA →

Diamond Head Rd.

U.S. Coast
Guard Res.

National Memorial Cemetery
of the Pacific **14**
Nuuanu Pali Lookout **3**
Oahu Cemetery **5**
Pacific Aerospace Museum **1**
Puu Ualakaa State Park **16**
Queen Emma Summer Palace **3**
Royal Mausoleum **4**
U.S. Army Museum **18**

USS *Arizona* Memorial
at Pearl Harbor **1**
USS *Bowfin* Submarine Museum
& Park **1**
Waikiki Aquarium **22**

Oahu Cemetery. 2162 Nuuanu Ave. (north of Judd St.). ☎ **808/538-1538.** Free admission. Daily 7am–6pm. TheBUS: 4.

Not Hawaii's oldest cemetery nor even the biggest, this 150-year-old, 35-acre cemetery is a burying place in America's rural, monumental tradition—more a garden than a Golgotha. It holds the earthly remains of Honolulu's "Who's Who" of days gone by. Here lies Honolulu history: advisors to kings, sugar barons and sea captains, musicians and missionaries, all buried in a reclaimed taro patch on the outskirts of the mud-and-grass-thatch village they helped transform into the city of Honolulu. Under shade trees beside old carriage trails are Damons, Judds, and Thurstons, the missionaries who stayed on in the islands; and patriarchs of Hawaii's first foreign families, whose names now appear on buildings and street signs: Blaisdell, Dudoit, Farrington, Magoon, Stangewald, Wilder. Here, too, lies Alexander Joy Cartwright Jr., who some consider to be the real father of baseball; he chaired the committee that adopted the rules of play in 1845 and set base paths at 90 feet, and he umpired in the first official game in 1846. A few grave markers give sketchy details of death: a British sea captain spilled from his horse; a 9-year-old girl drowned off Kauai; a Boston missionary, the victim of consumption; an Army private killed while looking for a leper in Kalalau. It's all there, carved in stone, old obituaries and grim reminders of timeless mortality.

Queen Emma Summer Palace. 2913 Pali Hwy. (at Old Pali Rd.). ☎ **808/595-3167.** Admission $5 adults, $3 seniors, $1 children. Daily 9am–4pm. TheBUS: 4.

"Hanaiakamalama," the country estate of Queen Emma and Kamehameha IV, was once in the secluded uplands of Nuuanu Valley. Now it sits adjacent to a six-lane highway full of 60 miles-per-hour cars that sound remarkably—if oddly—like the surf as they zip by. This simple, six-room New England–style house, built in 1847 and restored by the Daughters of Hawaii, holds an interesting blend of Victorian furniture and hallmarks of Hawaiian royalty, including feather cloaks and *kahili*, those bushy totems that mark the presence of *alii* (royalty). Other royal treasures include a canoe-shaped cradle for Queen Emma's baby, Prince Albert, who died at the age of 4. (Kauai's ultraritzy Princeville Resort is named for the little prince.)

Royal Mausoleum. 2261 Nuuanu Ave. (between Wyllie and Judd sts.). ☎ **808/536-7602.** Free admission. Mon–Fri 8am–4:30pm. TheBUS: 4.

In the cool uplands of Nuuanu, on a 3.7-acre patch of sacred land dedicated in 1865—and never surrendered to America—stands the Royal Mausoleum, the final resting place of King Kalakaua, Queen Kapiolani, and 16 other Hawaiian royals. Only the Hawaiian flag flies over this grave, a remnant of the kingdom.

WARTIME HONOLULU

✪ **USS *Arizona* Memorial at Pearl Harbor.** Pearl Harbor. ☎ **808/422-0561.** Daily 7:30am–5pm (boat shuttles run 8am–3pm). Closed Thanksgiving, Christmas, and New Year's Day. Free admission. Children under 12 must be accompanied by an adult. You must wear shoes; no slippers allowed. Drive west on H-1 past the airport; take the USS *Arizona* Memorial exit, and follow the green-and-white signs; there's ample free parking. TheBUS: 20, or Arizona Memorial Shuttle Bus, which picks up at Waikiki hotels 6:50am–1pm ($6 round-trip); ☎ 808/839-0911.

On December 7, 1941, while moored in Pearl Harbor, the USS *Arizona* was bombed in a Japanese air raid. The 608-foot battleship sank in 9 minutes without firing a shot, taking 1,177 sailors and Marines to a fiery death—and plunging the United States into World War II.

Nobody who visits the memorial will ever forget it. The deck of the ship lies 6 feet below the surface of the sea. Oil still oozes slowly up from the Arizona's engine room to stain the harbor's calm blue water; some say the ship still weeps for its lost crew. The memorial is a stark white 184-foot rectangle that spans the sunken hull of the ship; it was designed by the late Alfred Pries, a German architect interned on Sand Island during the war. It contains the ship's bell, recovered from the wreckage, and a shrine room with the names of the dead carved in stone.

Today, free U.S. Navy launches take visitors to the *Arizona.* Try to arrive early at the Visitors Center, operated jointly by the National Park Service and the U.S. Navy, to avoid the huge crowds. Waits of 1 to 3 hours are common; no reservations are taken. While you're waiting for the shuttle to take you out to the ship—you'll be is-sued a number and time of departure, which you must pick up yourself—you can explore the arresting museum, with personal mementoes, photographs, and histori-cal documents. A 20-minute film precedes your trip to the ship. Allow at least 4 hours to visit the memorial. Shirts and shoes are required; no swimsuits or flip-flops are al-lowed (shorts are okay). Wheelchairs are gladly accommodated.

USS *Bowfin* Submarine Museum & Park. 11 Arizona Memorial Dr. (next to the USS *Arizona* Memorial at Pearl Harbor). ☎ **808/423-1342.** Fax 808/422-5201. E-mail: bowfin@ aloha.net. Admission $8 adults, $6 active duty military, $3 children 4–12. Daily 8am–5pm. Closed Thanks-giving, Christmas, and New Year's Day. Drive west on H-1 past the airport; take the USS *Arizona* Memorial exit, and follow the green-and-white signs; there's ample free parking. TheBUS: 20, or Arizona Memorial Shuttle Bus, which stops at Waikiki hotels 6:50am–1pm ($6 round-trip); ☎ 808/839-0911.

Next to the *Arizona* Memorial Visitor Center is the USS *Bowfin,* one of only 15 World War II submarines still in existence today. You can go below deck of this fa-mous submarine—nicknamed the "Pearl Harbor Avenger" for its successful retalia-tory attacks on the Japanese—and see how the 80-man crew lived during wartime. The *Bowfin* Museum has an impressive collection of submarine-related artifacts. The Waterfront Memorial honors submariners lost during World War II.

National Cemetery of the Pacific. Punchbowl Crater, 2177 Puowaina Dr. (at the end of the road). ☎ **808/541-1434.** Free admission. Daily 8am–5:30pm; Mar–Sept to 6:30pm. TheBUS: 15.

Go in the morning when the air is still and listen. Except for the occasional sob of a sad widow, Punchbowl is silent as a tomb.

The National Cemetery of the Pacific, as it's officially known, is an ash-and-lava tuff cone that exploded about 150,000 years ago—it's like Diamond Head, only smaller. Early Hawaiians called it Puowaina, or "hill of sacrifice." The old crater is a burial ground for 35,000 victims of three American wars in Asia and the Pacific: World War II, and the Korean and Vietnam wars. Among the graves you'll find many unmarked ones with the date December 7, 1941 carved in stone. Some will be un-known forever. Others are famous, like that of war correspondent Ernie Pyle, killed by a Japanese sniper in April of 1945 on Okinawa; still others buried here are remem-bered only by family and surviving buddies, now in their mid-70s. The Courts of The Missing, white stone tablets, bear the names of 28,788 Americans missing in action in World War II.

Survivors come here often to reflect on the meaning of war and remember those, like themselves, who stood in harm's way to win peace a half century ago. Some fight back tears, remembering lost buddies, lost missions, and the sacrifice of all who died in "the last good war."

3 Fish, Flora & Fauna

✪ **Foster Garden.** 50 N. Vineyard Blvd. (at Nuuanu Ave.). ☎ **808/522-7065.** Fax 808/ 522-7050. Admission $5 adults, $1 children 6–12. Daily 9am–4pm; guided tours Mon–Fri at 1pm. TheBUS: 2, 4, or 13.

A leafy oasis amid the high-rises of downtown Honolulu, this 14-acre garden on the north side of Chinatown was born in 1853 with a single tree planted by German physician and botanist William Hillenbrand on Royal land. Today, it's the showcase of 24 native Hawaiian trees and the last stand of several rare trees, including an East African whose white flowers only bloom at night. There are orchids galore, a primitive cycad garden, a palm collection, plus all kinds of spices and herbs.

Honolulu Zoo. 151 Kapahulu Ave. (between Paki and Kalakaua aves.), at the entrance to Kapiolani Park. ☎ **808/971-7171.** Fax 808/971-7173. E-mail: nordic@aol.com. Admission $6 adults, $1 children 6–12, when accompanied by an adult (if a child isn't with an adult, he or she pays adult fee; children under 6 are not allowed in without an adult). Daily 9am–4:30pm. TheBUS: 2, 8, 19, 20, or 47.

Nobody comes to Hawaii to see an Indian elephant, or African lions and zebras. Right? Wrong. This 43-acre municipal zoo in Waikiki attracts visitors in droves, who come to see the new African Savannah, a 10-acre wild preserve exhibit with more than 40 uncapped African critters roaming around in the open. The zoo, which now offers night walks—when the nocturnal beasties are out—also has a rare Hawaiian nene goose, a Hawaiian pig, and Mouflon sheep. (Only the goose, an evolved version of the Canadian honker, is considered to be truly Hawaiian; the others are imported from Polynesia, India, and elsewhere.)

For a real treat take the "Zoo by Moonlight" tour, which offers you a rare behind-the-scenes look into the lives of the zoo's nocturnal citizens. Tours are offered 2 days before, during, and 2 days after the full moon from 7pm to 9pm; the cost is $7 for adults and $5 for children.

Kapiolani Park. Bordered by Kalakaua Ave. on the ocean side, Monsarrat Ave. on the Ewa side, and Paki Ave. on the mountain side. TheBUS: 2.

In 1877 King David Kalakaua gave 130 acres of land to the people of Hawaii and named it after his beloved wife, Queen Kapiolani. This truly royal park has something for just about everyone: tennis courts, soccer and rugby fields, archery, picnic areas, wide open spaces for kite flying and frisbee throwing, and a jogging path with aerobic exercise stations. On Sundays in the summer, the Royal Hawaiian Band plays in the bandstand, just like they did during Kalakaua's reign. The Waikiki Shell, located in the park, is host to a variety of musical events from old Hawaiian songs to rock and roll.

Lyon Arboretum. 3860 Manoa Rd. (near the top of the road). ☎ **808/988-7378.** Fax 808/ 988-4231. $1 donation requested. Mon–Sat 9am–3pm. TheBUS: 5.

Six-story-tall breadfruit trees . . . yellow orchids no bigger than a bus token . . . ferns with fuzzy buds as big as a human head: Lyon Arboretum is 125 budding acres of botanical wonders. A whole different world opens up to you along the self-guided 20-minute hike through Lyon Arboretum to Inspiration Point. You'll pass more than 5,000 exotic tropical plants full of birdsong in this cultivated rain forest (a research facility that's part of the University of Hawaii) at the head of Manoa Valley.

Guided tours for serious plant lovers are offered one or two Saturdays a month. Led by a resident botanist, the tour may take up to 3 hours and focus on one species. Call ☎ **808/988-3177** for tour schedule and reservations.

○ **Waikiki Aquarium.** 2777 Kalakaua Ave. (across from Kapiolani Park). ☎ **808/923-9741.** Fax 808/923-1771. Admission $6 adults, $4 seniors and students, $2.50 children 13–17. Daily 9am–5pm. Closed Christmas Day. TheBUS: 19 or 20.

Behold the chambered Nautilus, nature's submarine and inspiration for Jules Verne's *20,000 Leagues Under the Sea.* You may see this tropical cephalopod mollusk with its many-chambered spiral shell any day of the week at the Waikiki Aquarium.

This tropical aquarium Diamond Head of Waikiki is worth a peek if only to see the only living Chambered Nautilus born in captivity. Its natural habitat is the deep waters of Micronesia; but Bruce Carlson, director of the aquarium, succeeded not only in trapping the pearly shell in 1,500 feet of water by dangling chunks of raw tuna, but also managed to breed this ancient relative of the octopus. The aquarium was also the first to successfully display the cuttlefish and Hawaii's own mahimahi.

There are plenty of other fish as well in this small but first-class aquarium, located on a live coral reef. Owned and operated by the University of Hawaii, the aquarium, after a $3 million upgrade, now features a Hawaiian reef habitat with sharks, eels, a touch tank, and habitats for the endangered Hawaiian monk seal and green sea turtle. Recently added: a rotating Biodiversity Special Exhibit featuring a look at the diversity of sea life and interactive exhibits focusing on corals and coral reefs.

IN NEARBY EAST OAHU

Sea Life Park. 41-202 Kalanianaole Hwy. (at Makapuu Point), Honolulu. ☎ **808/259-7933.** Admission $19.95 adults, $15.95 seniors 65 and over, $9.95 children 4–12, children under 4 free. Daily 9:30am–5pm, Fri to 10pm. TheBUS: 22 or 58.

This 62-acre ocean theme park is one of Oahu's main attractions. It features orca whales from Puget Sound, Atlantic bottle-nosed dolphins, California sea lions, and penguins going through their hoops to the delight of kids of all ages. There's a Hawaiian Reef Tank full of tropical fish, a "touch" pool where you can grab a real sea cucumber (commonly found in tide pools), and a Bird Sanctuary where you can see birds like the red-footed booby and Frigate bird that usually fly overhead. There's also a whaling museum that tells how New England whalers harpooned whales and made scrimshaw out of their bones. The chief curiosity, though, is the world's only "wolphin"—a cross between a false killer whale and an Atlantic bottle-nosed dolphin. On site, marine biologists from the National Marine Life Fisheries operate a recovery center for endangered marine life; during your visit, you'll be able to see the restored Hawaiian monk seals and seabirds.

4 Spectacular Views

Diamond Head. Diamond Head Rd. Daily 6am–6pm. To get there from Waikiki take Kalakaua Ave. toward Kapiolani Park. Turn left onto Monsarrat Ave. at the Park. Monsarrat Ave. is renamed Diamond Head Rd. after Campbell Ave. Continue on Diamond Head Rd. to turnoff to crater. Turn right into turnoff, follow to parking lot. TheBUS: 22 or 58

The 360-degree view from atop Diamond Head Crater is worth the 560-foot hike and is not to be missed. You can see all the way from the Koko Crater to Barbers Point and the Waianae Mountains. The 760-foot-tall volcano, which has become the symbol for Hawaii, is about 350,000 years old. The trail to the summit was built in 1910 to service the military installation along the crater, it's about a 30-minute hike, but quite manageable by anyone of any age.

Diamond Head has always been considered a "sacred sight" by Hawaiians. According to legend Hi'iaka, the sister to the volcano goddess Pele, named the mountain

Leahi (meaning the brow of the ahi) when she saw the resemblance to the yellow fin tuna (called "ahi" in Hawaiian).

Kamehameha the Great built a "luakini heiau" on the top where human sacrifices were made to the god of war, Ku.

The name Diamond Head came in to use around 1825 when a group of British sailors (some say they were slightly inebriated) found some rocks sparkling in the sun. Absolutely sure they were rich, the sailors brought these "diamonds" back into Honolulu. Alas, the "diamonds" turned out to be calcite crystals. The sailors didn't become fabulously rich, but the name Diamond Head stuck.

Lanikai Beach. Mokulua Dr., Kailua. To get there from Honolulu, take Hi. 61 (Pali Hwy.) into Kailua. Follow the street (which becomes Kailua Rd., then becomes Kuulei Rd.) until it ends. Turn right on Kalaheo Ave. (which will be renamed in a few blocks to Kwawiloa Rd.). Follow the road over the canal. At the stop sign turn left on Kaneapu Pl. At the fork in the road, bear left on the one-way Aalapapa Dr. Turn right at any cross street onto Mokulua Dr. No bus service.

This is one of the best places on Oahu to greet the sunrise. Watch the sky slowly move from pitch black to wisps of gray to burnt orange as the sun begins to rise over the two tiny offshore islands of Mokulua. This is a five sense experience: birds singing, gentle breezes on your face, the taste of salt in the air, the smell of the ocean, the sand and the fragrant flowers near by, and the kaleidoscopic colors as another day dawns.

✪ Nuuanu Pali Lookout. Near the summit of Pali Hwy. (Hi. 61). To get there directly from downtown Honolulu, turn left off Nimitz Hwy. (Hi. 92) onto Nuuanu Ave. or Bishop St. Follow it to Pali Hwy., which will take you to the Lookout. No bus service.

Sometimes gale-force winds howl through the mountain pass at this 1,186-foot-high perch guarded by 3,000-foot peaks, so hold on to your hat—and small children. But if you walk up from the parking lot to the precipice, you'll be rewarded with a view that'll blow you away—no pun intended. At the edge, the dizzying panorama of Oahu's windward side is breathtaking: clouds low enough to pinch scoot by on trade winds; pinnacles of the *pali* (cliffs), green with ferns, often disappear in the mist. From on high, the tropical palette of green and blue runs down to the sea. Definitely take a jacket with you. On very windy days the water in the waterfalls, blown by the wind, looks as if it is flowing uphill.

This road up to the Lookout dates back to 1898 when John Wilson built it using 200 laborers. Before the road, the Nuuanu Pali (which translates as cool heights) was infamous for the legend of Kamehameha the Great's last battle. Although some academic scholars scoff at this, the story alleges that Kamehameha pursued Oahu's warriors up Nuuanu to these cliffs and waged a battle to unite the Hawaiian islands in 1795. The Oahu defenders supposedly were driven over the cliffs by Kamehameha's warriors. Some say the battle never happened, some say it happened but there were just a few men fighting, some say there were thousands who were forced over the side to their deaths. And still others say, at night, you can still hear the cries of these long dead warriors coming from the valley below.

Puu O Mahuka Heiau. One mile past Waimea Bay; take Pupukea Rd. mauka off Kamehameha Hwy. at Foodland, and drive $^7/_{10}$ of a mile up a switchback road. TheBUS: 52 and walk up Pupukea Rd.

Once the largest sacrificial temple on Oahu, today Puu O Mahuka Heiau is a National Historical Landmark. Located on a 300-foot bluff, the heiau encompasses some 5 acres. People still come here to pray—you may see offerings such as ti-leaves, flowers, and fruit left at the Heiau. Don't disturb the offerings or walk on the stones (it's very disrespectful). The view from this 300-foot bluff is awe-inspiring: from Waimea Bay all the way to Kaena Point.

Go around sundown to feel the *mana* of this sacred Hawaiian place. The construction of the site is attributed to the *menehune* (the legendary small people who accomplished amazing building feats). Chiefesses were sent here to give birth. But the largest sacrificial temple on Oahu, became infamous with the great kahuna Kaopulupulu, who sought peace between Oahu and Kauai. The prescient *kuhuna* predicted that the island would be overrun by strangers from a distant land. In 1794, three of Capt. George Vancouver's men of the *Daedalus* supposedly were sacrificed here. In 1819, the year before New England missionaries landed in Hawaii, King Kamehameha II ordered all idols at the heiau to be destroyed.

From this 18th-century heiau overlooking Waimea Bay, you can see 25 miles of Oahu's wave-lashed north coast—all the way to Kaena Point, where the Waianae Range ends in a spirit leap to the other world. The heiau appears as a huge rectangle of rocks twice as big as a football field (170 feet by 575 feet), with an altar often covered by the flower and fruit offerings left by native Hawaiians.

✪ **Puu Ualakaa State Park.** Round Hill Dr. To get there from H-1 Freeway take Punahou St. exit (Exit 23). Turn left on Punahou. Make a left onto Wilder Ave. Turn right on Makaki St. When the road forks, bear left onto Round Top Dr. The park entrance is 2¹/₂ miles up Round Top from Makaki. Once in the park it is a half mile to the lookout. No bus service.

Don't miss the sweeping panoramic views from this 1,048-foot hill, which extend from Diamond Head across Waikiki and downtown Honolulu, over the airport and Pearl City, all the way to the Waianae Range. There are great photo opportunities during the day, romantic sunset views in the evening, and starry skies at night. Puu Ualakaa translates into "rolling sweet potato hill," which was how the early Hawaiians harvested the crop. The park gates open at 7am and close at 6:45pm (7:45pm in the summer).

5 More Museums

Aliiolani Hale. 417 S. King St. (between Bishop and Punchbowl sts.). ☎ **808/539-4999.** Fax 808/539-4996. Free admission. Mon–Fri 10am–3pm; reservations for group tours only. TheBUS: 1, 2, 3, 4, 8, 11, or 12.

Don't be surprised if this place looks familiar; you probably saw it on "Magnum P.I." or "Hawaii Five-O." Hollywood always uses it as the Honolulu Police Station, although the made-for-TV movie *Blood and Orchids* correctly used it as the courthouse where Clarence Darrow defended the perpetrators in the famed Massie case in 1931. This gingerbread Italianate, designed by Australian Thomas Rowe in Renaissance Revival–style, was built in 1874 and was originally intended to be a palace. Instead, Aliiolani Hale ("House of Kings" in Hawaiian) became the Supreme Court and Parliament government office building.

Aliiolani Hale operates a **Judiciary History Center,** open Monday through Friday from 10am to 3pm. The Center, located on the ground floor of the building, is free and features a multimedia presentation, a restored historic courtroom, and exhibits tracing Hawaii's transition from Hawaiian law (pre-western contact) to western law.

Contemporary Museum. Spalding Estate, 2411 Makiki Heights Dr. ☎ **808/526-0232.** Admission adults $5; senior citizens and students, $3; children free. The third Thursday of each month is free. Ask about their daily docent-led tours. Tues–Sat 10am–4pm, Sun noon–4pm. From Waikiki take Kalakaua Ave. to Beretania. Make a left on Beretania and go 1 block to Makaki. Turn right on Makaki and follow it up the hills. Make a left on Makiki Heights Dr. and wind around the hills to the museum. TheBUS: 15.

Housed in an old kamaaina estate in one of Honolulu's most prestigious residential communities, the Contemporary Museum remains a peerless cultural resource

Especially for Kids

Shop the Aloha Flea Market *(see p. 242)*   Most kids hate to shop. But the Aloha Flea Market, a giant outdoor bazaar at Aloha Stadium on Wednesday, Saturday, and Sunday, is more than shopping: It's an experience akin to a carnival, full of strange food, odd goods, and bold barkers. Nobody ever leaves this place empty-handed—or without having had lots of fun.

Explore the Bishop Museum *(see p. 202)*   There are some 1,180,000 Polynesian artifacts; 13,500,000 different insect specimens; 6,000,000 marine and land shells; 490,000 plant specimens; 130,000 fish specimens; 85,000 birds and mammals all in the Bishop Museum. Kids can explore interactive exhibits, see a 50-foot sperm whale skeleton, and check out a Hawaii grass hut. There's something for everyone here.

Walk Through a Submarine *(see p. 207)*   The USS *Bowfin* Submarine Museum Park offers kids an interactive museum to experience a real submarine that served in some of the fiercest naval battles in World War II. Kids can explore the interior of the tightly packed submarine that housed some 90 to 100 men, and see the stacked shelves where they slept, the radar and electronics in the command center, and the storage place of the torpedoes.

Dream at the Hawaii Maritime Center *(see p. 218)*   Kids will love the Kalakaua Boathouse, the two-story museum of the Maritime Center. Exhibits include the development of surfing, the art of tattooing, and the artifacts from the whaling industry. Next door is the fully-rigged, four-masted *Falls of Clyde*. Built in 1878, this vessel served as a cargo and passenger liner and a sailing tanker before being declared a National Historic Landmark; it is permanently docked as a museum. If

in Hawaii. TCM, as it's called, is renowned for several features: its $3^{1}/_{2}$ acres of Oriental gardens with reflecting pools, sun-drenched terraces, views of Diamond Head, and stone benches for quiet contemplation; the Cades Pavilion, housing David Hockney's *L'Enfant et les Sortileges,* an environmental installation of his sets and costumes for Ravel's 1925 opera; six galleries representing significant work and artists of the last four decades; and its excellent cafe and gift shop. Equally prominent is the presence of contemporary Hawaii artists in the museum's programs and exhibitions.

Honolulu Academy of Arts. 900 S. Beretania St. (between Victoria St. and Ward Ave.). ☎ 808/532-8701. Admission $5 per adult, with discounts for seniors and military personnel. Tues–Sat 10am–4:30pm, Sun 1–5pm. TheBUS: 1, 2.

The Honolulu Academy of Arts claims one of the finest Asian art collections in the country, as well as an acclaimed collection of American and European masters and prehistoric works that include Mayan, Greek, and Hawaiian art. Special exhibitions and annual events have received international recognition. The Moorish structure is a paragon of graciousness, with curved, tiled roof lines, open courtyards and lily ponds, and wide hallways leading to sensitively organized galleries. The Academy's setting, art collections, Garden Cafe, gift shop, and theater make this a must for any resident or visitor.

Damien Museum. 130 Ohua St. (between Kuhio and Kalakaua aves., behind St. Augustine's Catholic Church, on Kalakaua Ave.). ☎ 808/923-2690. Donations accepted. Mon–Fri 9am–3pm, Sat 9am–noon. Closed holidays. TheBUS: 8, 19, or 20.

it's not out sailing, moored next to the *Falls* is the *Hokule'a,* the re-creation of a traditional double-hulled sailing canoe, which in 1976 made the 6,000-mile round-trip voyage to Tahiti using only ancient navigation techniques—the stars, the wind, and the sea.

Watch the Fish and Sharks at the Waikiki Aquarium *(see p. 209)* Much more than just a big fish tank, the Waikiki Aquarium will astound and at the same time educate your youngsters. They can probably sit for hours staring at the sharks, turtles, eels, rays, and fish swimming in the main tank. For a few laughs, wander out to the monk seal area and watch the antics of these sea-going clowns.

Snorkel in Hanauma Bay *(see p. 229)* Kids will be enthralled with the teeming tropical fish and the underwater world at this marine park. The shallow waters near the beach are perfect for neophyte snorkelers to learn in. The long (2,000-foot) beach has plenty of room for kids to take off and run on. Get there early; it can get very crowded.

Hike to the top of Diamond Head Crater *(see p. 209)* The entire family can make this easy 1.4-mile round trip walk to the top of the 750-foot volcanic cone with its rewarding view of Oahu. Bring a flashlight for the entry tunnel and a camera for the view.

Explore the Depths in a Submarine Dive *(see p. 179)* Better than a movie, more exciting than a video game, the Atlantis or Voyager Submarines journey down to 100 feet below the waves and explore the Neptunian world of tropical reef fish, huge oceangoing pelagics, and even an occasional shark or two.

This is a tiny museum about a large subject in Hawaii's history: Father Damien's work with leprosy victims on the island of Molokai. The museum contains prayer books used by Father Damien in his ministry as well as his personal items. Don't miss the award-winning video on Damien's story.

Pacific Aerospace Museum. In the Central Waiting Lobby, Honolulu International Airport, 300 Rodgers Blvd., Honolulu, HI 96819. ☎ **808/839-0767.** Fax 808/836-3267. Admission $3 adults; $2.50 children 6–12, military, and students; children under 5 free. Daily 9am–6pm. TheBUS: 19 or 20.

While you're waiting for your flight to depart, check out the history of flight in the Pacific at this $3.8 million shrine to flying. You can trace elapsed time and distance of all direct flights from Honolulu on a 6-foot globe using fiber optics; watch old film clips of NASA astronauts splashing down in Hawaiian waters after landing on the moon; see models of early planes and flying boats (including a life-size replica of the Flight Deck of the space shuttle *Challenger*), and hear the heroic stories of the aviators who pioneered sky routes to the islands and beyond.

U.S. Army Museum. Fort DeRussy Park. ☎ **808/955-9552.** Free admission. Tues–Sun 10am–4:30pm. TheBUS: 8.

This museum was built in 1909 and used in defense of Honolulu and Pearl Harbor. Inside are military memorabilia ranging from ancient Hawaiian warfare to the hi-tech munitions of present day. On the upper deck, the Corps of Engineers Pacific Regional Visitors Center graphically shows how the corps works with the civilian community in managing water resources in an island environment.

WALKING TOUR:
Historic Chinatown

Chinese laborers from the Guangdong Province first came to work on Hawaii's sugar and pineapple plantations in the 1850s. Once their plantation contracts were completed, a few of the ambitious ones started up small shops and restaurants in the area around River Street. At the time, the community wasn't much—mainly a handful of dirt streets—but it was in a good location, close to the docks and the newly developing businesses around Iolani Palace in downtown Honolulu.

Chinatown reached its peak in the 1930s. In the days before air travel to the islands, visitors arrived by cruise ship, and they often headed straight for the exotic shops and restaurants of Chinatown. In the 1940s, military personnel on leave flocked to Chinatown looking for excitement in the form of pool halls, beer parlors, tattoo joints, and houses of ill-repute. Over the years Chinatown deteriorated into a tawdry red-light district with seedy bars, drug dealing, and homeless people, but it has recently undergone extensive urban renewal. There's still just enough sleaze on the fringes (a few peep shows and topless bars) to keep it from being a novelty tourist attraction.

Today Chinatown is a jumble of streets that come alive every day with bustling residents and visitors from all over the world; a cacophony of sounds, from the high-pitched bleating of vendors in the open market to the lyrical dialects of the retired men talking story over a game of mahjong; and a combination of brilliant reds, blues, and greens trimming buildings and goods everywhere you look. This isn't quite Hawaii, but it's not really a microcosm of China, either—rather, what you'll find is a mix of Asian cultures.

Getting There: From Waikiki, take TheBUS no. 2 or 20 toward downtown; get off on North Hotel Street (after Maunakea Street). If you're driving, take Ala Moana Boulevard and turn right on Smith Street; make a left on Beretania Street and a left again at Maunakea Street. The City parking garage (50¢ per hour) is located on the Ewa (west) side of Maunakea Street, between North Hotel and North King streets.
Start: North Hotel and Maunakea streets.
Finish: Same intersection.
Time: Approximately 1 to 2 hours, depending on how much time you spend browsing.
Best Times: Daylight hours.

   Start your walk on the Ewa (west) side of Maunakea Street at:

1. **Hotel Street.** During World War II, Hotel Street was synonymous with "good times." Pool halls and beer parlors lined the blocks and prostitutes were plentiful. Today the nefarious establishments have been replaced with small shops, from art galleries to specialty boutiques, and urban professionals; and recent immigrants now walk where the sailors once roamed, looking for bargains.

   Once you're done wandering through the shops, head back to the intersection with Maunakea Street. Turn right on Maunakea; proceed to the corner of King Street and the:

2. **Bank of Hawaii.** At King and Maunakea streets sits this very unusual-looking bank; not the conservative edifice you'd expect, but one guarded by two fire-breathing dragon statues.

   Continue down King Street. As you go, you'll pass the shops of various Chinese herbalists, such as the:

3. **Viet Hoa Chinese Herb Shop,** 162 N. King St. Chinese herbalists act as both doctors and dispensers of herbs. Patients come in and tell the herbalist what ails them; the herbalist then decides which of the myriad herbs he'll mix together.

Walking Tour: Historic Chinatown

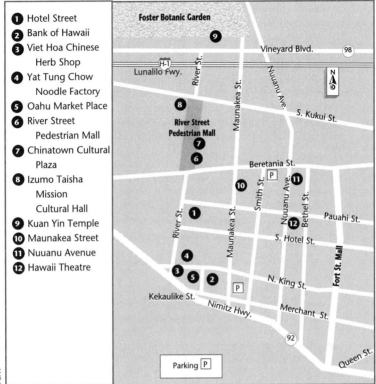

1. Hotel Street
2. Bank of Hawaii
3. Viet Hoa Chinese Herb Shop
4. Yat Tung Chow Noodle Factory
5. Oahu Market Place
6. River Street Pedestrian Mall
7. Chinatown Cultural Plaza
8. Izumo Taisha Mission Cultural Hall
9. Kuan Yin Temple
10. Maunakea Street
11. Nuuanu Avenue
12. Hawaii Theatre

Usually there's a wall of tiny drawers all labeled in Chinese characters; the herbalist pulls various ground, powdered, and dried things from the drawers that range from dried flowers and ground-up roots to such exotics as mashed antelope antler. The patient then takes the concoction home to brew into a strong tea.

Another interesting shop on North King Street is the:

4. **Yat Tung Chow Noodle Factory,** 150 N. King St. The delicious, delicate noodles that star in numerous Asian dishes are made here, ranging from threadlike noodles (literally no thicker than embroidery thread) to fat, wide udon noodles. There aren't any tours of the factory, but you can look through the window, past the white cloud of flour that hangs in the air, and watch as dough is fed into rollers at one end of the noodle machines, and perfectly cut noodles emerge at the other end.

On the Ewa side of Kekaulike Street, on King Street, lies the most visited part of Chinatown, the open-air market known as:

5. **Oahu Market Place.** If you're interested in Asian cooking, you'll find everything you could possibly want here, including pig's heads, poultry (some still squawking), fresh octopus, salted jellyfish, pungent fish sauce, fresh herbs, and thousand-year-old eggs. The friendly vendors are happy to explain their wares and give instructions on how to prepare these exotic treats. The market is divided into meats, poultry, fish, vegetables, and fruits. Past the open market are several grocery stores with fresh produce on display on the sidewalk. You're bound to spot some varieties here that you're not used to seeing at your local supermarket.

Follow King down to River Street and turn right toward the mountains and the:

6. River Street Pedestrian Mall. A range of inexpensive restaurants line River Street from King Street to Beretania Street. You can get the best Vietnamese and Filipino food in town in these blocks, but go early—lines for lunch start at 11:15am. At Beretania Street, River Street ends and the pedestrian mall begins with the **statue of Chinese revolutionary leader Sun Yat-Sen.** The wide mall, which borders the Nuuanu Stream, is lined with shade trees, park benches, and tables where senior citizens gather to play mahjong and checkers. Plenty of take-out restaurants are nearby if you'd like to eat outdoors.

Along the River Street Mall, extending nearly a block over to Maunakea Street, is the:

7. Chinatown Cultural Plaza. This modern complex is filled with shops featuring everything from tailors to calligraphers (most somewhat more expensive than their street-side counterparts), as well as numerous restaurants—a great idea, but in reality people seem to prefer wandering Chinatown's crowded streets to venturing into a modern mall. The plaza does have one excellent feature, though: In the center is the **Moongate Stage,** the site of many cultural presentations, especially around Chinese New Year.

Continue up the River Street Mall and cross the Nuuanu Stream via the bridge at Kukui Street, which will bring you to:

8. Izumo Taisha Mission Cultural Hall. This small wooden Shinto shrine, built in 1923, houses a male deity (look for the X-shaped crosses on the top). Members of the faith ring the bell out front as an act of purification when they come to pray. Inside the temple is a 100-pound sack of rice, symbolizing good health. During World War II, the shrine was confiscated by the city of Honolulu and wasn't returned to the congregation until 1962.

If temples are of interest to you, walk 1 block toward the mountains to Vineyard Boulevard; cross back over Nuuanu Stream, past the entrance of Foster Botanical Gardens, to:

9. Kuan Yin Temple. This Buddhist temple, painted in a brilliant red with a green ceramic-tiled roof, is dedicated to Kuan Yin Bodhisattva, the goddess of mercy, whose statue towers in the prayer hall. The piquant aroma of burning incense is your clue that the temple is still a house of worship, not an exhibit, so enter with respect and leave your shoes outside. You may see people burning paper "money," which is for prosperity and good luck, or leaving flowers and fruits at the altar (also gifts to the goddess). A frequent offering is the *pomelo,* a grapefruit-like fruit that's a fertility symbol as well as a gift indicating a request for the blessing of children.

Continue down Vineyard the turn left toward the ocean on:

10. Maunakea Street. Between Beretania and King streets are numerous lei shops (with lei makers working away right on the premises) on both sides of the street. The air is heavy with the aroma of flowers being woven into beautiful treasures. Not only is this the best place in all of Hawaii to get a deal on leis, but the size, color, and design of the leis made here are exceptional. Wander through all the shops before you decide which lei you want.

If you have a sweet tooth, stop in at **Shung Chong Yuein,** 1027 Maunakea St. (near Hotel Street), for delicious Asian pastries like moon cakes and almond cookies, all at very reasonable prices. They also have a wide selection of dried and sugared candies (like ginger, pineapple, lotus root) that you can eat as you stroll, or give as an exotic gift to friends back home.

Turn up Hotel Street in the Diamond Head direction, and walk to:

11. Nuuanu Avenue. You may notice that the sidewalks on Nuuanu Avenue are made of granite blocks; they came from the ballast of ships that came from China to Hawaii in the 1800s. On the corner of Nuuanu Avenue and Hotel Street is the **Chinatown Police Station,** located in the Perry Block building. Built in 1888, it looks like something straight out of a film noir.

Across the street from the Police Station is the **Lai Fong Department Store,** a classic Chinatown store owned by the same family for more than three-quarters of a century. Walking into Lai Fong is like stepping back in time. The old store sells everything from precious antiques to god-awful knickknacks to rare turn-of-the-century Hawaiian postcards—but it has built its reputation on the fabulous selection of Chinese silks and brocades and custom dresses it carries.

Between Hotel and Pauahi streets is the **Pegge Hooper Gallery,** 1164 Nuuanu Ave., where you can admire Pegge's well-known paintings of beautiful Hawaiian women.

At Pauahi Street, turn toward Diamond Head and walk up to Bethel Street and the:

12. Hawaii Theatre. This restored 1920 art deco theater is a work of art in itself. It hosts a variety of programs, from the Hawaii International Film Festival to beauty pageants (see "Oahu After Dark," in chapter 11, for details on how to find out what's on while you're in town).

Walk toward the ocean on Bethel Street and turn right on Hotel Street, which will lead you back to where you started.

WALKING TOUR
Honolulu Waterfront

For a walk into Honolulu's past from the days when Polynesians first came to Hawaii, take this leisurely stroll along the waterfront and the surrounding environs.

Until about 1800, the area around Honolulu Harbor (from Nuuanu Avenue to Alakea Street and from Hotel Street to the ocean) was known as Koa. Some scholars say it was named after a dedicated officer to Chief Kakuhihewa of Oahu; others say it comes from the kou tree, which flourishes in this area. In 1793, Captain William Brown, on the British frigate *Butterworth,* sailed the first foreign ship into Honolulu harbor. Like most British explorers, he didn't bother asking the name of the harbor and just renamed the area. He called it Fair Haven. Other ships that followed started to call the harbor "Brown's Harbor." Luckily the name the Hawaiians gave the harbor, Honolulu, which translates into "sheltered bay," became the popular name.

The waterfront area played a vital role in the history of Honolulu. King Kamehameha I moved his royal court here in 1809 to keep an eye on the burgeoning trade from the numerous ships that were coming here. The royal residence was at the makai end of Bethel Street, just 1 block from the start of our tour at the Aloha Tower.

Getting There: From Waikiki take Ala Moana Boulevard in the Ewa direction. When Ala Moana ends turn left on Nimitz Highway. There is parking on the ocean side of Nimitz at Bishop Street. TheBUS: 19 or 20.

Start: Aloha Tower, ocean end of Fort Street Mall at Pier 9.

Finish: Waterfront Plaza and Restaurant Row, Punchbowl Street / Ala Moana Boulevard.

Time: About 1 to 2 hours, depending on how long you linger in museums and shops.

Best Time: Daylight, when Hawaii Maritime Museum is open (8:30am to 5pm daily).

Park in the parking lot on Bishop Street and Nimitz Highway and walk over to Pier 9.

1. Aloha Tower. One of the reasons that the word aloha is symbolic with Hawaii today is the Aloha Tower. Built in 1926 (for the then-outrageous sum of $160,000), this 184-foot, 10 story tower (until 1959 the tallest structure in Hawaii) has clocks on all four sides of the monolith and the word "aloha" under each clock. Aloha, which has come to mean the greeting of hello and farewell, was the first thing that passengers of steamships saw when they entered the Honolulu Harbor. In the days when tourists arrived by steamer, "boat days" were a very big occasion. The Royal Hawaiian band would be on hand to play, crowds would gather, flower leis were freely given, and Honolulu came to a standstill to greet the visitors.

Go up the elevator inside the Aloha Tower to the 10th floor observation deck for a bird's-eye view from Diamond Head and Waikiki to the downtown and Chinatown area and the harbor coastline to the airport. On the ocean side you can see the harbor mouth, Sand Island, the Honolulu reef runway, and the Pearl Harbor entrance channel.

No charge to see the view; the Aloha Tower is open Sunday through Wednesday, 9am to 6pm and Thursday through Saturday 9am to 10pm.

2. Aloha Tower Marketplace. In the early 1990s the city fathers had the great idea to renovate and restore the waterfront with shops, restaurants, and bars to bring back that feeling of the "boat days." Eventually this area will be fabulous, but now it is in a transition area with everything from video games and carnival rides on one side to upscale shops and restaurants on the other. There seems to be a temporary cash flow problem, and the developers have "temporarily" rented space to the carny rides and video people to stay afloat. The shops, restaurants, and bars inside the two-story Aloha Marketplace offer an array of cuisines, one-of-a-kind shops, and even a microbrewery. Most shops open at 9am daily and the restaurants and bars don't shut down until the wee hours of the morning.

From the Aloha Tower Marketplace walk in the Diamond Head direction along the waterfront to the Maritime Museum on Pier 7.

3. Hawaii Maritime Center, which is composed of three entities: the museum in the **Kalakaua Boathouse,** the *Falls of Clyde,* the four-masted ship moored next door and the *Hokule'a,* the 60-foot Polynesian sailing canoe, also moored at Pier 7.

The Kalakaua Boathouse is filled with relics from the past, exhibits of Hawaii's maritime history, and an auditorium with videos of Hawaii's seagoing culture.

When you enter the two-story Boathouse, stop to look at the glass case of trophies and artifacts from the days when the boathouse really did belong to King David Kalakaua. Don't miss the great exhibits on whaling, the history of surfing in the islands, and the cultural art of tattooing; there's also a reproduction of a Matson Liner stateroom.

4. *Falls of Clyde.* The world's only remaining fully rigged, four-masted ship is on display as a National Historic Landmark. Still afloat, the 266-foot, iron-hulled ship was built in 1878 in Glasgow, Scotland. Matson Navigation bought the ship in 1899 to carry sugar and passengers between Hilo and San Francisco. When that become economically unfeasible, in 1906 the boat was converted into a sail-driven oil tanker. After 1920, it was dismantled and became a floating oil depot for fishing boats in Alaska.

Walking Tour: Honolulu Waterfront

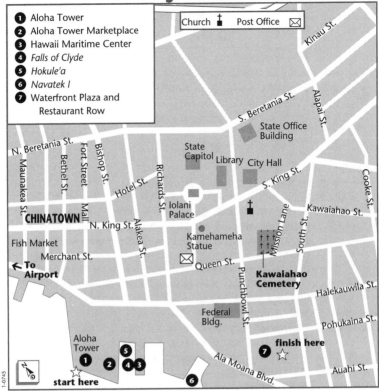

1. Aloha Tower
2. Aloha Tower Marketplace
3. Hawaii Maritime Center
4. *Falls of Clyde*
5. *Hokule'a*
6. *Navatek I*
7. Waterfront Plaza and Restaurant Row

Church   Post Office

Kinau St.

S. Beretania St.

Alapai St.

N. Beretania St.

State Office Building

State Capitol   Library   City Hall

Fort Street

Bethel St.

Bishop St.

Hotel St.

Richards St.

Cooke St.

S. King St.

Kawaiahao St.

Maunakea St.

Mall

CHINATOWN

N. King St.

Alakea St.

Iolani Palace

Kamehameha Statue

Mission Lane

South St.

Fish Market

Merchant St.

Queen St.

Kawaiahao Cemetery

← To Airport

Halekauwila St.

Federal Bldg.

Punchbowl St.

Pohukaina St.

Aloha Tower

5

finish here

7 ☆

1

2

4 3

Ala Moana Blvd.

Auahi St.

start here

6

She was headed for the scrap pile when a group of Hawaii residents raised the money to bring her back to Hawaii in 1963. Eventually she was totally restored and visitors can wander across her decks and through the cargo area below.

5. ***Hokule'a.*** When it is in town, it will be moored next to *Falls of Clyde,* but the 60-foot Polynesian sailing canoe is often out on jaunts. This reproduction of the traditional double-hulled sailing canoe proved to the world in 1976 that Polynesians could have made the 6,000-mile round-trip from Tahiti to Hawaii, navigating only by the stars and the wave patterns. Living on an open deck (9 feet wide by 40 feet long), the crew of a dozen, along with a traditional navigator from an island in the Northern Pacific, made the successful voyage. Since then there has been a renaissance in the Pacific among native islanders to relearn this art of navigation.

6. ***Navatek I.*** From ancient Polynesian sailing canoes to today's high-tech, on Pier 6 is the latest in naval engineering, the 140-foot-long *Navatek I* isn't even called a boat; it's actually a SWATH (Small Waterplane Area Twin Hull) vessel. That means the ship's superstructure—the part you ride on—rests on twin torpedolike hulls that cut through the water so you don't bob like a cork and spill your Mai Tai. It's the smoothest ride in town and guarantees you will not get seasick.

From Pier 6 walk down Ala Moana Boulevard and turn mauka at Punchbowl.

7. **Waterfront Plaza and Restaurant Row.** Eateries from gourmet Hawaiian regional cuisine to burgers, shops, and theaters fill this block-long complex. This is a great place to stop for lunch or dinner or for a cool drink at the end of your walk.

WALKING TOUR
Historic Honolulu

The 1800s were a turbulent time in Hawaii's history. By the end of the 1790s Kamehameha the Great had united all of the islands. Then foreigners began arriving by ship—first explorers, then merchants, and in 1820, missionaries. The rulers of Hawaii were hard-pressed to keep up. By 1840 it was clear that the capital had shifted from Lahaina, where the Kingdom of Hawaii was centered, to Honolulu where the majority of commerce and trade was taking place. In 1848, the Great Mahele (division) enabled commoners and eventually foreigners to own crown land. In two generations more than 80% of all private lands had shifted to foreign ownership. With the introduction of sugar, foreigners prospered and in time they put more and more pressure on the government.

The monarchy had run through the Kamehameha line by 1872, and in 1873 David Kalakaua was elected to the throne. Known as the "Merrie Monarch," Kalakaua redefined the monarchy by going on a world tour, building Iolani Palace, having a European-style coronation, and throwing extravagant parties. By the close of the 1800s, however, the foreign sugar growers and merchants had become extremely powerful. With the assistance of the U.S. Marines, they orchestrated the overthrown of Queen Liliuokalani, Hawaii's last reigning monarch, in 1893. The United States declared Hawaii a territory in 1898.

You can witness these turbulent years in just a few short blocks in Honolulu.

Getting There: From Waikiki take Ala Moana Boulevard in the Ewa direction. Ala Moana Boulevard ends at Nimitz Highway. Turn right on the next street on your right (Alakea Street). Park in the parking garage across from St. Andrews Church after you cross Beretania Street. TheBUS: 1, 2, 3, 4, 11, 12, or 50.
Start: St. Andrew's Church, Beretania/Alakea streets
Finish: Same place
Time: 2 to 3 hours depending on how long you linger in museums
Best Times: Wednesday through Saturday daytime when the Iolani Palace has tours

Cross the street from the church parking lot and venture back to 1858 when you enter:

1. **St. Andrew's Church.** The Hawaiian monarchs were greatly influenced by the royals in Europe. When King Kamehameha IV saw the grandeur of the Church of England, he decided to build his own cathedral. He and Queen Emma founded the Anglican Church of Hawaii in 1858. However, he didn't live to see the church completed; he died on St. Andrew's Day, 4 years before King Kamehemeha V oversaw the laying of the cornerstone in 1867. The church was named St. Andrew's in honor of King Kamehameha IV's death. This French-Gothic structure was shipped in pieces from England and reassembled here. Even if you aren't a fan of visiting churches, you have to see the floor-to-eaves hand-blown stained-glass window that faces the setting sun. In the glass is a mural of Reverend Thomas Staley, the first bishop in Hawaii; King Kamehameha IV; and Queen Emma. There also is an excellent thrift shop on the grounds with some real bargains, open Monday, Wednesday, and Friday 9:30am to 4pm and Saturday 9am to 1pm.

Next walk down Beretania Street in the Diamond Head direction to the gates of the:

2. **Washington Place.** Today this is the residence of the Governor of Hawaii (sorry, no tours; just peek through the iron fence), but it occupies a distinguished place in Hawaii's history. Originally the colonial-style home was built by a U.S.

Walking Tour: Historic Honolulu

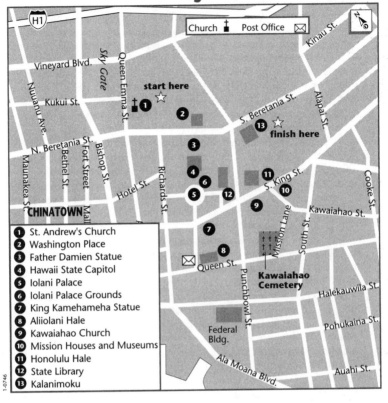

Church † Post Office ⊠

CHINATOWN

1 St. Andrew's Church
2 Washington Place
3 Father Damien Statue
4 Hawaii State Capitol
5 Iolani Palace
6 Iolani Palace Grounds
7 King Kamehameha Statue
8 Aliiolani Hale
9 Kawaiahao Church
10 Mission Houses and Museums
11 Honolulu Hale
12 State Library
13 Kalanimoku

start here
finish here

Kawaiahao Cemetery
Federal Bldg.

sea captain named John Dominis. The sea captain's son, also named John, married a beautiful Hawaiian princess, Lydia Kapaakea, who later became Hawaii's last queen, Liliuokalani. When the Queen was overthrown by U.S. businessmen in 1893, she moved out of Iolani Palace and into her husband's inherited home, Washington Place, where she lived until her death in 1917. On the left side of the building, near the sidewalk, is a plaque inscribed with the words to one of the most popular songs written by Queen Liliuokalani, *Aloha Oe* (Farewell to Thee).

Cross the street and walk to the statue in front of the Hawaii State Capitol.

3. Father Damien Statue. The people of Hawaii have never forgotten the sacrifice this Belgian priest made to help the sufferers of leprosy when he volunteered to work with them in exile on the Kalaupapa Peninsula on the island of Molokai. After 16 years of service, Father Damien died of leprosy, at the age of 49. Frequently the statue is draped in leis in recognition of Father Damien's humanitarian work.

4. Hawaii State Capitol. Behind Father Damien's statue is the building where Hawaii's state legislators work from mid-January to the end of April every year. This is not your typical white dome structure, but a building symbolic of Hawaii. Unfortunately it symbolizes more of Hawaii than the architect and the state legislature probably bargained for. The building's unusual design has palm tree–shaped pillars, two cone-shaped chambers (representing volcanoes) for the legislative bodies, and in the inner courtyard, a 600,000-tile mosaic of the sea (Aquarius) created by a local artist. A reflecting pool (representing the sea) surrounds the entire structure. Like a lot of things in Hawaii it was a great idea, but no one considered the logistics. The reflecting pond also draws brackish water, which rusts the hardware; when it rains, water pours into the rotunda, dampening government business; and the Aquarius floor mosaic became so damaged by the elements it became a hazard. The entire building shut down for a couple of years (forcing the legislature to set up temporary quarters in several buildings) while the entire building (built in 1969) had to be redone in the early 1990s. It's open again and you are welcome to go into the rotunda and see the woven hangings and murals at the entrance, or take the elevator up to the fifth floor for a spectacular view of the city's historical center.

Walk down Richards Street toward the ocean and stop at Honolulu's palace.

5. Iolani Palace. Hawaii is the only state in the union to have not one, but two royal palaces; one is in Kona where the royals went during the summer, and the second is the Iolani Palace (Iolani means royal hawk). Don't miss the opportunity to see this grande dame of historic buildings. You must book in advance; tours are limited (Wednesday through Saturday, 9am to 2pm; admission $8 adults, $3 children 5 to 13) and very popular.

In ancient times this area was a heiau. When it became clear to King Kamehameha III that the capital should be transferred from Lahaina to Honolulu, he moved to a modest building here in 1845. The construction of the palace began in 1879 by King David Kalakaua and was finished 3 years later at a cost of $350,000 (a fortune in those days). The king spared no expense: You can still see the glass and iron work imported from San Francisco. The palace had all the modern conveniences for its time: electric lights were installed 4 years before the White House in Washington, D.C., had them; every bedroom had its own full bath with hot and cold running water and copper-lined tubs, flush toilet, and a bidet. The king had a telephone line from the palace down to his boathouse on the water a year after Alexander Graham Bell introduced it to the world.

It was also in this palace that Queen Liliuokalani was overthrown and placed under house arrest for 9 months. The territorial, and later the state government, used the palace until it outgrew it. When the legislature left in 1968, the palace was in shambles and has since undergone a $7 million overhaul to restore it to its former glory. Tours are Wednesday through Saturday; call ☎ **808/522-0832** in advance for a reservation.

6. Iolani Palace Grounds. You can wander around the grounds at no charge and visit the Hawaii of yesteryear. The ticket window to the palace and the gift shop are in the former barracks of the Royal Household Guards. The domed pavilion on the grounds was originally built as a Coronation Stand by King David Kalakaua (9 years after he took the throne, he decided to have a formal European-style coronation ceremony where he crowned himself and his queen, Kapiolani). Later he used it as a Royal Bandstand for concerts (King Kalakaua, along with Herni Berger, the first Royal Hawaiian Bandmaster, wrote "Hawaii Pono'i," the state anthem). Today the Royal Bandstand is still used for concerts by the Royal Hawaiian Band. The more modern building on the grounds is the State Archives, built in 1953, which hold records, documents, and photos of Hawaii's people and its history.

From the Palace, walk makai to King Street, and cross the street to the:

7. King Kamehameha Statue. At the juncture of King, Merchant, and Mililani streets is this replica of the man who united all of the Hawaiian Islands. The striking black and gold bronze statue is magnificent. The best day to see the statue is on June 11 (King Kamehmeha Day), when it is covered with leis in honor of Hawaii's favorite son.

The statue of Kamehameha I was cast by Thomas Gould in 1880 in Paris. However, it was lost at sea around the Falkland Islands, so the insurance money was used to pay for a second statue. The original statue was then recovered and sent to the town of Kapaau on the Big Island, the birthplace of Kamehameha. The second statue was placed in Honolulu in 1883, as part of King David Kalakaua's coronation ceremony, and a third statue (all said to be from the same mold, but all are very different) now stands in Washington, D.C., erected when Hawaii became a state in 1959.

8. Aliiolani Hale. Behind the Kamehameha statue is Aliiolani Hale (House of Heavenly Kings), the distinctive building with a clock tower, which now houses the State Judiciary Building. King Kamehameha V originally wanted to build a palace here and commissioned the Australian architect Thomas Rowe in 1872. However, it ended up as the first major government building for the Hawaiian monarchy. Kamehameha V didn't live to see it completed, and King David Kalakaua dedicated the building in 1874. Ironically, less than 20 years later, on January 17, 1893, Stanford Dole, backed by other prominent sugar planters, stood on the steps to this building and proclaimed the overthrow of the Hawaiian monarchy and the establishment of a provisional government.

Tours Tuesday through Thursday, 10am to 3pm, no charge.

Walk toward Diamond Head on King Street; at the corner of King and Punchbowl, stop in at the church that played a big role in Hawaii's history.

9. Kawaiahao Church. When the missionaries came to Hawaii, the first thing they did was build churches. The thatched grass shacks that were the first churches on this site (one measured 54 feet by 22 feet and could seat 300 people on lauhala mats; the last thatched church held 4,500 people) were not what the Rev. Hiram Bingham had in mind.

Four thatched grass churches had been built through 1837 when the good reverend finally got his wish and began building a "real" church, a New England–style congregational church with Gothic influences. Between 1837 and 1842, the building of the church required some 14,000 giant coral slabs (some weighing more than 1,000 pounds). Hawaiian divers literally raped the reefs, digging out huge chunks of coral in the reefs, causing irreparable environmental damage.

Hawaii's oldest church, Kawaiahao was the scene of numerous historical events such as a speech made by King Kamehameha III in 1843, an excerpt from which become Hawaii's state motto ("Ua mau ke ea o ka aina i ka pono," which translates as "The life of the land is preserved in righteousness.")

The clock tower in the church, which was donated by King Kamehameha III and installed in 1850, continues to tick today. The church is open Monday through Saturday, from 8am to 4pm; you'll find it to be very cool in temperature. Don't sit in the pews in the back, marked with kahili feathers and velvet cushions; they are still reserved for the descendants of royalty. Sunday service (in Hawaiian) 10:30am.

10. Mission Houses and Museums. Across the street from Kawaiahao Church on the corner of King and Kawaiahao streets are the original buildings of the Sandwich Islands Mission Headquarters: the **Frame House** (built in 1821), the **Chamberlain House** (1831), and the **Printing Office** (1841). The complex is open Tuesday through Saturday from 9am to 4pm; admission is $6 adults, $5 seniors, $3 college students, $2 children. The tours are often lead by descendants of the original missionaries to Hawaii.

Believe it or not, the missionaries brought their own prefab house along with them when they came from Boston around Cape Horn to Hawaii in 1819. The structure was designed for New England winters with small windows (it must have been stifling hot inside). Finished in 1921 (the interior frame was left behind and didn't arrive until Christmas 1920), it is Hawaii's oldest wooden structure.

The Chamberlain House, built in 1931, was the storehouse for the missionaries; back in the 1800s you could buy a gallon of oil for 25 cents. The missionaries felt the best way to spread the message was to learn the Hawaiian language and then to print literature for the Hawaiians to read. So it was the missionaries who gave the Hawaiians a written language. The Printing House on the grounds was where the lead-type Ramage press (brought from New England, of course) printed the Hawaiian Bible.

Cross King Street and walk in the Ewa direction to the corner of Punchbowl and King.

11. Honolulu Hale. The Honolulu City Hall, built in 1927, was designed by Honolulu's most famous architect, C. W. Dickey. His Spanish mission–style building has an open-air courtyard, which is used for art exhibits and concerts. Open weekdays.

Cross Punchbowl Street and walk mauka to the:

12. State Library. Anything you want to know about Hawaii and the Pacific can be found here, the main branch of the state's library system. Located in a restored historic building, there is an open-air garden courtyard in the middle of the building, great for stopping for a rest on your walk.

Head mauka up Punchbowl to the corner of Punchbowl and Beretania streets.

13. Kalanimoku. This beautiful name, Ship of Heaven, has been given to this dour state office building. Here you can get information on hiking and camping (from the Department of Land and Natural Resources) in state parks.

Retrace your steps in the Ewa direction down Beretania to Alakea to the parking garage.

WALKING TOUR
Kapiolani Park

On June 11, 1877, King Kamehameha Day, then-King David Kalakaua donated some 140 acres of land to the people of Hawaii for Hawaii's first park. He asked that the park be named after his beloved wife, Queen Kapiolani, and celebrated the opening of this vast grassy area with a free band concert and "high stakes" horse races (the king loved gambling) on the new horse-racing oval he had built below Diamond Head.

At the turn of the century a wave of antigambling sentiment and the temperance movement led to the outlawing of horse races, but the park—and the free band concerts—have lived on. Just a coconut's throw from the high-rise concrete jungle of Waikiki lies this now-133-acre park (the Paki playground and fire station used up the remaining acreages) of grassy lawns dotted with spreading banyans, huge monkeypod trees, blooming royal poincianas, and swaying ironwoods. Among the open spaces are jogging paths, tennis courts, soccer fields, cricket fields, even an archery range. People come to the park to listen to music, watch ethnic dancing, exercise, enjoy team sports, take long meditative walks, picnic, buy art, smell the roses, and just plain veg out. The park is the site of international kite-flying contests, the finishing line for the Honolulu marathon,

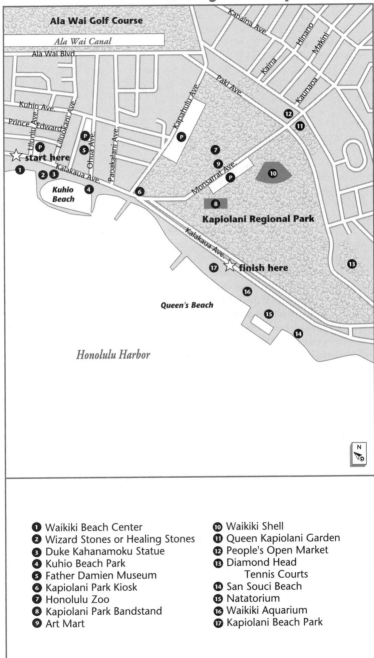

1 Waikiki Beach Center
2 Wizard Stones or Healing Stones
3 Duke Kahanamoku Statue
4 Kuhio Beach Park
5 Father Damien Museum
6 Kapiolani Park Kiosk
7 Honolulu Zoo
8 Kapiolani Park Bandstand
9 Art Mart
10 Waikiki Shell
11 Queen Kapiolani Garden
12 People's Open Market
13 Diamond Head
      Tennis Courts
14 San Souci Beach
15 Natatorium
16 Waikiki Aquarium
17 Kapiolani Beach Park

and the home of yearly Scottish highland games, Hawaiian cultural festivals, and about a zillion barbecues and picnics every year.

Getting There: From Waikiki walk toward Diamond Head on Kalakaua Avenue. If you are coming by car, the cheapest parking is metered street parking on Kalakaua Avenue adjacent to the park. TheBUS: 19 or 20.

Start: Waikiki Beach Center, Kalakaua Avenue, Diamond Head side of the Sheraton Moana Hotel, across the street from the Hyatt Regency and Uluniu Avenue.

Finish: Kapiolani Beach Park.

Time: 4 to 5 hours, allow at least an hour each for walking around the Park, wandering around the Zoo, reviewing the Aquarium, and snapping photos at the Kodak Hula Show, plus all the time you want for the beach.

Best Time: Tuesday to Thursday mornings if you want to catch the Kodak Hula Show.

1. **Waikiki Beach Center,** on the ocean side of Kalakaua Avenue, next to the Sheraton Moana Hotel is a complex of rest rooms, showers, surfboard lockers, and rental concessions, which includes the Waikiki police substation.

2. **Wizard Stones or Healing Stones,** on the Diamond Head side of the police substation are four basalt boulders, weighing several tons apiece, sitting on a lava rock platform, surrounded by plants and framed by a fancy wrought-iron fence. This sanctuary holds four stones held sacred by the Hawaiian people.

   Sometime before the 15th century, four powerful healers from Moaulanuiakea, in the Society Islands, named Kapaemahu, Kahaloa, Kapuni, and Kihohi, lived in the Ulukoa area of Waikiki. After years of healing the people and the alii of Oahu, they wanted to return home. They asked the people to erect four monuments made from bell stone, a basalt rock that was in a Kaimuki quarry and produced a bell-like ringing when struck. The healers then spent a month in ceremony transferring their spiritual healing power, or their mana, into the stones. The great mystery is how the boulders were transported from Kaimuki to the marshland near Kuhio Beach in Waikiki! The stones eventually became buried beneath a Waikiki bowling alley built on the spot. After the bowling alley was torn down in the 1960s, tourists used the stones to eat lunch on or to drape their wet towels over. In 1997 the stones were once again given a place of prominence with the construction of the $75,000 shrine that now surrounds them. Since then the stones have become something of a mecca for students and patients of traditional healing.

3. **Duke Kahanamoku Statue,** just west of the stones is the bronze statue of Hawaii's most famous athlete, the man known as the father of modern surfing. Duke (1890–1968) won Olympic swimming medals in 1912, 1920, 1924, and 1928. He was enshrined in both the Swimming Hall of Fame and the Surfing Hall of Fame. He also traveled around the globe promoting surfing. Interestingly, when the city of Honolulu first erected the statue of this lifelong water man they placed it with his back to the ocean. There was public outcry—no one familiar with the ocean would ever stand with his back to the ocean. The city moved the statue closer to the sidewalk to appease the outcry.

4. **Kuhio Beach Park.** Diamond Head of the statue are two small swimming holes in the ocean, the Kuhio Beach Park, named after Prince Kuhio, who actually lived in this area. His house was finally torn down in 1936 to expand the beach area. These pools are great for swimming; just heed the warning sign WATCH OUT FOR HOLES. There actually are deep holes in the sandy bottom, where you may suddenly find yourself in very deep water. The best pool for swimming is the one in the Diamond Head end, but the circulation of the water is questionable—there

sometimes appears to be a layer of suntan lotion floating on the surface. If the waves are up, watch the boogie boarders surfing by the sea wall. They ride right towards the wall and at the last minute veer away with a swoosh. After watching the surfers, cross Kalakaua Avenue and walk mauka down Ohua Avenue, behind St. Augustine's Church and you'll find the:

5. **Father Damien Museum.** This small museum is a tribute to the priest who worked with the sufferers of leprosy on Molokai. Open Monday through Friday from 9am to 3pm, and Saturday from 9am to noon; admission is free. After spending some time watching the video of Father Damien and the leprosy colony and wandering around the museum, go back to Kalakaua Avenue and walk towards Diamond Head to the entrance of Kapiolani Park.

6. **Kapiolani Park Kiosk,** at the corner of Kalakaua and Kapahulu avenues, is a small display stand that contains brochures and actual photos of the history of the park and information on upcoming events at the various sites within the park (Aquarium, Zoo, Waikiki Shell, Kodak Hula Show, and Kapiolani Bandstand). A very informative map will help to orient you to the park grounds. Continue up Kapahulu Avenue to the entrance of the:

7. **Honolulu Zoo.** The city's 42-acre zoo is open every day from 9am to 4:30pm, but the best time to go is as soon as the gates open—the animals seem to be more active and it is a lot cooler than walking around midday in the hot sun.

    You can walk or ride the tram to view the animals from around the globe, stopping at the new African Savannah, a 10-acre wild preserve exhibit with more than 40 uncaged African critters (including lions, cheetahs, white rhinos, giraffes, zebras, hippos, and monkeys) roaming around in the open. There's also a petting zoo of various farm animals for kids, an aviary for Hawaii's rapidly disappearing native birds, and a very interesting collection of Hawaii's native plants. Admission is $6 adults, $1 children 6 to 12 when accompanied by an adult (if a child isn't with an adult, he or she pays adult fee; children under 6 are not allowed in without an adult).

    For a real treat take the "Zoo by Moonlight" tour, which allows you a rare behind-the-scenes look into the lives of the zoo's nocturnal citizens. Tours are offered 2 days before, during, and 2 days after the full moon from 7pm to 9pm; the cost is $7 for adults and $5 for children. Trace your steps back to Kapahulu and Kalakaua avenues and head mauka down Monsarrat Avenue to the:

8. **Kapiolani Park Bandstand,** where, on the mauka side of the Bandstand, the **Kodak Hula Show** has been presenting the hula for visitors since 1937 (and a few of the senior ladies in the show have been dancing since the show started). Some 3,000 people fit into the bleachers around a grassy stage area (with the sun to your back for perfect picture taking). If you forget your camera or run out of film, Kodak has cameras for rent and plenty of film for sale. For a good seat, get there by 8am; to get into the show, be there no later than 9am. Once the show starts, they will only admit people between acts. The show is nonstop entertainment with hula dancers, bedecked in ti-leaf skirts and flower leis, swaying to an assortment of rhythms. The grand finale consists of all the dancers lining up on the stage and spelling out A-L-O-H-A and H-A-W-A-I-I with placards, so save plenty of film to shoot everyone's favorite postcard. The performances are Tuesday through Thursday, 10am to 11:15am, and are free.

9. **Art Mart,** across Monsarrat Avenue, on the fence fronting the Honolulu Zoo, provides an opportunity to get some of the best deals on local art. The Art Mart, or the new official name, Artists of Oahu Exhibit, is where local artisans come and

actually hang their work on the fence for the public to view and buy. Not only do you get to meet the artists, but you have an opportunity to buy artwork at a considerable discount from the prices in galleries. Exhibits are Saturday, Sunday, and Wednesday, 10am to 4pm.

Back across Monsarrat Avenue, you'll find the:

10. Waikiki Shell. Mauka of the Kodak Hula Show is the open-air amphitheater that hosts numerous musical shows from the Honolulu Symphony to traditional Hawaiian music.

Now walk down to the end of the block to the corner of Monsarrat and Paki avenues to:

11. Queen Kapiolani Garden. You'll see a range of hibiscus plants and dozens of varieties of roses, including the somewhat rare Hawaiian rose. The tranquil gardens are always open and are a great place to wander and relax.

Across the street on a Wednesday morning, you'll find the:

12. People's Open Market. Open from 10am to 11am, the farmer's market with its open stalls will prove an excellent spot to buy fresh produce and flowers. After you make your purchases, continue in the Diamond Head direction down Paki Avenue to the:

13. Diamond Head Tennis Courts. Located on the mauka side of Paki Avenue, the free City and County tennis courts open for play during daylight hours 7 days a week. Tennis etiquette suggests that if someone is waiting for a court, limit your play to 45 minutes. After watching or playing, turn onto Kalakaua Avenue and begin the walk back to Waikiki.

Continue on Kalakaua Avenue back toward Waikiki to:

14. San Souci Beach. Next to the New Otani Kaimana Beach Hotel, this is one of the best swimming beaches in Waikiki. The shallow reef close to shore keeps the waters calm and protected from waves. Further out there is good snorkeling in the coral reef by the Kapua Channel. Facilities include outdoor showers and a lifeguard. After a brief swim, keep walking toward Waikiki until you come to the:

15. Natatorium. This huge concrete structure by the beach is both a memorial to the soldiers in World War I and a 100-meter saltwater swimming pool. Opened in 1927, when Honolulu had hopes of hosting the Olympics, the ornate swimming pool fell into disuse and disrepair after World War II, and was finally closed in 1979. After about 2 decades of the state and the City and County of Honolulu arguing about what to do with the Natatorium, the Mayor of Honolulu released some $11.5 million in 1997 to rebuild the seawalls, renovate the men's and women's locker rooms, and bring the pool back to its former glory. The plans call for the pool to reopen in 1998 with a small fee (estimated $2) for swimmers. There are proposals to use the Natatorium as a training facility for police and firefighters, a venue for swimming programs for children, and perhaps evening water shows for visitors. After a brief stop here, continue on to the:

16. Waikiki Aquarium, located at 2777 Kalakaua Ave. Try not to miss this stop— the tropical aquarium is worth a peek if merely to see the only living Chambered Nautilus born in captivity. Its natural habitat is the deep waters of Micronesia; but Bruce Carlson, director of the aquarium, succeeded not only in trapping the pearly shell in 1,500 feet of water by dangling chunks of raw tuna, but also managed to breed this ancient relative of the octopus. The aquarium was also the first to successfully display the cuttlefish and Hawaii's favorite food fish, the mahimahi. There are plenty of other fish as well in this small but first-class aquarium, located at the edge of a live coral reef. Owned and operated by the University of Hawaii, the aquarium, after a $3 million upgrade, now features a Hawaiian reef habitat with sharks, eels, a touch tank, and habitats for the endangered Hawaiian monk seal and green sea turtles. Recently added: a rotating Biodiversity Special Exhibit featuring a look at the diversity of sea life and interactive exhibits focusing on corals and coral reefs. Admission $6 adults, $4 seniors and students, $2.50 children 13 to 17. Daily 9am to 5pm. Closed Christmas Day.

17. **Kapiolani Beach Park** is your final stop. Relax on the stretch of grassy lawn alongside the sandy beach, one of the best-kept secrets of Waikiki. This beach park is much less crowded than the beaches of Waikiki, plus it has adjacent grassy lawns, barbecue areas, picnic tables, rest rooms, and showers. The swimming is good here year-round, offshore is a surfing spot known as "Public's," and there's always a game going at the volleyball courts. The middle section of the beach park, in front of the pavilion, is known as Queen's Beach, or Queen's Surf, and is popular with the gay community.

6 Beyond Honolulu: Exploring the Island

The moment always arrives—usually after 2 or 3 days at the beach, snorkeling in the warm blue-green waters of Hanauma Bay, enjoying sundown Mai Tais, listening to the mellifluous tones of Sonny Kamahele and the Sunset Serenaders at the Halekulani—when a certain curiosity kicks in about the rest of Oahu, largely unknown to most visitors. It's time to find the rental car in the hotel garage and set out around the island. If you don't have a car, you can explore the island via TheBUS. There are two buses that "circle the island": no. 52, which goes around the island clockwise, and no. 55, which goes around the island counterclockwise. Both run about every 30 minutes. However, be aware that at Turtle Bay Hilton, just outside of Kahuku, the no. 52 becomes the no. 55 and returns to Honolulu via the coast, and the no. 55 becomes the no. 52 and returns to Honolulu on the inland route. Translation: You have to get off and switch buses to complete your island tour, which takes about 4 hours, not including stops. If there is one specific area you want to go to, there are express buses to certain destinations (no. 54 to Pearl City; no. 46 to Kailua-Kaneohe; and nos. 57 and 58 to Sea Life Park); Call **TheBUS** for more information at ☎ **808/848-5555.**

For great places to stop for a bite to eat while you're exploring, see "Oahu Dining," in chapter 7. You also might want to check out "Shopping," in chapter 10.

OAHU'S SOUTHEAST COAST

Some head immediately to the North Shore, but you might want to go south because, believe it or not, you'll get out of town faster. Once you clear suburban Hawaii Kai and the Kalanianaole Highway (Hi. 72), head uphill to Hanauma Bay; you're on one of the last unspoiled coasts on Oahu. It's a great little getaway, especially if you spin around the south coast and loop back to town on the Pali Highway (Hi. 61).

Around **Koko Head,** Oahu looks like Arizona-by-the-sea; it's an arid moonscape with prickly pears and, in winter, spouting whales cavorting in the water. Some call it the south shore, others "Sandy's," after the mile-long beach here, but Hawaiians call it **Ka Iwi,** which means "the bone"—no doubt because of all the bone-cracking shore break along this popular bodyboarding coastline. The beaches here are long, wide, and popular with local daredevils.

This open, scenic coast is the best place on Oahu to watch sea, shore, and even land birds. It's also a good whale-watching spot in season, and the night sky is ideal for amateur astronomers to watch meteors, comets, and stars.

The jagged lava coast itself spouts sea foam at the ✪ **Halona Blowhole.** Look out to sea from Halona over Sandy Beach and across the 26-mile gulf to neighboring Molokai, and the faint triangular shadow of Lanai on the far horizon. **Sandy Beach** (see "Beaches," in chapter 8) is Oahu's most dangerous beach; it's the only one with an ambulance always standing by to whisk injured wave catchers to the hospital. Bodyboarders just love it.

The coast looks raw and empty along this stretch, but the road weaves past old Hawaiian fishponds and past the famous formation known as **Pele's Chair,** just off Kalanianaole Highway (Hi. 72) above Queen's Beach. From a distance, the lava-rock outcropping looks like a mighty throne; it's believed to be the fire goddess's last resting place on Oahu before she flew off to continue her work on other islands.

Ahead lies 647-foot-high **Makapuu Point,** with a lighthouse that once signaled safe passage for arriving steamship passengers from San Francisco. The automated light now brightens Oahu's south coast for passing tankers, fishing boats, and sailors. You can take a short hike up here for a spectacular vista.

If you're with the kids, you may want to spend the day at **Sea Life Park,** a marine amusement park; see "Fish, Flora & Fauna" above.

Turn the corner at Makapuu and you're on Oahu's windward side, where cooling trade winds propel windsurfers across turquoise bays and the waves at **Makapuu Beach Park** are perfect for bodysurfing. For more details, see "Beaches," in chapter 8.

Ahead, the coastal vista is a profusion of fluted green mountains and strange peaks, edged by golden beaches and the blue, blue Pacific. The 3,000-foot-high sheer green Koolau Mountains plunge almost straight down, presenting an irresistible jumping-off spot for hang-glider pilots, who catch the thermals on hours-long rides.

Winding up the coast, Kalanianaole Highway (Hi. 72) leads through rural **Waimanalo,** a country beach town of nurseries and stables, fresh fruit stands, and some of the island's best conch and triton shell specimens at roadside stands. Nearly 4 miles long, **Waimanalo Beach** is Oahu's longest beach, and the most popular for bodysurfing. Take a swim here or head on to **Kailua Beach,** one of Hawaii's best beaches (see "The Windward Coast," above, and "Beaches," in chapter 8).

If it's still early in the day, you can head up the lush, green Windward Coast by turning right at the Castle Junction, Hi. 72, and Hi. 61 (which is also Kailua Road on the makai side of the junction, Kalanianaole Highway on the mauka side of the junction), and continue down Kailua Road (Hi. 61). After Kailua Road crosses the Kaelepulu Stream, the name of the road changes to Kuulei Road. When Kuulei Road ends, turn left on to Kalaheo Avenue. After Kalaheo Avenue crosses the Kawainui Channel, the name of the road changes to Kaneohe Bay Drive. Follow this scenic drive around the peninsula until it joints the junction of Kaneohe Bay Drive and Kamehameha Highway (Hi. 83). Turn right and continue on Kamehameha Highway for a scenic drive along the ocean

If you're in a hurry to get back to Waikiki, turn left at Castle Junction and head over the Pali Highway (Hi. 61), which becomes Bishop Street in Honolulu and ends at Ala Moana. Turn left for Waikiki; it's the second beach on the right.

THE WINDWARD COAST

From the **Nuuanu Pali Lookout,** near the summit of Pali Highway (Hi. 61), you get the first hint of the other side of Oahu, a region so green and lovely that it could be an island sibling of Tahiti or Moorea. With many beaches and bays, the scenic 30-mile Windward Coast parallels the corduroy-ridged, nearly perpendicular cliffs of

Eastern Oahu & The Windward Coast

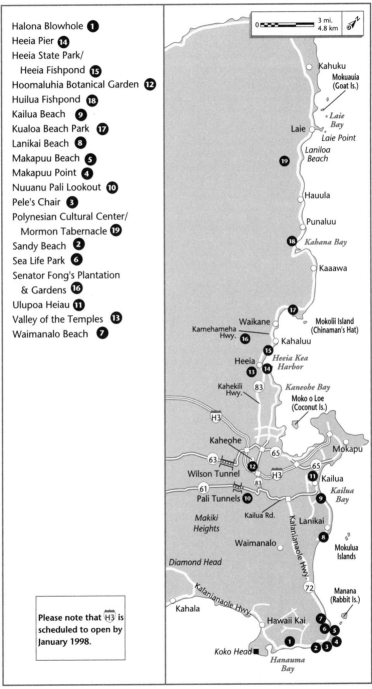

0   3 mi.
     4.8 km

Kahuku
Mokuauia
(Goat Is.)

Laie Bay

Laie   Laie Point

Laniloa Beach
19

Hauula

Punaluu

18   *Kahana Bay*

Kaaawa

Waikane   **17**   Mokolii Island
Kamehameha   (Chinaman's Hat)
Hwy.   **16** Kahaluu
       15
Heeia **13** **14** *Heeia Kea Harbor*
Kahekili
Hwy.   83   *Kaneohe Bay*
                Moko o Loe
                (Coconut Is.)
H3
Kaheohe   Mokapu
       12
63   65
Wilson Tunnel   H3   65   **11** Kailua
       61   83
Pali Tunnels **10**   **9** *Kailua Bay*
*Makiki   Kailua Rd.
Heights*
                Lanikai
       Waimanalo
                    8   Mokulua
Diamond Head   Islands

Kalanianaole Hwy.   Manana
                      72   (Rabbit Is.)
Kahala   **7**
              Hawaii Kai **6** **5**
                       1   **4**
Please note that H3 is   **2** **3**
scheduled to open by Koko Head *Hanauma Bay*
January 1998.

1-0712

231

the Koolau Range, which separates the windward side of the island from Honolulu and the rest of Oahu.

From the Pali Highway, to the right is **Kailua,** Hawaii's biggest beach town, with more than 50,000 residents and two special beaches, **Kailua** and **Lanikai,** begging for visitors (for more details, see "Beaches," in chapter 8). Funky little Kailua is lined with $1 million houses next to tar-paper shacks, antique shops, and bed-and-breakfasts. Although the Pali Highway (Hi. 61) proceeds directly to the coast, it undergoes two name changes, becoming first Kalanianaole Highway—from the intersection of Kamehameha Highway (Hi. 83)—and then Kailua Road as it heads into Kailua town—the road remains Hi. 61 the whole way. Kailua Road ends at the T-intersection at Kalaheo Drive, which follows the coast in a northerly and southerly direction. Turn right on South Kalaheo Drive to get to Kailua Beach Park and Lanikai Beach. No signs point the way, but you can't miss them.

If you spend a day at the beach here, stick around for sunset, when the sun sinks behind the Koolau Range and tints the clouds pink and orange. After a hard day at the beach you work up an appetite and Kailua has several great, inexpensive restaurants (see "Oahu Dining," in chapter 7). And don't forget to stop by the Agnes Portuguese Bake Shop, **A Panadaria** (35 Kainehe, Rm. 108, Kailua ☎ **808/ 262-5367**). Don't go snorkeling after eating two or three of these weighty treats, or you'll sink to the bottom.

As you descend on the serpentine Pali Highway beneath often-gushing waterfalls, you'll see the nearly 1,000-foot spike of **Olomana,** the bold pinnacle that always reminds us of that mountain in *Close Encounters,* and beyond, the Hawaiian village of **Waimanalo.** If you want to skip the beaches this time, turn left on North Kalaheo Drive, which becomes Kaneohe Bay Drive as it skirts Kaneohe Bay and leads back to Kamehameha Highway (Hi. 83), which then passes through **Kaneohe.** The suburban maze of Kaneohe is one giant strip mall of retail excess that mars one of the Pacific's most picturesque bays. After clearing this obstacle, the place begins to look like Hawaii again.

Incredibly scenic **Kaneohe Bay** is spiked with islets, and lined with gold-sand beach parks like **Kualoa,** a favorite picnic spot (see "Beaches," in chapter 8). The bay has a barrier reef and four tiny islets, one of which is known as **Moku o loe,** or Coconut Island. Don't be surprised if it looks familiar—it appeared in "Gilligan's Island." It's now the United States' only tropical marine research laboratory on a coral reef.

Little poly-vowelled beach towns like **Kahaluu, Kaaawa, Punaluu,** and **Hauula** pop up along the coast, offering passersby shell shops and art galleries to explore. Famed hula photographer Kim Taylor Reece lives on this coast; his gallery at 53-866 Kamehameha Hwy., near Sacred Falls (☎ **808/293-2000**), is open Sunday through Tuesday, from 10am to 6pm. There are also working cattle ranches, fisherman's wharves, and roadside fruit and flower stands vending ice-cold coconuts (to drink) and tree-ripened mangoes, papayas, and apple bananas.

At **Heeia State Park** (☎ **808/247-3156**) is **Heeia Fishpond,** which ancient Hawaiians built by enclosing natural bays with rocks to trap fish on the incoming tide. Heeia Fishpond is now being restored. The 88-acre fishpond, made of lava rock, which had four watchtowers to observe fish movement and several sluice gates along the 5,000-foot-long wall, is now in the process of being restored.

Stop by the **Heeia Pier,** which juts onto Kaneohe Bay. You can take a snorkel cruise here, or sail out to a sandbar in the middle of the bay for an incredible view of Oahu that most people, even those who live here, never see. If it's Tuesday through Saturday between 7am and 6pm, stop in and see Ernie Choy at the **Deli on Heeia Kea Pier** (☎ **808/235-2192**). Ernie Choy has served fishermen, sailors, and kayakers the beach town's best omelets, plate lunches, and loco mocos at reasonable prices since 1979.

Everyone calls it Chinaman's Hat, but the tiny island off the eastern shore of Kualoa Regional Park is really **Mokolii.** It's a sacred *puu honua,* or place of refuge, like the restored Puu Honua Honaunau on the Big Island of Hawaii. Excavations have unearthed evidence that this area was the home of ancient *alii* (royalty). Early Hawaiians believed the island of Mokolii (or "fin of the lizard") is all that remains of a *mo'o,* or lizard, slain by Pele's sister, Hiiaka, and hurled into the sea. At low tide, you can swim out to the island, but keep watch on the changing tide, which can sweep you out to sea. The islet has a small sandy beach and is a bird preserve, so don't spook the red-footed boobies.

Farther along, on the east side Kahana Bay by Kamehameha Highway, is **Huilua Fishpond.** This National Historic Landmark is one of Windward Oahu's most beautiful fishponds and the easiest to see. Once fed by a freshwater spring and refreshed by the ocean, this pond proved ideal for raising mullet and milk fish.

Sugar, once the sole industry of this region, is gone. But **Kahuku,** the former sugar plantation town, has new life as a small aquaculture community with prawn and clam farms that supply island restaurants.

From here, continue along Kamehameha Highway (Hi. 83) to the North Shore.

ATTRACTIONS ALONG THE WINDWARD COAST

Hoomaluhia Botanical Gardens. 45-680 Luluku Rd., Kaneohe. ☎ **808/233-7323.** Free admission. Daily 9am–4pm. From Honolulu, take H-1 to the Pali Hwy. (Hi. 61); turn left on Kamehameha Hwy. (Hi. 83); at the fourth light, turn left onto Luluku Rd. TheBUS: 55 or 56 will stop on Kamehameha Hwy.; you'll have a 1^{1}/2-mile walk to the Visitors Center.

This 400-acre botanical garden at the foot of the steepled Koolau Mountains is the perfect place for a *mauka* picnic. Its name means "a peaceful refuge." That's exactly what the Army Corps of Engineers created when they installed a flood-control project here, which resulted in a 32-acre freshwater lake and the garden. Just unfold a beach mat, lay back, and watch the clouds race across the rippled cliffs of the majestic Koolau Range. It's one of few public places on Oahu that provides a close-up view of the steepled cliffs. The park has hiking trails, and—best of all—the island's only free inland campground. (See "Oahu's Campgrounds & Wilderness Cabins," in chapter 6.) Guided nature hikes start at 10am Saturdays and 1pm Sunday from the Visitors Center.

Valley of the Temples. 47-200 Kahekili Hwy. (across the street from Temple Valley Shopping Center), Kaneohe. ☎ **808/239-8811.** Admission $2 adults, $1 children under 12, and seniors 65 and older. Daily 8:30am–4:30pm. From Honolulu, take the H-1 to the Likelike Fwy. (Hi. 63); after the Wilson Tunnel, get in the right lane and take the Kahekili Hwy. (Hi. 63); at the sixth traffic light is the entrance to the cemetery (on the left). TheBUS: 65.

The people of Honolulu bury their pets and their grandparents in this graveyard. Awhile back, Ferdinand Marcos, the exiled Filipino dictator, was also here; he occupied a temporary mausoleum until the Philippines relented and let him be buried in his native land. Marcos may be gone now, but dogs and cats and a lot of local folks remain. In a cleft of the pali, the graveyard is stalked by wild peacocks and about 700 curious people a day, who pay to see the 9-foot meditation Buddha, 2 acres of ponds full of more than 10,000 Japanese Koi (carp), and a replica of Japan's 900-year-old Byodo-in Temple of Equality. The original, made of wood, stands in Uji, on the outskirts of Kyoto; the Hawaiian version, made of concrete, was erected in 1968 to commemorate the 100th anniversary arrival of the first Japanese immigrants to Hawaii. It's not the same as seeing the original, but it's worth a detour. A 3-ton brass temple bell brings good luck to those who can ring it—although the gongs do jar the Zen-like serenity of this Japan-like setting.

Senator Fong's Plantation & Gardens. 47-285 Pulama Rd., Kaaawa. ☎ **808/239-6775.** Admission $8.50 adults, $5 children 5–12. Hour-long tours daily from 10:30am; last tour 3pm. From Honolulu, take the H-1 to the Likelike Hwy. (Hi. 63); turn left at Kahekili Hwy. (Hi. 83); continue on to Kaaawa, and turn left on Pulama Rd. TheBUS: 55; it's a mile walk uphill from the bus stop.

Senator Hiram Fong, the first Chinese-American elected to the U.S. Senate, served 17 years before retiring to tropical gardening years ago. Now you can ride an open-air tram through five gardens named for the American presidents he served. His 725-acre botanical garden includes 75 plants and flowers. It's definitely worth an hour—if you haven't already seen enough botanics to last a lifetime.

Ulupoa Heiau. Behind the YMCA on the Kaneohe side of 1200 Kailua Rd. (Hi. 61), at the end of Manuoo Rd. TheBUS: 56 or 57 will get you to the YMCA.

On a street lined with contemporary Christian churches, out of sight behind a YMCA gym and pool, is one of Oahu's most sacred ancient sites, where some believe the world began. Built of stacked rocks, the 30-by-40-foot temple is believed to have been an agricultural temple, since it's next to Kawainui Marsh, the largest body of fresh-water in Hawaii. Its name roughly translates to "night inspiration," so go there during a full moon to get the full, eerie effect. Remember, Hawaii's *heiau* are sacred, so don't walk on the rocks or dare to move one.

✪ **Polynesian Cultural Center.** 55-370 Kamehameha Hwy., Laie. ☎ **800/367-7060** or 808/293-3000. Waikiki office: 2255 Kuhio Ave., Suite 1601. ☎ 808/923-2911. Mon–Sat 12:30pm–9:30pm. Admission only $27 adults, $16 children 5–11. Admission, buffet, and nightly show $44 adults, $27 children. Admission, IMAX, luau, and nightly show $59 adults, $37 children. Ambassador VIP (deluxe) tour $92 adults, $61 children. From Honolulu, take the H-1 to the Pali Hwy. (Hi. 61) and turn left on Kamehameha Hwy. (Hi. 83). TheBUS: 55, or Polynesian Cultural Center Coaches for $15 round trip; book at numbers above.

If you, like most people, have reached the end of your geographical leash in Hawaii, then you can satisfy your curiosity about the rest of the far Pacific all in a single day here. The Polynesian Cultural Center makes it easy (and relatively inexpensive, considering the time and distance involved to see the real thing) to experience the authentic songs, dance, costumes, and architecture of seven Pacific islands. The 42-acre lagoon park re-creates villages of Hawaii, Tonga, Fiji, Samoa, the Marquises, New Zealand, and Easter Island.

You "travel" through this kind of living museum of Polynesia by canoe on a man-made freshwater lagoon. Each village is "inhabited" by native students from Polynesia, who attend Hawaii's Bright Young University. Operated by the Mormon Church, the park also features a variety of stage shows, including "Manna! The Spirit of Our People," and "Pageant of the Long Canoes," which celebrate the music, dance, history, and culture of Polynesia. There's also a luau every evening. Since a visit can take up to 8 hours, it's a good idea to arrive before 2pm.

Just beyond the center is a replica of the **Mormon Tabernacle,** built of volcanic rock and concrete in the form of a Greek cross with reflecting pools, formal gardens, and royal palms. It was the first Mormon temple built outside of Salt Lake City.

CENTRAL OAHU & THE NORTH SHORE

If you can afford the splurge, rent a bright, shiny convertible—the perfect car for Oahu since you can tan as you go—and head for the North Shore and Hawaii's surf city: **Haleiwa,** a quaint turn-of-the-century sugar plantation town designated as a historic site. A collection of faded clapboard stores with a picturesque harbor, Haleiwa has evolved into a surfer outpost and major roadside attraction with art galleries, restaurants, and shops that sell hand-decorated clothing, jewelry, and sports gear (see chapter 10, "Shopping").

Getting there is half the fun. You have a choice: cruise up the H-2 through Oahu's broad and fertile central valley, past Pearl Harbor and Schofield Barracks of *From Here to Eternity* fame, and on through the red-earthed heart of the island where pineapple and sugarcane fields once stretched from the Koolau to the Waianae mountains. Or, meander north along the lush Windward Coast, through country hamlets with roadside stands selling mangos, bright tropical pareaus, fresh corn, and pond-raised prawns (see "The Windward Coast," above).

TAKING THE CENTRAL OAHU ROUTE

If you take the central route, the tough part is getting on and off the H-1 freeway from Waikiki, which is done by maneuvering along convoluted neighborhood streets. Try McCully Street off Ala Wai Boulevard, which is always crowded but usually the most direct route.

Once you're on H-1, stay to the right side; the freeway tends to divide abruptly. Keep following the signs for the H-1 (it separates off to Hi. 78 at the airport, and reunites later on; either way will get you there), then the H-1/H-2. Leave the H-1 where the two "interstates" divide; take the H-2 up the middle of the island, headed north toward the town of Wahiawa. That's what the freeway sign will say—not North Shore or Haleiwa, but Wahiawa.

The H-2 runs out and becomes a two-lane country road about 18 miles out of downtown Honolulu, near Schofield Barracks. The highway becomes Kamehameha Highway (Hi. 99 and later Hi. 83) at Wahiawa. Just past Wahiawa, about half an hour out of Honolulu, the **Dole Pineapple Plantation,** 64-1550 Kamehameha Hwy. (☎ **808/621-8408,** fax 808/621-1926; daily 9am to 6pm), offers a rest stop with pineapples, pineapple history, pineapple trinkets, and pineapple juice (TheBUS no. 52 also can get you here). "Kam" Highway, as everyone calls it, will be your road for most of the rest of the trip to Haleiwa.

CENTRAL OAHU ATTRACTIONS

On the central plains of Oahu, tract homes and malls with factory outlet stores are now spreading across abandoned sugarcane fields. Before the sugarcane, sandalwood grew at the foot of Mount Kaala, the mighty summit of Oahu. Hawaiian chiefs sent commoners into the thick forests to cut down the trees, which were then sold to China traders for small fortunes. The scantily clad natives caught cold in the cool uplands, and many died.

In the 1800s, planters began growing sugarcane and pineapple, and a man named James Campbell discovered artesian wells to irrigate the fields that changed Hawaii forever. In 1908, also on the central plain, the U.S. army pitched a tent on the site that became Hawaii's biggest and most beautiful fort. On December 7, 1941, Japanese pilots came screaming through Kolekole Pass to shoot up the art deco barracks at Schofield, sending soldiers running for cover in their skivvies, and then flew on to sink ships at Pearl Harbor.

On those plains in the 1950s, an out-of-work pop singer named Sinatra made a Hollywood comeback portraying Maggio, a soldier at Schofield on the eve of World War II in the film classic *From Here to Eternity.*

U.S. Army Schofield Barracks.

James Jones called Schofield Barracks "the most beautiful army post the U.S. has or ever had." The *Honolulu Star Bulletin* called it a country club. More than 1 million soldiers have called Schofield Barracks home. With broad, palm-lined boulevards and art deco buildings, this old army calvary post is still the largest operated by the U.S. Army outside of the continental United States. And it's still one of the best places to be a soldier.

Named for Lt. Gen. John M. Schofield, commanding general of the U.S. Army from 1888 to 1895, who first saw Hawaii's strategic value in the Pacific, the 17,597-acre post sprawls across central Oahu on an ancient Hawaiian battlefield where chieftains once fought for the supremacy of Oahu. In the 1930s, the buildings were erected in the art deco style then popular. The red-tile–roofed post office, built in 1939, reflects Hawaii's version of Mediterranean architecture.

The history of Schofield Barracks and the 215th Infantry Division is told in the small **Tropic Lightning Museum,** Schofield Barracks (☎ **808/655-0438;** free admission; Tuesday through Saturday 10am to 4pm). Artifacts range from relics of the War of 1812 to a replica of Vietnam's infamous Cu Chi tunnels.

Kukaniloko Birthing Stones. Off Kamehameha Hwy. between Wahiawa and Haleiwa, opposite the road to Whitmore Village.

Two rows of 18 lava rocks once flanked a central birthing stone, where women of ancient Hawaii gave birth to potential *alii* (royalty). The rocks, according to Hawaiian belief, held the power to ease the labor pains of childbirth. Birth rituals involved 48 chiefs who pounded drums to announce the arrival of newborns likely to become chiefs. Children born here were taken to the now-destroyed Holonopahu Heiau in the pineapple field, where chiefs ceremoniously cut the umbilical cord.

Used by generations of Oahu's alii, the *pohaku* (or rocks), many in bowl-like shapes, now lie strewn in a coconut grove in a pineapple field at this, the most sacred site in central Oahu. Some think it also may have served as an ancient astronomy site, sort of a Hawaiian Stonehenge. Petroglyphs of human forms and circles appear on some of the stones.

SURF CITY: HALEIWA

Only 28 miles from Waikiki is Haleiwa, the funky ex–sugar plantation town that's the world capital of big-wave surfing. This beach town really comes alive in winter, when big waves rise up, light rain falls, and temperatures dip into the 70s. Then, it seems, every surfer in the world is here to see and be seen, surfing the big swells.

Officially designated a Historic Cultural and Scenic District, Haleiwa thrives in a time warp recalling the turn of the century, when it was founded by sugar baron Benjamin Dillingham. Dillingham built a 30-mile railroad to link his Honolulu and North Shore plantations, and opened a hotel named Haleiwa, or "house of the Iwa," after the tropical seabird often seen here.

The turn-of-the-century Victorian-style hotel and railroad are gone, but Haleiwa, which was rediscovered in the late 1960s by hippies, resonates with rare rustic charm. Tofu, not taro, is a staple in the local diet. Arts and crafts, boutiques, and burger stands line both sides of the town; there's a busy fishing harbor full of charter boats and captains who hunt the Kauai Channel daily for tuna, mahimahi, and marlin. And, the bartenders at Jameson's mix the best Mai Tais (made according to the original recipe by Trader Vic Bergeron) on the North Shore.

Once in Haleiwa, the hot and thirsty traveler reports directly to the nearest shave-ice stand, usually **M. Matsumoto Store,** 66-087 Kamehameha Hwy. For 40 years, this small, humble shop operated by the Matsumoto family has served a popular rendition of the Hawaii-style snow cone flavored with tropical tastes. The cooling treat is also available at neighboring stores, some of which still shave the ice with a hand-crank device.

Central Oahu & The North Shore

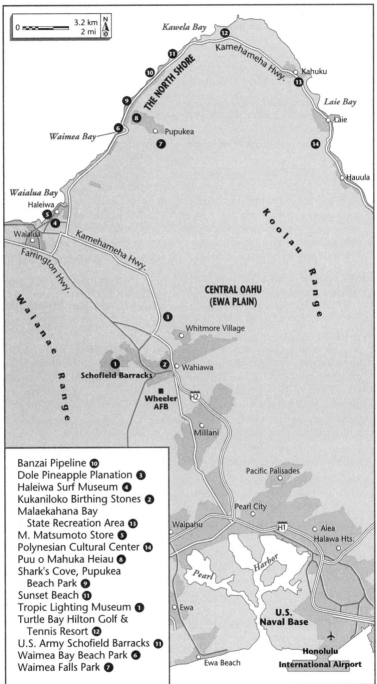

0 — 3.2 km
2 mi
N

Kawela Bay ⑫

Kamehameha Hwy.

⑪

THE NORTH SHORE

⑩

Kahuku ⑬

⑨

Laie Bay

⑧

Laie

⑥ *Waimea Bay*

Pupukea

⑦

⑭

Hauula

Waialua Bay

Haleiwa

⑤

④

Waialua

Kamehameha Hwy.

Koolau Range

Farrington Hwy.

Waianae Range

CENTRAL OAHU
(EWA PLAIN)

③

Whitmore Village

② Wahiawa

① Schofield Barracks

Wheeler AFB H2

Mililani

Pacific Palisades

Pearl City

Waipahu H1 Aiea
Halawa Hts.

Pearl *Harbor*

Ewa

U.S.
Naval Base

Ewa Beach

Honolulu
International Airport

Banzai Pipeline ⑩
Dole Pineapple Planation ③
Haleiwa Surf Museum ④
Kukaniloko Birthing Stones ②
Malaekahana Bay
  State Recreation Area ⑬
M. Matsumoto Store ⑤
Polynesian Cultural Center ⑭
Puu o Mahuka Heiau ⑧
Shark's Cove, Pupukea
  Beach Park ⑨
Sunset Beach ⑪
Tropic Lighting Museum ①
Turtle Bay Hilton Golf &
  Tennis Resort ⑫
U.S. Army Schofield Barracks ⑪
Waimea Bay Beach Park ⑥
Waimea Falls Park ⑦

Just down the road are some of the fabled shrines of surfing—**Waimea Bay, Banzai Pipeline, Sunset Beach**—where the world's largest waves, reaching 20 feet and more, rise up between November and January. They draw professional surfers as well as reckless daredevils and hoardes of onlookers, who jump in their cars and head north when word goes out that "surf's up." Don't forget your binoculars. (For more details on North Shore beaches, see "Beaches," in chapter 8.)

Haleiwa Surf Museum. North Shore Marketplace, 66-250 Kamehameha Hwy. (behind Kentucky Fried Chicken), Haleiwa. ☎ **808/637-3406.** Free admission. Daily 10am–6:30pm. TheBUS: 52.

When surfers aren't hanging ten at Sunset Beach or Pipeline, they're probably hanging out at John E. Moore's nifty little museum, which celebrates the sport of Hawaiian kings. Even if you've never set foot on a surfboard, you'll want to visit Oahu's only surf museum to trace the sport. His collection of memorabilia includes vintage surfboards (a 1915 redwood longboard owned by North Shore surfer Jerry Kermode is a treasure), classic 1950s surf meet posters, 1960s surf music album covers, old beach movie posters starring Frankie Avalon and Sandra Dee, the early black-and-white photos by legendary surf photographer LeRoy Grannis, and a killer 1950 Ford Woody that every surfer we know once had and wishes he had kept.

MORE NORTH SHORE ATTRACTIONS

✪ **Waimea Falls Park.** 59-864 Kamehameha Hwy. ☎ **800/767-8046,** 808/638-8511, or 808/942-5700. Admission $19.95 adults, $9.95 children 6–12. Daily 10am–5:30pm. TheBUS: 52. Free shuttle service from some Waikiki hotels; call number above for reservations.

If you only have a day to spend on Oahu and want to see an ancient hula, sniff tropical flowers, go kayaking along the shore or hiking to archaeological sites and a waterfall, and play the games of ancient Hawaii (spear-throwing, lawn bowling), there's only one place to be: Waimea Falls Park. This is the perfect family place—it takes a whole family to do everything. You can explore remnants of the old Hawaiian settlements in a scenic 1,800-acre river valley that's full of tropical blooms. Or watch authentic demonstrations of the ancient (*kahiko*) hula by the park's own *halau* (school), and see cliff divers swan-dive into a pool fed by a 45-foot waterfall. Everyone is invited to explore the valley. You can ride a mountain bike, paddle a kayak, or run the Elehaha River on an all-terrain vehicle into the jungle.

✪ **Puu O Mahuka Heiau.** One mile past Waimea Bay; take Pupukea Rd. mauka off Kamehameha Hwy. at Foodland, and drive 7/10 of a mile up a switchback road. TheBUS: 52; then walk up Pupukea Rd.

Go around sundown to feel the mana of this sacred Hawaiian place, the largest sacrificial temple on Oahu, associated with the great kahuna Kaopulupulu, who sought peace between Oahu and Kauai. The prescient *kuhuna* predicted that the island would be overrun by strangers from a distant land. In 1794, three of Captain George Vancouver's men of the *Daedalus* were sacrificed here. In 1819, the year before New England missionaries landed in Hawaii, King Kamehameha II ordered all idols at the heiau to be destroyed.

A National Historical Landmark, this 18th-century heiau, known as the "hill of escape," sits on a 5-acre, 300-foot bluff overlooking Waimea Bay and 25 miles of Oahu's wave-lashed north coast—all the way to Kaena Point, where the Waianae Range ends in a spirit leap to the other world. The heiau appears as a huge rectangle of rocks twice as big as a football field (170 feet by 575 feet), with an altar often covered by the flower and fruit offerings left by native Hawaiians.

Shopping

by Jocelyn Fujii

In this land of the alluring outdoors, few people like to admit that shopping is a major activity—or, some would say, distraction. With bodysurfing, hiking on volcanoes, and other invigorating, exotic adventures beckoning, spending time in a shopping mall seems so, well, bourgeois. Truth be known, the proliferation of topnotch made-in-Hawaii products, the vitality of the local crafts scene, and the unquenchable thirst for mementos of the islands lend a new respectability to shopping here. And Oahu (Maui, too) is a haven for mall mavens. From T-shirts to Versace, posh European to down-home local, avant-garde to unspeakably tacky, Oahu's offerings are wide-ranging indeed. But shopping on this island is slightly schizophrenic. You must sometimes wade through oceans of schlock to arrive at the mother lode. Nestled amid the Louis Vuitton, Chanel, and Prada boutiques on Waikiki's Kalakaua Avenue are plenty of tacky booths hawking air-brushed T-shirts, gold by the inch, and tasteless aloha shirts that require sunglasses to behold.

The section that follows is not about finding cheap souvenirs or tony items from designer fashion chains. You can find these on your own. Rather, we offer a guide to finding those special treasures that lie somewhere in between.

1 Shopping In & Around Honolulu & Waikiki

ALOHA WEAR

One of Hawaii's lasting afflictions is the penchant tourists have for wearing loud, matching aloha shirts and muumuus. We applaud such visitors' good intentions (to act local), but they are not Hawaiian. No local resident would be caught dead in such a getup. Muumuus and aloha shirts are wonderful, but the real thing is what island folks wear on Aloha Friday (every Friday, to the Brothers Cazimero Lei Day Concert [every May 1st]), or to work (where allowed). It's what they wear at home (not in matching sets) and to special parties where the invitation reads "aloha attire." Our favorites in aloha shirts include the famous **Avanti** label (see below), sold at many retail outlets throughout Hawaii, and the other manufacturers mentioned below. They prove that aloha, indeed, can be worn.

At the stores listed below, look for the ubiquitous **Kahala Sportswear,** a label that has revolutionized the aloha shirt genre by translating the work of fine artists into the medium of textile. Kahala has faithfully reproduced, with astounding success, the linoleum-block prints of noted Big Island artist Avi Kiriaty. Designs include Mandarin-style dresses, tank dresses, and distinctive aloha shirts bearing scenes of fishing, canoeing, farming, and other idyllic Polynesian pursuits. Watch Kahala: It's found two hot new contemporary artists, both avid surfers, for fabric print designs that show as much promise as Kiriaty's. Kahala is sold in department stores (from Liberty House to J C Penney and Nordstrom), surf shops, and stylish boutiques throughout Hawaii and the mainland.

For the most culturally correct aloha wear, check out the aloha shirts, dresses, and pareus of **Sig Zane Design** available at **Martin & MacArthur** (☎ 808/524-6066) in Aloha Tower Marketplace. Zane, an accomplished hula dancer married to one of Hawaii's most revered hula masters, has an unmistakable visual style and profound knowledge of Hawaiian culture. These levels of expertise bring depth and meaning to his boldly styled renditions of the ti plant, 'ohia, kukui, 'ie'ie, koa, kauna'oa, and other prominent Hawaiian flora. Each Sig Zane pareu and aloha shirt, in pure cotton, tells a story. No wonder it's the garb of the cultural connoisseurs, who also buy fabrics by the yard to bring the rain forest into their homes.

The mainland-based **Tommy Bahamas** is also making a splash in the aloha shirt business. The stylish line and aggressive marketing have made this shirt ubiquitous on the mainland and in Hawaii, where, though not Hawaiian, its quirky designs and carefree spirit are widely admired. Another name to watch for is the locally designed and manufactured **Tutuvi,** whose T-shirts, dresses, and pareus are distinctive for their brilliant color combinations and witty juxtaposition of design motifs. Tutuvi designs, as well as a wide selection of attractive aloha shirts, T-shirts, and other Hawaii-themed fashions, can be found at **Products of Hawaii Too,** in Waikiki's Hyatt Regency; the **Hula Supply Center** at the corner of King and Isenberg streets; **Native Books and Beautiful Things** in downtown Honolulu; and at the **Bishop Museum,** and other locations. You can also visit the **Tutuvi studio** by appointment, 2850 S. King St. (☎ 808/947-5950).

If you love the vintage look, but are not so wild about vintage price tags, the kamaaina label of **Tori Richard** has come out with an attractive line called Pau Hana, a series of retro prints and styles for women. Pau Hana and other Tori Richard designs can be found at most department stores throughout Hawaii.

Well-known muumuu labels in Hawaii include **Mamo Howell,** who has boutiques in Kahala Mall and Ward Warehouse; **Princess Kaiulani** and **Bete** for the dressier muus, sold along with many other lines at Liberty House and other department stores; and **Sun Babies** for casual styles, also found at Liberty House.

Our favorite retail stores for aloha shirts include:

✪ **Avanti Fashion.** 2229 Kuhio Ave. ☎ **808/924-1688.** Also at 2270 Kalakaua Ave., Waikiki Shopping Plaza. ☎ 808/922-2828.

This is the leading retro aloha shirt label, which turns out stunning silk shirts and dresses in authentic 1930s to 1950s fabric patterns. The shirts are the ne plus ultra of aloha shirts, with all the qualities of a vintage silkie minus the high price and the web-thin fragility of authentic antique shirts. For about $60, you can find a stylish shirt that is wearable long after you leave Hawaii. Women's dresses, high-collared tea timers from the 1930s, pant sets, and many other styles are the epitome of comfort and nostalgic good looks. The line is distributed in better boutiques and department stores throughout Hawaii, but the best selections are at its two Waikiki retail stores.

Bailey's Antiques and Aloha Shirts. 517 Kapahulu Ave. ☎ **808/734-7628.**

A large selection (hundreds!) of vintage, secondhand, nearly new, inexpensive, and expensive (rock-star prices) aloha shirts and other collectibles fill this eclectic emporium. It looks like the owners regularly scour Hollywood movie costume departments for old ball gowns, feather boas, fur stoles, leather jackets, 1930s dresses, and scads of other garments from periods past, including one of the largest vintage aloha shirt collections in Honolulu. Prices range from inexpensive to sky-high. Old Levi's jeans, Mandarin jackets, vintage vases, household items, shawls, purses, and an eye-popping assortment of bark cloth fabrics (the real thing, not repros) are among the mementos in this monumental collection of high junque to great finds.

Hilo Hattie. 1450 Ala Moana Blvd., Ala Moana Center. ☎ **808/973-3266.** Also at 700 N. Nimitz Hwy., ☎ 808/544-3500.

Hilo Hattie, the largest manufacturer of Hawaiian fashions, attracted more than a million visitors to its six outlets throughout the state, and that number is rising daily since the large new Ala Moana store opened where the old HOPACO used to be. The new store is a jump up in image, quality and range of merchandise, and overall shopping options. You can find great gifts here, from coconut utensils to food products and aloha shirts in all price ranges and motifs. Hilo Hattie offers complimentary daily shuttle service to most of its stores, including service from Waikiki to its sprawling retail outlet on Nimitz Highway in Iwilei. (No free Hilo Hattie shuttle to Ala Moana yet, though.) There are some inexpensive silk aloha shirts as well as brand-name aloha shirts like Tommy Bahamas and the store's own Hilo Hattie label. Also offered here are macadamia nuts, Hawaiian coffees, jewelry, aloha wear, and other Hawaii souvenirs, as well as live Hawaiian entertainment and free Kona coffee samples.

J C Penney. 1450 Ala Moana Blvd., Ala Moana Center. ☎ **808/946-8068;** and other locations throughout Hawaii.

This chain department store has come into its own with a respectable aloha shirt selection that includes all the name brands, and more. Racks and racks of aloha shirts fill the floor with vintage looks, Hawaiian heritage designs, and the usual surf-oriented motifs. Kahala is a big seller here.

Liberty House. 1450 Ala Moana Blvd., Ala Moana Center. ☎ **808/941-2345.**

If it's aloha wear, Liberty House has it. The extensive aloha shirt and muumuu departments of Liberty House stores feature every label you can conjure, with a selection that changes with the times, and in all price ranges.

Reyn's. 1450 Ala Moana Blvd., Ala Moana Center. ☎ **808/949-5929.** Also at 4211 Waialae Ave., Kahala Mall. ☎ 808/737-8313.

The reverse-print aloha shirt, the uniform of downtown boardrooms, was popularized by Reyn's, which has also jumped aboard the vintage-look bandwagon with its old-Hawaii cotton fabric prints, some of them in attractive two-color pareu patterns. Reyn's used to a stodgy line but has stepped up its selection of women's and men's aloha wear with contemporary fabric prints and stylings, appealing to the under-40 crowd as well.

ANTIQUES & COLLECTIBLES

Antiques hunting on Oahu is usually an eclectic endeavor, a treasure hunt for Asian, European, Hawaiian, and South Pacific antiquities.

Aloha Antiques and Collectibles. 926 Maunakea St. ☎ **808/536-6187.**

You may find a priceless Lalique antique among the tchotchkes that fill every square inch of this dizzying shop. But you'll have to look hard, because there are so many items they literally spill out onto the sidewalk. Upstairs, downstairs, in adjoining

Oahu's Vibrant Art Scene

Passionate art lovers find solace and serenity in Hawaii's two top cultural resources, the **Contemporary Museum** (at Spalding Estate, 2411 Makiki Heights Dr., ☎ 808/526-0232) and the **Honolulu Academy of Arts** (900 S. Beretania St., ☎ 808/532-8701). The vastly differing collections are housed in two of Hawaii's most memorable settings, both the legacy of one woman, Mrs. Charles Montague Cooke, who built the Alice Cooke Spalding house in 1925 and named it after her daughter. Two years later, Cooke founded the Academy, a beacon in the arts to this day. The Alice Cooke Spalding house became the Contemporary Museum in 1988. One shudders to think what Hawaii's art world would have been without these two kamaaina legacies.

The Honolulu Academy of Arts claims one of the finest Asian art collections in the country, as well as an acclaimed collection of American and European masters and prehistoric works that include Maya, Greek, and Hawaiian art. Special exhibitions and annual events have received international recognition. The Moorish structure is a paragon of graciousness, with curved, tiled roof lines, open courtyards and lily ponds, and wide hallways leading to sensitively organized galleries. The Academy's setting, art collections, Garden Cafe, gift shop, and theater make this a must for any resident or visitor. Open Tuesday through Saturday from 10am to 4:30pm and Sunday from 1 to 5pm. Admission is $5 per adult, with discounts for seniors and military personnel; members free.

Located up on the slopes of Tantalus, one of Honolulu's most prestigious residential communities, the Contemporary Museum, established in 1988, is renowned for several features: its 3¹/₂ acres of Oriental gardens with reflecting pools, sun-drenched terraces, views of Diamond Head, and stone benches for quiet contemplation; the Cades Pavilion, housing David Hockney's L'Enfant et les Sortileges, an environmental installation of his sets and costumes for Ravel's 1925 opera; its excellent cafe and gift shop; and six galleries representing significant work and artists of the last 4 decades. Equally prominent is the presence of contemporary Hawaii artists in the museum's programs and exhibitions. Open Tuesday through Saturday from 10am to 4pm, Sunday from noon to 4pm. A 1-day membership for adults is $5; seniors and students, $3; members and children free. The third Thursday of each month is free. Ask about their daily docent-led tours.

Galleries   Longevity matters in Hawaii's art world. Like restaurants, galleries come and go in Chinatown, where well-meaning efforts to revitalize the area have moved in fits and spurts, especially in recent years. Two exceptions are the **Ramsay Galleries** in the striking brick Tan Sing Building (1128 Smith St., ☎ 808/537-2787), celebrating nearly 200 exhibitions and its 18th year in 1998, and the **Pegge Hopper Gallery** (1164 Nuuanu Ave., ☎ 808/524-1160). Both are housed in historic Chinatown buildings that have been renovated and transformed into stunning

rooms, around corners—the place defies inventory. Jewelry, vintage aloha shirts, vases, silver, ephemera, and countless eclectic items make up this mind-boggling collection of junk, treasures, and nostalgia.

✪ **Aloha Flea Market.** Aloha Stadium. ☎ 808/486-1529.

Our advice is to go as early as possible, take a hat, and wear sunscreen. It gets very hot in this world of unshaded, heat-retaining macadam, and with more than 1,000 showplaces for their and other artists' work. Nationally known quill-and-ink artist Ramsay, who has drawn everything from the Plaza in New York to most of Honolulu's historic buildings, maintains a vital monthly show schedule featuring her own work as well as one-person shows of her fellow Hawaii artists. The finest names in contemporary crafts and art have appeared here, in media ranging from photography to sculpture to glass, painting, prints, and, yes, computer art. When Ramsay's work is exhibited, each drawing is displayed with a magnifying glass to invite intimate viewing of the rich details.

Pegge Hopper's widely collected paintings of Hawaiian women with broad, strong features, shown in simple lines and colors in relaxed poses, are displayed in her attractive two-story gallery. One of Hawaii's most popular artists, Hopper has works that can be viewed at the Honolulu International Airport, Aloha Tower Marketplace, and at the Hawaii Theatre.

The darling of Hawaii's ceramics world, Gail Bakutis, gathered 11 other artists in varied media and formed **Art à la Carte in Ward Centre** (1200 Ala Moana Blvd., ☎ 808/597-8034). The gallery celebrates its 12th anniversary in 1998. What's there: paper, clay, scratch board, oils, acrylics, watercolors, collage, woodblock, lithographs, and Bakutis's award-winning raku- and pit-fired ceramics, known throughout Hawaii. You can browse among the two-dimensional fine art, select greeting cards to go with them, and order table-length floral runners, made of haku-lei–style (plaited or wound) flowers, seeds, and vines, which the gallery will ship to the mainland.

Hawaii's most unusual gallery is perched on the slopes of Punchbowl. It is the **Tennent Art Foundation Gallery** (203 Prospect St., ☎ 808/531-1987), devoted to the oeuvre of internationally esteemed artist Madge Tennent, whose work hangs in the National Museum of Women with the work of Georgia O'Keeffe. In its dozens of Tennent originals, the gallery traces the artist's development. Tennent's much-imitated style depicts Polynesians throughout the 1920s to the 1940s in bold, modernist strokes that left an indelible influence on Hawaii art. The gallery is open only limited hours or by appointment.

In windward Oahu, flush against the lush Koolau Mountains, the garden idyll of Hart Tagami and **Powell Gallery and Gardens** (Kahaluu, ☎ 808/239-8146; please call before going) turns out to be the most memorable Oahu stop for many visitors. The gallery, showcasing works by local artists—including Hiroshi Tagami and Michael Powell, both well known for their inspired paintings of Hawaii—is itself a work of art, a place of simple majesty where art and nature converge. The paintings, hand-turned bowls of native woods, ceramics, and sculptures by the best of Hawaii's artists are arranged in a serene environment surrounded by lush gardens. Tagami, an inveterate gardener, planted every tree himself, and has introduced several magnificent botanical species to Hawaii.

vendors sprawling across the stadium floor, it can be exhausting as well. You'll find the more interesting individuals and estates offering vintage treasures interspersed among produce stands and tacky stalls with cheap sunglasses and T-shirts. But you never know when that extra-special 1940s tablecloth, Matson liner menu, John Kelly print, vintage silkie aloha shirt, or Roseville pottery vase will appear. These treasures are snatched up quickly by flea market habitués, so serious collectors had best go early. Admission is 50¢ per person. Open Wednesday, Saturday, and Sunday from 6am to 3pm.

Anchor House Antiques. 471 Kapahulu Ave. ☎ **808/732-3884.**

This highly eclectic collection of Hawaiian, Oriental, and European pieces, located here for 28 years, sprawls over its hidden corner of Kapahulu. You'll find wooden calabashes, camphor chests, paintings, Hawaiian artifacts, and trinkets, priced from $10 to $2,000.

Antique Alley. 1347 Kapiolani Blvd. ☎ **808/941-8551.**

Antique Alley is chockablock with the passionate collections of several vendors under one roof. And with its expanded collection of old Hawaiian artifacts and surfing and hula nostalgia, it's a sure winner for eclectic tastes. The showcases include estate jewelry, antique silver, Hawaiian bottles, collectible toys, pottery, Depression glass, linens, plantation photos and ephemera, and a wide selection of nostalgic items from Hawaii and across America. Salt-and-pepper shakers, Pillsbury dough-boy statuettes, old phones, radios, ivory, china, and cameras spill out across the narrow shop. At the rear is a small, attractive selection of Soiree clothing, made by Julie Lauster out of antique kimonos and obis.

Antique House. 2259 Kalakaua Ave., the Royal Hawaiian Hotel. ☎ **808/923-5101.**

Small but tasteful, the low-profile Antique House is hidden below the lobby level of this illustrious hotel. Come here for small items: Oriental antiques, Chinese and Japanese porcelains, and a stunning selection of snuff bottles, bronzes, vases, and china.

Garakuta-Do. 580 N. Nimitz Hwy., across from Gentry Pacific Center. ☎ **808/524-7755.**

If it's Japanese antiques you're after, it's worth driving to the industrial harbor area to view the late-Edo period (1800s through early 1900s) antiques collected and sold by cheerful owner Wataru Harada. A wide selection of gorgeous tansus, mingei folk art, Japanese screens, scrolls, Imari plates, bronze sculptures, kimono, obi, and stone objects fill the sprawling space.

✪ Kilohana Square. 1016 Kapahulu Ave., Kapahulu.

If there is any one destination that we would recommend for antiques, it would be this tiny square in Kapahulu. Kilohana's five antiques shops cover a rich range of Oriental art, Japanese and European antiques, and high-quality collectibles. Many of the shops have loyal clients across the country who know they can find authentic goods here, particularly Asian. Our favorites are **T. Fujii Japanese Antiques** (☎ **808/ 732-7860**), a long-standing icon in Hawaii's antiques world and an impeccable source for Ukiyoe prints, scrolls, obis, Imari porcelain, tansus, tea ceremony bowls, and screens, as well as contemporary ceramics from Mashiko and Kasama, with prices from $25 to $18,000; **Miko Oriental Art Gallery** (☎ **808/735-4503**), a large repository of Chinese, Japanese, Korean, and Southeast Asian ceramics, bronzes, and furniture, ranging in price from $50 to $22,000; **✪ Silk Winds** (☎ **808/735-6599**), a tasteful collection of Asian antiques, everything from beads and jewelry to cricket cages, jade sculptures, and porcelain; and **Carriage House Antiques** (☎ **808/ 737-2622**), whose owner is an expert in antique silver and European porcelain. Each shop has its own hours; call to be sure they're open.

✪ Robyn Buntin. 848 S. Beretania St. ☎ **808/523-5913.**

The gracious and authoritative Robyn Buntin is an expert in netsuke and a highly esteemed resource in Oriental art. Located not far from the Honolulu Academy of Arts, the 2,500-square-foot space, as much a gallery as an antiques store, radiates a tasteful serenity. The offerings include jade, netsuke, scholar's table items, Buddhist sculpture, Japanese prints, contemporary Chinese, Japanese, and Korean pictorial (graphic) art, and a large and magnificent collection of Hawaiiana. Some pieces are 5,000 years old, while many others are hot off the press from Tokyo, Seoul, and Beijing. Buntin represents several Japanese contemporary print artists, an artist from Seoul, and a handful of Hawaiian artists. The brilliant selection of netsuke and Japanese carving is complemented with Hawaiian works by John Kelly, Isami Doi, Avi Kiriaty, Guy Buffet, Mark Kadota, and others. Few people know that John Kelly's legacy includes Oriental works; they're here, along with rare etchings and prints that move swiftly to waiting collectors. Also known for his meticulous craftsmanship and taste in framing, Buntin has a framing operation in downtown Honolulu.

BOOKSTORES

Book Cellar. 222 Merchant St. ☎ **808/523-3772.**

It is definitely a cellar, located downtown for more than a decade, spilling over with used and rare books with a few new items. It's a good general used-book store with about 35,000 titles, mostly hardcovers but with a large selection of paperbacks. Hawaiiana, nonfiction, and books of the Pacific are among its stronger categories. Ask for CC (Carl Carroll, the man who knows the inventory).

Honolulu Book Shops. 1450 Ala Moana Blvd., Ala Moana Center. ☎ **808/941-2274;** and three other locations.

Children's books and Hawaiian and local titles are the strong suit of this longtime Honolulu bookstore, much smaller than the other giants mentioned but considerably bolstered by its nearly 1,000 titles in Hawaii-themed subjects. They try harder with discounts, too: 33% on the *NYT* best-selling hardcovers, 22% on the *NYT* best-selling paperbacks, and 11% off on the "category of the month." Honolulu Book Shops carries 80,000 titles at its Ala Moana store.

Pacific Book House. 1249 S. Beretania St. ☎ **808/591-1599.**

Dennis Perron, connoisseur of rare books, has moved his venerable Pacific Book House to a new location, kept and expanded the rare and out-of-print book inventory, and expanded into paintings, antiques, and estate jewelry. Literati still come here, however, for the finds in Hawaiiana, rare prints, collectible books (such as the first edition of Poe's *The Raven and Other Poems*), and other out-of-print treasures. Pacific Book House also handles book restoration that others are afraid to touch.

Rainbow Books and Records. 1010 University Ave. ☎ **808/955-7994.**

A little weird but totally lovable, especially among students and eccentrics (and insatiable readers), Rainbow Books is notable for its selection of textbooks, popular fiction, records, and Hawaii-themed books, secondhand and reduced. Because it's located in the university area, it's always bulging with textbooks, Hawaiiana, and popular music. It's about the size of a large closet, but you'd be surprised at what you'd find.

Tusitala Bookshop. 116 Hekili St., Kailua. ☎ **808/262-6343.**

Named after Robert Louis Stevenson, whose Samoan name, Tusitala, means "teller of tales," this Kailua mainstay has a loyal following among book lovers and book collectors. The quintessential specialty bookstore, it's been here for two decades with its strong selection of hard-to-find books on Hawaii and the South Pacific. All books here are used, rare, and out-of-print. There are more than 2,000 titles on Hawaii and the Pacific alone, and prices range from $10 to $20,000 for the eight-volume set of

Cook's Voyages from the 1700s. Nancy Abe knows the inventory and the stories that come with the volumes.

CONSIGNMENT SHOPS

comme ci comme ca. 3464 Waialae Ave., Kaimuki. ☎ **808/734-8869.**

It's barely larger than a closet, so all treasures are within arm's reach. Great finds abound here, especially if your timing is good. Brand-new Prada bags, old Hermès jackets and dresses in pristine condition, an occasional Ferragamo purse, Armani suits, and vintage fur-collared sweaters straight out of 1940s Hollywood are some of the pleasures awaiting. Timing is paramount here; finds—such as a made-in-Italy, brand-new, mostly cashmere Donna Karan for Men jacket—disappear to the early birds.

Consignment Closet. 2970 E. Manoa Rd., Manoa. ☎ **808/988-7442.**

Manoa's neighborhood consignment store is cheaper (much) and funkier than most, with a small yet honorable selection of shoes, dresses, and separates. Don't forget the hidden back room with its racks and racks of secondhand goodies—silk blouses, blazers, separates, sweaters. An entire wall lined with dresses adds to the fun.

The Ultimate You. 851 Pohukaina St., Kakaako. ☎ **808/591-8388.**

As far as prices go, no one can beat the budget-saving Goodwill and Salvation Army stores. But don't compare them with a consignment store like The Ultimate You, a store that really thrills the woman with confidence enough to wear another person's cast-offs with neither apology nor announcement. This is a resale boutique, not a vintage or secondhand store, so the clothes are current and not always cheap, but always 50% to 90% off retail. When a red star appears on the tag, it means another big chunk off the bill. The joy is in the hunt here, as you peruse the selection of perfectly good clothes (all 2 years old or less, and freshly laundered or cleaned). This means designer suits and dresses, often new or barely worn, from such names as Escada, Chanel, Prada, Gianfranco Ferre, Donna Karan, Yves St. Laurent, Armani, Ralph Lauren, Laura Ashley, and Ann Taylor. You'll also find scads of separates, cashmere sweaters, dresses, shoes, scarves, and purses of equal (or greater) beauty and lesser renown. Yes, they also carry Gap, J. Crew, and Banana Republic clothing, as well as a handsome assortment of handbags and accessories. Shopaholics as far away as the West Coast send their new and barely used clothes here, so the inventory is always intriguing.

EDIBLES

In addition to the stores listed below, we also recommend **Executive Chef in the Ward Warehouse** and **Islands' Best** in the Ala Moana Center.

Asian Grocery. 1319 S. Beretania St. ☎ **808/531-8371.**

The influx of newcomers from Asia has spawned new sources of exotic food products. Asian Grocery supplies many of Honolulu's Thai, Vietnamese, Indonesian, and Indian eateries with the authentic ingredients of their native cuisines: spices, rices, noodles, produce, sauces, herbs, pastes, and countless new adventures for the western palate. Browse among the shallots, kaffir lime leaves, tamarind and fish sauces, red and green chiles, fresh basil, curry sauces, chutneys, jasmine and basmati rices, and shelf upon shelf of medium-to-hot chili sauces.

Daiei. 801 Kaheka St. ☎ **808/973-4800.**

Stands offering take-out sushi, Korean kal bi, pizza, Chinese food, flowers, Mrs. Fields cookies, and other items for self and home rim this huge emporium. Inside you'll find household products, electronics, cosmetics, a pharmacy, and inexpensive clothing, but it is the prepared foods and produce that excel. In the food department inside the store, the fresh seafood section is one of Honolulu's best bets, not far from where regulars line up for the bento lunches and individually wrapped sushi. When Ka'u navel oranges, macadamia nuts, Kona coffee, Chinese taro, and other Hawaii products are on sale in the produce department, savvy locals arrive in droves to take advantage of the high quality and good value.

Honolulu Chocolate Co. At Ward Centre. ☎ **808/591-2997.** Also at 500 Ala Moana Blvd., Restaurant Row. ☎ 808/528-4033.

Life's greatest pleasures are dispensed here with abandon: expensive gourmet chocolates made in Honolulu, chocolate-covered macadamia nuts, Italian and Hawaiian biscotti, boulder-size turtles (caramel and pecans covered with chocolate), truffles, chocolate-covered coffee beans, jumbo apricots dipped in white and dark chocolate. There are tinned biscuits, European candies, and sweets in a million disguises at this Honolulu people-pleaser.

✪ **Mauna Kea Marketplace Food Court.** 1120 Maunakea St., Chinatown. ☎ **808/524-3409.**

Hungry patrons line up in front of the no-nonsense food booths that offer Vietnamese, Thai, Italian, Chinese, Japanese, and Filipino food—booths proffering everything from pizza to plate lunches and many other types of quick, authentic, inexpensive ethnic cuisine. The best seafood fried rice comes from the woks of Malee Thai/Vietnamese Cuisine at the mauka end of the marketplace—generous, perfectly flavored, endowed with morsels of fish, squid, and shrimp. Walk the few steps down to the produce stalls (pungent odors, fish heads and chicken feet on counters: not for the squeamish) and join in the spirit of discovery. Fish counters and produce stalls vend everything from fresh ahi and whole snappers to mangoes, papayas, bananas, Southeast Asian durian (in season), yams and taro, seaweed, shellfish, and fresh fruits and vegetables of every shape and size.

Paradise Produce Co. 83 N. King St., Chinatown. ☎ **808/533-2125.**

Neat rows of mangoes, top-quality papayas, and reasonably priced and very fresh produce make this a paradise for food lovers. When asparagus is plentiful, it will be inexpensive and fresh. When mangoes are in season, you'll find Yee's Orchard Haydens set apart from the less desirable Mexican mangoes, and, if you're lucky, a stash of ambrosial Piries that will sell out quickly. Chinese taro, bok choy, basil, litchis in season, local eggplant, and dozens of types of fruit and vegetables are offered up fresh, neat, and colorful.

✪ **People's Open Markets.** Various sites around town. ☎ **808/527-5167.**

Truck farmers from all over the island bring their produce to Oahu's neighborhoods in regularly scheduled, city-sponsored open markets. Among the tables of ong choy, choi sum, won bok, Okinawan spinach, opal basil, papayas, mangoes, seaweed, fresh fish, and litchis in season, you'll find homemade banana bread, Chinese pomelo (like large grapefruit), fresh fiddleheads (fern shoots) when available, and colorful, bountiful harvests from land and sea. The offerings change by the week and the season, but you will always find a satisfying sampling of Island-grown, inexpensive, freshly gathered greens. Call the number above to find the open market nearest you.

✪ **R. Field Wine Co.** 1200 Ala Moana Blvd., Ward Centre. ☎ **808/596-9463.**

Oenophile, gourmet, and cigar aficionado Richard Field combines all his interests in this ultrachic shop of culinary pleasures. His sophisticated selection includes exclusive, limited, hard-to-find vintages; the classic malts of Scotland; organic vine-ripened tomatoes; salmon mousse; poha and ohelo berry preserves; plum pudding; designer vinegars; Kulana "organic" beef; Langenstein estate Kona coffee; estate-grown, super-luxe Hawaiian Vintage Chocolate, grown on the Big Island; Petrossian caviar; Waimanalo baby greens; gourmet cheeses; and, of course, cigars. R. Field is synonymous with fine dining, good living, and healthful choices, and never ceases to expand and improve. Meat lovers, take note: Ostrich filets, venison, goose, duck, and buffalo meats are sold here, as well as fresh and prepared foie gras. Plans call for a full selection of microbrewed beers, a decadent line of R. Field ice creams, and the sale of melt-in-your-mouth Kobe beef here. Regular wine and cigar tastings, annual culinary festivals, a radio program, and ongoing efforts to expand and elevate his customers' dining experiences make this an epicurean center of Hawaii—not quite Dean & DeLuca, but growing.

Shirokiya. At Ala Moana Shopping Center. ☎ **808/973-9111.**

Shirokiya's upstairs food department is well-known throughout Honolulu as the marketplace for Japanese treats. Food samples hot off the grill or oven are offered from the counters: fish, mochi, pickled vegetables, and black beans fill the air with briny, smoky scents. A separate take-out food department sells sushi, udon and noodle soups, and many varieties of boxed bento lunches. Tables are available, or you can order the food to go. In the retail food department surrounding all this, exotic assortments of rice crackers, deluxe dried shiitake mushrooms, Japanese teas, dried seaweeds and bonito, pickled plums, candies, biscuits, and snacks and seasonings galore call out for your attention.

✪ Strawberry Connection of Hawaii. 1931 Kahai St., Kalihi. ☎ **808/842-0278.**

If you love food enough to search for it in the bowels of industrial Honolulu, give this place a try. Foodies in the know swear by Strawberry Connection, the most stunning showcase of Hawaii food products in the state (aside from culinary festivals and annual fairs). Shopping here is an adventure. If you don't bring a jacket, they'll loan you one: The walk-in chill rooms are cold, and you have to enter them to pick the best portobello or shiitake mushrooms, flawless asparagus spears, plump strawberries, Waimanalo gourmet greens, and stacks of designer produce from all the Hawaiian islands. Sections of prepared foods (preserves, sauces, dressings, seasonings, rice, pasta, cheeses, chocolates, Sierra bean soups, cholesterol-free New York flatbread, frozen and freeze-dried vegetarian meals) appear in front of and inside the retail space. Friendly service, good prices, and regular culinary classes and demonstrations are part of the deal.

Bakeries

The **Saint-Germain bakeries** in Shirokiya at Ala Moana Shopping Center (☎ **808/955-1711**), near Times Supermarket (11296 S. Beretania St., ☎ **808/593-8711**), and at Pearlridge Center (☎ 808/488-4967) are the best in town for French breads, baguettes, country loaves, and oddball delicacies, such as mini mushroom and spinach pizzas in Danish-type shapes and dough. How good are the breads? Many of the fine restaurants in Honolulu serve their French loaves at candlelit tables.

In Ward Warehouse, **Mary Catherine's** (☎ **808/591-8525**), the darling of the gourmet bakeries, still turns out sinful cakes, fruit tarts, and cookies despite its smaller, more modest, less European space—and prices that are nothing to sneeze at. In Kaimuki, the newest rave is **Cafe Laufer** (3565 Waialae Ave., ☎ **808/735-7717;** see chapter 7, "Oahu Dining"), where the baked goods compete with the towering, made-to-order soufflés and inexpensive sandwiches. Nearby, old-timers still line up at **Bea's Pies & Deli** (1117 12th Ave., ☎ **808/734-4024**), which often runs out of pies (custard-pumpkin is a must) by noon. Across the Pali in Kailua town, **Agnes Portuguese Bake Shop** (35 Kainehe St., ☎ **808/262-5367**) is the favorite of the malassada mavens. These sugary Portuguese dumplings, like doughnuts without holes, fly out of the bakery along with a full variety of specialty pastries, cookies, scones, Portuguese bean and other soups, and local and European-style breads that infuse the neighborhood with irresistible aromas.

Fish Markets

Safeway on Beretania Street has a seafood counter with fresh choices and a staff that takes pride in its deftness with prepared foods. (If you're curious, don't be shy about asking for a taste.) The prepared foods (fresh ahi poke, seaweed salad, shrimp cocktail, marinated crab) are popular items among busy working folks heading home, or for potluck gatherings. **Foodland** on Beretania Street also offers good buys on live lobster and Dungeness crab, fresh ahi and aku poke, ahi sashimi and steaks, and a wide variety of fresh fish and shellfish, including whole snappers and oysters when available.

Tamashiro Market. 802 N. King St., Kalihi. ☎ **808/841-8047.**

You'll think you're in a Fellini movie amid the tanks of live lobsters and crabs, and the dizzying array of counters glistening with fresh slabs of ahi, opakapaka whole and in fillets, onaga, and ehu. Point and ask if you don't know what you're looking at, and one of the many fish cutters will explain, then clean and fillet your selection. Good service and the most extensive selection in Honolulu make Tamashiro the grandfather of fish markets and the ace-in-the-hole for home chefs with bouillabaisse or paella in mind. Also a magnet for shoppers is the separate counter of seaweed salads, prepared poke, lau lau, lomi salmon, Filipino and Puerto Rican ti-wrapped steamed rice, Japanese pickles, fresh produce, and dozens of other ethnic foods.

Yama's Fish Market. 2203 Young St., Moiliili. ☎ **808/941-9994.**

Neighbor islanders have been known to drive directly from the airport to Yama's for a plate lunch, one of the best in Honolulu. Robust Hawaiian plates with pork or chicken lau lau (20 combinations!), baked ahi, chili, beef stew, shoyu chicken, and dozens of other varieties stream out to those who line up at the counter and to offices who order by the dozen. But Yama's is also known for its inexpensive fresh fish (fresh mahimahi is always less expensive here than in the supermarkets), tasty poke (ahi, aku, Hawaiian-style, Oriental-style, with seaweed), lomi salmon, and many varieties of prepared seafood. Chilled beer, boiled peanuts, and fresh ahi they'll slice into sashimi are popular for local-style gatherings, sunset beach parties, and festive pau hana (end of work) celebrations.

Health Food

Down to Earth. 2525 S. King St., Moiliili. ☎ **808/947-7678.**

Located in the university district, Down to Earth is a respectable source of organic vegetables and bulk foods, with a strong selection and good prices in supplements, herbs, and cosmetic products. Everything here is vegetarian, down to the last vitamin pill or drop of tincture. Cereals, bulk grains and nuts, breads, many varieties of honey, nonalcoholic beer, teas, snacks, environment-friendly paper and household products, and a vegetarian juice and sandwich bar are among the reasons shoppers of all ages come here.

Hou Ola. 1541 S. Beretania St. ☎ **808/955-6168.**

Tiny but powerful, with a loyal clientele that has stuck by it through management and name changes and a hefty dose of parking problems, Hou Ola has competitive prices and a wide and user-friendly selection of health-food supplements. The supplements are good enough reason to shop here. No produce, but there are frozen vegetarian foods, cosmetics, bulk grains, and healthy snacks.

Huckleberry Farms. 1613 Nuuanu Ave., Nuuanu. ☎ **808/524-7960.**

Located in Nuuanu across town from the university area, Huckleberry Farms has a wide selection of produce, vitamins, cosmetics, and books, with a serviceable selection of prepared vegetarian foods. A few doors down from the Huckleberry Farms grocery store is the new beauty and vitamin retail outlet, a large and dizzyingly stocked room dedicated to beauty creams, cosmetics, nutritional supplements, and nonperishable, nongrocery health products.

Kokua Market. 2643 S. King St., Moiliili. ☎ **808/941-1922.**

Kokua is Honolulu's best source of healthy grinds in all categories but vitamin supplements. Voluminous, leafy organic vegetables; an excellent variety of cheeses; pastas and bulk grains; sandwiches, salads, and prepared foods; and a solid selection of organic wines elevate Kokua to a special place in the hearts of health-minded shoppers. Ample parking is offered behind and makai (toward the beach) of the store.

FLOWERS & LEIS

For a special-occasion, top-of-the-line, designer bouquet or lei, you can't do better than Michael Miyashiro of **Rain Forest Plantes et Fleurs** (1550 Rycroft St., near Ala Moana Center, ☎ **808/942-1550**). He is a nature-loving, ecologically aware, and highly gifted lei maker—pricey, but worth it. His nontraditional leis include one-of-a-kind garlands made from ma'o flowers (Hawaiian cotton) entwined with pikake, pakalana with a new twist, a New Guinea blossom brand-new to the islands, or strands of regal ilima. He custom designs the lei for the person and the occasion, and the personalized attention shows.

The other primary sources for flowers and leis are the shops lining the streets of Moiliili and Chinatown. Moiliili favorites include **Rudy's Flowers** (2722 S. King St., ☎ **808/944-8844**), a local institution with the best prices on roses, Micronesian ginger lei (they can go as low as $8.50 here while others sell them for $15), and a variety of cut blooms. Across the street, **Flowers for a Friend** (2739 S. King St., ☎ **808/955-4227**) has a limited lei selection but occasionally has good prices on cut flowers. In Chinatown, lei vendors line Beretania and Maunakea streets, and the fragrances of their wares mix with the earthy scents of incense and ethnic foods. Our top picks in Chinatown are **Lita's Leis** (59 N. Beretania St., ☎ **808/521-9065**), which has fresh puakenikeni, gardenias that last, and a supply of fresh and reasonable leis; **Sweetheart's Leis** (69 N. Beretania St., ☎ **808/537-3011**), with a worthy selection of the classics at fair prices; **Lin's Lei Shop** (1017 A Maunakea St., ☎ **808/537-4112**), with creatively fashioned, unusual leis (Kauai mokihana in season, Hilo maile, stefanotis, baby roses); and **Cindy's Lei Shoppe** (1034 Maunakea St., ☎ **808/536-6538**), a household word with terrific sources for unusual lei such as feather dendrobium, firecracker combinations, and everyday favorites such as ginger, tuberose, orchid, and pikake, which may be purchased in quantity. At this and other lei shops, simple leis sell for $3 and up, deluxe leis, $10 and up. Ask Cindy's about their unique "curb service," available with advance phone orders. Give them your car color and model, and you can pick up your lei at curbside—what a convenience, especially on this street.

HAWAIIANA/GIFT ITEMS

Our top recommendations in this category are the ✪ **Academy Shop** at the Honolulu Academy of Arts (900 S. Beretania St., ☎ **808/523-8703**) and the

✪ **Contemporary Museum Gift Shop** (2411 Makiki Heights Rd., ☎ 808/ 523-3447), two of the finest shopping stops on Oahu and worth a special trip whether or not you're in a museum mood. As the retail operations of Hawaii's two finest art museums, each is stocked with the best in books, cards, and ethnic and contemporary gift items. The Academy Shop offers art books, jewelry, basketry, beadwork, ikats, saris, ethnic fabrics from all over the world, posters and books, native crafts, and fiber vessels and accessories. The Contemporary Museum shop focuses on contemporary arts and crafts, such as avant-garde jewelry, cards and stationery, books, home accessories, and gift items made by artists from Hawaii and across the country.

Other good sources for quality gift items are the **Little Hawaiian Craft Shop** (in the Royal Hawaiian Shopping Center) and **Martin and MacArthur** (in the Aloha Tower Marketplace).

✪ **Following Sea.** 4211 Waialae Ave. ☎ **808/734-4425.**

The buyers scour the country for the best representations of fine American craftsmanship in everything from candles and bath products to sculpture, fiber art, jewelry, ceramics, glassware, and functional and nonfunctional works of wood. Hawaii is well represented in the collection, with handsome hand-turned bowls made of native and introduced woods, jewelry, ceramics, handmade paper and hand-bound books, and a notable selection of koa boxes. Bread boards, koa mirrors, hair sticks, chopsticks of fine woods, and Hawaii-inspired jewelry in gold and silver are among the offerings of local artists.

Hula Supply Center. 2346 S. King St., Moiliili. ☎ **808/941-5379.**

Hawaiiana meets kitsch in this shop's marvelous selection of Day-Glo cellophane skirts, bamboo nose flutes, T-shirts, hula drums, shell leis, feathered rattle gourds, lauhala accessories, fiber mats, and a wide assortment of pareu fabrics. Although hula dancers shop here for their dance accoutrements, it's not all serious shopping. This is fertile ground for finding souvenirs and memorabilia of Hawaii, a selection well-balanced between irreverent humor and cultural integrity.

✪ **Island Provision Co. at Vagabond House.** 1200 Ala Moana Center, Ward Centre. ☎ **808/593-0288.**

This Ward Centre newcomer celebrates the island lifestyle with its 1,700 square feet of home accessories, gift items, one-of-a-kind island crafts, and multicultural treasures collected from the owners' travels. Amber tones, the fragrances and textures of natural fibers, the warmth of dark, gleaming woods, fine porcelain and pottery, children's books, and a touch of whimsy highlight this shop of wonders. Leave time to browse, because shopping here is more like a journey through an island-style kamaaina home. Luxury soaps and bath products, unique photo frames, hand-screened and hand-painted table linens, clothing, cushion covers, coconut kitchen accessories, teapots, pottery, toys, china, furniture, and enhancements for home and self are some of the gifts to be found.

✪ **Native Books & Beautiful Things.** 222 Merchant St., Downtown. ☎ **808/599-5511.** Also at 1525 Bernice St., Kalihi, at Bishop Museum.

The enormous success of this hui (association) of artists and crafters under one roof, called Native Books & Beautiful Things in downtown Honolulu, led to the establishment of another location at the Bishop Museum, next door to Shop Pacifica, the museum's gift and book shop. Come to either location to be enveloped in a love of things Hawaiian, from musical instruments to calabashes, jewelry, lei, books, and items of woven fibers—beautiful things, indeed. You'll find the best selection of

Hawaii-themed books here, as well as contemporary and Hawaiian clothing, hand-made koa journals, leis made of wiliwili, Hawaii-themed home accessories, lauhala handbags and accessories, jams and jellies, and wide-ranging, high-quality gift items. Favorites include the cotton tablecloths and napkins by Skinny Dip, hand-painted in cheerful plant and fruit motifs, and the handpainted tiles, platters, and candle-sticks of Hawaiian themes and motifs, also by Skinny Dip. Some of Hawaii's finest artists in all craft media have their works available here on a regular basis, and the Hawaiian-book selection is tops in Hawaii.

✪ **Nohea Gallery.** At Ward Warehouse. ☎ **808/596-0074.** Also at Kahala Mandarin Oriental Hawaii, 5000 Kahala Ave. ☎ 808/737-8688.

A fine showcase for contemporary Hawaii art, Nohea celebrates the islands with thoughtful, attractive selections in all media, from pit-fired raku and finely turned wood vessels to jewelry, glassware, fabrics (including Hawaiian-quilt cushions), and furniture. Ninety percent of the works are by Hawaii artists. Handcrafted koa rock-ers by Marcus Castaing and Mike Riley; raku teapots by Gail Bakutis; koa calabashes by Jack Straka; low-fired ceramics by Vicky Chock; glass by Kurt McVay; and gleam-ing koa accessories, from hair sticks to jewelry boxes, grace the pleasing showrooms.

Nui Mono. 2745 S. King St., Moiliili. ☎ **808/946-7407.**

We love the kimono clothing and accessories and the contemporary clothes made from ethnic fabrics, sold in this tiny shop in Moiliili. Handbags made of patchwork vintage fabrics and priceless kimono silks, drapey Asian shapes and ikat fabrics, richly textured vests and skirts, and warm, rich colors are the Nui Mono signature—and it's all moderately priced.

Quilts Hawaii. 2338 S. King St., Moiliili. ☎ **808/942-3195.**

Handmade Hawaiian quilts drape the shop from top to bottom, in traditional Hawaiian and contemporary patterns. Hawaiian-quilt cushions (much more afford-able than full-sized quilts, which run, understandably, in the thousands of dollars) and quilt-sewing kits can also be found here. You can also custom-order the larger works.

Shop Pacifica. 1335 Kalihi St. (in the Bishop Museum). ☎ **808/848-4158.**

Local crafts, lauhala and Cook Island woven coconut, Hawaiian music tapes and CDs, pareus, and a vast selection of Hawaii-themed books anchor the museum's gift shop. Hawaiian quilt cushion kits, jewelry, glassware, seed and Niihau shell leis, silk-screened dish towels, cookbooks, and many other gift possibilities will keep you oc-cupied between stargazing in the planetarium and pondering the shells and antiquities of the esteemed historical museum.

SHOPPING CENTERS

Ala Moana Center. 1450 Ala Moana Blvd. ☎ **808/946-2811.**

Ala Moana Center, a teeming megalopolis of consumerism, also has airline ticket counters (in Sears), a foreign exchange service (Thomas Cook, street level), a dry cleaners (Al Phillips, street level), a Honolulu Satellite City Hall (street level), a U.S. Post Office (street level), several optical companies (including 1-hour service by LensCrafters), the Foodland Supermarket, a pharmacy, and several services for quick photo processing. Its 200 shops and restaurants sprawl over several blocks, catering to every imaginable need, from over-the-top upscale (Tiffany, Dior, Cartier, Polo/Ralph Lauren, Agnes b, Prada, Ermenegildo Zegna, Chanel, Armani, Versace), to mainland chains such as The Gap, The Body Shop, Banana Republic, Sharper Im-age, Sam Goody, Williams-Sonoma, and J C Penney. Departments stores such as

Liberty House and the endlessly entertaining **Shirokiya** sell fashion and household needs, and Longs Drugs has everything from film, sunscreen, and cosmetics to eagerly awaited sales on macadamia nuts. One of the best stops for Hawaiian gifts is **Islands' Best,** a small, wonderful street-level store that spills over with Hawaiian-made foodstuffs, ceramics, fragrances, and more. **Splash! Hawaii** is a good source of women's swimwear; for men's swimwear, try **Liberty House, Town & Country Surf,** or the terminally hip **Hawaiian Island Creations.** Lovers of Polynesian wear and pareus should not miss **Tahiti Imports,** and shoppers in hot pursuit of aloha shirts should head straight for Reyn's, Liberty House, and J C Penney. To go with the island garb, **Slipper House** has kick-up-your heels footwear, everything from lauhala-and-velveteen to fashion sandals and reefwalkers. For noshing on the run, **Fishmonger's Wife** on the mall level is a great stop for sandwiches and seafood, and the **Makai Market Food Court** (see chapter 7, "Oahu Dining") is the fast-foods emporium nonpareil—everything from pizza and Thai to Patti's Chinese Kitchen, our favorite Tsuryua Noodle House, Schlotzsky's Deli, and Little Cafe Siam.

Open Monday through Saturday from 9:30am to 9pm, Sunday from 10am to 6pm. You can get there on the Ala Moana Shuttle Bus, running daily every 15 minutes from eight spots in Waikiki; or take TheBUS no. 8 (Ala Moana Center), no. 19 (Airport or Airport/Hickam AFB), or no. 20 (Airport/Halawa Gate). The Waikiki Trolley also stops at Ala Moana from various Waikiki locales; an all-day pass costs $15.

Aloha Tower Marketplace. 1 Aloha Tower Dr., on the waterfront between piers 8 and 11, Honolulu Harbor. ☎ **808/528-5700.**

Despite valet parking and trolley stops, parking is a discouraging aspect of shopping at Aloha Tower. Once you get to the new harborfront complex, however, a sense of nostalgia, of what it must have been like in the "Boat Days" of the 1920s to 1940s, will inevitably take over. Sleek ocean liners still tie up across the harbor, and the refurbished Aloha Tower stands high over the complex, as it did in the days when it was the tallest structure in Honolulu. Dining and shopping diversions abound. Places we love include Martin & MacArthur, for its Sig Zane clothing, kupee shell and wiliwili leis, and kamaaina-style accents and furnishings; Oceania, for its comfortable island-style clothing and accessories; and topnotch fragrance maven Caswell Massey, even though it is a chain store. Open Sunday through Thursday from 9am to 9pm, Friday and Saturday from 9am to 10pm. Various Honolulu trolleys stop at the Marketplace, but if you want a direct ride from Waikiki, take the $2 Aloha Tower Marketplace Express, which continues on to Hilo Hattie's in Iwilei.

Kahala Mall. 4211 Waialae Ave. ☎ **808/732-7736.**

Chic, manageable, unfrenzied, Kahala Mall is home to some of Honolulu's best shops. Located past Kaimuki, in the posh neighborhood of Kahala, the Kahala Mall has everything from Liberty House (smaller and more limited than Ala Moana, but complete enough for basic needs) to chain stores such as Banana Republic, The Body Shop, and The Gap. One of the town's more popular coffee counters, Starbucks Coffee, is here along with some 90 other restaurants and specialty shops. Some of our favorites include Riches, a tiny kiosk with a big, bold selection of jewelry; **Rafael,** for sleek, chic women's wear; **The Compleat Kitchen,** a salvation for culinary needs; and **Eyewear Hawaii,** for sunglasses from dawn to dusk. Look also for the **Liberty House Men's Store** at the mauka corner of the mall, under a separate roof from the main store. Our picks for the mall's best and brightest are **Corner Loft,** ablaze with estate jewelry, depression glass, antique crystal, vintage beads and baubles, and dazzling collectibles; **Paradizzio,** for accessories for the home; and the **Following Sea** (see "Hawaiiana/Gift Items," above), a gallery of fine crafts and gift items from Hawaii and across the mainland. Open Monday through Saturday from 10am to 9pm, Sunday from 10am to 5pm.

Royal Hawaiian Shopping Center. 2201 Kalakaua Ave. ☎ **808/922-0588.**

This 3-block shopping complex in the heart of Waikiki occupies 6¹/₂ acres and, if you let it, it could absorb your entire Hawaii budget. Upscale is the operative word here. Although there are drugstores, lei stands, many restaurants, and food kiosks, the most conspicuous stores are the **European designer boutiques** (Chanel, Loewe, Celine, Cartier, Hermès, Gianni Versace, Prada, Van Cleef & Arpels) that cater largely to visitors from Japan. One of our favorites stops is the **Little Hawaiian Craft Shop** (☎ 808/926-2662), which features a fabulous collection of Niihau shell leis, museum replicas of Hawaiian artifacts, and works by Hawaii artists, as well as South Pacific tapa, fiber bags and handicrafts, and Papua New Guinea shields and masks. **Beretania Florist,** located in the hut under the large banyan tree, will ship cut tropical flowers (anthuriums, bromeliads, orchids, gingers) anywhere in the United States. A favorite fashion stop is **McInerny Galleria,** a cluster of boutiques under one roof, with such big names as DKNY, Ralph Lauren, Coach, and Armani. Open daily from 9am to 11pm.

Waikele Center. 94–790 Lumiaina St., Waikele. ☎ **808/676-5858.**

Hawaii's first outlet shopping center opened in 1993, and within 2 years had established itself as one of the top 18 outlet markets in the U.S. There are two sections to this sprawling shopping mecca: the **Waikele Factory Outlets,** some 51 retailers and a cafe; and the **Waikele Value Stores** across the street, with 25 stores and eateries, including a food pavilion. Recently purchased by a New Jersey–based company, the 64-acre complex has made discount shopping a major activity and a travel pursuit in itself, with shopping tours for visitor groups and carloads of neighbor islanders and Oahu residents making virtual pilgrimages from all corners of the state. They come to hunt down bargains on everything from perfumes, luggage, and hardware, to sporting goods, fashions, china, and footwear. Anchored by **Borders Books and Music, Eagle Hardware & Garden, and Kmart,** Waikele attracts busloads of Japanese tourists as well as car- and busloads of value-conscious shoppers eager to purchase Geoffrey Beene, Donna Karan, Saks Fifth Ave., Anne Klein, Guess, Max Studio, Mikasa, Levi's, Converse, BCBG, Kenneth Cole, and dozens of other name brands at a fraction of retail.

Open Monday through Friday from 9am to 9pm, Sunday from 10am to 6pm. To get there by car, take H-1 West toward Waianae and turn off at exit 7. To get there on TheBUS, take the no. 2 from Waikiki and transfer at King and Beretania streets to the no. 48, which drops you off directly in front of the center. The companies offering shopping tours with Waikiki pick-ups include **Apple Tour** (☎ 808/395-8557); **E Noa Tours** (☎ 808-591-2561); **Da Shopping Shuttle** (☎ 808/924-8882); **Polynesian Adventure Tours** (☎ 808/833-3000); and two others specializing in the Japanese market. Waikele is approximately 20 miles outside of urban Honolulu.

Ward Centre. 1200 Ala Moana Blvd. ☎ **808/591-8411.**

Although it has a high turnover and a changeable profile, Ward Centre, formerly a yuppie haven, is still a standout for several reasons, mostly gastronomic. It holds a concentration of good restaurants, including coffee bar and health-food haven Mocha Java (see chapter 7), Keo's Thai Cuisine, Ryan's Grill (the happy-hour hangout), the new Bernard's Deli, and dining mecca A Pacific Cafe Oahu (see chapter 7), as well as gift shops and galleries, including **Tropical Clay** for island-themed ceramics,

Island Provision Co. at Vagabond House (see "Hawaiiana/Gift Items," above) for unique home accessories; **Honolulu Chocolate Company** (see "Edibles," above); the very attractive **Art à la Carte.** The most popular stop is the reader-friendly **Borders Books & Music** (see "Bookstores," above), always bustling with browsers and music lovers, and with its own program of musical and artistic events. The center is open Monday through Saturday from 10am to 9pm, Sunday from 10am to 9pm.

Ward Warehouse. 1050 Ala Moana Blvd. ☎ **808/591-8411.**

Older than its sister property, Ward Centre, and endowed with an endearing patina and rustic quality that are very unmallish, Ward Warehouse remains a popular stop for dining and shopping and is one of five sister centers in the area, collectively called Victoria Ward Centers. (Ward Centre is also part of Victoria Ward Centers.) Sports Authority across the street, Borders Books & Music at Ward Centre, and nearby Computer City are a part of this Kakaako complex, still a work in progress and covering several large blocks. Recommended stops in the low-rise brown wooden structure include the ever-colorful **C. June Shoes,** returning to its original location after years in Waikiki, with flamboyant designer women's shoes and handbags (tony, expensive, but oh so entertaining!); **Executive Chef,** for gourmet Hawaii food items and household accessories; **Pomegranates in the Sun,** for creative, colorful sportswear; **Out of Africa,** for pottery, beads, and interior accents; **East of Sun, West of Moon,** for its sensuous array of fragrances, linens, music, bath products, bedspreads, candles, and accessories for body, home, and spirit; **Kamuela Hat Company** and **Indo-Pacific Trading Co.,** for clothing and home accessories; **Yes! Perfumes,** with its hundreds of brand name fragrances; **Mamo Howell,** for distinctive aloha wear; and **Private World,** for delicate sachets, linens, and fragrances. For T-shirts and swimwear check out the **Town & Country Surf Shop,** and for an excellent selection of sunglasses, knapsacks and footwear to take with you from the beach to the ridgetops, don't miss **Thongs 'N Things.** Another favorite shop is the **Nohea Gallery** (see "Hawaiiana/Gift Items," above), one of the finest sources in the state for quality Hawaii-made arts and crafts.

SURF & SPORTS

The surf-and-sports shops scattered throughout Honolulu are a highly competitive lot, with each trying to capture your interest (and dollars). The top sources for sports gear and accessories in town are **McCully Bicycle & Sporting Goods** (2124 S. King St., McCully, ☎ 808/955-6329), with everything from bicycles and fishing gear to athletic shoes and accessories, and a stunning selection of sunglasses; and **The Bike Shop** (1149 S. King St., near Piikoi St., ☎ 808/596-0588), excellent for cycling and backpacking equipment for all levels, with major bike lines such as Diamondback and Specialized, and major camping lines such as North Face, MSR, and Kelty. **The Sports Authority** (333 Ward Ave., ☎ 808/596-0166, and at Waikele Center, ☎ 808/677-9933) is a megaoutlet offering clothing, cycles, accessories, and equipment at a discount.

Surf shops, centers of fashion as well as definers of daring, include **Local Motion** (1714 Kapiolani Blvd., ☎ 808/955-7873, and other locations in Waikele, Windward Mall, and Koko Marina) and **Hawaiian Island Creations** (Ala Moana Shopping Center, ☎ 808/941-4491). Local Motion is the icon of surfers and skate-boarders, both professionals and wannabes. The shop offers surfboards, T-shirts, aloha shirts, dresses and casual wear, skateboards, boogie boards, and every imaginable accessory for life in the sun. Its competitor, Hawaiian Island Creations, is another super-cool surf shop offering sunglasses, sun lotions, surf wear, bicycles, and accessories galore.

VINTAGE CLOTHING

It costs big bucks to wear old clothes if they're in good shape and have a past—$600 to $1,000, say, for a vintage silkie in perfect condition. Take a peek in **Bailey's Antiques and Aloha Shirts** (517 Kapahulu Ave., ☎ 808/734-7628; see listing above) and check out vintage finds from the tatty to the sublime: old lamps, cushions, movie costumes, vintage jewelry, salt and pepper shakers, figurines, fur stoles, hats, and a dizzying selection of clothing for serious collectors and neophytes. A vintage rayon Chinese-style muu with pointed long sleeves, called a "pake muu," or any vintage schmatte in perfect condition could fetch $600 and up, but you may be able to turn up some cheaper options. Prices begin below $20 and a lucky hunter could find a velvet dress or sarong skirt for under $50. Also in Kapahulu, **Coconut Bay** (3114 Monsarrat Ave., ☎ 808/737-2699) is a neighborhood hit with its unique Hawaiian wear and Southeast Asian imports. Its clothing looks vintage, and pulls it off with panache. Quilts, clothing, retro Hawaiian wear, and scads of men's shirts, not to mention a coffee shop next door, have gained this Kapahulu newcomer a lot of fans.

2 Shopping Around the Island

WINDWARD OAHU

KAILUA

Longs Drugs and **Liberty House,** located side-by-side on Kailua Road in the heart of this windward Oahu community, form the shopping nexus of the neighborhood—the one-stop convenience stores that no Kailua resident can live without. Except for food, these two stores provide all the basic needs, from film and cosmetics and household products to apparel and gift items. For maps, books, and food for thought, the **Honolulu Book Shop** in the Kailua Shopping Center provides great books and good service.

Heritage Antiques & Gifts. 767 Kailua Rd. ☎ 808/261-8700.

Heritage has been a Kailua landmark for more than 2 decades, known for its large selection of Tiffany-style lamps (from $200 to $2,000), many of which are hand-carted back to the mainland. The shop's mind-boggling selection also includes European, Asian, local, American, and Pacific Island collectibles. It's fun, the people are friendly, and the selection is diverse enough to appeal to the casual as well as serious collector. Glassware, china, furniture, and estate, costume, and fine jewelry are among the items of note. Heritage has its own jeweler who custom-designs, repairs, and resurrects jewelry, while a stable of wood craftsmen turn out custom-made koa rockers and hutches to complement the antique furniture selection.

KANEOHE

Windward Mall, 46–056 Kamehameha Hwy. (☎ 808/235-1143), is basically a suburban mall serving windwardites. Its more than 100 stores and services include health stores, department stores (Liberty House, Sears, J C Penney), airline counters, surf shops, The Hobby Company craft shop, LensCrafters, and dozens of other retail businesses spread out over windward Oahu's largest shopping complex. The star of the mall is gift-and-craft gallery Kauila Maxwell (see below). A small food court serves pizza, Chinese food, tacos, and other morsels for the dine-and-dash set. Open Monday through Saturday from 9:30am to 9pm, Sunday from 10am to 5pm.

Kauila Maxwell. 46–056 Kamehameha Hwy. ☎ 808/235-8383.

The shop specializes in serious, top-quality Hawaiian crafts and gift items and in educating shoppers on their value and cultural significance. Everything is made in

Hawaii, from the tools, paddles, adzes, and other reproductions of traditional implements to the extensive selection of calabash bowls in koa, milo, kamani, mango, Norfolk pine, and other gleaming woods. The 1,000-square-foot shop also specializes in Niihau shell leis, made by a couple from Niihau and beautifully displayed in the shop with generous educational literature. Jewelry, locally made tropical perfumes (plumeria, gardenia, orchid), rare kou wood sculptures, koa jewelry boxes, hula implements, and a few pieces of Liliuokalani-style koa rockers round out the selection.

3 Shopping the North Shore: Haleiwa

Haleiwa means serious shopping for the growing cadre of townies who drive an hour each way just to stock up on wine and clothes at its stores of growing renown. (I know; I'm one of them.) I always bring a cooler, in case I find that Bordeaux I can't live without, or for storing the picnic lunch that I'll inevitably assemble along the way. It's not a good idea to store valuables in the car or trunk, so I always cross my fingers that my North Shore stash (wine from Fujioka's, clothes and accessories from Silver Moon and Bella Luna) will make it home with me intact, because if not, I would turn right around and start over again. Here are our Haleiwa highlights:

ART, GIFTS & CRAFTS

Haleiwa's seven galleries display a combination of marine art, watercolors, sculpture, and a multitude of crafts trying to masquerade, not always successfully, as fine art. This is the town for gifts, crafts, fashions, and surf stuff rather than fine art, despite some price tags (Wyland, for example) in the hundreds of thousands of dollars. **The Art Plantation** (66–521 Kamehameha Hwy., ☎ 808/637-2343), located in a historic wooden storefront, displays works of more than 70 artists. The nearby **Kaala Art** (66–4556 Kamehameha Hwy., ☎ 808/637-7065) has scaled down its Thai and Indonesian fabrics and clothing (pareus to die for) to focus on acrylics, prints, silk screens, and other mostly new-agey works by local artists.

The two locations of **Global Creations** (66–079 Kamehameha Hwy., ☎ 808/637-1505), across the street from each other, offer clothing (hemp is cheap, sturdy, and attractive here), shoes, caps, backpacks, and other accessories for top to toe. Also offered are international imports for the home, including Balinese bamboo furniture and lamps as well as colorful Yucatan hammocks and gifts and crafts by local potters, painters, and designers.

At the high end of the gallery scene, the indomitable **Wyland,** a North Shore resident who made a name throughout Hawaii and other locales with his large "whaling walls," has his largest Hawaii gallery at 66–150 Kamehameha Hwy. (☎ 808/637-7498). The eponymous **Thomas Deir Galleries** (66–208 Kamehameha Hwy., ☎ 808/637-7431) displays the artist's marine paintings and hand-painted tiles along with the works of more than a dozen other artists, most of them from the islands. Pottery, oils, acrylics, and sculptures in themes ranging from seascapes to goddesses to strong Hawaiian women go for $30 to $250,000.

EDIBLES

Haleiwa is best known for its roadside shave-ice stands: the famous **M. Matsumoto** (66-087 Kamehameha Hwy.), with the perennial queue snaking along Kamehameha Highway, and nearby **Aoki's.** Shave ice is the popular Island version of a snow cone, a heap of shaved ice topped with your choice of syrups, such as strawberry, rainbow, root beer, vanilla, or passion fruit. Aficionados order it with a scoop of ice cream and sweetened black azuki beans nestled in the middle.

For food-and-wine shopping, our mightiest accolade goes to **Fujioka Super Market** (66–190 Kamehameha Hwy., ☎ 808/637-4520). Oenophiles and tony wine clubs from town shop here for the best prices on California reds, coveted Italian reds, and a growing selection of Cabernets, Merlots, and French vintages that are thoughtfully selected and unbelievably priced. So popular is this store that it makes once-weekly deliveries to corporate clients in town. Fresh produce and no-cholesterol, vegetarian health foods, in addition to the standards, fill the aisles of this third-generation store.

Tiny, funky **Celestial Natural Foods** (66–443 Kamehameha Hwy., ☎ 808/637-6729) is the health foodies' Grand Central for everything from wooden spine-massagers to health supplements, produce, cosmetics, and bulk foods.

FASHION

Although Haleiwa used to be an incense-infused surfer outpost in which zoris and tank tops were the regional uniform and the Beach Boys and Ravi Shankar the music of the day, today it's one of the top shopping destinations for those with unconventional tastes. Iconoclasts and renegades love Haleiwa, but so do the urban refugees and gentrified expats who now have a presence in this North Shore outpost. Specialty shops abound here. Top-drawer **Silver Moon Emporium** (North Shore Marketplace, 66–250 Kamehameha Hwy., ☎ 808/637-7710) in its new larger location is still an islandwide phenomenon with the terrific finds of buyer/owner Lucie Talbot-Holu. Exquisite clothing and handbags, reasonably priced footwear, hats straight out of Vogue, jewelry, scarves, and a full gamut of other treasures pepper the attractive boutique. Down the road, at its original location amid banana trees and picnic tables in the shade of a towering monkeypod tree, Silver Moon's sister store, **Bella Luna** (66–037 Kamehameha Hwy., ☎ 808/637-5040) still captures our hearts with its Victorian dresses, drop-dead–gorgeous French Connection dresses, and affordable Italian footwear. Nearby **Oceania** (66–218 Kamehameha Hwy., ☎ 808/637-1516) also has some treasures among its racks of casual and leisure wear. Foldable straw hats, sequined retro-hula shirts by Faith, diaphanous dresses, dressy T-shirts, friendly service, and good prices are what we've found at Oceania. **Oogenesis Boutique** (66–249 Kamehameha Hwy., ☎ 808/637-4580) located in the southern part of Haleiwa, features a storefront lined with vintage-looking dresses that flutter prettily in the North Shore breeze.

Highlights of the new and growing North Shore Marketplace include **Patagonia** (☎ 808/637-1245) for nationally renowned, high-quality surf, swim, hiking, kayaking, and all-around adventure wear. Also in the Marketplace, **Jungle Gems** (☎ 808/637-6609) is the mother lode of gemstones, geodes, crystals, silver, and beadwork.

Among all these Haleiwa newcomers, the perennial favorite remains **H. Miura Store and Tailor Shop** (66–057 Kamehameha Hwy., ☎ 808/637-4845). You can custom-order swim trunks, an aloha shirt, or a muumuu from the bolts of Polynesian-printed fabrics that line the store, from tapa designs to two-color pareu prints. They will sew, ship, and remember you years later when you return. It's the most versatile tailor shop we've ever seen, with coconut-shell bikini tops, fake hula skirts, aloha shirts, and heaps of cheap and glorious tchotchkes lining the aisles.

SURF SHOPS

Haleiwa's ubiquitous surf shops are the best on earth, surfers say. At the top of the heap (15 shops at last count) is **Northshore Boardriders Club** (66–250 Kamehameha Hwy., North Shore Marketplace, ☎ 808/637-5026), the mecca of the board-riding elite, with sleek, fast, elegant, and top-of-the-line boards designed by North Shore legends such as longboard shaper Barry Kanaiaupuni; John Carper; Jeff Bushman; and Pat Rawson. Kanaiaupuni's other store, **B K Ocean Sports** (66–215 Kame-hameha Hwy., ☎ 808/637-4966), located in the old Haleiwa Post Office, is a more casual version, appealing to surfers and watersports enthusiasts of all levels. Across the street, **Hawaii Surf & Sail** (66–214 Kamehameha Hwy., ☎ 808/637-5373) offers new and used surfboards and accessories for surfers, bodyboarders, and sailboarders.

Strong Current Surf Design (66–250 Kamehameha Hwy., North Shore Marketplace, ☎ 808/637-3406), is the north shore's nexus for memorabilia and surf nostalgia because of the passion of its owners, Bonnie and John Moore. Moore, a lifetime collector and surfer since 1963, expanded the commercial surf-shop space to encompass the **Haleiwa Surf Museum** within the same walls. From head level down in its 1,200 square feet of space, Strong Current sells shorts, jewelry, and ocean sportswear; from head level up, the walls and ceilings are lined with vintage boards, posters, and pictures from the 1950s and '60s. Although Strong Current is a longboard surf shop, the current popularity of longboarding among all age groups makes this less an esoteric than a popular stop. World-famous north shore shapers Dick Brewer and Mike Diffenderfer are among the big names who design the fiberglass and balsa wood boards.

Also in the North Shore Marketplace, **Raging Isle Surf and Cycle** (66–250 Kamehameha Hwy., ☎ 808/637-7707) is the surf-and-cycle center of the area, with everything from wet suits and surfboards to surf gear and clothing for men, women, and children. The adjoining surfboard factory, Bill Barnfield Performance, puts out custom-built boards of high renown. Cyclists also hightail it here because of its large inventory of mountain bikes, one of the largest on Oahu, for rent and sale. Marin, Kona, and Electra are among the name brands in their mountain bike inventory.

Willis Brothers Surfboards (66–119 Kamehameha Hwy., ☎ 808/637-1980) and **Hawaiian Surf** (66–250 Kamehameha Hwy., North Shore Marketplace, ☎ 808/637-7600) are among the familiar names for surfers, with boards and accessories for sale.

A longtime favorite among oldtimers is the newly expanded **Surf & Sea Surf Sail & Dive Shop** (62–595 Kamehameha Hwy., ☎ 808/637-9887), a flamboyant roadside structure just over the bridge, with old wood floors, fans blowing, and a tangle of surf and swim wear, T-shirts, surfboards, boogie boards, fins, watches, sunglasses, and countless other miscellany. You can also rent surf and snorkel equipment there. **Tropical Rush** (62–620-A Kamehameha Hwy., ☎ 808/637-8886) is a surfer haven with its huge inventory of surf and swim gear, much of it for rent: longboards and Perfect Line surfboards, Reef Brazil shoes and slippers, swimwear for men and women, T-shirts, visors, sunglasses and scads of cool gear. An added feature is the shop's surf report line for the up-to-the-minute lowdown on wave action, ☎ 808/638-7874, updated daily and quite entertaining, covering surf and weather details for all of Oahu.

11

Oahu After Dark

by Jocelyn Fujii

One of my favorite occasions in life is sunset at Ke Iki Beach, in the thatched, open-sided hale of my friend Alice Tracy's vacation rental, Ke Iki Hale. The entire day builds up to sunset—shopping for the Mai Tai ingredients, checking the angle of the sun, swimming with the knowledge that the big salty thirst will soon be quenched with a tall, homemade Mai Tai on the beach I love most in the world. When the sun is low, we make our mix: fresh lime juice, fresh lemon juice, fresh orange juice, passion-orange-guava juice, and fresh grapefruit juice if possible. We pour this mix on ice in tall, frosty glasses, then add Meyer's rum, in which Tahitian vanilla beans have been soaking for days. (Add cinnamon if desired, or soak a cinnamon stick with the rum and vanilla beans.) A dash of Angostura bitters, a few drops of Southern Comfort as a float, a sprig of mint, a garnish of fresh lime, and voila! The homemade Ke Iki Mai Tai, a cross between Planter's Punch and the classic Trader Vic's Mai Tai. As the sun sets, we lift our glasses and savor the moment, the setting, and the first sip—not a bad way to end the day.

In Hawaii, the Mai Tai is more than a libation. It's a festive, happy ritual that signals holiday, or vacation, or a time of play, not work. Computers and Mai Tais don't mix. Mai Tais and hammocks do. Mai Tais and sunsets go hand in hand.

1 It Begins with Sunset . . .

Nightlife in Hawaii begins at sunset, when all eyes turn westward to see how the day will end and revelers begin planning their technicolor venue to launch the evening's festivities. Like seeing the same pod of whales or school of spinner dolphins, sunset viewers seem to bond in the mutual enjoyment of a natural spectacle. People in Hawaii are fortunate to have a benign environment that encourages this cultural ritual.

On Fridays and Saturdays at 6:30pm, as the sun casts its golden glow on the beach and surfers and beachboys paddle in for the day, Kuhio Beach, where Kalakaua Avenue intersects with Kaiulani, eases into evening with a torch-lighting ceremony and hula dancing. This is a thoroughly delightful, free weekend offering. Start off earlier with a picnic basket and your favorite libations and walk along the oceanside path fronting Queen's Surf, near the Waikiki Aquarium. (You can park along Kapiolani Park or near the Honolulu Zoo.)

There are few more pleasing spots in Waikiki than the benches at the water's edge at this Diamond Head end of Kalakaua Avenue, where lovers and families of all ages stop to peruse the sinking sun. A short walk across the intersection of Kalakaua and Kapahulu avenues, where the seawall and daring Boogie boarders attract hordes of spectators, takes you to the Duke Kahanamoku statue on Kuhio Beach. There you can view the torch-lighting and hula and gear up for the strolling musicians who amble down Kalakaua Avenue every Friday evening from 8pm to 10pm. The musicians begin at Beachwalk Avenue at the Ewa end of Waikiki and end up at the Duke Kahanamoku statue.

This launches you fully—and with only the cost of a picnic dinner—into evening. Waikiki's beachfront bars offer many possibilities, from the Royal Hawaiian Hotel's **Mai Tai Bar,** a few feet from the sand, to the ever-enchanting **House Without a Key** at the Halekulani, where the breathtaking Kanoelehua Miller dances hula to the riffs of Hawaiian steel-pedal guitar under a century-old kiawe tree. With the sunset and ocean glowing behind her and Diamond Head visible in the distance, the scene is straight out of Somerset Maugham—romantic, evocative, nostalgic. It doesn't hurt, either, that the Halekulani happens to make the best Mai Tais in the world. Halekulani has the after-dinner hours covered, too, with light jazz by the mellifluous Loretta Ables Trio and elegant libations by the glass at Lewers Lounge, at the foot of the stairs leading to La Mer.

The **Aloha Tower Marketplace** (1 Aloha Tower Dr., on the waterfront between piers 8 and 11, Honolulu Harbor, ☎ 808/528-5700, Entertainment and Events Hotline ☎ 808/566-2339 for daily updates) has its own version of sunset from Honolulu Harbor. The landmark Aloha Tower at Honolulu Harbor, once Oahu's tallest building, has always occupied Honolulu's prime downtown location—on the water, at a naturally sheltered bay, near the business and civic center of Honolulu. Since the Aloha Tower Marketplace was constructed, it's also become the spot for entertainment and nightlife, with more than 100 shops and restaurants, including several venues for Honolulu's leading musical groups.

It's too soon to tell if it will succeed, but the new **Studio 1 Hawaii** (☎ **808/ 531-0200**) at Aloha Tower Marketplace shows lots of ambition in its plans to become an upscale supper club and multipurpose nightclub. The $10-a-year-membership fee allows for free or discounted admission at its shows year-round, and the dress code encourages the "dress-up-and-be-seen" mentality. Although ties are not required, jackets are encouraged, and verboten items include T-shirts, halter tops, shorts, athletic shoes, and slippers. What does Studio 1 offer? A sleek industrial motif, two floors, a 400-room showroom, five VIP rooms upstairs, a billiards and cigar room, a 75-seat lounge, a bar that seats 30, booths, and state-of-the-art technical equipment that includes 85 television screens. The 5pm to 8pm happy-hour is a draw, as is the house band with the extraordinary saxophonist. So far the shows have included local talent such as Orlando Sanchez and Salsa Hawaii and Azure McCall.

Unlike Waikiki, there are no swaying palm trees at your fingertips at Aloha Tower Marketplace, but you'll see tugboats and cruise ships from the popular open-air **Pier Bar** and from various venues throughout the marketplace offering live entertainment during happy hour and beyond. The Pier Bar's main stage, **Gordon Biersch Brewery,** and the **Atrium Center Court** feature ongoing programs of foot-stomping good times. Sunday is jazz day at the Pier Bar, Friday is Hawaiian music day, and on Saturday the dance music rocks and rolls like the swells of Honolulu Harbor. At Gordon Biersch Brewery and Restaurant, diners swing to jazz on Wednesdays, the rhythm-and-blues of Nueva Vida and Big Thang on Thursday, and a lively mix on weekends, including reggae or alternative music on Sunday. **Buffalo Bud's Bar & Grill**

Mai Tai, Anyone?

Most Mai Tais served in Hawaii today are too strong, too sweet, and, at $7 and up, too expensive. They're pale imitations of the original, by a legendary California restaurateur, the late Vic Bergeron, of Trader Vic's fame. Some taste like gasoline, others like cough syrup; they burn the throat, produce terrible headaches, and generally give Hawaii a bad name. They should be served with a Surgeon General's warning. These tacky concoctions have little in common with a real Mai Tai, and should be avoided at all costs.

The classic Mai Tai is an unforgettable cocktail, an icy Jamaican rum and fresh lime juice drink with a subtle hint of oranges and almonds and a sprig of fresh mint for garnish. Now, that's a Mai Tai. As long as they don't alter the basic ingredients, variations on the original theme are perfectly acceptable, and can be excellent.

Of course, where you sip a Mai Tai is almost as important as the ingredients. This tropical drink always tastes better in a thatch hut on a lagoon, with coco palms lining the shore. A great Mai Tai in, say, the Tonga Room of San Francisco's Fairmont Hotel is not the same as a great Mai Tai on Waikiki Beach. Here are the best places to enjoy the premier Hawaii Mai Tai experience:

• **Halekulani's House Without a Key** ($7.25): The search for the perfect Mai Tai begins and ends here. It's as close to the original as you'll find in Waikiki. This sophisticated version is comprised of a fine blend of two rums, lemon and lime juice, and sweet orange curaçao. A purple Vanda orchid adds a splash of color.

• **Jameson's by the Sea** ($5): Up on the North Shore, big waves may draw surfers from around the world, but Mai Tai connoisseurs pack the lanai at Jameson's at sundown to catch the wave of Mai Tais prepared by head barman Jim Bragaw. The best in Surf City.

• **New Otani Kaimana Beach Hotel** ($5.75): Go on Aloha Friday, when the exotic sounds of Arthur Lyman waft across the golden sand, and ask veteran bartender Clara Nakachi for a classic Mai Tai. Sit under the tree where Robert Louis Stevenson wrote poems to Princess Kaiulani. Take a sip, stare out to sea and wonder, is this not paradise?

—Rick Carroll

dances to a different beat: satellite-live football on Monday, live deejay and top-40s music on Wednesday and Thursday, and a mix of dance rhythms and top-40s the rest of the nights.

Names to watch for, here and throughout Honolulu, include jazz singer Azure McCall, voted Honolulu's favorite singer in a *Honolulu Weekly* survey; riveting rhythm-and-blues chanteuse Alisa Randolph; Mojo Hand, unbeatable blues-and-dance music for those too hip for the Clyde Pound Orchestra and too sophisticated for a warehouse rave; Willie K., unspeakably versatile, a virtuoso Hawaiian falsetto who also belts out blues, rock, and ballads; Henry Kapono, contemporary Hawaiian music; Rolando Sanchez & Salsa Hawaii; and Nueva Vida, Honolulu's darling of rhythm-and-blues and jazz. Nueva Vida gives two different presentations: Nueva Vida Big Thang, rhythm-and-blues and dance music; and Nueva Vida Jazz Thang. Hula, guitar concerts, jazz nights, and special events such as Cinco de Mayo parties, magic shows, Sunday afternoon jazz jam sessions, and Tower Thursday "sunset specials" make Aloha Tower Marketplace a major entertainment venue from sunset well into the night.

HAWAIIAN MUSIC

Oahu has several key spots for Hawaiian music. Although they have left their former venue, the Bishop Museum, the **Brothers Cazimero** remain one of Hawaii's most gifted duos (Robert on bass, Roland on 12-string guitar). Watch the local dailies or ask the hotel concierge if the Brothers Caz, as they're called, are giving a special concert (as they do every May 1 at the Waikiki Shell), or if they've found a new venue. Theirs is an enchanting blend of ancient chant, hula, and contemporary Hawaiian music.

Waikiki is also peppered with casual, lively nightspots into which you can saunter spontaneously for consummate entertainment, which often includes impromptu hula and spirited music from the family and friends of the performers. Foremost among these choices is the Hilton Hawaiian Village's ✪ **Paradise Lounge,** which (despite its pillars) serves as a large living room for the full-bodied music of Haunani Apoliona, Jerry Santos, and Wally Suenaga, known as **Olomana.** A venerated songwriter and 12-string guitar player, Apoliona is a musical icon in Hawaii, and—especially when singing in harmony with Santos—makes goose-bump music that stays with you. They play on Friday and Saturday, from 8pm to midnight, no cover charge. At **Duke's Canoe Club** at the Outrigger Waikiki Hotel, it's always three deep at the beachside bar when the sun is setting and the fabulous **Moe Keale** is playing with his trio. **Del Beazley, Brother Noland, Ledward Kaapana, Henry Kapono,** and other top names in Hawaiian entertainment appear at Duke's, where extra-special entertainment is a given. Usually the entertainment is from 4pm to 6pm on Friday, Saturday, and Sunday evenings, but call ☎ **808/923-0711** to see if there's anything cooking later in the evening.

Nearby, the Sheraton Moana Surfrider offers a regular program of Hawaiian music in the **Banyan Veranda** that surrounds an islet-sized canopy of banyan tree and roots where Robert Louis Stevenson loved to linger. (*Hot tip:* Drinks, though not as elegantly presented, cost much less from the ground-level bar than from the elegant veranda with the high-backed chairs, and you still get to enjoy the music.) At the Outrigger Prince Kuhio, the **Cupid's Lounge** piano bar is home to the venerable **Mahi Beamer,** a foremost Hawaiian composer, pianist, and descendant of the famed musical dynasty of Helen Desha Beamer.

Our best advice for lovers of Hawaiian music is to scan the local dailies or the *Honolulu Weekly* to see if and where the following Hawaiian entertainers are appearing: **Ho'okena,** a symphonically rich quintet featuring Manu Boyd, one of the most prolific songwriters and chanters in Hawaii; **Hapa,** an award-winning contemporary Hawaii duo; **Keali'i Reichel,** premier chanter, dancer, and award-winning recording artist, voted "Male Vocalist of the Year" in the 1996 Na Hoku Hanohano Awards; **Robbie Kahakalau,** "Female Vocalist of the Year" in the same awards; **Kapena,** contemporary Hawaiian music; **Na Leo Pilimehana,** a trio of angelic Hawaiian singers; the **Makaha Sons of Niihau,** pioneers in the Hawaiian cultural renaissance; **Israel Kamakawiwoole,** a brilliant, soulful Hawaiian recording artist and big local favorite; and slack-key guitar master **Raymond Kane.** Consider the gods beneficent if you happen to be here when the hula halau of **Frank Kawaikapuo-kalani Hewett** is holding its annual fund-raiser in windward Oahu. It's a rousing, inspired, family effort for a good cause, and it always features the best in ancient and contemporary Hawaiian music. For the best in ancient and modern hula, it's a good idea to check the dailies for halau fund-raisers, which are always authentic, enriching, and local to the core.

Showroom acts that have gained a following are led by the tireless, 67-year-old **Don Ho**, who still sings "Tiny Bubbles" and who reportedly is experiencing a comeback in his Waikiki Beachcomber Hana Hou showroom nightly except Saturday and Monday. Across Kalakaua Avenue in the Outrigger Waikiki on the Beach, the **Society of Seven**'s nightclub act (a blend of skits, Broadway hits, popular music, and costumed musical acts) is into its 28th year—no small feat for performers.

BLUES

The best news for blues fans is the growing network of dyed-in-the-wool blues lovers here who have their own newsletter, blues festivals, club gigs, and the indomitable leadership of Louie Wolfenson of the **Maui Blues Association** (☎ 808/879-6123), the primary source for information on blues activities throughout the state. The blues are alive and well in Hawaii, with quality acts both local and from the mainland drawing enthusiastic crowds in even the funkiest of surroundings. Junior Wells, Willie & Lobo, War, and surprise appearances by the likes of Bonnie Raitt are among the past successes of this genre of big-time licks. The best-loved Oahu venue is **Anna Bannanas** (2440 S. Beretania St., ☎ 808/946-5190).

THE CLASSICS

You can also drape yourself in Donna Karan and high-step it to the opera, theater, or symphony for quality entertainment in a healthy performing arts scene. Aloha-shirt-to-Armani is what we call the night scene in Honolulu, mostly casual but with ample opportunity to dress up if you dare to part with your flip-flops. The May 1996 opening of the ✪ **Hawaii Theatre** (1130 Bethel St., downtown, ☎ 808/528-0506) following a 4-year, $22-million renovation introduced a glittering new venue for Hawaii's performing arts. The neoclassical beaux-arts landmark features a 1922 dome, 1,400 plush seats, a hydraulically elevated organ, a mezzanine lobby with two full bars, Corinthian columns, and gilt galore. Breathtaking murals, including a restored proscenium centerpiece lauded as Lionel Walden's "greatest creation," help to produce an atmosphere that is making the theatre a leading multipurpose center for the performing arts.

The **Honolulu Symphony Orchestra** has booked some of its performances at the new theatre, but it still performs at the Waikiki Shell and the Neal Blaisdell Concert Hall. Meanwhile, opera lovers, the highly successful **Hawaii Opera Theatre,** in its 37th season (past hits have included La Bohème, Carmen, Turandot, Rigoletto, Aida), still draws fans to the Neal Blaisdell Concert Hall (as do many of the performances of Hawaii's four ballet companies: **Hawaii Ballet Theatre, Ballet Hawaii, Hawaii State Ballet,** and **Honolulu Dance Theatre**). Contemporary performances by **Dances We Dance** and the **Iona Pear Dance Company,** a strikingly creative Butoh group, are worth tracking down if you love the avant-garde.

JAZZ

Yes, folks, there is a Jazz Hawaii Big Band and a jazz scene that keeps the saxophones and pianos in tune and Hawaii's gifted musicians accessible. **Jazz Hawaii** (☎ 808/737-6554) has an updated list of who's playing where. Big names and regular venues include **Duc's Bistro** (1188 Maunakea St., Chinatown, ☎ 808/531-6325), where the silky-smooth chords of Azure McCall deliver everything from "Paradise Cafe" to "Stormy Weather," from 10pm to 1am Fridays and Saturdays. Duc's also features nightly dinner music by Tennyson Stevens, from 7pm. At the entrance to

Waikiki, **Coconuts** (Ilikai Hotel Nikko Waikiki, 1777 Ala Moana Blvd., ☎ 808/
949-3811) offers Big Band live jazz on Monday evenings from 7pm to 10pm and
Latin disco on Wednesday nights. Tops in taste and ambience is the perennially
alluring **Lewers Lounge** in the Halekulani (2199 Kalia Rd., ☎ 808/923-2311),
where the Loretta Ables Trio attracts a sophisticated audience of music lovers who
sip vintage ports and expensive champagnes by the glass.

ALTERNATIVE CLUBS

The club scene is abuzz with rave reviews on **1739 Kalakaua Nightclub Lounge**
(1739 Kalakaua Ave., ☎ 808/949-1739), near the Hard Rock Cafe and the soon-
to-be-completed Hawaii Convention Center. The music themes at 1739 differ by the
night, but their calendar readings give you an idea: jazzy and hip-hop live music;
gothic-industrial dance with deejays; alternative, new-wave 1980s music, cheesy and
campy; progressive house music; deejay house music; jungle ambient and trip-hop;
wine, women, and song; Nat King Soul; mood music; old school; and more jazz and
hip-hop. So, whether you're into hip-hop or trip-hop, there's humor and cult appeal
here. Open 9pm to 2am nightly, and on Friday to Saturday, additionally from
2:30am to 8am. The cover charge depends on the group.

Anna Bannanas (see "Blues," above) still packs them in, with bands known to gen-
erate the most perspiration on the most enthusiastic dance floor in Honolulu. This
indomitable and much-loved club is a venue for groups with roots in reggae, blues,
world music, and alternative music. Most shows start at 9:30pm, and cover charge
depends on the show. **Nimitz Hall** (1130 N. Nimitz Hwy., behind the new Eagle
Café, ☎ 808/536-4255), formerly The Groove, is Honolulu's prevailing concert hall
for parties, raves, and ultra-hip (not hip-hop) special events. Jethro Tull, LL Cool J,
Chemical Brothers, The Toasters, Big Mountain, Primus, Porno for Pyros, and Hall
and Oates are among the name groups that have played to a full house in the large
industrial-chic hall. Raves with names like "Moon in the Seventh House," with
deejays-cum-icons, draw a heavily hip, young, alternative music crowd.

The Jungle (311 Lewers, Waikiki, ☎ 808/922-7808) is the hot scene for alternative music these days, a disco with occasional live entertainment, open from 10pm
to 4am. You can be as cheesy as you want here, and no one will notice. **The Wave
Waikiki** (1877 Kalakaua Ave., Waikiki, ☎ 808/941-0421) is rough around the
edges but still popular, serving up alternative music to the heavily body-pierced crowd
on the same stage that Grace Jones once spat from. Oh yes—**Hard Rock Cafe** (1837
Kapiolani Blvd., Waikiki, ☎ 808/955-7383), the bastion of decibels run amok, is
doing more than displaying rock memorabilia. It's offering live entertainment on
many, but not all, Friday and Saturday nights from 10:30pm to 12:30am. These no-
cover events bring out a hip crowd for the local alternative, reggae, and classic rock
bands.

DISCOS

Maharaja (2255 Kuhio Ave., 7th floor, Waikiki Trade Center, ☎ 808/922-3030)
is the mirrored wonder of the disco world, the chicest of them all (and snobby, too),
with dinner and dancing on a state-of-the-art floor and peerless sound and light sys-
tems. Dress up and be seen. But it's **Nicholas Nickolas** (410 Atkinson Dr., Ala
Moana Hotel, ☎ 808/955-4466) that has the best view. From the 36th floor of the
hotel (take the express elevator), watch the Honolulu city lights wrap around the
room and cha-cha-cha to the vertigo! Live music and dancing nightly, and an appetizer menu nightly from 5pm. Downstairs in the lobby of the same hotel, **Rumours
Nightclub** (☎ 808/955-4811) is the disco of choice for those who remember that

Paul McCartney was a Beatle before Wings. The themes change by the month, but generally it's the "Big Chill" '60s, '70s, and '80s music on Fridays, the "Little Chill" on Saturdays, ballroom dancing in the earlier hours of Sundays and Wednesdays, country and western on Tuesdays, "after-work office party" 5pm to midnight on Thursdays, and Ladies' Night 9pm to 4am on Thursdays. Open Tuesday through Sunday, from 5pm to closing. A spacious dance floor, good sound system, and top-40s music draw a mix of generations.

Across town in Waikiki, the sister restaurant of Nicholas Nickolas, **Nick's Fishmarket** (2070 Kalakaua Ave., Waikiki Gateway Hotel, ☎ 808/955-6333), is another sophisticated spot, with live entertainment nightly in its cozy lounge—mild jazz or top-40 contemporary hits. At Restaurant Row, **Ocean Club** (500 Ala Moana Blvd., Restaurant Row, ☎ **808/526-9888)** has taken over the former Studebaker's, and is currently the Row's hottest, hippest, and coolest spot. Good seafood appetizers, attractive happy-hour prices, a fabulously quirky interior, and passionate deejays in alternative garb make up a sizzlingly successful formula. For more information, see chapter 7 "Oahu Dining."

COMEDY

Local comedian **Frank DeLima** is the laugh doctor of Honolulu—raucous, outrageous, flamboyant, and completely uninhibited (but clean) in matters of ethnic humor. You can't be too politically correct if you go to his **Frank De Lima and Glenn Medeiros Show** (Polynesian Palace in the Outrigger Reef Tower Hotel, 227 Lewers St., ☎ **808/923-7469)**, 9:30pm from Tuesdays through Saturdays. His humor mirrors the best and worst of Hawaii, and his local vocabulary and point of view may make it difficult for a nonislander to get all the jokes. Nevertheless he is brilliant, popular, big-hearted, and somewhat of a local hero, one of Waikiki's entertainment staples. Although multicultural Hawaii is his material, universal, and therefore familiar, themes and characters populate his skits. Glenn Medeiros is a crooner from Kauai who's gone from top-40s local heartthrob to his highly successful niche as De Lima's sidekick. Cost is $19.50 per adult, $15 for children under 12, and $17.50 for those 12 to 20 years old.

Coconuts, listed above in the Ilikai Hotel, puts on its comedy hat nightly except Monday with its live comedy show, **Comedy Cow,** featuring big laughs from the mainland TV and comedy-club circuit. Only 6 months old at this writing, Comedy Cow is a valiant attempt to keep stand-up comedy alive since the Honolulu Comedy Club closed in this location. Names such as Kevin Hughes, the "comedy sex therapist," Rich Ceisler, Willie Barcena, and others from HBO, Showtime, and MTV have gotten things rolling at the club. Cost is $12 per person, with a two-drink minimum. The shows go on at 8pm nightly except Monday, and on Fridays and Saturdays at 10pm as well.

FILM

A quick check in both dailies and the *Honolulu Weekly* will tell you what's playing where in the world of feature films. For film buffs and esoteric movie lovers, **The Movie Museum** (3566 Harding Ave., ☎ **808/735-8771)** has special screenings of vintage films and also rents a collection of hard-to-find, esoteric, and classic films. The **Honolulu Academy of Arts Theatre** (900 S. Beretania St., ☎ **808/532-8768)** is the film-as-art center of Honolulu, offering special screenings, guest appearances, and cultural performances, as well as noteworthy programs in the visual arts.

Additionally, major movie theater complexes throughout Oahu bring celluloid to the masses more conveniently. In the heart of Waikiki, on Kalakaua Avenue and on

Seaside Avenue, three **Waikiki Theatres** are among the largest and most luxurious in multiplex-plagued Honolulu, showing major, mainstream feature films. In the university area of Moliili, the **Varsity Twins,** at University Avenue near Beretania Street, specializes in the more avant-garde, artistically acclaimed releases. Not far away, at King Street near Kalakaua, the **Cinerama Theatre** is the big-screen lover's delight. The Kahala Mall's **Kahala 8-Plex** and **Kapolei Megaplex** (a 16-theater complex), in west Oahu near the Ko Olina Resort, are the biggest movie theater complexes on the island.

At the nine **Wallace Theatres** on Restaurant Row near downtown Honolulu, free parking in the evenings, discount matinees, and special $5 midnight shows take a big step toward making movies friendlier and more affordable.

2 . . . And More

It's true that Elvis and Marilyn didn't die. They're still wowing fans through their impersonators, having achieved entertainment immortality with skillful makeup and voice coaches. Watch Madonna, Michael Jackson, Roy Orbison, Diana Ross, Janet Jackson, The Artist Formerly Known As Prince, Whitney Houston, Marilyn Monroe, Elvis, and other entertainment icons at the **Legends in Concert** show at the Aloha Showroom of the Royal Hawaiian Shopping Center in Waikiki (☎ 808/971-1400). The recently revamped dinner show has added a magic act, new china and menu (steak and scampi), and a finely tuned cast of impersonators in a $10-million showroom with laser lights, smoke effects, and high-tech stage and sound systems. At least five personalities are featured at each performance, with Elvis, performed by uncanny look-alike Jonathan Von Brana, and Madonna, performed by Von Brana's real-life wife, Eileen Fairbanks, among the show's staples. Two shows (6:25pm and 9pm) are featured 7 nights a week at $29 for cocktails, $65 for dinner show, and $99 for deluxe dinner show, with reduced children's rates available.

Finally, for late-night schmoozing, with a theater complex nearby, the **Restaurant Row's Row Bar** (500 Ala Moana Blvd., Restaurant Row, ☎ 808/528-2345) always seems to be full, smoky, and somewhat, if impersonally, convivial, except after the theaters have emptied from an Oliver Stone movie.

DINNER CRUISES

The best news in the dinner cruise world is the brilliant move by *Navatek I* (Pier 6, ☎ 808/848-6360) to introduce Hawaii Regional Cuisine on its cruises. Noted chef George Mavrothalassitis, formerly of Halekulani's La Mer and now the executive chef at the Five-Diamond Four Seasons Resort Wailea, has developed the menu for the *Navatek*'s nightly dinner cruises off the coast of Waikiki. This means that the 140-foot-long, ultra-stable SWATH (Small Waterplane Area Twin Hull) vessel not only promises spill-proof Mai Tais and a bob-free, seasick-less ride, it is now in the gourmet dinner arena.

There are several structures to the *Navatek* cruises, involving number of courses, upper-deck or lower-deck seating, and time of cruise, but generally the offerings are: Sunset Dinner Cruise, daily from 5pm to 7:30pm, $145.85 for a five-course meal (lobster salad, mahimahi bouillabaisse, asparagus flan, beef tournedos, and dessert) five drinks, and a contemporary jazz show; Moonlight Dinner Cruise, called La Lumiere, daily 8:15pm to 10:15pm, $130.20 for a four-course dinner, four drinks on the upper deck; Skyline Dinner Cruise on the main deck, 8:15pm to 10:15pm, $78.10 for four-course dinner (salmon roulade, tiger shrimp salad, beef tournedos, dessert) and three drinks. The food, views of sunset and the Waikiki skyline, and occasional dolphin and turtle sightings are infinitely more enjoyable on a stable, state-of-the-art craft like *Navatek*.

For a less expensive alternative, many choose the **Windjammer Cruises** (Pier 7, ☎ 808/537-1122), the prominently lit tall ship that's visible from Waikiki nightly. It looks like a sailboat but is motorized, with one sail daily from 5:15pm to 7:30pm. Tickets range from $39 for a buffet dinner to $99 for steak-and-lobster dinner and tableside service, as well as Polynesian entertainment and dancing.

LUAU!

Regrettably, there's no commercial luau on this island that comes close to Maui's Old Lahaina Luau, or Hawaii Island's legendary Kona Village luau. The two major luaus on Oahu are **Germaine's** (☎ 808/941-3338) and **Paradise Cove Luau** (☎ 808/973-LUAU), both located about a 40-minute drive away from Waikiki on the leeward coast. Bus pickups and drop-offs in Waikiki are part of the deal. Athough Germaine's tries awfully hard and is a much smaller and more intimate affair, Paradise Cove (itself a mixed bag, with 600 to 800 guests a night) is a more complete experience. The small thatched village makes it more of a Hawaiian theme park, with Hawaiian games, hukilau net throwing and gathering, craft demonstrations, and a beautiful shoreline looking out over what is usually a storybook sunset.

O'Brian Eselu's hula halau has been entertaining luau goers here for years. Tahitian dance, ancient and modern hula, white-knuckle fire dancing, and robust entertainment make this a fun-filled evening for those who don't expect an intimate gathering, and who are spirited enough to join in with the corny audience participation. The food is safe, though not breathtaking. Hawaiian kalua pig, lomi salmon, poi, and coconut pudding and cake are provided, but for the less adventurous, there is always a spread of teriyaki chicken, mahimahi, pasta salad, potato salad, and banana bread. Paradise Cove costs $49.50 for adults and $29.50 for children 6 to 12 years old. For $10 more, the Royal Alii Service will ensure table service instead of the usual buffet, pitchers of Mai Tais and Blue Hawaii cocktails on the table, and seating close to the stage. To attend Germaine's, the cost is $46 per adult, $25 for children. Although these luaus can be crowded, commercial affairs, everyone seems to have fun.

Visitors who attend a Polynesian revue in a dinner-showroom setting often find it a reasonable alternative to a luau and a lot of fun as well, minus the palm-tree silhouettes and picture-perfect sunsets. **Kalo's South Seas Revue** at the Hawaiian Hut Theater Restaurant (410 Atkinson Dr., ☎ 808/941-5205) lights up the 500-seat room with flames, fast-beating drums, and swaying hips in a wide-ranging program of Polynesian entertainment. Hula, fire dance, Tahitian dance, and Hawaiian, Maori, Tongan, and other Pacific traditions make this a fast-paced show. It's a commercial show, however, not an intimate backyard affair, so expect more entertainment than cultural enlightenment. The show includes a prime rib buffet dinner; $49 covers the show, dinner, and a double standard or a single exotic drink, and the show only costs $27. Dinner show at 5:30pm daily; show only at 6:30pm.

General Index

See also separate Accommodations and Dining indexes, below.

ACCOMMODATIONS

WHEREVER YOU TRAVEL, *H*ELP IS NEVER FAR AWAY.

From planning your trip to providing travel assistance along the way, American Express® Travel Service Offices are always there to help you do more.

Hawaii

OAHU
American Express Travel Service
Honolulu
808/536-3377

Hilton Hawaiian Village
Honolulu
808/947-2607

Hyatt Regency Waikiki
Honolulu
808/926-5441

American Express Travel Service
Honolulu
808/946-7741

BIG ISLAND OF HAWAII
Hilton Waikoloa Village
Kamuela
808/885-7958

MAUI
Westin Maui Hotel, Shop #101
Lahaina
808/661-7155

Ritz Carlton Kapalua
Lahaina
808/669-6018

Grand Hyatt Wailea
Wailea
808/875-4526

do more AMERICAN EXPRESS

Travel

http://www.americanexpress.com/travel